The dark side of globalization

CIGI

The Centre for International Governance Innovation

Centre pour l'innovation dans la gouvernance internationale

The Centre for International Governance Innovation (CIGI) is an independent, non-partisan think tank that addresses international governance challenges. Led by a group of experienced practitioners and distinguished academics, CIGI aims to anticipate emerging trends in international governance and to strengthen multilateral responses to the world's most pressing problems. CIGI advances policy ideas and debate by conducting studies, forming networks and convening scholars, practitioners and policy makers. By operating an active program of publications, events, conferences and workshops, CIGI builds capacity to effect change in international public policy. CIGI was founded in 2001 by Research In Motion (RIM) co-CEO and philanthropist Jim Balsillie, who serves as CIGI's chair. CIGI is advised by an International Advisory Board.

www.cigionline.org

The dark side of globalization

Edited by Jorge Heine and Ramesh Thakur

United Nations University Press
TOKYO • NEW YORK • PARIS

Synergy Books
India

First published in 2011 by the United Nations University Press,
The United Nations University, 53-70 Jingumae 5-chome,
Shibuya-ku, Tokyo 150-8925
For copyright reasons, this edition is for sale in South Asia only.

ISBN: 978-93-82059-00-4

Indian edition 2012 by:

Synergy Books India

(A Unit of M/s Bookwell Publication)
24/4800 Ansari Road, Darya Ganj
New Delhi-110002
Phone: 011-23268786, 23257264
Fax: 011-23281315
E-Mail: synergybooks@gmail.com
bookwell@vsnl.net

Printed at : DK FINE ART PRESS (P). LTD. DELHI-92

Endorsements

"This remarkably fine book constitutes the elegant bridge between academic theorizing about globalization and the inspired anecdotage of Thomas Friedman. It leaps beyond the frenzied celebration and denunciation (so frequently found in this field), to illuminate the vast human breakage that is an incidental result of compressing time and space without a corresponding growth in transnational mechanisms for limiting the malignant consequences of globalization ('the dark side'), which not only scar but can in the longer term limit globalization's desirable effects."

Tom Farer, *University Professor and past Dean, Josef Korbel School of International Studies, University of Denver*

"A bold step addressing the unattractive baggage that comes with the more desirable elements of globalization. An excellent collection that breaks away from conventional thinking to address globalization's unsavory elements."

Diana Tussie, *Director, Department of International Relations, FLACSO, Argentina*

"Timed just right! This book will be welcome reading in classrooms and policy circles worldwide in which globalization is a problem as well as a solution to the ongoing financial and economic crisis. All aspects of the issue are dissected by an unusual group of contributors. These international voices are not the usual suspects. Indispensable reading for anyone who wants to understand the full range of contents and discontents caused by globalization."

Thomas G. Weiss, *Director, Ralph Bunche Institute of International Studies, CUNY and past president, International Studies Association*

Contents

Figures and tables

Figure

Tables

Contributors

M. J. Akbar is a leading Indian journalist and author. He is the founder and former editor-in-chief and managing director of *The Asian Age*, a daily multi-edition Indian newspaper with a global perspective. He has written several non-fiction books, including *Byline* (New Delhi: Chronicle Books, 2003), a biography of Jawaharlal Nehru entitled *Nehru: The Making of India*, a book on Kashmir titled *Kashmir: Behind the Vale*, *Riot after Riot* and *India: The Siege Within*. He also authored *The Shade of Swords*, a cohesive history of jihad. Akbar's recent published book is *Blood Brothers*, a family saga covering three generations and packed with information of events in India and the world, particularly the changing Hindu–Muslim relations. In 2006, Akbar joined the Brookings Institution as a Visiting Fellow in the Brookings Project on US Policy Towards the Islamic World.

Gustavo Almeira is Researcher at the National Water Institute, Argentina. He is a meteorologist from the University of Buenos Aires and a Political Science PhD Candidate at the National University of San Martín. He is currently serving as a weather researcher at the National Water Institute and is conducting PhD research on environmental politics and climate change discourse in Argentina.

Rekha Chowdhary is a Professor of Political Science at the University of Jammu, India. She was formerly Head of the Department of Political Science (January 1999–December 2001) and Honorary Director of the Centre for Strategic and Regional Studies (until August 2003). She has been working in the areas of Indian and State Politics, specializing in the Politics of Jammu and Kashmir. She is currently the Coordinator of the USG Special Assistance Program on

Jammu and Kashmir. In addition to being the author of several academic publications, she also contributes regularly to the *Indian Express* and the *Kashmir Times*.

William D. Coleman holds the CIGI Chair in Globalization and Public Policy at the Balsillie School of International Affairs and is Professor of Political Science at the University of Waterloo. He has written five books, including *The Independence Movement in Quebec, 1945–1980* (Toronto: University of Toronto Press, 1984), *Business and Politics: A Study in Collective Action* (Montreal: McGill-Queen's University Press, 1988) and (with Michael M. Atkinson) *The State, Business and Industrial Change in Canada* (Toronto: University of Toronto Press, 1989). This book was awarded the Charles H. Levine Prize for the best book in the fields of public administration and public policy by the Structure of Government Research Committee of the International Political Science Association. The two most recent books are *Financial Services, Globalization and Domestic Policy Change: A Comparison of North America and the European Union* (Basingstoke: Macmillan, 1996) and (with Wyn Grant and Timothy Josling) *Agriculture in the New Global Economy* (Cheltenham: Edward Elgar, 2004).

Dorcas Ettang is Program Officer at the African Centre for the Constructive Resolution of Disputes in Durban, South Africa. Prior to this appointment she was a Research Assistant in the Conflict Prevention, Management and Resolution Department at the Kofi Annan International Peacekeeping Training Centre. She joined the KAIPTC in September 2007 as a research intern under the United Nations Association in Canada Junior Professional Consultant Program. She is a graduate of the University of Windsor (Canada) with a Masters of Arts in Political Science. Her research interests include conflict management and resolution, governance, human security and resource politics.

Kirsten Foot is Associate Professor of Communication at the University of Washington. Her research focuses on the reciprocal relationship between information/communication technologies and society. As co-director of the WebArchivist.org research group, she is developing new methods for studying social and political action on the web. She is the co-author of *Web Campaigning* (MIT Press, 2006), and co-editor of *The Internet and National Elections* (Routledge, 2007).

Charles Goredema heads the Organised Crime and Money Laundering programme of the Institute for Security Studies in Cape Town. After teaching criminal justice at universities in Zimbabwe and South Africa between 1987 and 2000, Charles Goredema joined the Institute in mid-2000. Since 2000, he has contributed ideas and publications to various organizations and institutions, including the Law Society of Zimbabwe, the Eastern and Southern Africa Anti-Money Laundering Group (ESAAMLG), the Inter-Governmental Action Group against Money Laundering in West Africa, PricewaterhouseCoopers, and the Institute for Justice and

Reconciliation. He has arranged or participated in training workshops for anti-money laundering agencies in Namibia, Zimbabwe, Malawi, Mozambique and Zambia.

Ricardo A. Gutiérrez is Professor and CONICET (Consejo Nacional de Investigaciones Científicas y Técnicas) Researcher at the National University of San Martín, Argentina. Gutiérrez received his PhD in Political Science from Johns Hopkins University. He is currently involved with the Masters in Development Management and Policy, a combined programme between Georgetown University and the National University of San Martín. His current research programme deals with different aspects of environmental politics and policy in Latin America.

Nasra Hassan has worked for the United Nations (1981–2008) at the UN Headquarters in New York and in Vienna, as well as in the Middle East, the Balkans and Central Asia. She previously served as Director, United Nations Information Service. Nasra Hassan has served in a number of UN organizations, including the Department of Public Information (DPI), the United Nations Children's Fund (UNICEF), the United Nations Relief and Works Agency for Palestine Refugees in the Near East (UNRWA), the Department of Peacekeeping Operations (DPKO), and at the United Nations Office on Drugs and Crime (UNODC). Her ongoing research on Muslim suicide terrorism and on jihadist militancy is widely cited in academic and other fora.

Jorge Heine holds the CIGI Chair in Global Governance at the Balsillie School of International Affairs, is Professor of Political Science at Wilfrid Laurier University and is a Distinguished Fellow at the Centre for International Governance Innovation. He has served as Vice-President of the International Political Science Association (IPSA). Previously, he served as Chile's Ambassador to India, Bangladesh and Sri Lanka (2003–7), as Ambassador of Chile to South Africa (1994–9), as well as a cabinet minister in the Chilean government. Dr Heine has been a Visiting Fellow at St Antony's College, Oxford and a Research Associate at the Wilson Center in Washington DC. He is the author, co-author or editor of nine books, including *Which Way Latin America? Hemispheric Politics Meet Globalization* (UNU Press, 2009), *The Last Cacique: Leadership and Politics in a Puerto Rican City* (Pittsburgh University Press, Choice Magazine Outstanding Academic Book of 1994), *A Revolution Aborted: The Lessons of Grenada* (Pittsburgh University Press, 1991) and *Cross Currents and Cleavages: International Relations of the Contemporary Caribbean* (Holmes and Meier, 1988), and has published some 70 articles in journals and symposium volumes. His opinion pieces have been published in the *New York Times*, the *Washington Post* and the *International Herald Tribune*.

Edgardo Lander is Professor of Social Sciences at the Universidad Central de Venezuela in Caracas. He is a member of the editorial board of the academic journal *Revista*

Venezolana de Economía y Ciencias Sociales. Currently he is part of the steering committee of the Hemispheric Council of the Social Forum of the Americas. He participated in the negotiations of the Free Trade Agreement of the Americas (FTAA) as part of the Venezuelan delegation. He is a member of the Latin American Social Science Council's (CLACSO) research group on Hegemonies and Emancipations, and part of the Latin American network on Modernity and Coloniality. Among other publications, his work includes *Contribución a la crítica del marxismo realmente existente: Verdad, ciencia y tecnología*; *La ciencia y la tecnología como asuntos políticos: Límites de la democracia en la sociedad tecnológica*; *Neoliberalismo, sociedad civil y democracia: Ensayos sobre América Latina y Venezuela*; and *La colonialidad del saber: Eurocentrismo y ciencias sociales*.

Garth le Pere was the Executive Director of the Institute for Global Dialogue in South Africa from 1993 to 2009. The IGD is dedicated to the research and study of international affairs and to the practical promotion of South Africa's foreign and international relations. In 2008, Dr le Pere was appointed Extraordinary Professor of Political Science at the University of Pretoria. He holds a PhD in Political Science from Yale University. His postgraduate areas of interest concentrated on public policy, African studies, comparative politics and international relations. His doctoral thesis examined the interface between the politics of resistance in South Africa and international opposition to apartheid from 1960 to 1985.

Ajay K. Mehra is Professor of Minority Studies at Jamia Millia Islamia University in New Delhi. He is a Ford Foundation Professor at the Centre for Dalit Studies there. Previously Senior Lecturer at Shaheed Bhagat Singh College, New Delhi, he is also the Honorary Director of the Centre for Policy Research, New Delhi. Professor Mehra is the author, co-author or editor of some seven books, including *Emerging Trends in Indian Politics* (Routledge India, 2010); *The Indian Parliament: A Comparative Perspective* (Konark, 2003); and *Political Parties and Party Systems* (Sage, 2003).

S. D. Muni is currently a Visiting Senior Research Fellow at the Institute of South Asian Studies. Prior to this appointment he held the position of Senior Visiting Scholar at the Institute for Defence Studies and Analyses, New Delhi. He was also Editor of the *Indian Foreign Affairs Journal*. He superannuated from Jawaharlal Nehru University, New Delhi, in 2006 after 33 years of service. At JNU he was Chairman of the Centre for South, Central and Southeast Asian Studies (1991–3) and held the prestigious Appadorai Chair of International Relations and Area Studies. He also served as India's Special Envoy (2005–6) to Southeast Asian countries on UN Security Council Reforms and was India's Ambassador in Lao PDR from November 1997 to December 1999. In 2005, the Sri Lankan President bestowed on him "Sri Lanka Ratna", the highest Sri Lankan national honour for a non-national.

Saskia Sassen is the Robert S. Lynd Professor of Sociology at Columbia University, a member of the Committee on Global Thought there and Centennial Visiting Professor at the London School of Economics. She taught previously at the University of Chicago. Her research focuses on globalization, immigration, global cities, the new networked technologies, and changes within the liberal state. She is known for zeroing in on the unexpected and the counterintuitive to cut through established "truths". She is the author of nine books, translated into 16 languages. They include *A Sociology of Globalization* (Norton, 2007), *Territory, Authority, Rights: From Medieval to Global Assemblies* (Princeton University Press, 2006), *The Global City* (Princeton University Press, 2nd ed, 2001), and *The Mobility of Labor and Capital* (Cambridge University Press, 1988). Her edited volumes include *Deciphering the Global: Its Spaces, Scales and Subjects* (Routledge, 2006), and *Digital Formations: New Architectures for Global Order* (Princeton University Press, 2006). She was involved with the 2006 Venice Biennale of Architecture, which for the first time focused on cities, and wrote the lead essay in the catalogue. Her opinion pieces have appeared in the *Financial Times*, the *New York Times*, the *International Herald Tribune* and *Newsweek International.*

Tiziana Scaramagli is Assistant to the Representative of the United Nations University office in Paris (UNU-OP) at UNESCO and M.Phil/Ph.D. candidate at the Department of War Studies, King's College London. She previously spent two years working as Research Assistant to the Director of the United Nations University Institute on Comparative Regional Integration Studies (UNU-CRIS) in Bruges, Belgium. Before that, Ms. Scaramagli worked for a Brussels-based think tank as Project Manager of a Programme devoted to European Security and Defence. She holds an M.A. in EU International Relations and Diplomacy Studies from the College of Europe in Bruges and an M.A. in International Politics and Diplomacy from the University of Padua (Italy), from where she also graduated with a degree in Political Sciences and International Relations, which included six months of study at Sciences Po in Paris.

Ramesh Thakur is Professor of International Relations, Asia-Pacific College of Diplomacy, Australian National University, and Adjunct Professor at the Institute of Ethics, Governance and Law at Griffith University in Brisbane, Australia. Previously, Dr Thakur was Vice Rector and Senior Vice Rector of the United Nations University (and Assistant Secretary-General of the United Nations) from 1998 to 2007. Educated in India and Canada, he was a Professor of International Relations at the University of Otago in New Zealand and Professor and Head of the Peace Research Centre at the Australian National University, during which time he was also a consultant/adviser to the Australian and New Zealand governments on arms control, disarmament and international security issues. He was a Commissioner and one of the principal authors of *The*

Responsibility to Protect (2001), and Senior Adviser on Reforms and Principal Writer of the United Nations Secretary-General's second reform report (2002). The author and editor of over 30 books and 300 articles and book chapters, he also writes regularly for quality national and international newspapers around the world. His most recent books include *The United Nations, Peace and Security: From Collective Security to the Responsibility to Protect* (Cambridge University Press, 2006) – winner of the ACUNS (Academic Council on the United Nations System) 2008 Award for the best recent book on the UN system – and *The United Nations and Nuclear Orders* (UNU Press, 2009). His latest book is *Global Governance and the United Nations: An Unfinished Journey* (Indiana University Press, 2010).

Luk Van Langenhove is Director of the Comparative Regional Integration Studies Programme of the United Nations University (UNU-CRIS) in Bruges and teaches at the Vrije Universiteit Brussel (VUB), Université Libre de Bruxelles (ULB) and the College of Europe. He was Deputy Secretary-General of the Belgian Federal Services for Scientific, Technical and Cultural Affairs, a post he occupied from May 1995 till September 2001. From 1992 until 1995, he was Deputy Chief of Cabinet of the Belgian Federal Minister of Science Policy. Before that he worked as a researcher and a lecturer at the VUB. He is Vice-President of the International Social Sciences Council.

Brendan Vickers is Senior Researcher: multilateral trade at the Institute for Global Dialogue (IGD) in Johannesburg, South Africa. His research agenda focuses on South Africa's multilateral, regional and bilateral trade policy and negotiations; regional integration in Southern Africa; and global governance and public policy debates. Prior to joining the IGD, Brendan Vickers worked as the deputy director responsible for International Relations and Trade in an advisory unit attached to the Office of President Thabo Mbeki. He has also taught International Relations at several South African universities, namely Johannesburg, Pretoria, Vista and Nelson Mandela Metropolitan. Brendan holds a PhD in Politics from the University of London.

Marisa von Bülow has been a Professor at the Political Science Institute, University of Brasilia, Brazil, since 1996. Her current research areas are civil society and globalization, social networks and collective action, and trade agreement negotiations in the Americas. Von Bülow coordinates the research group Civil Society and International Negotiations at the University of Brasilia, which is currently analysing the challenges and impacts of civil society participation in the Southern Common Market (MERCOSUR) since 1992. She also coordinates the work of a group of students who are analysing various aspects of the World Social Forum, ranging from debates about internal democracy to the identity of the Forum and discussions about its future. She holds a PhD from Johns Hopkins University.

Foreword: In the penumbra of globalization

Saskia Sassen

This is a book we need. Together, the authors cover a range of global dynamics either not usually included in books on globalization or studied in isolation. What makes this book unique is that it gives us an across-the-board engagement with a range of illicit, illegal, uncivil global processes and actors. The authors do so from many different disciplines and backgrounds. In the editors' hands – that is in the introduction and conclusion – it becomes a thick tapestry of what takes place in the penumbra of corporate economic globalization. The more we have focused, analysed, dissected the high-visibility components of globalization, especially corporate, the more impenetrable the realities that operate on the dark side.

Asymmetric interdependence and uneven distribution of the benefits of globalization are key underlying conditions contributing to the dark side of globalization. They are not the only source, and they do not only lead to negative outcomes. But they are a structural condition that can have multiple negative consequences. And they function both among as well as within states.

Such inter- and intrastate asymmetries are at the heart of the current phase of globalization. Inequality within countries has increased perhaps even more than inequality between countries. Thus the sharp increase in a new prosperous middle class in India, estimated to number c.300 million, evolved alongside a sharpening impoverishment of the poor, and of the 600,000 villages where most Indians live.

These and other such intrastate asymmetries actually feed the formation of new geographies of centrality that cut across some of the old

South–North divides. Among the constituents of these new geographies of centrality are global elites, financial networks, the hundred of thousands of affiliates of global firms spread around the world. International banking, the new global transport capabilities, the network of global cities, the international standardizing of more and more features of our economies, all of these are the infrastructure for those new geographies of centrality that cut across old divides.

But they are also infrastructures for the dark side of globalization – the traffic in drugs, people and arms, and so many other aspects described in this book. As the book describes, the illegal trade in drugs, people and arms is estimated to be up to 10 per cent of global GDP – US$54 trillion. Chapter after chapter in the book makes these diverse submerged economies concrete, and brings them to life for the reader.

As the book brilliantly shows us, the dark side of globalization goes well beyond these three submerged economies. It extends to the lingering histories of colonialism, with their many murderous legacies. Thus several chapters engage the fact that much of the killing in the global South is inflicted by guns brought in through illegal trafficking. Further, the book examines how the unjust treatment of indigenous peoples by the old colonial powers persists in diverse ways – in the law, in custom, in culture. Thus the exclusion of the Amerindian population was formalized in legal and constitutional structures, freezing it across time. This is also a dark side of globalization. Latin America's recent radical political change and the new constitutions are one response to that legacy. Significant sectors of the indigenous peoples in Bolivia and Ecuador, and the popular sector in Venezuela, all long excluded, have now become political actors.

The book concludes with a subject of critical importance for the future, particularly if we aspire to a better future. Much, though not all of the dark side is a consequence of the often extreme asymmetry between the thickening world of global practices and the inadequate and thin capabilities for their global governing. The book makes clear that global governing will have to deal with national states, and that this is necessary, inevitable, and not always bad.

London, June 2010

Acknowledgements

Globalization has ushered in unprecedented wealth as well as much illicit activity. Spurred by advances in communication, transportation and myriad other technologies, today's globalized world faces new challenges. Many of these challenges – such as illicit trafficking of goods, people and weapons – have existed before. Others, like internet crime, are newly to the fore. In the networked world of the early twenty-first century, these activities are not easy to detect and curtail. Global "uncivil" society represents the dark side of globalization. How to overcome the global governance deficits that continue to facilitate its activities was the driving force behind this volume.

It was with this purpose that the Centre for International Governance Innovation (CIGI) and the Globalization Studies Network (GSN) co-sponsored the Uncivil Society conference, in Waterloo, Ontario, Canada on 25–27 August 2008. This meeting brought together specialists from across the world to analyse this issue. Participants included Jan Aart Scholte, Pamela Mbabazi, Saied Ameli, Peter I. Hajnal, Mawaki Chango, Alla Glinchikova, Ren Xiao, Tasansu Turker, Edgardo Lander, John Forrer, William D. Coleman, Diana Brydon, Luk Van Langenhove, Ragayah Haji Mat Zin, Josephine C. Dionisio, Sarah Raymundo, Nicole Curato, Grazielle Furtado Alves da Costa, Garth le Pere, Dana Marie Morris, Lucy Eugene, Suzette Haughton, Jessica Byron, Rodrigo Álvarez, Marisa von Bülow, Enrique Peruzzotti, Ricardo A. Gutiérrez, Gabriel Tati, Hany Besada, Jonathan Mafukidze, Dominique Gomis, Ram Rattan Sharma, Paul James, Zhang Jiadong, Rekha Chowdhary, S. D. Muni, Kirsten

Foot, Dorcas Ettang, Matiu Adejo, Marlon Anatol, Akongbowa Bramwell Amadasun, and Ajay K. Mehra.

The conference would not have been possible without the dedication and commitment of CIGI staff. Anne-Marie Sanchez, Breanne Carter, Anne Blayney and Briton Dowhaniuk should all be commended for their efforts. Anne-Marie also deserves a good deal of credit for the research and management expertise that she brought to getting this collected edition started. Deanne Leifso shepherded the project through its second stage and provided excellent editing and structural advice. Joe Turcotte then managed the final stages of the manuscript development and provided the research, editing and project management necessary to finish the volume. Two anonymous readers for UNU Press provided some excellent editorial input. Special thanks need to be given to the high-quality work of Ann Bone, who delivered a comprehensive copy-edited version of the MS. We must also thank Saskia Sassen for providing the Foreword.

The original conference and the subsequent process of converting conference papers into a coherent and credible set of chapters for a worthwhile book would not have been possible without the fulsome support of John English, the then executive director of CIGI. We are grateful that Thomas A. Bernes, CIGI's acting executive director and vice-president of programs, provided uninterrupted support to ensure the completion of the project output in the form of this book. CIGI was founded in 2001 by Jim Balsillie, co-CEO of RIM (Research-in-Motion) and collaborates with and gratefully acknowledges support from a number of strategic partners, in particular the Government of Canada and the Government of Ontario.

South African painter Joe Joubert, born in the Kalahari District, who is known for his vivid and surreal work, was kind enough to authorize the use of his *Gourmet* for the cover, thus providing a dramatic front for this collection.

The final thanks are for Naomi Cowan and her colleagues at United Nations University Press, whose enthusiastic support made it possible to bring our original vision into reality.

Jorge Heine and Ramesh Thakur
Waterloo, Ontario, July 2010

Abbreviations

ANFSU(R)	All Nepal Free Students Union (Revolutionary)
ANNISU(R)	All Nepal National Independent Students' Union (Revolutionary)
ASEAN	Association of Southeast Asian Nations
AU	African Union
CARU	Uruguay River Administration Commission/Comisión Administradora del Río Uruguay
CEDHA	Centro de Derechos Humanos y Ambiente/Center for Human Rights and Environment (Argentina)
CFSP	Common Foreign and Security Policy (EU)
CIA	Central Intelligence Agency
CICAD	Inter-American Drug Abuse Control Commission
CINC	commander-in-chief (US regional)
CONFILAR	International Confederation for Liberty and Regional Autonomy
CPI	Communist Party of India
CPI(ML)	Communist Party of India (Marxist-Leninist)
CPM	Communist Party of India (Marxist)
CSO	civil society organization
DDR	disarmament, demobilization and reintegration
DRC	Democratic Republic of the Congo
ECOWAS	Economic Community of West African States
ESDP	European Security and Defence Policy
EU	European Union
FBI	Federal Bureau of Investigation
FDI	foreign direct investment
FTAA	Free Trade Area of the Americas

GATT	General Agreement on Tariffs and Trade
GIABA	Inter-Governmental Action Group against Money Laundering in West Africa
GTAN	Bilateral High-Level Technical Group/Grupo Técnico de Alto Nivel (Argentina/Uruguay)
Hizb	Hizb-ul-Mujahideen
HIV/AIDS	human immunodeficiency virus/acquired immune deficiency syndrome
HP	Himachal Pradesh
HSA	Hemispheric Social Alliance
ICJ	International Court of Justice
IMF	International Monetary Fund
INA	National Water Institute (Argentina)
IPKF	Indian Peacekeeping Force
IT	information technology
JKLF	Jammu and Kashmir Liberation Front
KPCS	Kimberley Process Certification Scheme
LTTE	Liberation Tigers of Tamil Eelam
MERCOSUR	Southern Common Market
MNC	multinational company
MODEL	Movement for Democracy (Liberia)
MP	Madhya Pradesh
NAFTA	North American Free Trade Agreement
NATO	North Atlantic Treaty Organization
NGO	non-governmental organization
NIE	National Intelligence Estimate (US)
NRN	Non-Resident Nepalese
OAS	Organization of American States
OSCE	Organization for Security and Co-operation in Europe
PIF	Pacific Islands Forum
RIM	Revolutionary International Movement
RUF	Revolutionary United Front (Sierra Leone)
SALW	small arms and light weapons
SC	Scheduled Castes
SEZ	Special Economic Zones
SOFA	Status of Forces Agreement
SSR	security sector reform
ST	Scheduled Tribes
UAE	United Arab Emirates
UK	United Kingdom
ULFA	United Liberation Front of Assam
UN	United Nations
UNCTAD	UN Conference on Trade and Development
UNODC	UN Office on Drugs and Crime
UNPoA	UN Programme of Action to Prevent, Combat and Eradicate the Illicit Trade in Small Arms and Light Weapons in All Its Aspects
UNSC	UN Security Council

UP	Uttar Pradesh
UPA	United Progressive Alliance (India)
URL	uniform (or universal) resource locator
US	United States
VAT	value added tax
WTO	World Trade Organization
ZIMRA	Zimbabwe Revenue Authority

Introduction: Globalization and transnational uncivil society

Jorge Heine and Ramesh Thakur

This changing world presents us with new challenges. Not all effects of globalization are positive; not all non-State actors are good. There has been an ominous growth in the activities of the drug-traffickers, gun-runners, money-launderers, exploiters of young people for prostitution. These forces of "uncivil society" can be combated only through global cooperation, with the help of civil society.

UN Secretary-General Kofi Annan, 1998

It has been said that being against globalization is like being against the sun coming up every morning, and about as fruitful. That may or may not be the case, but there is little doubt that globalization, that is, the increased flow of goods, services, capital, data and cultural products across international borders, has been one of the driving forces of international affairs over the past 30 years.[1] In the light of the 2008–9 world financial crisis, some questions have been raised as to whether this will continue to be the case – the World Trade Organization reported a 12.2 per cent drop in world trade in 2009 (WTO 2010) – or whether we will enter a process of "deglobalization". However that may be, since the Third Industrial Revolution was launched in 1980, when the first personal computer and round-the-clock television news from CNN came on the market, information technology (IT) and telematics have been bringing the world closer together and deterritorializing it. We may not be living at a time of "the end of history", as Francis Fukuyama famously argued (1992), but a case can be made that we are moving towards "the end of geography" as we had known it. The effective, "real" cost of a telephone call from New Delhi to Denver is no different from one made from New Delhi to Mumbai.

Many regard globalization as both a desirable and an irreversible engine of commerce that will underpin growing prosperity and a higher standard of living throughout the world. Others recoil from it as the soft underbelly of corporate imperialism that plunders and profiteers on the basis of unrestrained consumerism. From one point of view, globalization has been occurring since the earliest trade expeditions (e.g. the Silk Road). International trade, as a proportion of total production in the world economy, was about the same in the 1980s as in the last two decades of the Gold Standard (1890–1913) (Bhaduri and Nayyar 1996: 67). Thus the process itself is not fundamentally new. Nevertheless, the current era of globalization is unique in the rapidity of its spread and the intensity of the interactions in real time that result.

The primary dimension of globalization concerns the expansion of economic activities across state borders, which has produced increasing interdependence through the growing volume and variety of cross-border flows of finance, investment, goods and services, and the rapid and widespread diffusion of technology. Other dimensions include the international movement of ideas, information, legal systems, organizations and people, as well as cultural exchanges.

This volume is not a comprehensive book that reviews the scholarly field of globalization.[2] Instead, it bridges the policy–scholarship divide and addresses globalization from many of its various sides. Yet there is the need to clarify and articulate our understanding of globalization for the purposes of this volume; to specify the different dimensions of globalization at different levels of analysis; to be explicit about the unattractive baggage that might come with the desirable elements of globalization (e.g. the threats to cultural and policy autonomy) in the uneven impact of globalization, on the one hand, and the elements that are regarded as harmful and undesirable by all parties, such as trafficking. This volume, then, examines globalization from various contexts: (1) as a project, (2) as a process, (3) as international and transnational processes, (4) through state responses to these different levels of globalization, and (5) civil society responses to them.

Globalization refers both to the process and to the results or end-state. By addressing the "dark side" of globalization, the benefits of the process/project can be realized with minimal negative impact with respect to consequences. As a project, moreover, it refers to the vision of an idealized end-state and the initiation of particular processes in order to hasten the achievement of that end-state by those who embrace the vision. The process/project debate will be bridged to demonstrate how globalization is characterized by elements of both: globalization is not a natural process, rather it is implemented by humans for specific aims.

Still, even in this age of globalization, the movement of people continues to be restricted and strictly regulated. Moreover, growing economic interdependence is highly asymmetrical: the benefits of linking and the costs of delinking are not equally distributed among partners. Industrialized countries are highly interdependent in relations with one another; developing countries are largely independent in economic relations with one another; and developing countries are highly dependent on industrialized countries. Contrary to public perceptions, compared to the postwar period, the average rate of world growth decelerated during the age of globalization: from 3.5 per cent per capita per annum in the 1960s, to 2.1, 1.3, and 1.0 per cent in the 1970s, 1980s and 1990s, respectively (Nayyar 2006: 137–59, 153–4). And there has been a growing divergence, not convergence, in income levels between countries and peoples, with widening inequality among and within nations (2006: 153–6). Assets and incomes are more concentrated. Wage shares have fallen while profit shares have risen. Capital mobility alongside labour immobility has reduced the bargaining power of organized labour. The rise in unemployment and the increase in informal sector employment has generated an excess supply of labour and depressed real wages in many countries.[3] In the developed countries, too, globalization came to be blamed for the destruction of the manufacturing base and a "scam" by corporations to exploit cheap labour. The widespread public anger against the top financial and banking executives in 2009–10 was rooted in a powerful sense of unfairness at the stringent austerity imposed on workers and retirees while the senior executives continued to award themselves lavish bonuses. The result was that at the January 2010 World Economic Forum gathering in Davos – the very symbol and bastion of globalization – some of the most powerful delegates challenged the basic tenets of globalization (Bremmer 2010; Ignatius 2010).

Thus globalization creates losers as well as winners and entails risks as well as provides opportunities. As an International Labour Organization blue-ribbon panel noted, the problems lie not in globalization per se, but in the "deficiencies in its governance" (World Commission on the Social Dimension of Globalization 2004: xi). The deepening of poverty and inequality – prosperity for a few countries and people, marginalization and exclusion for many – has implications for social and political stability, again among as well as within states (Nayyar 2002). The rapid growth of global markets has not seen a parallel development of social and economic institutions to ensure their smooth and efficient functioning, labour rights have been less assiduously protected than capital and property rights, and the global rules on trade and finance are unfair to the extent that they produce asymmetric effects on rich and poor countries.

This is why many countries, especially developing countries, were worried even before the financial crisis of 2008–9 that the forces of globalization would impinge adversely on their economic sovereignty, cultural integrity and social stability. "Interdependence" among unequals amounts to the dependence of some on international markets that function under the dominance of others. The 2008–9 crisis confirmed dramatically that, in the absence of effective regulatory institutions to underpin them, globalization and liberalization can cause weak civil society to be overwhelmed by rampant transnational forces.

Globalization has brought many benefits. The proportion of people under the poverty line in the world has dropped considerably since 1980. This has been driven in part by the high growth rates in Asia – especially, but not only, in the Asian giants, China and India. The emergence of these and other emerging powers, like Brazil, South Africa, Turkey and Indonesia, is not unrelated to the capacity of these nations to navigate the treacherous waters of an increasingly globalized economy. There are countless ways in which the internet and IT have facilitated access and made the life of peasants and poor people across the developing world easier and better.

The purpose of this book, however, is to deal with the dark side of globalization – that is, the negative forces unleashed as a result of the compression of space and time made possible by modern technology. The forces of globalization have also let loose the infrastructure of uncivil society and accelerated the transnational flows of terrorism, drug trafficking, organized crime and diseases like AIDS. "Uncivil society" is a portmanteau term for a wide range of disruptive and threatening elements that have emerged in the space between the individual and the state and that lie outside effective state control. It merges into "the dark side of globalization" as it becomes transnationalized.[4] According to former United Nations Secretary-General Kofi Annan, networks of terrorism, drug trafficking and organized crime are all forces of global uncivil society that are rapidly growing as a result of the transnationalization of uncivil forces. In the words of another UN official, Sandro Calvani, the dark side of globalization is best thought of as the "unrelenting growth of cross-border illegal activities ... that threaten the institutions of the State and civil society in many countries".[5] Calvani's list of criminal activities on the dark side of globalization included human, drugs and arms trafficking; money laundering; and piracy (Calvani 2000).[6]

What to do?

A key challenge for developing nations at the beginning of the twenty-first century therefore is how to contend with globalization. Two extremes can be found in this regard: one is the outright rejection of globalization and the retreat towards a national cocoon of sorts (along the lines of what Burma, i.e. Myanmar, has done); the other is the full embrace of globalization and all it entails, somewhat along the lines of what countries like Ecuador and El Salvador did at one point earlier in this decade by adopting the US dollar as their national currency and giving up a monetary policy of their own. This challenge is not limited to nations of the global South. As Iceland, Latvia, Lithuania and Estonia found out to their chagrin in 2008–9, the notion that all you have to do to foster economic growth and investment is to open up your economy and do away with all capital controls has proven to be quite wrong – as a result of the global financial crisis the GDP of these small nations experienced double-digit "negative growth" in 2009. This was followed in 2010 by the severe debt crisis in Greece that threatened the viability of the entire eurozone.

Most observers would agree with the proposition that to cope effectively with the forces of globalization, developing nations need policies that are somewhere in between those two extremes. Lowering all barriers to the tides of the global economy may end up drowning much of local production. Raising barriers that are too high may be counterproductive, if not downright futile. Those countries that are able to find that golden middle – like, say, Singapore, or, to a lesser extent, Chile – tend to thrive and to make the most of their international environment, channelling the enormous opportunities offered by an expanding world economy for the benefit of their own citizens. Those unable to find that middle – like many in West and Central Africa – end up being marginalized and left behind, if not taken over by the "dark side" of globalization. The case of Guinea-Bissau, described by some as the world's first "narco-state", is a good example.

The challenge posed by globalization is a double one. On the one hand, it is vital for nations today to harness the positive forces of globalization for their own benefit. Many opportunities that were unavailable before have now come to the fore. Micro-states like Antigua and Barbuda, for example, have found a niche in such a specialized and even arcane activity as internet gambling – something that did not exist as recently as 20 years ago. This entails finding the right balance between openness and regulation, a balance often difficult to strike. On the other hand, it implies keeping an ever watchful eye over that "dark side", that is, the illegal if not downright criminal activities that thrive in the interstices of the national and the international, and that have been facilitated by technological progress. Facilitating trade can also be a way of facilitating smuggling – of guns, illegal drugs or people.

According to some estimates, this illicit trade may reach anywhere from 1 to 3 trillion dollars in value; some consider it may be as high as 10 per cent of the global product, and it is growing at seven times the rate of growth of legal trade (see Naím 2005). This growth in transnational flows, in turn, has not been matched by an equivalent growth in global governance mechanisms to cope with them and what they entail. In addition to the challenge posed by globalization to individual states, then, there is a "collective action" problem. No single state can hope to deal successfully with global warming or with international crime syndicates. And this leads us to the broader issue of the link between the great powers, globalization and empire.

Globalization and imperialism

It is easy for Westerners to ignore or downplay the lingering shadows of colonialism on the memories and policies of the countries that were colonized. Afro-Asian countries achieved independence on the back of extensive and protracted nationalist struggles. The parties and leaders at the forefront of the fight for independence helped to establish the new states and shape and guide the founding principles of their foreign policies. The anti-colonial impulse was instilled in the countries' foreign policies and survives as a powerful sentiment in the corporate memory of the elites. In their worldview, the European colonizers came to liberate the "natives" from their local tyrants, yet stayed to rule as foreign oppressors. In the name of enlightenment, they defiled lands, plundered resources and expanded their empires. Some, like the Belgians in the Congo, left only ruin, devastation and chaos whose dark shadows continue to blight. Others, like the British in India, left behind ideas, ideals and structures of good governance and the infrastructure of economic development alongside memories of national humiliation. This is why the formerly colonized countries still look for the ugly reality of geostrategic and commercial calculations camouflaged in lofty rhetoric in the actions and policies of many Western countries.

On the occasion of the Great Recession of 2008–9, there was much talk about "the end of the neoliberal era", the 30-year period that started with the elections of Margaret Thatcher in the United Kingdom and Ronald Reagan in the United States and ended with the inauguration of President Barack Obama. A strong belief in the need to roll back the power of the state and in the mantra of what came to be known in the 1990s as "the Washington Consensus" (described by others as "the Washington Contentious") was its hallmark. Though there is some dispute about the paternity of this neoliberal revolution (the supporters of General Augusto Pinochet in Chile claim that it was launched earlier – by Chile's military government in 1973[7]), there is, in any event, an interesting overlap between this neoliberal programme based on deregulation, privatization and the opening up of economies, and the onset of globalization, which many would posit was launched in 1980 with the Third Industrial Revolution.

And that is the gist of William Coleman's argument in the lead chapter of this volume, "Globalization, imperialism and violence". Coleman describes an increasingly interlinked world based on networks of global finance, trade and business, whose key pivot is the absolute mobility of capital, something that goes hand in hand with ever greater constraints on labour. In this perspective, globalization is framed as an extension of neoliberal ideals. Underpinning this neoliberal expansion is an imperialist endeavour supported by a network of US military bases across the world. Militarism and imperialism coexist, and "globalization creates the material and cultural basis for permitting imperialism to become globally more extensive and intensive". Globalization is driven by communications technologies, which allow the creation and maintenance of elaborate worldwide networks, but do not allow for an unequivocal leader. The very nature of the structure of globalized networks, which intertwine global actors and interests, ensures that no single power – including the United States – is able to maintain its position within this newly emerging global order without making compromises with other global players.

Imperialism and colonialism have, of course, left their imprint in the global South. Although many countries in Latin America greeted the bicentennial of their independence from Spain in 2010, this does not mean that the colonial legacy of the Spanish *conquista* has vanished. In the course of the first decade of the twenty-first century, Latin America has undergone a process of radical political change that has left many foreign observers puzzled as to its meaning and implications, as it questions the very basis of the premise that the post-Cold War era would also be the one of the End of Ideology.[8]

In a fascinating essay centred on these processes of change in Bolivia, Ecuador and Venezuela, Edgardo Lander traces the origins of the movements behind this trend. Far from those who categorize them simply as populist throwbacks to an earlier era of the region's history, he identifies the significant sectors of the population – in the case of Bolivia and Ecuador, mostly the indigenous peoples, in Venezuela the popular sector at large that had been largely excluded from the political system and the official discourse – that have now come into their own. The fact that Bolivian President Evo Morales, elected in 2005, is the first elected head of state in Latin America of Amerindian origin (he is a native Aymara) speaks volumes about this exclusion (see Van Cott 2005).

The dark side of colonialism, a precursor of contemporary globalization, was the treatment meted out to colonial subjects, something which, amazingly, persists in Latin America even today. For the colonial enterprise was framed by Eurocentric lenses and categories, within which the aboriginal populations did not fit. The exclusion of and discrimination against the Amerindian population was thus kept alive long into the Latin American republics' independence. It was formalized in their legal and constitutional structures, thus freezing in time social hierarchies that privilege the social classes and ethnic groups associated with Northern elites. The new constitutions in Bolivia, Ecuador and Venezuela, whatever their shortcomings, set forth a radical re-evaluation of the role and nature of the state that seeks to address, if not overcome, these historical inequalities. The enormous changes we are witnessing in Latin America, where a former metal worker and trade union leader, who lost one of his fingers on the factory floor, has become president of Brazil, where women have been elected to the presidency in Argentina and Chile, and where an Aymara high-school dropout has become president of Bolivia, are as much cultural as they are political. They are helping to leave behind one the darkest legacies of colonialism: the exclusion of vast sectors of the population from public life.

Africa, on the other hand, home to 36 of the 50 least developed states, is in many ways a paradigm of how state weakness opens the door to transnational crime and terrorism. Arguing that weak states are particularly prone to illegal transnational ventures, Garth le Pere and Brendan Vickers highlight six areas that are prevalent in the continent: the illegal exploitation of natural resources, terrorism, the drug trade, illegal migration and human trafficking, gunrunning and money laundering. They posit that transnational criminal activity as well as terrorism have "become inextricably interwoven in the fabric of globalization". The three chapters in this introductory part lay out the changes and consistencies demonstrated between contemporary globalization and the legacy of colonialism and imperialism. Historic relationships between states and civilians are being altered in a contemporary landscape that is increasingly interconnected, leading to new challenges that transcend national boundaries and authorities.

The nature of the challenges

Part II of this volume explores many of the varying challenges facilitated by the dark side of globalization. While not an exhaustive list of the complications arising from globalization, these chapters serve as a representative sample of the pressing issues emerging today and shed light on the factors that facilitate them. How do the various expressions of what has been called "uncivil society" manifest themselves? How do they take advantage of the opportunities offered by globalization? What is it exactly that they do to make the most of the "global village"?

Much of the killing that takes place throughout the global South is inflicted by guns, many of them of illegal origin. West Africa, an area where some of the most brutal civil wars in the past two decades have taken place, has been especially afflicted by the thriving business undertaken by gunrunners, often operating on a continental basis. In a tragic twist, guns are not only produced in several of these countries and imported from abroad, but also *recycled* from one African conflict to another. Weapons thus find their way seamlessly from the Congo to Liberia and Sierra Leone, and back. Weak African states, unable to patrol their porous borders, are thus at the mercy of arms traffickers. Dorcas Ettang argues that sustainable security sector reforms are key to putting an end to this tragic predicament, a venture in which, in addition to the state, civil society must be enlisted.

Moving from West to Southern Africa, Charles Goredema assesses how the most prosperous region of the continent has witnessed the rise of elaborate transnational crime organizations. The illegal trafficking in narcotics, mineral resources, ivory, counterfeit products and stolen property (particularly automobiles) is thriving. International crime syndicates exploit government weaknesses to make huge profits. Illegal migration and money laundering rob the state of valuable human and material resources, in a region that desperately needs them.

A different kind of challenge is posed by insurgencies that often thrive as a result of the inequalities created by globalization. One of the countries that has made the most of the opportunities offered by IT and telematics technology has been India, a world leader in IT-enabled services, and whose 5 per cent yearly growth rate in the 1980s climbed to 6 per cent in the 1990s and to 7 per cent in the course of the first decade of this century. Yet this progress has gone hand in hand with an ever greater gap between the prosperity of urban, middle-class Indians (estimated to have reached some 300 million) and the squalor still seen in many of its 600,000 villages, where the majority of Indians still reside. In the 12-year period 1997–2008 inclusive, a total of 199,132 suicides of farmers were recorded by the National Crime Records Bureau, or an average of 16,594 per year (Sainath 2010). One reason is the vicious debt trap caused by the removal of quantitative restrictions under the WTO regime which has left the country's small and marginal farmers exposed to the volatility of international markets and prices. With no access to crop insurance, they are easy prey for usurious moneylenders.

It is this "development dichotomy" that has allowed the Naxalite movement, originally founded in West Bengal in the late 1960s, not only to persist in much of northern and central India, but to grow as it propounds its oddly out-of-date Maoist ideology, a belief system left behind even by the People's Republic of China, where it originated. Ajay Mehra frames this "old" revolutionary movement in a new context. The contrast between those states and areas where the "New India" shines and those where the "Old India" remains, exacerbating the differences between high-level consumption and prosperity patterns, on the one hand, and extreme deprivation, on the other, has generated discontent and resentment to fuel these guerrilla movements. It has also often been the aboriginal populations (the Adivasis), or scheduled tribes, and the members of the lowest caste or Dalits (the oppressed) that have suffered the most as a result of the population displacements induced by major development projects like dams. Uprooted from their ancestral lands and unable to adapt to the demands of a modern economy, they often see revolutionary redemption as the only way out of their predicament.

The Indian Naxalite insurgency does have parallels in neighbouring countries. In Nepal, the Maoist guerrilla movement was so successful that it gained power, abolished the monarchy, established a republic, and installed its leader, Prachanda, as prime minister, albeit for only a brief period. In Sri Lanka, the Liberation Tigers of Tamil Eelam (LTTE) waged a savage civil war against the Sri Lankan state for a quarter of a century (from 1983 to 2009), a war that cost 70,000 lives (including those of one Sri Lankan president, one foreign minister, and that of a former Indian prime minister), but was ultimately defeated. As S. D. Muni points out, these insurgencies differ in that the Nepalese was driven by essentially political reasons, and the Sri Lankan by ethnic ones (by the Tamil minority, which comprises some 13 per cent of the population against the Sinhala majority, which reaches 80 per cent), but also in the manner in which they interacted with global forces.

Although originally linked up with the Indian Naxalite movement, the Nepalese Maoists ended up cutting those ties so as not to alienate India, a country on which Nepal heavily depends, and waging a much more traditional, nationally based guerrilla war against the Nepalese monarchy. The latter was defeated as much because of the political ineptitude of King Gayendra as because of anything else.

The LTTE, on the other hand, may well have been one of the most globalized terrorist movements anywhere. Part of the reason for its considerable, if temporary, success was the effective way it relied on the Sri Lankan Tamil diaspora both to obtain resources and to marshal political support for its cause. It is estimated that it was able to raise somewhere between US$200 million and US$300 million a year for its operations, all collected from the Tamil diaspora, largely in Europe and North America. It made effective use of the latest IT and telecommunications technology, and has been the only terrorist movement to date with its own navy and air force. Ironically, much as its deployment of global networks ensured its success, while it lasted, it was also global forces that spelled its end.

After 9/11, the existence of a terrorist movement relying on global financing, however nested it might be in an island state off the Indian coast, became unacceptable to the international community. The LTTE was banned in 32 countries, many states became ready to supply arms to the Sri Lankan government to fight it, and it became only a matter of time before its time was up.

On the other hand, Rekha Chowdhary warns against the ahistorical conception of terrorism and terrorist movements that has emerged after 9/11. Focusing on Kashmir, she argues that Kashmiri militants (the word of choice in Kashmir to refer to the insurgents there, some of whom fight for an independent Kashmir and others for one that would join Pakistan) employed various tactics before resorting to violence. Of special interest is the tension she examines between local Kashmiri militant groups and foreign jihadists. The efforts of the latter to impose the Wahabi conception of Islam on Kashmiris found stiff resistance among the population of the Valley. Once again, the complex dialectic of the global and the local, a recurrent theme in this volume, plays itself out in unexpected ways in the province that has been at the heart of the simmering conflict between India and Pakistan for six decades now.

A valuable insight into the mind of jihadis is given to us by Nasra Hassan, who has been interviewing them for many years now. Hassan draws a parallel between globalization and *jihad*, arguing that both are focused on opening borders and on bringing about progress. Jihadists have excelled at using contemporary IT and telecoms technology to promote their cause and foster their objectives – from websites to satellite phones. Transnational crime – often in the illegal drugs trade – provides the financial resources that allow them to continue to build their networks and bring about their terrorist attacks. As Mahmoud Mamdani has observed, this link between the drug trade and terrorism is, of course, one pioneered by the CIA (see Mamdani 2004). First in South East Asia during the Vietnam War, then in Central America to finance the Contras against the Sandinistas, and then in Afghanistan to raise additional resources for the mujahedin in their fight against the Soviet Union, it was always seen as a welcome, off-budget mechanism to raise funds to help US allies. Jihadis have also perfected into an art form the international transfer of funds in ways that are essentially untraceable, by relying on ancient mechanisms that replicate the old-fashioned way Osama bin Laden gets his information – through pieces of paper brought to him by hand by loyal messengers – which is one reason he remains at large.

One product of the so-called "global war on terror" was the US-led invasion of Iraq in March 2003. Many wondered how an attack on the most secular of all Arab states was supposed to contribute to the struggle against a fundamentalist Islamic group like Al Qaeda. Moreover, the notion of "bringing democracy to Iraq", in a country in which 60 per cent of the population is Shia, would logically imply the establishment of a Shia majority government – and thus one in close alignment with Iran. Predictably, this is exactly what happened, as M. J. Akbar, one of India's leading Muslim public intellectuals, argues in the final chapter of this part of the volume. By bringing to an end Saddam Hussein's regime, the traditional "balancer" of Iran's power in the broader Middle East, the United States has unwittingly enhanced the power of the Islamic Republic of Iran, a country it once denounced as part of the so-called "axis of evil".

Coping with the dark side

Faced with the many challenges facilitated by contemporary globalization it is easy to lose sight of the possibilities for response. Globalization per se is not the problem – rather it is the lack of effective mechanisms of transnational governance and cooperation that provides spaces for illicit transnational organization to exploit. Responding to these actors and filling these spaces with good governance tools is essential to ensure security and stability.

One response to the global governance gaps that have made these illegal activities possible has been regionalism. In their chapter, Luk Van Langenhove and Tiziana Scaramagli argue that the transfer of state functions to supranational forms of regional governance enhances the capacity of individual states to combat the endeavours of uncivil society. This would be especially valid for neighbouring countries sharing similar security concerns, such as those associated with smuggling and other cross-border illegal activities. The sharing of expertise, institutions, policy tools, personnel and other resources can go a long way in stemming the tide of these activities. Van Langenhove and Scaramagli examine the cases of the European Union, the Economic Community of West African States, the Association of Southeast Asian Nations, the Pacific Islands Forum, the Andean Community and the Organization of American States. They focus on the normative goals of the integration movement and highlight how and why intraregional security is paramount to protect the interests of society at large and of its individual members.

A key tension often arises between intraregional cooperation and claims of state sovereignty. Yet, one of the paradoxes of contemporary globalization is how civil society organizations can use the tools of transnationalism to further seemingly old-fashioned notions of national sovereignty. One such case is that of the Hemispheric Social Alliance (HSA), analysed by Marisa von Bülow. The HSA took on the Free Trade Area of the Americas (FTAA) and mobilized labour and other civil society organizations across the hemisphere to stop the project. In so doing, it often brought together parties from the opposite ends of the political spectrum. The experience of the HSA demonstrates the difficulties inherent in harnessing the energies of disparate organizations and uniting them in a common cause. However, it also shows that such seemingly motley groups can succeed even when taking on a pet foreign policy project of the world's last remaining superpower. The FTAA, whose deadline for completion was 2005, was effectively dead long before that.

Another fascinating aspect of globalization is "glocalization", that is, the interaction between the local and the global. A key challenge for local activists with a stake in an international issue is to generate sufficient interest from the national government to garner its support. In theory, conflicting issues of an international nature that involve two or more member states of a regional integration scheme should be resolved by whatever conflict resolution mechanisms that particular scheme has chosen for itself. Yet that is not always the case, as the conflict between Argentina and Uruguay over the Uruguay River paper mills shows. Although both countries are founding members of MERCOSUR, the Southern Common Market, the latter entity was unable to resolve the issue, which ended up at the International Court of Justice in The Hague. Ricardo Gutiérrez and Gustavo Almeira show how local environmental protests in the Argentine province of Entre Ríos managed, through a variety of imaginative techniques, to induce a change in Argentina's foreign policy. A deft use of the media and of "public diplomacy" was part of the reason they succeeded, creating the most serious rift in decades between two countries that have had historically very friendly relations. The communications technology that drives globalization can also be deployed to counteract global forces by local communities – in this case a Finnish foreign direct investment project in a paper mill in Uruguay challenged by environmental activists in a small town in Argentina.

Human trafficking is one of the darkest aspects of the dark side of globalization, turning human beings into commodities that are bought and sold in the international marketplace. In so doing it inflicts untold suffering on some very vulnerable people. Women and children are among the most exposed to it. How can it be countered? Undertaking a thorough survey of websites campaigning against human trafficking, Kirsten Foot explores the myriad ways non-governmental organizations from all continents attempt to cope with this nefarious activity, and report on those involved in it.

The dark side of globalization

It remains to be seen whether the 2008–9 global financial crisis has brought to an end not only the neoliberal era that was kick-started by

Margaret Thatcher and Ronald Reagan around 1980, but also globalization as we have known it during these three decades. The collapse of the Doha Round, the first time a multilateral trade round had failed, and the 12 per cent drop in global trade in 2009 would seem to indicate, at the very minimum, a slowing down in the tempo and rate at which global flows will grow in the near future. But there is little doubt that the "dark side" of globalization, the subject of this volume, will remain with us. A better understanding of this "downside" of the transnational forces that are pulling the world together is imperative if we want to manage this complex process better. That is the purpose of this book. The chapters lay out a variety of the challenges affecting states and citizens. Though geographically and topically diverse, the challenges and responses illustrate that the dark side of globalization raises both domestic and international issues. Though facilitated by transnational and global forces, the effects are most often felt by the citizens of sovereign states. There are ample ways in which civil society can fight the negative aspects of globalization and the emergence of uncivil society at the local level. Transnational governance reforms must go hand in hand with responses from civil society.

Notes

1. A standard source on globalization is Held et al. 1999.
2. Doing so falls outside of the scope of this project. For various examinations of globalization from such a perspective, see Castells 2004; Meyer 2000; 2007; Robertson and Khonder 1998; Lechner 2009; Holton 1998; 2005.
3. For an informed perspective on this and other aspects of the economic impact of globalization, see Stiglitz 2002.
4. For a study of how organized crime syndicates have become increasingly interconnected and interdependent on a worldwide basis, see Glenny 2008. See also Naím 2005
5. Both Annan and Calvani are cited in Rumford 2001: para. 2.2.
6. At the time, Calvani was the UN Representative in East Asia and the Pacific for Drug Control and Crime Prevention, based in Bangkok.
7. See Büchi 1993.
8. On this, see *Journal of Democracy* (2006), with a dossier entitled "A 'left turn' in Latin America?". See also Cooper and Heine 2009; Silva 2009.

REFERENCES

Annan, Kofi A. (1998) "Secretary-General describes emerging era in global affairs with growing role for civil society alongside established institutions", Press Release SG/SM/6638, United Nations, 14 July. At <http://www.un.org/News/Press/docs/1998/19980714.sgsm6638.html> (accessed 10 Sept. 2009).

Bhaduri, Amit and Deepak Nayyar (1996) *The Intelligent Person's Guide to Liberalization*. New Delhi: Penguin.

Bremmer, Ian (2010) "At Davos, the globalizers are gone", *Washington Post*, 30 Jan.

Büchi, Hernán (1993) *La transformación económica de Chile: Del estatismo a la libertad*. Bogotá: Norma.

Calvani, Sandro (2000) "Facing the dark side of globalization: Rotten apples or banana peels?" (May). At <http://www.sandrocalvani.it/docs/20080917_Articles_rotten_apples.pdf> (accessed June 2010).

Castells, Manuel, ed. (2004) *The Network Society: A Cross-cultural Perspective*. Cheltenham, UK: Edward Elgar.

Cooper, Andrew F. and Jorge Heine, eds (2009) *Which Way Latin America? Hemispheric Politics Meets Globalization*. Tokyo: United Nations University Press.

Fukuyama, Francis (1992) *The End of History and the Last Man*. New York: Free Press.

Glenny, Misha (2008) *McMafia: A Journey through the Global Criminal Underworld*. New York: Knopf.

Held, David, Anthony McGrew, David Goldblatt and Jonathan Perraton (1999) *Global Transformations: Politics, Economics and Culture*. Stanford: Stanford University Press.

Holton, Robert J. (1998) *Globalization and the Nation State*. Basingstoke: Macmillan.

Holton, Robert J. (2005) *Making Globalization*. Basingstoke: Palgrave Macmillan.

Ignatius, David (2010). "Populism popular at the World Economic Forum in Davos", *Washington Post*, 31 Jan.

Journal of Democracy (2006) "A 'left turn' in Latin America", *Journal of Democracy*, 17(4) (Oct.).

Lechner, Frank J. (2009) *Globalization: The Making of a World Society*. Oxford: Wiley-Blackwell.

Mamdani, Mahmoud (2004) *Good Muslim, Bad Muslim: America, the Cold War and the Roots of the War on Terror*. New York: Pantheon.

Meyer, John W. (2000) "Globalization: Sources and effects on national states and societies", *International Sociology*, 15(2) (June): 233–48.

Meyer, John W. (2007) "Globalization: Theory and trends", *International Journal of Comparative Sociology*, 48(4): 261–73.

Naím, Moisés (2005) *Illicit: How Smugglers, Drug Traffickers and Copycats are Hijacking the Global Economy*. New York: Doubleday.

Nayyar, Deepak, ed. (2002) *Governing Globalization: Issues and Orientations*. Oxford: Oxford University Press.

Nayyar, Deepak (2006) "Globalisation, history and development: A tale of two centuries", *Cambridge Journal of Economics*, 30(1): 137–59.

Robertson, Roland and Habib Haque Khonder (1998) "Discourses of globalization: Preliminary considerations", *International Sociology*, 13(1) (Mar.): 25–40.

Rumford, Chris (2001) "Confronting 'uncivil society' and the 'dark side of globalization': Are sociological concepts up to the task?", *Sociological Research Online*, 6(3) (30 Nov.). At <http://www.socresonline.org.uk/6/3/rumford.html> (accessed 30 Aug. 2009).

Sainath, P. (2010) "Farm suicides: A 12-year saga", *The Hindu*, 25 Jan.

Silva, Eduardo (2009) *Challenging Neoliberalism in Latin America*. New York: Cambridge University Press.

Stiglitz, Joseph (2002) *Globalization and Its Discontents*. New York: Norton.

Van Cott, Donna Lee (2005) *From Movements to Parties in Latin America: The Evolution of Ethnic Politics*. New York: Cambridge University Press.

World Commission on the Social Dimension of Globalization (2004) *A Fair Globalization: Creating Opportunities for All*. Geneva: International Labour Organization.

WTO (2010) "Trade to expand by 9.5% in 2010 after dismal 2009, WTO reports", Press Release: International Trade Statistics, World Trade Organization, 26 Mar. At <http://www.wto.org/english/news_e/pres10_e/pr598_e.htm> (accessed June 2010).

Part I

Domination and fragmentation

1

Globalization, imperialism and violence

William D. Coleman

The twentieth century was the most violent in human history. Relative to total population, more persons were killed, wounded, displaced or left mentally fraught than at any other period. Nor did war-fighting cease with the end of the Second World War and the founding of the United Nations. Some four decades later, when the violence of the Cold War came largely to an end, the world anticipated, but still has not seen, a significant decline in physical violence.

In discussing the remarkable physical violence that has occurred, discussions focus upon the "violence" of poverty, displacement and other economic and social effects of neoliberal globalization. A number of scholars have observed that the intensification of globalization that has taken place in the last two decades of the twentieth century has been accompanied by remarkable violence, with more of it taking intrastate or civil forms. Arjun Appadurai posed the question well:

> [W]hy should a decade dominated by a global endorsement of open markets, free flow of finance capital, and liberal ideas of constitutional rule, good governance, and active expansion of human rights have produced a plethora of examples of ethnic cleansing on one hand and extreme forms of political violence against civilian populations (a fair definition of terrorism as a tactic) on the other? (2006: 3)

Many scholars and pundits have offered answers to this question.

I begin this chapter with a short definition of globalization as a way to considering the question. I understand the word *global* as a reference to scale and to phenomena that are somehow transplanetary, to use Scholte's (2005) term. I also hold that the spread of transplanetary phenomena is not confined to the economic sphere (as is often assumed in popular discourse) but includes the political, cultural, military, and non-human spheres as well (Held et al. 1999). The growth of transplanetary relationships, the core of the diverse processes grouped under the term *globalization*, is uneven: it is more pronounced in wealthier countries than in poorer ones and differentially articulated spatially even within wealthier countries. Transplanetary phenomena have been evident and have grown in importance over several centuries. A simple glance over the past 150 years suggests that these phenomena became more pronounced between 1870 and 1914 but then receded considerably until perhaps the early 1980s (Streeter, Weaver and Coleman 2009).

The growth of transplanetary connections has accelerated since the Second World War, particularly since the late 1970s. There are various explanations for this acceleration. At the heart of most of them is the dynamism of capitalism that resulted from the rapid growth of fully global financial markets. The predominant position of finance capital has led to a type of global capitalism not seen before (Castells 1996). This change in capitalism is linked in complex ways with innovations in information and communication technologies that have permitted transplanetary connections to become more supraterritorial: these connections are less bound by the physical location or the nation-state boundaries within which people live. As a result, the growth of planet-wide connections has led to ever greater intrusions of global relationships into the daily lives of more persons than ever before (taking into account the caveats about inequalities in distribution noted above).

In his extensive study of globalization, Manuel Castells argues that compared to long-standing vertical social forms, "network societies", as new social structures, have become more efficient due to their flexibility, their scalability and their survivability (2004: 7). We have witnessed the network structural form become increasingly predominant in the economy as evidenced by global financial markets, transformations in international trade, regionalization of production and the emergence of the "network enterprise" and global business networks. It has also become more important in the realm of culture. Cultural expressions of all kinds are fundamentally changed and reshaped as networks permit the formation of an electronic hypertext that enables television, radio, print media, film, video, art and the internet to be integrated and networked into an increasingly global system. This global system, influenced by networks, departs from the hierarchical approaches of the past in being interactive.

The particularly neoliberal form of globalization that has been dominant for the past 30 years has been accompanied by widening divisions of wealth, both between states and within states in the world system. In response to the network character of this globalization, those movements that seek to challenge it find it more optimal to work through their own networks. I speak here not only of the global justice movement, but also of movements and networks promoting and using violence like Al Qaeda, Kurdish nationalists, the Tamil Tigers, the Patriot movement in the United States, and private militias and mercenary corporations.[1]

In seeking to develop a new vocabulary and conceptual tools for understanding globalization, neither Castells nor Appadurai refer very much, if at all, to imperialism. Amartya Sen, in his 2006 book *Identity and Violence,* while locating the problem in social developments and favouring social and political organization based upon a singular identity, sees globalization in more positive terms than do these two authors. Again, imperialism is not invoked as any kind of expression of globalization that might create situations favouring physical violence. Many scholars assume that imperialism is in the past and that globalizing processes as defined above have gone beyond imperialism. Other scholars disagree.

In this chapter, I focus on a small number of globalization scholars and their discussions of contemporary forms of imperialism in an effort to add understanding to the debate. I argue that imperialism is part of the phenomenon of neoliberal globalization and is built on a historically unique, networked military structure controlled by the United States, but often coordinated with the militaries of other states favouring neoliberal globalization. In short, there is a hard, military infrastructure undergirding contemporary globalization that needs to become more integrated into our consideration.

I develop this argument in three steps. First, I consider the work of several globalization scholars who seek to integrate the study of empires and imperialism into the study of globalization, noting the similarities and differences in their respective analyses. Second, I turn in some detail to the research of Chalmers Johnson, a US political scientist who argues that the US has developed a new form of empire, a militarist one, distinctive from its nineteenth-century counterparts. Third, I reflect upon the analysis in the first two sections for the study of globalization and our understanding of contemporary forms of violence.

Globalization, empires and imperialism

Globalizing processes are not new phenomena, but ones that have been taking place for a long time, while accelerating in intensity and extensity. Historically, they have often been linked to empire-building and imperialism. The British Empire, for example, accelerated the process of globalization by breaking down geographic, political and economic barriers throughout the world (Parsons 1999: 119–20). British rule and informal influence precipitated these developments by joining diverse regions and peoples on every continent. British imperialism brought about the diffusion of a diverse array of peoples, cultures, flora and fauna around the globe. Given its decentralized character, the most common point of reference for the peoples involved was British culture and the economic demands of British imperialism. The British created a global network of unequal exchanges, a network where their control was never total or absolute.

In these respects, the British Empire conformed to a particular form: a political unit that controlled an extensive amount of territory and a heterogeneous mix of subject peoples. Territories located overseas were often known as colonies, especially if they were settled by migrants from the dominant group in an empire. There were also informal parts of empires where colonies did not formally exist, but where British naval power and commercial dominance led to serious surrenders of sovereignty by particular states.

A number of scholars suggest, however, that the relationship between globalization, empires and imperialism has shifted considerably over the past 60 years, but has not yet ended. In interpreting the nature of these shifts, there are different points of view about the nature of empires and the role of the dominant power of this period, the United States of America, as an imperial power. This literature is extensive and developing and I cannot survey all of it here. Instead, I summarize briefly three positions on questions that both complement and differ from one another.

The focus of the debate is on how imperial control works and what its nature is. Globalization creates the material and cultural basis for permitting imperialism to become globally more extensive and intensive. Michael Hardt and Antonio Negri, in *Empire* (2000), take pains to distinguish the contemporary situation from earlier forms of empire: globalization involves multiple processes that are neither unified nor univocal; economic processes involve the development of world markets and include huge transnational corporations that sit astride these markets; and there are changes in production, particularly the idea of production taking place in a global frame of reference, where nation-state boundaries are less relevant. They lay particular stress on the contemporary construction of global money, or financial markets, and how these markets, in turn, deconstruct national financial and thereby economic markets (Hardt and Negri 2000: 345–6).

Hardt and Negri reject the views of world-systems perspectives that would see these developments as a continuation of long-standing historical tendencies towards a world market and expanding capitalist development. There are two developments that are crucial to understanding their position that the situation is "fundamentally new" and "a significant historical shift" (2000: 8). First, they note that communication networks, made possible by information and communication technologies, have an "organic relationship" to the new world order; "Communication not only expresses but also organizes the movement of globalization" (2000: 32). These networks are also crucial to the creation of subjectivities and to the transition from a "disciplinary society" to a "society of control". Communication networks create spaces not bounded by territory. Hardt and Negri make frequent use of the concept of "deterritorialization" in ways that are reminiscent of other globalization scholars like Jan Aart Scholte (2005) and John Thompson (1999).

Second, Hardt and Negri argue that the situation is significantly new because of a shift in global relations of power that brings together economic and political power. It is at this point that the concept of "Empire" comes into play.[2] They describe Empire as a "regime" that takes the form of "a decentred and decentralizing apparatus of rule that progressively incorporates the whole global realm within its open, expanding frontiers" (Hardt and Negri 2000: xii). Here, they refer to a process of political globalization that rests on a developing system of global law (a juridical regime), a system of administration, a global approach to policing, and a global system of ethics based on universal notions like human rights. Concepts of imperial command, imperial administration and imperial norms are developed in relation to this political process. This regime has no centre, nor does it have boundaries.

Therefore, "[t]he United States does not, and indeed no nation-state can today, form the centre of an imperialist project. Imperialism is over. No nation will be world leader in the way modern European nations were" (Hardt and Negri 2000: xv–xvi). In *Multitude: War and Democracy in the Age of Empire*, Hardt and Negri write:

> Not all the powers in Empire's network, of course, are equal – on the contrary, some nation-states have enormous power and some have none at all, and the same is true for the various other corporations and institutions that make up the network – but despite inequalities they must cooperate to create and maintain the current global order, with all of its internal divisions and hierarchies. (2004: xii)

Accordingly, "no nation-state, not even the most powerful one, not even the US, 'can go it alone' and maintain global order without collaborating with the other major powers in the network of Empire" (2004: xii).

From its inception, the US has claimed to be an exception to the corruption of European forms of sovereignty (Hardt and Negri 2004: 8). In this respect, the US continues to promote these characteristics by describing itself as the global leader, promoting democracy, human rights and the international rule of law. Conversely, US exceptionalism also means exception from the law. In this respect, it refers to the double standard of the most powerful; one who commands but does not need to obey. Such exception, Hardt and Negri add, is the basis of tyranny and makes the realization of freedom, equality and democracy truly impossible. Hence, the two conceptions contradict one another and US exceptionalism of the second sort legitimizes claims made by other states to a state of exception.

Ulf Hedetoft takes a different view from Hardt and Negri and sees the US as a dominant power in ways somewhat recognizant of nineteenth-century imperial powers (2009). He argues that the US has pursued a consistent neo-imperial line of policy and action since the Second World War and the Bretton Woods agreement. Thus the institutions, commitments and instruments put in place in the early postwar days are explicable in terms of American policy goals. He also argues that it is primarily the interaction of such continuity of purpose and shifts of instruments that has produced the kind of "accelerated globalization" we speak of today. In this respect, for Hedetoft, globalization actually means a system of open economies dominated by US and transnational corporate interests.

Hedetoft frames his argument in terms of neo-imperialism:

> the aggregate capacity to project power and interest beyond one's formal sphere of sovereign authority in such a way that other political units, other autonomies, are induced or coerced into pursuing choices in keeping with the interests and preferences of the neo-imperial sovereign, accommodating it in multiple ways by adapting to its agenda, and more often than not taking this road because it is viewed to be the lesser evil or the most beneficial way to protect and defend national interests. (2009: 252)

He distinguishes this neo-imperialism from earlier forms in three ways. First, where colonial empires are based on territorial conquest and domination, neo-imperialism relies on a wider and usually more "indirect" palette of instruments for the achievement of control and compliance. Second, the causal and reflexive relationship between globalization and empire has been reversed: colonial imperialism created many of the necessary conditions, economically, geopolitically, technologically, institutionally and culturally, for postwar globalizing processes, whereas today it is globalization that provides the basis for new forms of imperial politics. Third, whereas colonialism consisted of a curious mélange of imperial and national, state-driven and substate, political and cultural processes, largely uncoordinated and unorchestrated by any one central agency (though clearly with European powers in the forefront), the US now has a coordinating role. Here he takes a position distinct from that of Hardt and Negri, and writes: "The 'unipolar' structure of the world – the power and global reach of US interests – not only makes globalization a more coordinated process, but increasingly tends to conflate globalization and (American) empire" (Hedetoft 2009: 253). He adds: "Since World War II a peculiar creature has thus been born, wedding powerful nationalism, ultimate sovereign control, and 'homeland security' policies to global hegemonic ambitions and liberal-cosmopolitan agendas" (2009: 253).

Chalmers Johnson, a specialist in Chinese and Japanese politics, is an American political scientist who only began to write about American imperialism after a highly unsettling visit to Okinawa in 1995. He visited the complex of 38 US bases on the island and began asking why they were still there some 50 years after the Second World War had ended. This question prompted extensive research into US military bases around the world and their supporting structures. Johnson concludes that the US operates as an empire from the centre, similarly to Hedetoft.

Distinctive from Hedetoft, however, Chalmers emphasizes the military dimension of the empire. He agrees that the US Empire functions by "projecting" its power, but adds that a global network of military bases is the principal means for these actions. Central to his analysis is the distinction between "military" and "militarism". The former refers to "all the activities, qualities, and institutions required by a nation to fight a war in its defense" (Johnson 2004: 23). Having a military thus refers to a capacity to ensure national independence, a necessity for securing "personal freedom". In contrast, "militarism" refers to a situation where a nation's armed services:

> come to put their institutional preservation ahead of achieving national security or even a commitment to the integrity of the government structure of which they are a part ... [W]hen a military is transformed into an institution of militarism, it naturally begins to displace all other institutions within a government devoted to conducting relations with other nations. (Johnson 2004: 23–4)

Based upon a careful reading of official documents, Johnson estimates that the US had 737 bases outside the US in 2005 (2006: 139).[3] Maintaining bases *inside* one's own country is part of national defence; building and keeping them *outside* one's country is best understood as imperialism in Johnson's view. In a speech at West Point in 2002, then-President George W. Bush stated that the US had a unilateral right to overthrow any government in the world deemed a threat to its security. He added that the US must be "ready for pre-emptive action when necessary to defend our liberty and to defend our lives.... In the world we have entered, the only path to safety is the path of action. And this nation will act" (cited in Johnson 2004: 286). In this view, readiness for action requires military bases in enough places for the US armed forces to strike quickly and effectively when called upon to do so to defend their interests and empire.

To understand transnational violence, therefore, both Hedetoft and Johnson argue that we must understand American imperialism. Johnson adds that we must realize that this imperialism is a "militarist" one in ways not seen in the past: "The American network of bases is a sign not of military preparedness but of militarism, the inescapable companion of imperialism" (2004: 24). In contrast, Hardt and Negri link globalization and violence but argue that the linkages arise as part of a decentred system of rule where the US plays an important role while acting in company with other capitalist states and with transnational corporations, including those offering mercenary services.

The institutional structure of militarist imperialism

As anticipated by scholars like Castells and Appadurai, militarist imperialism follows a network logic in company with the networked structures and markets of contemporary global capitalism. The US network of army bases gradually emerged over the twentieth century, but was expanded considerably after the Second World War, particularly in Europe and East Asia, and has continued to grow since the end of the Cold War. The bases themselves are like "micro-colonies", according to Johnson, in that they are completely beyond the jurisdiction of the occupied nation-state. When a base is set up, the US almost always negotiates a Status of Forces Agreement (SOFA) with the host country. SOFAs are written so that national courts cannot exercise jurisdiction over US military personnel who commit crimes against local people, except in special cases where the US transfers them to local jurisdiction. Since members of the military are exempt from normal passport and immigration controls, the military often has the option of simply flying someone accused of a crime out of the country. In 2001, the US had publicly acknowledged SOFAs with 93 countries.[4] The US has also refused to accept the authority of the International Criminal Court. Thus neither domestic laws nor international laws have jurisdiction over US military personnel.

The system of bases, in turn, comes under the command of regional commanders-in-chief (CINCs). These regional commanders have accumulated more authority since the end of the Cold War, overseeing matters such as intelligence, special operations, space assets, nuclear forces, arms sales and military bases (Johnson 2004: 124). CINCs produce "theater engagement plans", which are miniature foreign policy statements for their respective region and include policies for cultivating close relations with local military organizations. In these respects, the CINCs have become more influential in the given regions than ambassadors. Thus the CINC in the Pacific region supervises the affairs of 43 countries. A CINC reports directly to the President and the Secretary of Defense, avoiding the normal chain of command. They exist for the Middle East, the Pacific, Europe, and Latin America.

Complementing these developments in Washington under the presidency of George W. Bush, the Department of Defense accelerated its gradual obscuring and displacement of the State Department as the primary agency for making and administering foreign policy. The US now stations more uniformed military officers in foreign countries than it does diplomats, aid workers and regional specialists.

The private sector is also extensively involved in this military network. Many US bases have come to depend on private contractors for their defence, amenities and operations. Presumably this approach is more cost effective, but as the Iraq War has shown, contracts often go to companies that are well connected to political authorities with competitive bidding largely absent. If one adds to these private contractors, university research and development centres, petroleum refiners and distributors, manufacturers of small-arms ammunition, multinational corporations like Boeing, the automobile companies, and so on, one can see how large and important the support for this imperial structure is in the US

When one looks at total military spending per year, at no time since 1955 has US defence spending declined to pre-Cold War, much less pre-Second World War, levels. More recently, if one includes privately outsourced services as well, Johnson estimates that the professional, permanent military costs about three-quarters of a trillion dollars per year (2006: 7), a figure that includes the Iraq and Afghanistan operations (US$120 billion), nuclear weapons (US$16.4 billion), pensions, hospital costs and disability payments for veterans (US$100 billion). When these figures are put into a world context, US military preponderance becomes evident.

Johnson speaks about the effects of militarism on the US republic, the atrophy of democracy, and the decline of Congress and the judiciary relative to the executive branch. At the end of the Cold War, the US no longer portrayed itself as a defensive power, seeking to ensure its own security and that of allied nations in the face of potential Soviet aggression. It did not declare victory and begin to demobilize its troops and close foreign bases. Rather, it began to recast its role as one of having a "responsibility to protect" other nations and societies from where "human rights" abuses and "genocide" were being committed. The US also claimed a responsibility to ensure that US-style democracy and its market economy were more widely adopted; Latin American drug cartels had to be beaten back, indigenous movements repressed, "rogue states" contained, and, of course, an endless "war on terrorism" pursued. Perhaps most important for our purposes is Johnson's summary statement of the five post-Cold War missions of the US military:

1 Maintaining absolute military preponderance over the rest of the world.
2 Eavesdropping on the communications of citizens, allies and enemies alike.
3 Attempting to control as many sources of petroleum as possible, both to service the country's demand for fossil fuels and the obvious needs of the military itself.
4 Providing work and income for the military-industrial complex (something he has termed "military Keynesianism" in more recent writings).
5 Ensuring that members of the military and their families live comfortably and are well entertained while serving abroad. (Johnson 2004: 151–2)

Having outlined these missions, he suggests that, taken together, they still do not explain the expanding empire of bases. He returns to militarism and imperialism, arguing that the bases reflect an impulse on the part of American leaders to dominate other peoples simply because they have the power to do so (2004: 152).

In fact, the US went to war more frequently after the Cold War ended than it had during the Cold War. In this period, the US acquired new bases in Eastern Europe, Iraq, the Persian Gulf, Pakistan, Uzbekistan, Afghanistan and Kyrgyzstan. These new bases permitted some scaling back of deployments in Germany, Turkey and Saudi Arabia, where opposition to bases had been increasing. Several very large bases are being built in Iraq and are expected, along with those in Kuwait, to replace those in Saudi Arabia in particular. Johnson suggests that a covert reason for the invasion of Iraq was to move the main focus of the US military installations in the Middle East to that country, also a major oil producer (2006: 156). The new ones in southern Eurasia will also provide a basis for a stronger influence over a region very rich in petroleum resources. Neoconservatives spoke openly about unilateral US domination and an imperial role, and their voices became even more influential as prominent proponents of the doctrine held highly important positions in the George W. Bush administration.

Militarist imperialism: Concluding observations

Several years before the attack on September 11, 2001, Johnson penned the first book in his trilogy entitled *Blowback*. The term was originally coined by officials in the Central Intelligence Agency to refer to the unintended consequences of policies that were kept secret from the American people (Johnson 2000: 8). "As a concept, blowback is obviously most easily grasped in its straightforward manifestations. The unintended consequences of American policies in country X lead to a bomb at an American embassy in country Y or a dead American in country Z" (2000: xi). Certainly, any number of Americans have wandered into situations of this kind; of hidden imperial scenarios about which they knew nothing. More generally, the concept refers to the local violent effects of militarism over time, associated racism and criminality, and the arrogance of power.

Understanding the forms of this violence is helped by globalization scholars like Castells and Appadurai who have remarked on the correspondence between network forms of neoliberal globalization and the cellular-like organizations fighting intercommunal, intrastate and transnational wars (Castells 2003; Appadurai 2006). By focusing also on the continuing linkages between globalization and imperialism, we also might come to see more clearly the material, military component of imperial rule and resulting blowback. Globalization fostered the idea of a "network society" and as such has led to open markets and global business and cultural networks as well as military networks, as embodied by the global network of military bases which form the American empire.

Johnson's research provides an opening and valued contribution for research. His work hints at more extensive collaboration between the US general staff and such staffs in the North Atlantic Treaty Organization (NATO) and other countries. Systematic networked military collaboration would be consistent with Hardt and Negri's understandings of Empire. NATO operations in Kosovo and Afghanistan fit with their thinking as well. Hedetoft would counter that such collaboration reflects US soft power and capabilities to project that power more than it does a "decentred" system of rule. Future research might resolve such differences.

When the US has utilized its power and operated as an empire, it has accelerated the speed of globalization. In addition to networked society, as has been argued, globalization has indirectly produced new forms of violence and networks of uncivil society as a way to combat US imperialism and the very forces of globalization, especially as the divide between the rich and poor grows. For that reason, to understand uncivil society, we must understand the origins and nature of networked society, and thus American imperialism and globalization as well. If an uncivil movement truly wants to challenge globalization and imperial violence, American or otherwise, it must develop and operate its own networks. Therefore, what remains clear is that globalization and imperialism remain joined, albeit in different ways than in the nineteenth and early twentieth centuries, and that imperial violence continues to beget violence.

Notes

1. For more on these and other similar questions, please see "Part II: Challenges" in this volume.
2. In addition to Empire, they use the word "imperial" in distinction with "imperialist" to make the contrast with the earlier European empires.
3. This estimate is a conservative one because it does not include bases in Kosovo, Serbia, Afghanistan, Iraq, Kyrgyzstan, Qatar, Uzbekistan and the United Kingdom. An honest count, he opines, would come to about 1,000 bases worldwide.
4. Johnson suspects the number is higher because these agreements are embarrassing to some countries, particularly Islamic ones, and thus their true number is not known (2004: 36).

REFERENCES

Appadurai, Arjun (2006) *Fear of Small Numbers: An Essay on the Geography of Anger*. Durham, NC: Duke University Press.

Castells, Manuel (1996) *The Rise of the Network Society*. Oxford: Blackwell.

Castells, Manuel (2003) *The Power of Identity*, 2nd edn. Oxford: Blackwell.

Castells, Manuel (2004) "Informationalism, networks, and the network society: A theoretical blueprint", in Manuel Castells, ed., *The Network Society: A Cross-cultural Perspective*, Cheltenham, UK: Edward Elgar, pp. 3–45.

Hardt, Michael and Antonio Negri (2000) *Empire*. Cambridge, MA: Harvard University Press.

Hardt, Michael and Antonio Negri (2004) *Multitude: War and Democracy in the Age of Empire*. New York: Penguin.

Hedetoft, Ulf (2009) "Globalization and US empire: Moments in the forging of the global turn", in Stephen Streeter, John Weaver and William Coleman, eds, *Empires and Autonomy: Moments in the History of Globalization*, Vancouver: University of British Columbia Press, pp. 247–72.

Held, David, Anthony G. McGrew, David Goldblatt and Jonathan Perraton (1999) *Global Transformations: Politics, Economics, and Culture*. Stanford: Stanford University Press.

Johnson, Chalmers (2000) *Blowback: The Costs and Consequences of American Empire*. New York: Holt.

Johnson, Chalmers (2004) *The Sorrows of Empire: Militarism, Secrecy, and the End of the Republic*. New York: Holt.

Johnson, Chalmers (2006) *Nemesis: The Last Days of the American Republic*. New York: Holt.

Johnson, Chalmers (2008) "Why the US has really gone broke: The economic disaster that is military Keynesianism", *Le Monde Diplomatique* (English edn), Feb. At <http://mondediplo.com/2008/02/05military> (accessed June 2010).

Parsons, Timothy (1999) *The British Imperial Century, 1815–1914: A World History Perspective*. Lanham, MD: Rowman and Littlefield.

Scholte, Jan Aart (2005) *Globalization: A Critical Introduction*, 2nd edn. London: Palgrave Macmillan.

Sen, Amartya K. (2006) *Identity and Violence: The Illusion of Destiny.* New York: Norton.

Streeter, S. M., John Weaver and William Coleman (eds) (2009) *Empires and Autonomy: Moments in the History of Globalization*. Vancouver: University of British Columbia Press.

Thompson, John (1999) *Globalization and Culture*. Chicago: University of Chicago Press.

2

New state structures in South America

Edgardo Lander

During the three hundred years of Iberian colonial rule over what is today known as Latin America, political participation was limited. Privileged positions in all realms of society, be it in the civil service, the Church, education, professions, etc., could only be occupied by Europeans or their "pure blood" descendants.[1] Those who did not fit into a particular category – that of the urban, educated, well-off, white male elite – were excluded from the ranks of civil society. The legacy of this history of exclusion and limited political participation is reflected in current projects of social transformation, democratization and inclusion – in essence, the decolonization of Latin American society – as well as in contemporary struggles against the established order. A critical understanding of civil society, democracy and citizenship in present-day Latin America requires recognition of the colonial imprint that these political categories left in the region. This chapter elaborates on some of the Latin American debates and experiences related to democracy, citizenship and civil society, and highlights the current conflicts related to these issues, with examples from Venezuela, Ecuador and Bolivia.

Latin American debates about democracy, civil society and citizenship have taken place at two levels. One is that of civilizational confrontations, or cultural wars – that is, the struggle between the modern/colonial modes of life and the multiple expressions of resistance, and the practical construction and reconstruction of cultural alternatives. This is the struggle for the decolonization of societies, which has come to the fore in recent years. Here the colonial and Eurocentric nature of liberal democracy in the continent is the central issue.

The other level can be found within the limits of "modern" Western democracy; confrontations and debates within the political spectrum from left to right. This is the dimension of the struggle for inclusion, for equality, for citizenship and for individual rights. This is the level within which political parties have operated. Within this overall framework, the most radical perspectives have led to the rejection of liberal democracy, characterized as a capitalist democracy that reproduces and legitimizes class domination.

The relations between these two levels have been complex and intertwined in diverse times and places. If either dimension is ignored, it is not possible to understand Latin American political history or the multiple meanings of democracy, civil society and citizenship.

The colonial imprint of democracy in Latin America

Even with political independence in most of the continent in the first decade of the nineteenth century, not much changed in relation to the preceding era of colonial rule. In what Aníbal Quijano has characterized as "political independence without a social revolution", the basic patterns of the "coloniality of power" – the structures of power, control and hegemony that emerged during the colonial era – were preserved (Quijano 2000a). The main component of the colonial structure of power, before and after independence, was the ranking of the population according to their so-called race, that is, their phenotypical characteristics, specifically the colour of their skin (Quijano 2000b). Despite its universalistic aspirations, liberal democracy embodies an alternative that does not exhaust the possibilities of the construction of plural and democratic coexistence between peoples.

The American and French revolutions are the paradigms of the political transformations that led to the creation of the modern democratic nation-state. At least in theory, the latter offered equal political rights and freedoms to all, despite slavery and huge economic disparities. What led to the Industrial Revolution and the American and European social revolutions had its roots in the "discovery" of America more than 500 years ago, the origin of the modern colonial world system. To examine the difference – the colonial difference – in the experience of modernity between the imperial North and the colonized South is the best way to approach the divergent experiences between contemporary Western Europe and Latin America in relation to liberal democracy (Mignolo 2000: 3–28).

The basic difference between the centre and the periphery, or North and South, is the colonial-imperial order of the modern world system. Without taking into account this difference, it is impossible to explain the historical experience of citizenship and democracy of some countries of Western Europe, and that of the colonized countries of the South. The limits to universal (liberal) citizenship and the democratization of peripheral societies are to be found in their subordination to the hegemonic colonial-imperial order, and in the preservation of the structures of colonial power.

As has been argued by Aníbal Quijano, Enrique Dussel, Walter Mignolo and others, the experience of modernity was radically different in the North and the South.[2] The "luminous nature" of modernity, as characterized by the philosophers of the Enlightenment – Kant, Hegel and more recently by Habermas – is the bright side of a worldwide historical process. Its dark underside lies in colonies, without which the bright side would not have been possible. In the North, modernity eventually led to material abundance, citizenship, democracy, science and technology. For the majority of the planet's population living in the colonized, subjugated South, modernity entailed imperial and colonial domination, genocide and slavery.

Given that the wars of independence in the Americas were fought in the name of liberty and the values of the Enlightenment, who, in the continent's new independent republics, were considered citizens? In the founding constitutions, strict limits were placed on citizenship. The vast majority of the population was excluded. Most of the criteria for exclusion were made explicit in the constitutional texts. With some variations, exclusions were defined in terms of religion (non-Catholics need not apply); education (a literacy requirement); income (certain thresholds of regular income); marital status (the requirement that citizens be married); occupation ("dependent" professions such as household servants were excluded). That women and most of the non-white population were not citizens was considered so obvious that there was no need to mention it. In any case, the sum of all of the other criteria all but guaranteed the exclusion of non-whites. In most countries, this limited citizenship to a small number of urban, educated, well-off, white male elites. This meant that the vast majority of the population – women, non-whites (Indians, blacks, "mixed-blood"), as well as poor whites, were not part of the polis of the new republics.[3] This is not a question of constitutional doctrine or design. It simply expresses and consolidates the pre-existing colonial structure of power.

The development of capitalism in Western Europe and in Latin America caused deep civilizational changes. The colonial difference explains why the outcomes of these transformations were so different. In Western

Europe, in spite of the traumatic experience suffered by most of the working population, the Industrial Revolution, while destroying the old economic and social order, created new modalities of social inclusion with the expansion of wage-earning labour and later, as a result of prolonged popular struggles, democratic citizenship.

The civilizational wars of capitalism/liberalism in Latin America occurred in the absence of two basic historical conditions of liberal democracy: a social revolution (or the destruction or significant weakening of the old order); and sovereign states. These cultural wars occurred without the possibilities of new forms of inclusion in a new economic and political order; neither wage labour nor citizenship with democratic rights were accessible to the vast majority.

The consequences have been severe for the indigenous peoples and Afro descendants. In most Latin American countries today half of the labour force is part of the "informal" sector of the economy; every year more than a million Latin Americans opt for (mainly illegal, strongly repressed) migration towards the United States or the European Union in search of better economic opportunities.

From the very beginning Latin American political systems were built on the basis of a colonial and Eurocentric grammar of politics. This grammar set precise limits on who was recognized as a social subject, what demands could be formulated, and what forms of organization and representation were possible. It established rules that limited who could speak and what could be expressed. Voices and demands outside these limits were not only considered illegitimate, but also nonsensical. In this colonial political grammar, the social classes seen as part of the "normal", "universal" historical experience of Western European industrial society (the bourgeoisie, landowners, the middle class, the working class and the peasantry) were recognized, at least potentially, as legitimate agents of political and social action. Their demands and aspirations, if not always accepted, were at least comprehensible. The Eurocentric patterns of this polity (left/right political cleavages, state/market conflict) and their organizational forms (political parties, labour unions, guilds and, later, interest groups and non-governmental organizations (NGOs)) became a straitjacket. They have allowed only for the recognition of certain parts of these societies (the so-called "modern" sectors), while making the rest invisible. These societies have high levels of structural heterogeneity with very diverse histories. They are multi-ethnic and multicultural and continue to have highly differentiated forms of production, language, knowledge, organization, authority and social norms.

Based on this linear, universalistic and Eurocentric view of history, the sort of citizenship constructed by this modern liberal political grammar has been highly one-sided. In denying the profound cultural/historical heterogeneity of these societies, this monocultural grammar has been part of a cultural war against those *others* whose very existence is not acknowledged and assumed to have nothing to contribute to the present or future of these nation-states.[4]

For the excluded majority, to aspire to be part of this kind of citizenship implied giving up their own culture, identity, community and history. To become a full citizen in this official state order required the assumption of liberal individualistic citizenship with its corresponding cultural values. In these conditions, the historical expulsions and the denial of access to the commons, due to the expansion of large-scale agricultural production and extractive activities, have implied a double-edged act of violence: the destruction of the material conditions of their own culture and the denial of the possibility of their incorporation into the dominant "modern" world.

To this historical experience, a new awareness has been added: the recognition of the ecological limits of the planet, and of the limits of liberal democracy in the age of neoliberal globalization. The promises of modernization, particularly over the last half century, have been associated with offers of material abundance and the consumer patterns of the American middle class, as portrayed by Hollywood and the global media. It has, however, become apparent that these destructive consumption patterns cannot be extended to the rest of the world's population. Even under current inequities in access to the common goods of the planet, in which millions don't have enough food or access to clean water, these consumption patterns are not sustainable and, as such, pose a direct and immediate threat to the continuation of human life. It has also become evident that, in spite of the fact that the poor in the South have contributed much less to climate change and other destructive life-menacing processes, they will bear the brunt of their negative impacts and have the least resources with which to deal with them.[5]

This raises many challenges for the continent, especially for the excluded indigenous peoples, Afro-descendants and peasants. On the one hand, the European cultural wars, by which liberal industrial society became dominant, were a new historical process. The global outcome could not be predicted. Now the consequences of those cultural wars are well known. The global expansion of the unregulated growth-oriented market economy, with its large-scale technology, is destroying the very conditions that make life possible. Many peasant, indigenous and Afro-descendant peoples and communities now realize that resistance is not just a cultural preference, but also one of survival.

At the same time, the promises of liberal democracy, especially of the model represented by postwar Western Europe, no longer seem attainable. During that period, liberal democracy achieved what now seems to be its maximum historical potential. Since the 1970s, the welfare state and its accompanying social and economic rights have been losing ground, even in the richest countries of the North. As a consequence of ecological and political/economic limits, the incorporation of the majority of the population into "modern", high-quality, wage-earning jobs no longer seems possible. The promises of "modernization", as represented by the consumption patterns of the North, have become less and less credible. This has all contributed to enormous cultural and political changes in popular political consciousness in Latin America over the last two decades.

The left and democracy in Latin America

The Latin American left has traditionally been critical of liberal democracy. For most of the left, the limits of liberal democracy are not necessarily its colonial character, but its class nature. It has been characterized as a formal, process-based model of democracy which privileges *negative rights* over *positive rights*, that is, formal political rights over social, economic and cultural rights. This perspective was prominent during the 1960s and 1970s, when, for many leftist organizations and intellectuals, a socialist revolution seemed to be on the cards.

However, after the military dictatorships in the 1970s and 1980s, a more positive view of the so-called "formal" aspects of liberal democracy emerged. The military dictatorships were the result of right-wing reactions, or counterrevolutions, against waves of popular movements and organizations struggling to change Latin American societies. Brutal repression coupled with neoliberal economic "structural adjustment" policies were the hallmark of these military regimes. In those conditions, democracy and basic human rights became banners for the left.

In the Latin American social sciences, the discourse about revolution gave way to a discourse about democracy and democratic transitions. A whole new academic discipline emerged: transitology (Lander 1997). This new discourse privileged negotiation, human rights, civil society, social movements and NGOs. The critique of the class character of liberal democracy all but disappeared in much of this transformed "democratic left". The colonial character of this model of democracy became a non-issue.

In spite of the initial emphasis on human rights and the need for a negotiated and peaceful transition to democracy, there were nonetheless broad popular expectations about alternatives to the neoliberal economic policies imposed by the right-wing military dictatorships. For some countries, transition to democracy was part of a negotiation that included guarantees that the basic orientations of the economic model would not be changed. In Chile, the constitution left by the Pinochet regime made it next to impossible to depart in any significant way from neoliberal policies. For other countries, the military dictatorships left huge foreign debts, as well as debt agreements with the International Monetary Fund and the World Bank, which implied that the basic orientations of neoliberal economic policies could not be altered. The new democratic governments had to act according to the dictates of these international financial institutions, even if this went against the will of the population. The limited character of these democracies soon became obvious. Unfulfilled expectations led to widespread frustration.

By the end of the 1980s, a new cycle of struggles and popular resistance against the effects of neoliberal structural adjustment policies began. The Caracazo in Venezuela (1989), the *levantamiento indígena* (indigenous uprising) in Ecuador (1990) and the Zapatista rebellion in Mexico (1994) were the most visible expressions of this new phase of popular resistance.[6] They soon spread to the rest of the region. The most significant feature of the popular struggles has been their diversity. The collapse of Soviet socialism led to the demise of a powerful historical influence on anti-capitalist struggles in Latin America (Lander 2004). It became easier to go beyond the Eurocentric demarcations and cleavages that the political projects, led by Marxist parties, had imposed on many popular struggles, based on the central role of the proletariat and a Eurocentric view of history. After the fall of the Berlin Wall, the new cycle of struggles in Latin America was weakened by the large variety of subjects and organizations involved: indigenous peoples and communities, Afro-descendant communities and organizations, peasants and landless rural workers, environmental groups, industrial workers, women's organizations, continent-wide campaigners against the Free Trade Area of the Americas (FTAA) and other free trade agreements, those struggling against the privatization of public services and enterprises, students and human rights organizations.[7]

New forms of politics are created, learned and shared in the collective experience. The diversity of subjects and the plurality of issues are celebrated as a virtue as they enrich the potential for a plural and democratic alternative social order. The construction of alternative social relations is not a task left for the future, but a day-to-day, present challenge.

The World Social Forum enriched this by facilitating face-to-face debates, creating and strengthening regional and global social and political networks, and by giving campaigns against issues such as the war in Iraq, free trade and water privatizations a global reach.[8] In the first decade of the twenty-first century, similar movements achieved significant levels of organization, mobilization and coordination and were able to achieve important victories, such as defeating the FTAA and reversing the privatization of public services, as in the case of water in Cochabamba, Bolivia. In chapter 1, William Coleman argues that network societies and the network mode succeed because of their flexibility, scalability and survivability. The above examples highlight this.

Socialism and/or decolonization

Until recently, even in countries where the majority of the population is indigenous, most of the struggles against the established order had remained within the limits imposed by the Eurocentric view. Other subjects, other demands and other forms of organization had no place within this logic.

An example of the difficulties faced by the left when confronted with realities that do not fit into this grammar is the case of the Bolivian revolution of 1952. In the view of the leaders of this revolutionary process, there was no space for Indian subjects or their demands. Thus the demands of Indians, a majority of the Bolivian population, had to be translated into the language and grammar of modern politics. The Indian peoples were assumed to be peasants: their demands for ancestral territories were translated into demands for agrarian reform and their traditional communal organizational forms were translated into peasant workers' unions. Only decades later were the Aymaras, Quechuas, Guarani and other Indian peoples and communities in Bolivia able to jettison these colonial constructs to struggle for their rights as Indian peoples. This requires different identities, including the right to be Aymaras, Quechuas, Guaranis, etc.; and different demands, including the right to their own cultures and languages, control over ancestral territories, and the reconstruction and/or strengthening of traditional basic community political units (the Ayllú in the case of the Aymaras). This signalled a new moment, especially in the Andean region, which could no longer be confined within the boundaries of the dominant liberal paradigm. Today, in Bolivia and Ecuador the struggle is for the overhaul of the monocultural colonial-liberal state and the creation of a pluricultural and plurinational state (Walsh 2008).

This new dynamic also reflects the new and complex relations between different groups: struggles carried out in the name of democratization and inclusion for all as citizens in a liberal capitalist order; anti-capitalist struggles aimed at the construction of what has been called "Twenty-First Century Socialism"; and struggles aimed at the decolonization of society. These different strands are present in diverse forms in different countries.[9] Often, these apparently contradictory struggles are present in the same political project.

The current so-called leftist governments in Latin America are very diverse in their political projects. In some countries like Chile, Uruguay, Argentina and Brazil, the governing parties, even if led by "socialists" or "workers", do not question the confines of capitalist liberal democracy and have abandoned any appeal to radical social change. They have combined neoliberal macroeconomic orientations, based on exports of agricultural and/or mineral commodities, with limited social democratic welfare state policies, aimed at improving the standard of living of the poor. Neither socialism nor decolonization is part of their political agenda.

Yet in Venezuela, Ecuador and Bolivia, attempts are being made to go beyond the limits of liberal democracy. In each of these countries, there are anti-capitalist and anti-colonial proposals that have a central role in current debates and governments' vision of the future of these societies. In this new context, there are new struggles over the meaning of the public, the private, democracy, citizenship and civil society. There are confrontations at all levels: theoretical, political, cultural and practical. There are struggles between attempts to question and subvert the class content and the universalistic colonial Eurocentric meaning (and practice) of these categories and attempts to reaffirm these meanings as universal. These are not well-delineated confrontations between clear-cut theoretical or political conceptions; rather, they reflect a complex practical, political and theoretical search for alternatives to the status quo.

What are the theoretical and political issues present in the constitutional debates and texts of these three countries?

These debates embody the challenges of creating new political grammars, new forms of state organizations, and alternative modes of production and of relations between humans and the rest of nature. They take place within the constraints of the present world system and take into account the reality of the present configuration of nation-states and the well-organized opposition to the proposed changes by its most privileged strata.

One initial thread to be found in these attempts to decolonize the idea and practice of democracy is the radical questioning of the separation between nature on the one hand, and the political, the economic and the social/cultural on the other. Democracy is thought to refer to the whole of life: a way of being as part of nature, in production, in culture, in knowledge, in languages, in diverse forms of decision-making and forms of public authorities. These efforts seek to decolonize the Eurocentric conception of democracy as one limited to the political arena. The new debates point to a democratic way of living in all spheres of existence.

The discussion that follows is based on the new constitutional texts of Venezuela (approved by a referendum in 1999), and those of Bolivia (approved in 2009) and Ecuador (approved in 2008).[10] No attempt is made here to explore the likely outcome of these efforts or to evaluate the political viability of these proposals.

Venezuela

In the 1999 Venezuelan constitution, the deepening of democracy is fostered through the introduction of various modalities of participatory democracy. Participatory democracy is not conceived as an overall substitute or alternative to representative democracy, but as a tool directed at expanding the limits of representative democracy. According to Article 70 of the constitution:

> Participation and involvement of people in the exercise of their sovereignty in political affairs can be manifested by: voting to fill public offices, referendum, consultation of public opinion, mandate revocation, legislative, constitutional and constituent initiative, open fora and meetings of citizens whose decisions shall be binding, among others. (Article 70)

Participatory democracy is not limited to politics. The same Article establishes diverse modalities of participation in social and economic affairs: "citizen service organs, self-management, co-management, cooperatives in all forms, including those of a financial nature, savings funds, community enterprises, and other forms of association guided by the values of mutual cooperation and solidarity" (Article 70). Over the past decade, this has led to an expansion of various forms of popular organization and participation across the country. Most of these deal with local issues (water, health, education, housing and land tenure, etc.). One new experience of popular organization and participation is the Communal Councils. In these the communities work in a territorial base to deal with their common problems. These entities carry out a diagnosis of the communities' most urgent needs and establish priorities that lead to a collective formulation of projects. These projects are financed by the national government without much bureaucratic hassle. The councils are in charge of carrying out or of supervising the projects, as well as being responsible for the administration of funds.

Bolivia and Ecuador

In the new Bolivian constitution, three forms of democracy are included:

1 Direct and participatory, by means of referenda, citizens' legislative initiatives, recall referenda, assemblies, town hall meetings and advance consultation, among others. Assemblies and town hall meetings to have a deliberative character.
2 Representative, by means of the election of representatives by universal, direct, secret vote, among others.
3 Communitarian, through the election, appointment or nomination of officers and representatives by rules and procedures of the nations and

peoples of indigenous origin and peasants, among others, according to Law. (Article 11)

The ideal of participatory democracy is also present in the new constitution of Ecuador: "Sovereignty belongs to the people, their will is the foundation of authority, a will exerted through the organs of public power and forms of direct participation" (Article 1).

However, in both the Bolivian and Ecuadorian constitutions the fundamental aim is not to increase participation within the existing state structures nor to add new forms of participation to the existing ones. The aim is to create new forms of participation within a radically transformed state. That is, to go beyond the monocultural liberal state towards the building of an intercultural, plurinational state based on the variety of peoples and cultures existing in these countries. These constitutional texts are part of a new alternative historical project, not only for the indigenous and Afro-American peoples and communities, but for the whole of the population.

These aims are expressed in many ways. One of these is found in Bolivia's constitutional project:

> We leave the colonial, republican and neoliberal State in the past. We assume the historical challenge of collectively constructing a united, social, communitarian plurinational state that integrates and articulates the aims of advancing towards a democratic, productive Bolivia, that inspires peace, and is tied to the goals of integral development and the free determination of the peoples. (Preamble)[11]

In the case of Ecuador:

> People have the right to build and to maintain their own cultural identity, to decide if they belong to one or more cultural communities and to express such options, [the right] to aesthetic freedom; the right to knowledge of the historical memory of their own cultures and [the right] to have access to their cultural patrimony; to divulge their own cultural expressions and to have access to them. (Article 21)[12]

The construction of a plurinational and pluricultural state recognizes that different peoples and communities within the nation-state speak different languages. In the Bolivian constitution, a total of 36 different languages, apart from Spanish, are recognized as official languages. Every level of government must use at least two official languages, one of them being Spanish (Article 5).

In Ecuador, two indigenous languages, the *kichwa* and the *shuar,* are official languages for "intercultural relations". The other ancestral languages are official languages for the indigenous people in zones where they live, and the state has the responsibility of protecting and promoting their conservation and use (Article 2). The state will guarantee freedom of education and the right of people to learn in their own language and in their own cultural setting.

This is part of a deep cultural transformation that questions the individualistic, hegemonic patterns of Western/capitalist civilization. It proposes a radically different path from the ideals of *progress* and *development* dominant in the modern world. This is not conceived as an imaginary utopia, but as an alternative rooted in the many cultural diversities and traditions existing in these countries. This is all subsumed under the ideas of *sumak kawsay* and *suma qamaña* (to live well).

In the case of Bolivia:

> The State assumes and promotes as ethical-moral principles of the plural society: *ama qhilla, ama llulla, ama suwa* (don't be lazy, don't be a liar, don't be a thief), *suma qamaña* (to live well), *ñandereko* (a harmonious life), *teko kavi* (a good life), *ivi maraei* (earth without evil) and *qhapaj ñan* (a noble way of life). II. The State is sustained in the values of unity, equality, inclusion, dignity, liberty, solidarity, reciprocity, respect, complementariness, harmony, transparency, balance, equality of opportunities, equal social and gender participation, common well-being, responsibility, social justice, and the distribution and redistribution of social goods and services in order to live well (*vivir bien*). (Article 8)

In the Ecuadorian text: .

> The idea of *sumak kawsay buen vivir* implies not only solidarity among humans, but also living in harmony with and in nature. In the words of Alberto Acosta, who chaired the Ecuadorian Constitutional Assembly during most of its debates: " 'living well' or *buen vivir* is born out of the collective life experience of the indigenous peoples and nationalities. It seeks a harmonious relation between human beings, and of them with nature.... It is a fundamental element in thinking a different society, a society that rescues popular knowledge and technologies, and solidarity based forms of organizing, of creating one's own answers ..." (cited in León 2008)

The role of the existing state

The construction of an intercultural, plurinational state offers the possibility of a radical redistribution of power relations within the state, as well as a redistribution in access to wealth and common goods for society as a whole. Otherwise, the recognition of the plurality of existing cultures would be limited to a multicultural recognition or even celebration of a diversity of unequals. Thus this historical project's key challenges are redistribution of wealth and access to common goods and the democratization of power relations. For this, the role of the state is crucial.

The nation-states established in Latin America were colonial states that responded more to the logic and interests of the colonizers and their descendants than to the cultures, territorial occupation or needs of the majority of the population. These states are seen as monocultural, authoritarian structures that have imposed the dominant Western culture on culturally and structurally heterogeneous societies. In Ecuador and Bolivia, the transformation of these societies can no longer be seen as part of the liberal tradition of inclusion and universal homogenizing of citizenship within the existing state structure. It requires a change towards a plurinational and pluricultural state.

However, these national states are considered to be necessary instruments of any possible transformation in these societies. The movements, leaders and parties that were pushing for more radical changes in these countries were elected. The majority of the population decided via a national referendum that a constitutional assembly should be convened. When elections for these assemblies were carried out, a huge majority of its members were in favour of changes to the established order.

In the political projects of Venezuela, Ecuador and Bolivia there is also the perceived need to strengthen the state so that it can be deployed in the process of social transformation. Three decades of neoliberalism weakened most of the Latin American states. As a result of the policies of structural adjustment, many public services were abandoned or privatized and the main state corporations – particularly, but not only, in the energy sector – were sold to transnational corporations.

Decentralization led to a significant weakening of the national states' capacity to deal with the external pressures from global financial institutions, governments of the North and transnational corporations. They were equally weakened in their capability to respond to the demands of their own population. Recovering control over the countries' oil and mineral resources and income, for example, is only possible with a stronger national state. This is also the case for redistributive policies. Fractured national states with little taxing capacity, where the privileged sectors of the population have controlled regional resources at the expense of the rest of the nation, as has been the case in Bolivia, have also led to the demand for strengthening the central national state. In the constitutions of all three countries, the strategic sectors of the economy, basic natural resources and main public services are reserved for the state.

Resistance to change

After five centuries of monocultural patterns of political organization that have ignored this plurality of cultures and peoples, the white and mestizo urban middle and upper classes see this as a threat to their historical privileges and denounce these processes as undemocratic, authoritarian or based on Indian fundamentalism.

In these confrontations, the Venezuelan case is quite typical. The stability of the Venezuelan democratic system, established after 1958, was based on the country's oil wealth and on the social democratic principles contained in the 1961 constitution. However, the national consensus started to unravel with the economic, political and institutional crisis that began in the late 1970s. One of the consequences of this crisis was the emergence of a neoliberal discourse that questioned the prevailing role of the state and political parties in Venezuelan society. This discourse led to a Manichean contrast between the *public* and the *private*. The state (together with political parties) is seen as the source of all evils, whereas civil society is considered to be the source of all virtues. The state is characterized as corrupt, paternalistic, inefficient and non-democratic. Civil society is characterized as creative, honest and efficient. Corporate media, which have become prominent political right-wing actors in most of Latin America, are seen as part of this virtuous civil society. Public policies that seek to include the excluded or expand access to health services and education are characterized as populist.

A new conception of citizenship emerged with this political discourse: from a democracy of parties to a democracy of citizens. This "modern citizen" is identified with middle-class and upper middle-class urban white Venezuelans. These citizens constitute "civil society" (Lander 1996). In this new polity, there was no place for the majority, the excluded popular strata of society. Ever since Chávez became president, as popular participation and organization have increased and society has become polarized, the confrontational use of the concept of civil society has become more frequent. Two meanings have come to the forefront: the association of civil society with the idea of being *civilized*, and an overt *racist* content. In this discourse, white, educated, middle- and upper-class, modern and civilized Venezuelans were threatened by primitive, uneducated, black and Indian hordes.

In current Venezuelan political discourse, "civil society" means middle- and upper-class opposition to the Chávez government. The left and popular social movements and organizations have given up any attempts to recover the concept of civil society. An appeal is made instead to *el pueblo* (the people), popular movements, popular organizations, etc.

The Latin American right and far right, as well as the US government, now view these trends as serious threats to "democracy". Right-wing think tanks, in Latin America, the United States and Europe, use a universalistic, Eurocentric paradigm of Western liberal democracy as a standard template with which to evaluate and discard every attempt to construct other alternative, historically and culturally rooted forms of political participation and organization, or any alternative conceptions of the state. The US State Department, through the National Endowment for Democracy, has given financial and political assistance to Venezuelan so-called civil society organizations such as *Súmate* that not only act as opposition political organizations, but also played an active role in the failed coup d'état against the Chávez government in April 2002.[13] Attempts to go beyond the historical patterns of limited democracy in Latin America are qualified as populist, authoritarian or "ethnic fundamentalist" threats to "democracy".

Likewise, resistance to the new constitutional proposals in Bolivia and Ecuador are made in the name of "civic" sectors, "civic organizations", and in an association between democracy and decentralization, between democracy and autonomy. Now that there is an attempt to use the administrative capacities and resources of the state to increase national autonomy and popular participation, the reaction appears in the discourse of opposition to a strong state, in the name of democracy, decentralization and civil society. The idea of civil society, and with it appeals to the civilized, has become a powerful political instrument in the hands of an opposition that, invoking the supposedly universal character of liberal "modern" democracy, questions the current constitutional processes as "primitive" and "premodern".

In Bolivia, decentralization and regional autonomy have become war cries for the right in order to control the resources of the richest regions in the country and oppose the government's policies. There is particularly violent opposition to any central state policies destined to control oil resources for redistributional purposes. The so-called statutes of autonomy seek to strip the central state of many of its powers. This has the express backing of the business community in the so-called Media Luna region of Bolivia, as well as of foreign landowners and transnational corporations involved in agribusiness and the energy sector. The threat of separatism, that is of breaking away from the rest of Bolivia, if their demands for autonomy are not granted, is permanently in the background.

In Ecuador, the right-wing/liberal opposition in Guayaquil – the richest part of the country – is claiming "full" autonomy from the central government (Calderón 2007). A similar, but weaker movement, the Committee for Liberty and Regional Autonomy, has been created in the oil-producing state of Zulia in Venezuela.

As part of a continental effort to coordinate struggles for regional autonomy, a new transnational organization has been created, the International Confederation for Liberty and Regional Autonomy (CONFILAR). For this organization, decentralization and regional autonomy go hand and hand with ultra-liberal policies and a minimal – Milton Friedman style – state. It has the backing of international liberal organizations and right-wing think tanks, like the Cato Institute in Washington

(Cato Institute 2006). One of the most radical leaders of the Bolivian right-wing opposition in Santa Cruz, Carlos Dabdoub, was named as the first president of this organization (Gobierno Departamental Autónomo Santa Cruz 2009).

Conclusion

There have been multiple meanings, debates and experiences of democracy, civil society and citizenship in the course of Latin American history. New policies of inclusion and new distinctions of what civil society is continue to emerge, as evidenced by current conflicts and projects of social transformation in Venezuela, Ecuador and Bolivia. Each nation must recognize the present configuration of the nation-state as it grapples with the challenge of decolonizing the idea and the practice of democracy and civil society. In this, the reshaping of the idea of participatory democracy and the meaning of "citizenship" towards the construction of intercultural and plurinational states is crucial.

Venezuela, Ecuador and Bolivia are going beyond the limits of Eurocentric liberal democracy and each has a new vision for the future of its society as illustrated in their respective constitutions. These policies have been articulated in diverse forms and in different countries that share similar colonial legacies. With a new political discourse, new struggles emerge over the meaning of democracy, citizenship and civil society.

Notes

1. For a detailed analysis of the case of Nueva Granada, see Gómez 2005.
2. See their essays in Lander 2000.
3. The notable exception was the revolution in Haiti, which was simultaneously anti-colonial, anti-slavery and anti-racist. The Constitution of 1816 is, in this sense, a remarkable historical document. It starts by prohibiting slavery (Article 1). The rights of men are declared to be liberty, equality and property (Article 6). "Equality does not admit any distinction based on birth, and inherited power" (Article 8). That was much more than the colonial powers could tolerate. This unique historical experience had to be squashed. The people of Haiti are still paying for the consequences.
4. This is what Johannes Fabian has characterized as "denial of coevalness"; see Fabian 1983.
5. For more on local and domestic environmental protests against global production projects in South America, specifically in Argentina and Uruguay, see chapter 13 by Ricardo Gutiérrez and Gustavo Almería in this volume.
6. To gain further perspective on uncivil and violent popular resistance movements that arise to challenge the status quo of neoliberal democracies, see chapter 1 above by William Coleman. Other popular resistance movements are analysed below by Mehra (chapter 6), Muni (chapter 7), Chowdhary (chapter 8) and Hassan (chapter 9).

7. In chapter 12, Marisa von Bülow examines the transnational alliances that were formed to protest the FTAA.
8. Marisa von Bülow's chapter details the organization, platform and participants of the World Social Forum.
9. These last two are usually identified with as anti-capitalist struggles.
10. See, for Venezuela <http://www.embavenez-us.org/constitution/intro.htm>; for Bolivia <http://www.bolivianconstitution.com/2009/06/new-constitution-of-bolivia-in-pdf.html>; for Ecuador <http://pdba.georgetown.edu/Constitutions/Ecuador/ecuador08.html> (all accessed Aug. 2010).
11. See also Article 1 and Article 2 for more examples of aims expressed.
12. See also Article 58 and Article 61.
13. See Lander 2002 and Golinger 2005.

REFERENCES

Calderón, Gabriela (2007) "Guayaquil con autonomía plena", *El Universo*, 9 Oct. At <http://www.elcato.org/node/2852> (accessed Aug. 2010).

Cato Institute (2006) "Por la libertad y la autonomía regional en Hispanoamérica", Washington, DC, 23 July. At <http://www.elcato.org/node/1761/> (accessed June 2010).

Fabian, Johannes (1983) *Time and the Other: How Anthropology Makes Its Object*. New York: Columbia University Press.

Gobierno Departamental Autónomo Santa Cruz (2009) "Carlos Dabdoub fue designado presidente de Confederación Internacional Autonómica". At <http://www.santacruz.gov.bo/index.php?option=com_content&task=view&id=97&Itemid=2> (accessed June 2010).

Golinger, Eva (2005) *El Código Chávez: Descifrando la intervención de los Estados Unidos en Venezuela*. Havana: Editorial de Ciencias Sociales.

Gómez, Santiago Castro (2005) *La hybris del Punto Cero: Ciencia, raza e ilustración en la Nueva Granada (1750–1816)*. Bogotá: Instituto Pensar, Pontifica Universidad Javeriana.

Lander, Edgardo (1996) "Urban social movements, civil society and new forms of citizenship in Venezuela", *International Review of Sociology*, 6(1): 51–65.

Lander, Edgardo (1997) *La democracia en las ciencias sociales latinoamericanas contemporáneas*. Caracas,: FACES/UCV: Biblioteca Nacional.

Lander, Edgardo, ed. (2000) *La colonialidad del saber: Eurocentrismo y ciencias sociales. Perspectives latinoamericanas*. Buenos Aires: CLASCO/UNESCO.

Lander, Edgardo (2002) "El papel del gobierno de los EE.UU. en el golpe de estado contra el Presidente Chávez: Una exploración preliminar", *Observatorio Social de América Latina*, 7 (June). At <http://bibliotecavirtual.clacso.org.ar/ar/libros/osal/osal7/lander.pdf> (accessed June 2010).

Lander, Edgardo (2004) "Sujetos, saberes, emancipaciones", in Emir Sade and Michael Brie, eds, *Reforma ou Revolução?*, São Paulo: Fundação Rosa Luxemburg and Laboratório de Políticas Públicas da UERJ, Expressão Popular, pp. 159–70.

León, Magdalena (2008) "El 'buen vivir': Objetivo y camino para otro modelo". At <http://alainet.org/active/26638&lang=es> (accessed June 2010).

Mignolo, Walter (2000) "Diferencia colonial y razón postoccidental," in Santiago Castro-Gómez, ed., *La reestructuración de las ciencias sociales en América Latina*, Bogotá: Colección Pensar, pp. 3–28.

Quijano, Anibal (2000a) "Colonialidad del poder, eurocentrismo y América Latina", in Edgardo Lander, ed., *La colonialidad del saber: Eurocentrismo y ciencias sociales. Perspectives latinoamericanas*, Buenos Aires: CLASCO/UNESCO, pp. 201–46.

Quijano, Anibal (2000b) "Colonialidad del poder y clasificación social", *Journal of World-Systems Research*, 11(2) (Summer–Fall): 342–86.

Walsh, Catherine (2008) "Interculturalidad y plurinacionalidad: Elementos para el debate constituyente", Conference, Montecristi, Universidad Andina Simón Bolívar, Sede Ecuador, Ecuador, Apr.

3

The African connection

Garth le Pere and Brendan Vickers

Globalization has introduced a range of centrifugal effects that render states and societies more vulnerable, especially in controlling the flows of goods and people across national boundaries. This is compounded and exacerbated by the problem of state legitimacy and authority, resulting in the inability of states to guarantee the provision of public goods where these concern social, political and economic well-being. A state-centric, Westphalian-based international system which functions according to the axioms of traditional geopolitics is thus an anachronism in today's world where geopolitics has been transcended, and in which territory, spatial relations and the constraints and privileges of sovereignty are far less compelling (see Ferguson and Mansbach 2004). It is a paradox that a permissive and highly liberalized international environment, underpinned by advances in technology, transportation and communications, has spawned transnational threats that would have been rather remote during the Cold War and which could not have been anticipated with its demise.

The global arena has become an extraordinary space for human development and progress, but also one that causes great disruption, instability and destruction. One threat that has proliferated as a consequence of accelerated global interaction is the spread of transnational criminal organizations and terrorist networks.[1] Particularly striking are the structural similarities between terrorism and organized crime. In both cases, states are the targets and, hence, collaboration is an increasingly attractive proposition. Their operational code is one of secrecy, and business is conducted in the dark reaches of the underworld; they use similar infrastructures to promote their activities; and they have recourse to the same networks for corruption and white-collar crime. Their tactical tools are also similar: cross-border smuggling, money laundering, counterfeiting, kidnapping, extortion and various forms of violence.[2]

Both transnational organized crime and terrorism are inextricably linked to the permissive spaces opened up by globalization and both seek to exploit the soft underbelly of contested state legitimacy and authority. It is for this reason, and not simply the need for maintaining law and order, that transnational organized crime and terrorism have become such potent security threats at this juncture of international relations (see van de Bunt, Siegel and Zaitch 2003). The purpose of this chapter is not only to examine these dynamics in their various manifestations, but also to cast the spotlight on how they play out in the African environment, which has been especially prone and vulnerable to the effects of terrorism and transnational crime.

The impact of globalization

Globalization has affected how international economic relations are organized around the world. As a process in a "borderless world", it influences both the social and political spheres of how governments, societies and ordinary people conduct themselves in their domestic interactions and foreign relations. Thus globalization is characterized by a complex set of interdependencies and interconnectivities, with an increasing number of actors vying to determine the outcomes of relations across a range of transnational activities. Such actors lay competing claims to resources, markets and legitimacy and are often engaged in issues that once belonged to the traditional or exclusive domain of the state. In short, globalization is an overarching modus operandi that shapes, defines and determines domestic politics and international dynamics, drawing virtually every country and society into its gravitational pull (Mittelman 1996).

However, this very same development facilitates a global political economy of illegality. Globalization has not only become the essential vector for the emergence of transnational organized crime, but has strengthened its operational fabric through the ease of international travel, the liberalization of emigration policies, the expansion of international trade, the spread of high technology communications systems and the underregulation of international financial networks. For example, one of the most dramatic impacts of the break-up of the Soviet Union has been the emergence of 14 newly independent states, which were previously inaccessible by air. While business linkages have flourished, these countries have also become hotbeds of organized crime by facilitating the movement of drug traffickers from areas of production to the large consumer markets of Western Europe and the United States, as well as among the nouveau riche in Russia. In turn, Russian criminal organizations, together with networks from their "near abroad" in Eastern and Central Europe, have been able to forge alliances with their South American and Caribbean counterparts in extending the geographical reach of drug trafficking, money laundering and arms trafficking. Similarly, West Africa has now become a major transhipment arc for drugs originating in Latin America and destined for Europe and the United States (Vulliamy 2008). These transregional alliances have provided a base for "thieves-in-law" collaboration in other criminal enterprises such as prostitution, international traffic in women, child pornography, usury, extortion, kidnapping, credit card fraud, counterfeiting and car theft (Farer 1999).[3]

All of this is made possible by the unprecedented mobility of people and changing migratory patterns. There are large numbers of people in poorer regions of the world who are haunted by poverty, famine, disease, violence, repression and conflict, and so seek better economic opportunities and a better life in the developed countries of Western Europe and the United States, by legal and illegal means. The ranks of migrants in both categories have swelled to 191 million in 2006, up from 176 million in 2000 (according to the International Organization for Migration). In one estimate, there are about 4 million people per year who cross the borders of developed and newly developing countries illegally, thus overwhelming the already overstretched systems of welfare, service delivery and law enforcement. Every year, thousands of desperate Africans, mostly young males, attempt the dangerous crossing of the Mediterranean from points in North Africa.

In this changing demographic labyrinth, there are members of criminal organizations who take their criminal skills and knowledge, affiliations and contacts with them. Thus diasporas and ethnic networks of China, Nigeria, Italy, Russia, Colombia, Venezuela and parts of Central and Eastern Europe have acquired and integrated significant criminal elements and have provided a foundation for serious criminal activities in their host countries. These diasporas provide cover, recruits and transnational linkages that lubricate the wheels of criminal activity and have an inbuilt security mechanism because they are not easily penetrated by law enforcement agencies (*Economist* 2001).[4]

International trade and its exponential growth also play an important part in providing a platform for expanding transnational criminal activity. The system of free trade, set up as a part of the General Agreement on Tariffs and Trade (GATT) after the Second World War, has resulted in the lowering of tariffs, the creation of free trade arrangements and the increasing integration of greater numbers of countries into global trade, especially since the establishment of the World Trade Organization (WTO) in 1995 (Hoekman and Kostecki 1995). This has caused a vast increase in the import and export of goods and services across and between countries and regions. The growth in international trade, aided by an exponential increase in shipping lanes and routes across international waters, has made it easier to hide illicit transactions, products and movements and to engage in theft and fraud. This has complicated problems of inspection and monitoring.

Ease of cross-border trade and communications has been supported by the growth of an international financial infrastructure that links countries, banks and financial institutions, such as brokerage houses and stock markets, currency and investment portfolios, in an exchange mechanism that operates continuously and is not subject to government control (Wagley 2006). This is part of a process of deregulation that has become synonymous with enhanced competitiveness and has been facilitated by technology and a massive increase in "megabyte" money transactions. A speculative economic regime has eclipsed real investment in driving what Susan Strange called "casino capitalism" (1994). The fluid interstices of this new global financial architecture and its low regulatory base offer a promiscuous environment for criminal activity where profits from illegal transactions can be transferred with speed, ease and relative impunity. Controls are even more elusive because of a growing diversity of monetary instruments, the increasing number of transaction-based futures and derivatives, the use of representative offices and foreign branches and the growing use of cyber money and smart cards. All of this is made possible by anonymous trading, the rapid movement of money, obscuring origin and ownership, making it more difficult to distinguish between "clean" and "dirty" money (Grosse 2001).

The hard interface of the global financial system is computer and information technology. The ability to manipulate and penetrate the central nervous system by breaching security mechanisms and firewalls provides access to critical national and global information, which then allows for financial fraud and embezzlement. This is where organized crime intersects with white-collar crime in offering novel opportunities for extortion through theft of data and intellectual property. In a highly competitive business environment, companies which risk having their computer systems shut down or disrupted are increasingly vulnerable as targets of "cyber-extortion" (Nazario 2006).

In this environment, states and their authority are under threat and often cannot cope with the demands of globalization's darker side. The growth of informal and parallel economic activity and the rise of grey and black markets are indicative of the inability of states to prevent the flows of illicit products across their borders. There are also growing concerns about theft of intellectual property, the spread of transnational software piracy and counterfeiting of products and currencies (Nkanga 2007). Regulation and enforcement within and across borders have proven to be difficult and hence there is every incentive to expand and improve efficiencies in criminal supplier arrangements and chains since windfall profits can be made. Weak states and those in transition, therefore, provide the context in which organized crime can take root and flourish. Africa must rank as the paradigm case of how state weakness has created and fostered an enabling environment for the emergence and growth of criminality and transnational crime.

The anatomy of state–society relations in Africa

What is remarkable about the African state is its comparative weakness and fragmentation, notwithstanding the flourishing of electoral forms of democracy across the continent. The long-standing institutional weaknesses and fragility of most states in Africa thus provide fertile ground for flourishing transnational criminal networks. Under the banners of the "Washington consensus" and neoliberal market reforms, the African state's penetrative, extractive and regulatory capacities have been severely eroded (Lewis 1996). In the 1980s and 1990s, state authorities often found themselves bereft of the financial and institutional resources essential for combating the rise and expansion of transnational criminal activity within their territories. Law enforcement agencies remain woefully inadequate, underfunded and corrupt. Courts and prison systems are outdated, overwhelmed and dysfunctional. And high-level political corruption has continued apace, despite the neoliberal credo that liberalization would reduce the range of illicit and concealed profit opportunities. Nearly two decades of International Monetary Fund (IMF) and World Bank induced reform and austerity measures render African states even more incapable of combating transnational organized crime. The African sociopolitical environment provides ideal conditions for the rapid penetration and spread of transnational crime.

With a population of 770 million in sub-Saharan Africa, there are millions of underemployed and unemployed people in a vast, seething cauldron of poverty and underdevelopment, in which criminality and anti-social behaviour easily incubate and multiply. Africa is in the midst of a youth bulge where young adults (aged 15 to 29) make up 40 per cent or more of the total adult population in the majority of countries; in roughly 30 countries, they constitute more than half of the adult population. Against such a backdrop: "it is not hard to understand why many African youths might have a highly developed sense of grievance ... [S]hocking numbers of young Africans have at some point in their short lives fallen into one or more of the following unhappy categories: combatants, victims of atrocities, refugees, internally displaced persons, forced labourers, or street children" (Gavin 2008). In these highly atomized societies, recourse to criminal activities, including forms of organized crime, often becomes a rational survival strategy in the face of extremely limited life opportunities.

Weak, often corrupt and frequently illegitimate states have been unable to address the needs of those on the margins of their societies. Leaders struggle to acquire sufficient hegemony over society and, therefore, resort to patronage, nepotism and corruption to generate support for their rule. Such neopatrimonial regimes acquire their legitimacy and raison d'être more from patron–client networks than from any moral authority to govern. These norms of political behaviour thus undermine the very substance and neutrality of public power (Hyden 2006).

The modern African state is reduced to an instrumental role, as a compendium of resources that rulers and political elites use to enhance their power and status in society. As Chabal and Daloz explain: "The political system functions in the here and now, not for the sake of a hypothetical tomorrow ... In other words, its legitimacy rests with its immediate achievements, not with its long-term ambitions" (1999: 161). In this formulation, the statist character of development strategy, abuse of public resources, inadequate public institutions and lack of public accountability help to explain the poor state of social welfare in much of Africa. Instead, public resources are egregiously squandered on theatrical displays of statehood and sovereignty in the form of white-elephant development projects, imperial coronations, large armed forces and defence expenditures, glamorous presidential palaces, fleets of limousines and so on.

The marginality and disengagement of many economic sectors is mirrored in the symbiosis of state elites and the mainly urban formal sector. The prevalence of rentier activities fosters an intimate interdependence among state and private sector elites, thus blurring public–private boundaries and impeding the formation of autonomous means of accumulation not subject to state control. These are the dynamics that have led to the "criminalization of the state" (see Bayart, Ellis and Hibou 1999). Paradoxically, rentier activities lend themselves to criminal enterprises: they rely not only on collaboration with state officials, but also on the evasion of state regulation, taxation and oversight.

In Africa, alongside the ambiguities of rentier groups there is also an extensive zone of informal economic activity that exists outside the state domain. Large parallel economies have placed substantial resources outside the reach of the central state. The austerity codes of the World Bank and IMF's adjustment programmes have ensured the rapid expansion of the informal sector, and have contributed to a decline in real wages and a rise in joblessness (Bayart, Ellis and Hibou 1999: 178–9).

The rule of law is weakly articulated and subject to erosion in much of Africa. This has been caused by weak administrative capabilities of many states, the personalization of power and authority, and the tendency to subvert constitutions to entrench single party domination. State authority tends to be arbitrary, offering few guarantees to property, civil rights and free public expression and association. This directly affects the confidence of citizens in the judiciary and deprives them of ready access to justice. The impact of poor governance practices, non-delivering state institutions and fragile civil societies has been felt most severely in the economic and social arenas. Africa is characterized by low human development, grinding levels of poverty, extreme inequality and chronic disease, especially the HIV/AIDS pandemic which has cut a swathe of human destruction across countries. Cyclical drought, famine and food shortages add another layer of human insecurity to an already overburdened continent (Bayart, Ellis and Hibou 1999: 137–47).

There is also the question of politicized ethnicity and the role of ethnic entrepreneurs in fuelling ethnic and communal tensions. Local and ethnic affinities typically cut across or subsume other divisions, and consequently class identities have remained weak and embryonic. High levels of ethnic diversity have polarizing effects and are material in accounting for conflict, political instability and violence (Young 1982: 44–55). Indeed, the prevalence of invidious communal politics and politicized ethnicities have caused the types of social fragmentation that exclude large groups from an already thin public veil, thus providing an additional impulse for criminality and violent contestation for resources, which often fuel civil wars (Reno 2000).[5]

Economies which are dependent on the extraction of natural resources, such as oil and minerals, have been particularly vulnerable to disorder and violent competition among different claimants. This has given rise to a type of warlord capitalism and "Kalashnikov lifestyles", where increasing levels of crime, lawlessness and banditry have become the order of the day. According to Reno, "a turn away from conventional state structures, or warlordism, is a rational response to globalization in weak states" (1998: 28).

In much of Africa, there is a direct correlation between the turbulence in domestic politics, the upsurge of criminal activity and the growth of criminal organizations with a distinctly transnational reach and capacity. The breakdown of authority structures and the atrophy of institutions make for a chaotic and atavistic political environment that provides a congenial breeding ground for criminal activity. Organized criminal organizations find it relatively easy to take advantage of Africa's zones of turbulence and, in effect, they have a vested interest in perpetuating the cycle of state weakness and fragmentation.

Mapping "uncivil society" in Africa

Criminal syndicates and networks – whether organized or informal – have been adept at taking advantage of the African state's crisis of governance and institutional weaknesses in order to ply their trade, amid the widening and deepening of globalization processes. Total illicit *financial* outflows from Africa, conservatively estimated, were approximately US$854 billion from 1970 to 2008, although the cost of *all* illicit outflows from the continent (including the proceeds from smuggling) *may be* as high as US$1.8 trillion (see Kar and Cartwright-Smith 2010). These dynamics are illustrated below by the examination of six manifestations of uncivil society in West, East and Southern Africa: the plunder of natural resources; terrorism; the trafficking of drugs; the trafficking of humans; the trafficking of arms; and money laundering.

Case 1: The conflict-commodity-criminal nexus

The African continent is richly endowed with natural resources and mineral assets – from huge oil, gold, copper, cobalt, coltan, zinc and diamond deposits, to extensive tropical rainforests with vast timber, hardwood and rubber resources. Instead of acting as a catalyst for sustained economic growth and development, Africa's ostensible "resource curse" has fuelled state, human and ecological insecurity. In particular, the income from trade in conflict resources has been used to finance wars, with a direct link to illicit arms trade, clandestine transport systems, money laundering and transnational criminal networks (Bannon and Collier 2003). These conditions have perpetuated a noxious nexus between the illicit trade in African commodities, the emergence of intractable conflicts alongside human insecurity and underdevelopment, and the rise of organized criminality in the continent, with tacit links to "downstream crime".

The international community wields several instruments to obstruct and stem this pernicious exchange. These include targeted sanctions against persons, products or regimes; certification schemes that identify origin (such as the Kimberley Process Certification Scheme for diamonds); the Extractive Industries Transparency Initiative; and the creation of Expert Panels to investigate illicit commercial activities in conflict zones. Yet the incentives for shadow activities and illicit gains remain strong.

The Democratic Republic of the Congo (DRC) in central Africa typifies this abundance of natural wealth, which has long existed alongside both rentier and "war economies" (Duffield 2001). The DRC is home to 80 per cent of the continent's coltan deposits (mined mostly in Kivu, in the east of the country); it recently became the world's fourth largest diamond producer; it is relatively rich in gold deposits; and it has approximately 1.3 million square kilometres of forest. Notwithstanding this wealth, the DRC ranks among the poorest countries in the world and has a history riddled with endemic mismanagement, corruption and conflict. The most recent conflict, which erupted in 1998 and claimed an estimated 3 million lives, has been described as one of the deadliest since the Second World War, drawing in a host of regional conflict agents – *inter alia*, forces from Rwanda, Uganda, Angola, Chad, Namibia and Zimbabwe – and transcontinental smuggling networks. Under these conditions, the DRC typified a quintessential dysfunctional state.

Given the absence of authority in the DRC, rebels and related entrepreneurs of crime and violence realigned their military-strategic objectives towards the capture of major mineral deposits (particularly gold, diamonds, tantalum, niobium and tin ores); secured monopolies in the purchase and export of tantalum ore (subsequently abandoned); concluded mineral contracts with multinationals in return for financial support; exchanged mineral wealth for drugs and guns; and turned from ethnic protection to protection racketeering and economic exploitation of populations and resources. This linkage between conflict, criminality and the illegal exploitation of natural resources in the DRC has indeed been systematic, intimate and palpable.

In the DRC and elsewhere in the continent – including Angola, Sierra Leone, Liberia and Ivory Coast – the plunder of natural resources, conflicts over resource allocation and illicit trade in commodities are inextricably interwoven with the weakness and vulnerability of the state. This is well illustrated by several examples drawn from the continent's recent history.

The illicit trade in diamonds from Sierra Leone, largely through Liberia and Guinea, to the world market reportedly funded the armed rebellion of the Revolutionary United Front (RUF). With the creation of the certificate of origin scheme under the Kimberley Process, official diamond exports from Sierra Leone have increased. However, criminal networks are still able to smuggle diamonds with the complicity of neighbouring countries and international crime syndicates based in the cutting, polishing or marketing centres for these gems. The illicit extraction and sale of artisanal gold on world markets is also reported in Ghana, Liberia and the Ivory Coast, often with the complicity of government-backed militias.

In Liberia, former Movement for Democracy (MODEL) fighters are guilty of illicit rubber tapping in the eastern part of the country, with transportation to the Ivory Coast for processing and shipment. Also in Liberia, the imposition of international sanctions against the country's logging trade has done little to stem these operations. It is reported that timber is being stockpiled for shipment once sanctions are lifted, while logs are also transported to militias operating in the Ivory Coast.

Communal violence in oil-producing countries, such as Nigeria, has also sparked a growth in organized criminal and syndicate activities, ranging from oil "bunkering" (up to 100,000 barrels of oil are stolen each day in the Niger Delta, for sale on the black market in neighbouring countries), to piracy, banditry and kidnappings (Wannenburg 2005). In the 3,000 river waterways of Nigeria, piracy and armed robberies against ships are a common occurrence, as well as in other parts of West Africa (particularly the Gulf of Guinea and the Senegalese coast). According to the International Maritime Bureau, there were 293 piracy attacks globally in 2008, up from 263 the previous year. The more egregious of these recent cases have taken place off the Somali coast (DPA 2009). Organized crime groups are also targeting the fishing industry in West Africa, which is an important source of livelihood, subsistence and foreign exchange.

Case 2: Terrorism and Africa

Terrorism in Africa is best understood in two ways: one is related to the rise in international terrorism, the other is related to the continued reliance upon terror by local, national and regional groups (particularly in Algeria, Sudan, Somalia, Uganda, the DRC, Sierra Leone and Liberia). Subnational and state terror have been long-standing and endemic features of the African continent's fraught political landscape; rebels and governments alike have been terrifying civilians for years in numerous civil wars, often accompanied by elements of criminality. For example, the Liberian conflict unleashed armed groups and criminal gangs that destabilized the entire subregion. Some 250,000 people – at least half of whom were civilian non-combatants – are believed to have died in war-related circumstances in Liberia since 1989. In Burundi, some 300,000 people were killed over the past decade when fighting between the government and Hutu militias forced about 100,000 to flee their homes every month. In the DRC, an estimated 3 million people have died during the last three years of conflict, whereas in neighbouring Rwanda, 40 per cent of the population have been killed or displaced since 1994. The civil war in Sudan has claimed the lives of 2 million people and caused the greatest displacement of people in Africa, aggravated by the humanitarian crisis in Darfur (Cilliers 2003: 96–8). The root causes of this violence are complex, but speak to the nature of Africa's social system, characterized by its generalized regime of patrimonial rule, systematic clientelism and fragile statehood.

International terrorism in Africa is on the rise, although from a very low base. Between 1990 and 2002, only 6 per cent of international terrorist incidents took place on African soil. However, when measured in terms of human casualties, the reality is far more alarming. During this same period, Africa recorded 6,177 casualties from 296 acts of international terrorism, second only to Asia in terms of continental casualties. The year with the highest number of casualties – 5,379 – was 1998, due to the bombings in Kenya and Tanzania (Cilliers 2003: 93).

The continent may still come to play a central role in international terrorism, since the motivation, means and targets all exist: "Africa presents a proliferation of targets that would, symbolically, hit at the heart of the first world and those international instruments that serve to maintain it" (Cilliers 2003: 99). There has already been an increase in acts of terrorism directed against opportunity targets, including peacekeepers, aid and humanitarian workers, donor agencies and international offices. Africa is also replete with potentially much higher value targets, ranging from the massive oil investments (often by United States companies) in the Gulf of Guinea, to the burgeoning tourist industry in South Africa (host of the 2010 Football World Cup, the first "global" soccer spectacular in Africa).

In summary, the African continent provides a facilitating environment for international terrorism. Moreover, the same networks that support arms trafficking, mercenaries, drug trafficking, illegal human trafficking and money laundering also provide the means for terrorism. The relationship between international terrorism and transnational crime is so close that the United Nations Security Council (UNSC) Resolution 1373 (Article 4) emphasizes the need for increased regional and international cooperation against terrorism and against transnational organized crime. UNSC Resolution 1373 provides states with an incentive to sign the UN Convention against Transnational Organized Crime of 2000 (the Palermo Convention) and an obligation to prevent transnational organized crime to the extent that such crimes assist international terrorism (Cilliers 2003: 101).

Case 3: The transnational narcotics trade

An arc of weak or fragile post-conflict societies in West Africa have recently also emerged as key transit hubs for the shipment of narcotics to North America and Europe. The case of Guinea-Bissau in West Africa, the world's first ostensible "narco-state", is a sobering example of how transnational criminal elements, originating from South America, have effectively taken advantage of dysfunctional state structures and weak governance to ply their trade. Today, Guinea-Bissau is a major transit hub for the shipment of cocaine from South America into Europe (principally

Britain, Spain and Portugal), as well as the trafficking of heroin and hashish by African and Asian cartels to the United States. It is estimated that 1 tonne of pure Colombian cocaine leaves the country each day, most of it destined for Europe (Vulliamy 2008). With an indigent population of 1.5 million people (ranked fifth from bottom in recent human development indicators), dysfunctional state structures and a coastal labyrinth of navigable islands and inlets, it is unsurprising that Guinea-Bissau has been a target of the criminal underworld.

The intersection of government instability following the civil war in 1999, corruption and scant surveillance by authorities, and socioeconomic decline have combined to open a propitious space for Colombian drug cartels to capture the state and its institutions. Drug cartels have exploited the weaknesses of the law enforcement and criminal justice systems, integrating this coastal country into their global narcotics supply chain, chiefly for cocaine shipments. This represents a peculiar paradox: while this impoverished West African country is increasingly "globalized" into world exchange, the shape and form of this integration is essentially odious.

Several other West African coastal countries such as Guinea, Senegal, Nigeria, Togo and Ghana have also drawn attention as potential transit points, with cocaine from sunken vessels literally washing up on their shores. However, the cultivation and consumption of narcotics – notably cannabis and mandrax (methaqualone) – and their links to organized crime are also rife within the continent. As is now well documented, this illicit trade previously armed, financed and sustained rebellions in West Africa, particularly in the Ivory Coast, Liberia and Senegal. In the Southern African region, Zimbabwe, Mozambique, South Africa and Angola have historically been key centres for the production or trade in drugs, particularly cannabis. The latter countries have recently also emerged as important transit hubs to service the sharp rise in demand for cocaine, crack cocaine and mandrax. In fact, South Africa has become the largest drug market in the region (Wannenburg 2006: 319–23). Given the vast sums generated by the narcotics trade, drug trafficking is readily associated with money laundering throughout the East and Southern African regions. The drug industry is also known to influence trends in "downstream" crimes, notably motor vehicle theft, housebreaking and armed robbery (Goredema 2003).

Controlling the trafficking and abuse of illicit drugs is a well-established priority on the agenda of the African Union (AU). The first Plan of Action on Drug Control was adopted in 1996 by the AU's predecessor, the Organization of African Unity. In 2007, the AU adopted the Revised African Union Plan of Action on Drug Control and Crime Prevention (2007–2012), which recognizes the multifaceted dimensions of drug control in Africa. The continental body also aims to harmonize drug control and crime prevention programmes and activities, in pursuit of continental and global sustainable social and economic development and peace. However, without the appropriate enforcement mechanisms and large investments in improving policing, surveillance and detection, these initiatives are bound to prove ineffective.

Case 4: Illicit migration and human trafficking

As globalization processes widely transmit, spread and disperse discourses on fundamental political, socioeconomic and human rights, it is hard to believe that trafficking and trade in human life continues to exist as a form of modern-day slavery. Organized criminal syndicates and networks are estimated to recruit, transport, transfer, smuggle and trade approximately 700,000 women, children and undocumented persons across porous international borders every year. Many of the victims of these crimes are unwittingly peddled into conditions of forced labour, servitude, slavery or sexual exploitation, often with the connivance of families and friends. Poor intelligence on the numbers of people trafficked and the inherently clandestine nature of the activity mean the traffickers usually trade their human cargo without fear of repercussions. Trafficking in human beings is outlawed under the UN Protocol against Trafficking in Persons, which has been in effect since December 2003. However, scores of African countries have yet to sign up to this deal, lacking legislative instruments, capacity and means to afford the victims of trafficking adequate protection.

Thus human trafficking remains an intractable problem in many African countries, particularly in West and Central Africa. In this particular region, the major trafficking routes extend to Benin, the Ivory Coast, Gabon, Ghana, Mali, Nigeria, Togo, Cameroon, Burkina Faso, Guinea, Niger and Sierra Leone. This heinous crime finds fertile ground and fortune in many of the structural and contingent weaknesses, fragilities and realities of the post-colonial African state: civil wars, poor governance and legislation, refugees, internal displacement, the recruitment of child soldiers into rebel ranks and deteriorating economic conditions, particularly poverty. The ongoing dominance of patriarchal power relations, coupled with a dearth of equal representation and opportunity for women, further compounds the plight of those groups most vulnerable to human trafficking.

In West Africa, an estimated 200,000 to 300,000 children are smuggled and trafficked each year for forced labour and sexual exploitation. The trade is lucrative and returns 5 to 20 times the amount initially paid. Depending on the country trafficked to and the purpose served, merchants may receive US$10,000–20,000 for a child and US$12,000–50,000 for a woman (Wannenburg 2006: 122–3). In Nigeria, women and children are particularly vulnerable to this crime, with states such as Edo, Delta, Imo and Kano more seriously affected by child trafficking networks than others. Women and girls from the south-west of the country are usually trafficked to Europe (notably the Schengen states: Italy, Spain, Germany and the Netherlands) and the United States for prostitution. In one estimate, in Italy, 60 per cent of women trafficked for commercial sex are Nigerians. By contrast, in eastern Nigeria, boys are mainly sold into agricultural, domestic, trading and apprenticeship jobs (Ojukwu 2006). To stem this criminality, in June 2005, 26 member countries of the Economic Community of West African States (ECOWAS) and the Economic Community of Central African States launched a joint regional initiative to enhance cooperation and coordination in this area.[6]

In the East and Southern Africa regions, concerns have also been expressed about an upswing in human trafficking. Nigerian groups, which dominate organized trafficking networks, appear to have expanded their operations into South Africa. With the economic meltdown in Zimbabwe, there are also concerns about the growing number of vulnerable children who have crossed undocumented into South Africa. (An estimated 3 million Zimbabweans have left their homeland.) Lack of anti-trafficking legislation in the regions has allowed these merchants of life either to escape prosecution or only to be convicted of such crimes as rape, abduction or fraud; but beyond this, there are few national or regional mechanisms that afford the victims of this trade any protection (IRIN 2008).

Case 5: Small arms and light weapons trafficking

The African continent (particularly West, Central and Southern Africa) is awash with light weapons, the pernicious legacy of decades of protracted conflicts, civil wars and political strife. As Dorcas Ettang details in chapter 4 below, the combination of globalization and weak and porous borders has heightened arms trafficking in the African continent. There are an estimated 100 million small arms and light weapons presently in circulation in Africa (Cilliers 2003: 100). The regional dynamics of the West African conflicts – notably Sierra Leone and Liberia, with their contiguous and porous borders – have contributed to widespread ownership and recycling of both legal and illegal weaponry. In Liberia, for instance, it is estimated that there are between 80,000 and 100,000 firearms circulating in that country. There are also allegations that ECOWAS peacekeepers are responsible for selling some of their weapons to criminal elements or regional belligerents. Even more disconcerting are recent reports that the Chinese are peddling arms to West African countries in exchange for trade and commercial agreements that are not subject to restrictive conditions around governance (Wannenburg 2006: 136–40).

Several West African countries – notably Senegal, Ghana, Guinea and Nigeria – also possess the capacity for manufacturing weapons, which could be sold to their conflict-prone peers in the region. With weak or corrupt arms export controls (for example, false end-user certificates), many of these supplier countries have allegedly breached key UN-sanctioned arms embargoes on Liberia and Sierra Leone, or assisted with the transhipment of weapons.

State-sponsored support for rebellions and militias is widely documented in the West African region. By contrast, the extent and scale of organized criminal groups in arms trafficking is still unclear. Nonetheless, small arms continue to circulate widely in the continent, in regions prone to political, socioeconomic and ecological instability. But as Ettang shows, without stronger government and civil society oversight and scrutiny, the growing crisis of arms trafficking within African countries and the related economic and social implications will continue.

Case 6: Money or asset laundering

The final illustrative case of uncivil society in Africa relates to money laundering. In West, East and Southern Africa, asset or money laundering is occurring on a substantial scale. This is both a manifestation of organized criminal activity within and beyond the continent, and a catalyst for it. Indeed, in the countries which comprise the East and Southern African Anti-Money Laundering Group – Botswana, Kenya, Lesotho, Malawi, Mauritius, Mozambique, Namibia, the Seychelles, South Africa, Swaziland, Tanzania, Uganda, Zambia and Zimbabwe – organized economic crime of one form or another exists.

However, given the clandestine nature of money laundering, there is a dearth of accurate or available statistics on its exact scale and frequency. According to one estimate, in 1998 a total of US$22 billion was laundered through the financial systems of Southern Africa. Of this figure, US$15 billion was generated within the region, whereas US$7 billion was infused from outside the region (Goredema 2003: 15). In West Africa, crime groups typically use international money transfers – such as Western Union – to repatriate the proceeds of crime from abroad.

There are three broad dimensions to this illicit activity in Africa: internal money laundering, characterized by the laundering of proceeds of domestic crime or assets to be used in committing these crimes; incoming money laundering, in which the assets laundered are derived from crime committed abroad; and outgoing money laundering, in which the proceeds of crime committed within the country are exported for laundering (Goredema 2003: 3).

Money laundering in the Southern African region stems from a range of illicit activities: drug trafficking, armed robbery, currency speculation, commercial crime and fraud, and the evasion of tax and of customs duty. Drug trafficking (particularly the sale of cocaine, heroin, ecstasy, cannabis and mandrax) is the most cash-intensive, which makes money laundering an attractive – but also necessary – option. The lack of developed and deep financial institutions in many Southern African countries, which encourages a cash-based economy, provides a conducive environment for laundering the local proceeds of crime. In addition, the advent of hyperinflation in Zimbabwe (estimated to be over 2 million per cent) has exacerbated the vulnerability of commerce to money laundering. This is unsurprising: retailers involved in evading tax are unlikely to report retail transactions involving tainted funds.

The common avenues for laundering illicit funds include not only retail cash transactions, but also investment in motor vehicles, usually trucks, minibuses and pickups; employing legitimate bank accounts of family members or third parties; or the establishment of business entities, whether as shell or front companies. Shell companies are distinct from front companies in that they do not trade, but they can be used to open and operate accounts with financial institutions, such as banks and insurance houses. This is a particularly attractive option, since it costs little to establish such a venture. In South Africa, the initial financial outlay may be as little as 450 rand (US$60). By contrast, front companies are identifiable trading concerns, used as a medium through which to infuse criminal proceeds into the financial system. These regularly take the form of cash-based outlets such as taverns, restaurants, butcheries, dry cleaners, cash loan businesses and cell-phone shops. In Namibia, South Africa, Zambia and Kenya, commuter transportation fleets (popularly called the "matatu" business in Kenya) are commonly used as vehicles to launder the proceeds of crime.

Currency speculation has also become a major source of income in parts of the region, particularly those afflicted by foreign exchange shortages. While this practice is evident in Malawi and Kenya on a small scale, Zimbabwe represents a classic example, where speculating in foreign currency has become one of the most lucrative enterprises in the country. Participants in this trade range from street traders, cross-border traders and senior public officials, to bureaux de change and commercial banks (Goredema 2003: 7).

Another common problem in the region is the evasion of tax and customs duty, as well as transfer pricing, which is symptomatic of capacity weaknesses within regional state structures for effective surveillance. These activities, which are also strongly correlated with corruption, are particularly prevalent in Uganda, Malawi, Kenya and South Africa. To illustrate the scale of this activity, corruption cost the Kenyan government

US$1,693 billion in the period 1990–5. In the 1996/97 financial year alone, the loss amounted to over US$160 million, or one in every six schillings allocated by the Kenyan parliament (Goredema 2003: 9).

In significant ways, the deepening and widening of globalization processes, including the globalization of financial markets and trade, have directly encouraged the growth of this particular form of uncivil society. For instance, the development of offshore financial centres and free trade zones is also susceptible to incoming money laundering and manipulation. This represents a rather cruel twist, since transnational criminality feeds off the sincere efforts of African countries to attract scarce investment capital and to be perceived as investor-friendly, in line with globalization's imperatives.

Strengthening the regulatory and surveillance capacity and functions of the state is necessary to ensure that incoming funds and criminal proceeds are not laundered. Various initiatives are underway in West and Southern Africa to contain and outlaw criminal and terrorist financing and money laundering. The creation of anti-money laundering institutions, such as the Financial Intelligence Centres, is well underway. Under the auspices of ECOWAS, West African countries have established the Inter-Governmental Action Group against Money Laundering (GIABA), with support from Interpol, the African Development Bank and other international institutions.

However, combating money laundering confronts African authorities with both capacity and resource challenges at the national level. In Africa, this is a real problem in that there are competing demands with regard to the procurement and utilization of scarce resources. Innovative thinking may also be necessary in some respects, since the majority of the African economy is cash-based. This may entail the setting of entirely home-grown standards (Alweendo 2005).

Conclusion

Transnational criminality and terrorist activity have become inextricably interwoven in the fabric of globalization. Most insidious is that transnational criminal gangs and terrorist networks threaten the stability and effectiveness of states. They do so by targeting their functional and institutional underpinnings and by adapting the infrastructure of globalization to their nefarious ends, especially advances in technology, transportation, communication and financial systems. For example, the massive flow of illicit money out of Africa is facilitated by a global "shadow" financial system comprising tax havens, secrecy jurisdictions, disguised corporations, anonymous trust accounts, fake foundations, trade mispricing and money laundering techniques (see Kar and Cartwright-Smith 2010). This promotes a political economy of illegality that is violently competitive, highly malleable, adaptable and resilient, and depends on large measures of invisibility and secrecy for its efficacy.

Probably more so than in other regions, the manifestations of uncivil society have found fertile ground in the African continent and have developed a deep taproot. This is primarily due to the intersection of the globalization of criminality and criminal activity *and* state weakness and fragmentation. These effects are particularly pronounced in the African context and help to explain a range of pathologies in governance. These include territorial vulnerability and weak border controls; functional holes in regulatory frameworks and the criminal justice system; underdeveloped institutions of social control and corrupt neopatrimonial practices; and contested and tenuous state legitimacy. States face further threats from political entrepreneurs and rebel militias, who have developed new economic formations or what have been referred to as "shadow" or "surrogate" states by wresting partial territorial control in an often violent bid to seize power. This facilitates the establishment of transnational criminal networks that engage in trafficking in drugs and arms, money laundering, smuggling of and trafficking in people, and trading and plunder of natural resources. This amounts to what Ignatieff (2004) has called "opportunistic nihilism", motivated by greed, power and profit.

The scale and complexity of the problem of uncivil society in Africa will ultimately undermine the normative and ontological bases of the state system and its security. Functional cooperation arrangements and international instruments are important in combating the growth of transnational criminal and terrorist networks, but civil society proper must reassert and reinvigorate itself as a bulwark against the erosion of the state caused by its illegal counterpart. Hence, "only when ordinary African men and women have cause to reject the logic of personalized politics, seriously question the legitimacy of the present instrumentalization of disorder and to struggle for new forms of political accountability, will meaningful change occur" (Chabal and Daloz 1999: 162).

Notes

1. Rekha Chowdhary's contribution to this volume, chapter 8, provides a further overview of this.
2. For more on this particular topic, see Dorcas Ettang (chapter 4) in this volume.
3. By contrast, Luk Van Langenhove and Tiziana Scaramagli in chapter 11 below analyse regional and transregional alliances as a solution to cross-border illegal activities and argue that regional state integration can represent an important means through which states can better deal with globalized uncivil society.

4. This is closely related to S. D. Muni's analysis of South Asian insurgencies which focuses on the effective use by the Liberation Tigers of Tamil Eelam (LTTE) of the Tamil diasporas network and the limited use by the Nepal Maoists of the Nepal diasporas in pursuance of their political objectives.
5. Comparatively, for more on the colonial origins of social fragmentation see chapter 2 above by Edgardo Lander which focuses on the colonial and Eurocentric, and thus exclusive, nature of liberal democracy in Latin America.
6. Kirsten Foot, in chapter 14 below, attempts to remedy the lack of knowledge about the global anti-trafficking movement through a survey of regional and worldwide patterns in the types of actors engaged in anti-trafficking work.

REFERENCES

Alweendo, Tom K. (2005) "Crime and money laundering", Address by the Governor of the Bank of Namibia to the African Banking Congress, Johannesburg, 8–10 Mar.

Bannon, Ian and Paul Collier (2003) *Natural Resources and Violent Conflict: Options and Actions.* Washington, DC: World Bank.

Bayart, Jean-François, Stephen Ellis and Béatrice Hibou, eds (1999) *The Criminalization of the State in Africa.* London: James Currey.

Chabal, Patrick and Jean-Pascal Daloz (1999) *Africa Works: Disorder as Political Instrument.* Oxford: James Currey.

Cilliers, Jakkie (2003) "Terrorism and Africa", *African Security Review*, 12(4): 91–103.

Clapham, Christopher (1996) *Africa and the International System: The Politics of State Survival.* Cambridge: Cambridge University Press.

DPA (2009) "Piracy watchdog records 293 sea attacks in 2008", news agency report, 17 Jan. At <http://sify.com/news/crime/fullstory.php?id=14838980> (accessed June 2010).

Duffield, Mark (2001) *Global Governance and the New Wars: The Merging of Development and Security.* London: Zed Books.

Economist (2001) "A survey of illegal drugs: Stumbling in the dark," *The Economist*, 28 July, p. 3.

Farer, Tom, ed. (1999) *Transnational Crime in the Americas.* New York: Routledge.

Ferguson, Yale H. and Richard W. Mansbach (2004) "States and other polities", in *Remapping Global Politics: History's Revenge and Future Shock*, Cambridge: Cambridge University Press, pp. 107–42.

Gavin, Michelle (2008) "Africa's restless youth", *Global Dialogue*, 13(1) (Mar.): 27.

Goredema, Charles (2003) "Money laundering in East and Southern Africa: An overview of the threat", Paper 69, Institute for Security Studies, Apr.

Grosse, Robert E. (2001) *Drugs and Money: Laundering Latin America's Cocaine Dollars.* Westport, CT: Praeger.

Hoekman, Bernard and Michel Kostecki (1995) "Part I: The institution", in *The Political Economy of the World Trading System: From GATT to WTO*, Oxford: Oxford University Press, pp. 12–35.

Hyden, Goran (2006) "Big man rule", in *African Politics in Comparative Perspective*, Cambridge: Cambridge University Press, pp. 94–115.

Ignatieff, Michael (2004) *The Lesser Evil: Political Ethics in an Age of Terror*. Princeton: Princeton University Press.

International Organization for Migration (2008) "Migration facts and figures." At <http://www.iom.int/jahia/jsp/index.jsp> (accessed Aug. 2008).

IRIN (Integrated Regional Information Network) (2008) "Southern Africa: Human trafficking on the upswing", 23 Apr. At <http://irinnews.org/printReport.aspx?ReportID=77888> (accessed June 2010).

Jackson, Stephen (2003) "Fortunes of war: The coltan trade in the Kivus", in Sarah Collinson, ed., *Power, Livelihoods and Conflict: Case Studies in Political Economy Analysis for Humanitarian Action*, Humanitarian Policy Group Report 13 (Feb.). London: Overseas Development Institute.

Kar, Dev and Devon Cartwright-Smith (2010) *Illicit Financial Flows from Africa: Hidden Resource for Development*. Washington, DC: Global Financial Integrity.

Lewis, Peter (1996) "Economic reform and political transition in Africa: The quest for a politics of development", *World Politics*, 49(1): 92–129.

Mittelman, James H. (1996) "The dynamics of globalization", in James H. Mittelman, ed., *Globalization: Critical Reflections*, Boulder, CO: Lynne Rienner, pp. 1–19.

Nazario, Jose (2006) "Cyber extortion is now a very real threat – is your business at risk?", 28 Mar. At <http://www.continuitycentral.com/feature0322.htm> (accessed June 2010).

Nkanga, Efem (2007) "Waging war against software piracy in Nigeria", *ThisDay*, 9 Aug. At <http://allafrica.com/stories/200708090357.html>.

Ojukwu, Adeze (2006) "Nigeria/West Africa: Human trafficking", *Daily Champion*, 21 Sept. At <http://www.stopdemand.com/afawcs0112878/ID=180/newsdetails.html> (accessed June 2010).

Reno, William (1998) *Warlord Politics and African States*. Boulder, CO: Lynne Rienner.

Reno, William (2000) "Shadow states and the political economy of civil wars", in Mats Berdal and David M. Malone, eds, *Greed and Grievance: Economic Agendas in Civil Wars*, Boulder, CO: Lynne Rienner, pp. 54–64.

Strange, Susan (1994) "From Bretton Woods to the casino economy", in Stuart Corbridge, Ron Martin and Nigel Thrift, eds, *Money, Power and Space*, Oxford: Blackwell, pp. 49–62.

United Nations High Commission for Refugees (2006) *2005 Global Refugee Trends*. Geneva: UNHCR.

van de Bunt, H. G., D. Siegel and D. Zaitch, eds (2003) *Global Organized Crime: Trends and Developments*. The Hague: Kluwer Law International.

Vulliamy, Ed (2008) "How a tiny West African country became the world's first narco state", *The Observer*, 9 Mar. At <http://www.guardian.co.uk/world/2008/mar/09/drugstrade> (accessed June 2010).

Wagley, John R. (2006) "Transnational organized crime: Principal threats and US responses", Congressional Service Report, Library of Congress, 20 Mar.

Wannenburg, Gail (2005) "Organised crime in West Africa", *African Security Review*, 14(4). At <http://www.iss.co.za/pubs/ASR/14No4/F1.htm> (accessed June 2010).

Wannenburg, Gail (2006) *Africa's Pablos and Political Entrepreneurs: War, the State and Criminal Networks in West and Southern Africa*. Johannesburg: South African Institute of International Affairs.

Young, Crawford (1982) *Ideology and Development in Africa*. New Haven: Yale University Press.

Part II

Challenges

4

Arms trafficking in West Africa

Dorcas Ettang

Globalization has created new threats on the international scene. These threats have affected the security and stability of nations. It has created a wide range of losers, especially in the area of arms trafficking. The security of citizens is at risk, making them losers in the war against arms. Governments are also losing this war. In Africa, arms trafficking is a major threat, fuelled by weak and porous borders.[1] Weapons from past conflicts continue to be used in current and emerging conflicts. Arms trafficking has become an increasing force in the first decade of this century.

Apart from guns imported into many African countries, arms trafficking is created from the ground up: local communities produce, sell and transfer guns. In many cases, these gun-producing regions are poor, and many people depend upon the income generated from the sale and production of these guns. The role of civil society is significant in addressing the economic and social implications of arms trafficking at the local level. With closer access to the people and with initiatives that target the grass roots, there is a need for further civil society and local involvement in security sector reforms to curb and inhibit the sale and transfer of these weapons.

Dealing with the growing challenge of small arms and light weapons (SALW) in Africa remains an uphill task. Civil society institutions need to be strengthened and assisted to curtail these threats. Governments play a key role in aiding civil society, by including them in discourse, as well as partnering with them to stop arms trafficking, promote security sector reforms and combat the proliferation of small arms and light weapons in the long term. Cases of specific African countries that are experiencing various forms of conflicts will be presented to examine the existing gaps and challenges with regard to arms trafficking and the role which civil society can play in curbing its spread.

Background

The focus on states as the primary, or only, actors that provide or withhold security is insufficient given the presence of new and emerging non-state actors. In weak states, globalization has made these non-state actors, such as terrorists, warlords and private military entrepreneurs, more powerful and violent. Easy access to weapons has empowered them, allowing for challenges to state stability and security. Advances in technology and the ease of banking and financial transactions have increased global commerce and trade, facilitating deals and transactions across the world and the illegal sale, brokering and delivery of arms. Increasing interdependence among these non-state actors has also arisen as they share information, skills, finance, investment, ideas and human capacity.

In West Africa, globalization has deepened the problem of weak borders and made evident the inability of states to protect citizens within their boundaries. The free movement of people has allowed for the movement of guns and illegal ammunition. The weak security structures in many West African countries have also created political instability and conflict, making it difficult for their economies to grow. This unstable situation has also left many innocent lives in the hands of various actors that threaten their peace and security. Calls for an increased focus on security sector reform (SSR) in the region and the continent are therefore pertinent.

The challenge of SALW and arms trafficking mirrors that of the wider challenge when dealing with SSR in West Africa. When examining SSR in the region, a key issue is arms trafficking as it affects the security and stability of a state. Small arms and light weapons, irrespective of their size, continue to inflict serious harm. Their production is cheap and they are portable, easy to conceal and easy to use. This has made them a major threat in the world today, especially as they are recycled from one violent conflict to another.

Small arms include revolvers, pistols, rifles, carbines, submachine guns, assault rifles and light machine guns. Light weapons include heavy machine guns and portable anti-aircraft guns. With the easy movement, production and transfer of these small arms and light weapons within the region and the porous borders between countries, it is difficult to curb the spread of these arms. No part of the subregion is isolated from illicit small arms proliferation and its impact (Ebo 2003: 13). Small arms have been cast off from one conflict to another in the subregion as rebel groups, liberation armies and other actors use their close linkages and networks to supply them to each other.[2] All parties involved in arms trafficking benefit from conditions of insecurity and instability, which propels them to foster the further instability.

The proximity of West African countries to international waters without adequate and effective monitoring facilitates access to these weapons. Security forces do not have the equipment to carry out surveillance to track weapons moved by air or sea. Countries have been unable to control their borders to ensure that weapons are not allowed to circulate across them.

In addition to weak and porous borders, the effectiveness of border officials is limited by corruption. In November 2003, Nigerian customs officials seized a lorry carrying 170,000 rounds of ammunition concealed in a cargo of charcoal that had already crossed the border from Benin (IRIN 2006). Governments, such as those of Burkina Faso and Guinea, are large importers and exporters of guns, especially AK-47s. State-approved trade in small arms and light weapons on the black market has become standard and accounts for approximately 80 per cent to 90 per cent of the total (IRIN 2006).

The crisis is further exacerbated by the fact that small arms and light weapons are produced locally, making them cheap and accessible. A substantial percentage of factories in African states produce small arms or small arms ammunition. In Ghana, the key challenge is not from imported illegal industrially manufactured weapons, but from local production of weapons and their export (Vines 2005: 352). High levels of unemployment in Ghana have propelled many to arms manufacturing, which becomes the main source of livelihood for them and their extended family (Aning 2007: 207). The conflicts in the city of Jos in Nigeria have involved looting and theft as many use the opportunity to better their economic situations. In the Niger Delta region of Nigeria, economic marginalization has led to unrest as many fight for resources and development. This mirrors the wider challenge of the poverty and inequality that plagues African societies. Due to economic marginalization, other options for economic improvement are often absent and for many the production, sale, and use of weapons for criminal activities becomes an attractive option.

Politicians have been known to supply arms and finance non-state actors to promote their political agendas. Armed gangs and vigilante groups are some of the many recipients of these political handouts. In Nigeria, there are numerous reports of politicians funding gangs and groups and providing them with weapons to incite violence, as well as threatening and forcing citizens to vote for them during elections. In an interview conducted by Human Rights Watch, a former gang leader stated that "if the government would pass a law preventing the politicians from giving arms to our people, it would help Rivers [the River State area] a lot" (Human Rights Watch 2007: 89).

Private security forces and other authorized weapons users may also be involved in the supply and sale of arms to illegal actors. In the Niger Delta region of Nigeria, there have been reports of corrupt officials selling confiscated weapons back to armed groups (Duffield 2009b; see also Duffield 2009a). In other instances, such as in the Democratic Republic of the Congo (IRIN 2006), weapons from poorly guarded government supplies or, in some cases, recovered on the battlefield after combat are purchased or stolen and later reused. Other actors or sources of illegal SALW have included returning peacekeepers, leakages from official armouries, and illicit flows from warring neighbours (Agboton-Johnson, Ebo and Mazal 2004). According to field research conducted in Ghana, there were unconfirmed reports from arms manufacturers in the Volta Region of the exchange of skills and knowledge with established contacts in the Philippines and India (Aning et al. 2005).

Numerous actors continue to challenge the state, vying for control over resources. Armed gangs, revolutionary groups and local warlords need these weapons to fight government forces. The use of child soldiers has also increased with the need to provide human resources to use these weapons. These arms have also contributed to increased criminal activity. In some cases, gun manufacturers make weapons for criminal gangs involved in robberies and other illegal activities. Indeed, there is a strong relationship between SALW availability and armed robbery (Agboton-Johnson, Ebo and Mazal 2004).

The failure of the state to protect its citizens means they must do so themselves. Citizens are thus reluctant to surrender their only source of protection, "arms". Minor conflicts in Africa have been exacerbated due to the presence of SALW. This has led to a huge loss in lives and has destroyed many societies.

International and regional legal underpinnings

At the global and regional level, much legal attention has been paid to arms trafficking, with the main goal of curbing the production, sale and transfer of illicit weapons. A variety of international and regional legal frameworks have been set up to bring countries together in the fight against arms trafficking. These efforts, made by international organizations such as the United Nations (UN) and regional organizations like the Economic Community of West African States (ECOWAS), all address arms trafficking in West Africa.[3]

Prominent efforts include the 2001 UN Conference on the Illicit Trade in Small Arms and Light Weapons in All Its Aspects (or UN Small Arms Conference), which focused on ensuring that illegal arms are not sold and transferred to non-state actors. There is also the UN Programme of Action to Prevent, Combat and Eradicate the Illicit Trade in Small Arms and Light Weapons in All Its Aspects (UNPoA), arising from the international conference on small arms in July 2001. The UNPoA provides member states with the measures needed to prevent and control black market transfers in their various countries. It has been criticized for not being effective and comprehensive enough to deal with other emerging actors that are involved in arms trafficking. Most significantly, the UN Protocol Against the Illicit Manufacture of and Trafficking in Firearms, Their Parts and Components and Ammunition tackles the challenge of arms trafficking and their production. As of 2010, only 8 of the 15 member states of ECOWAS have signed this UN Firearms Protocol.

The ECOWAS Convention on the Importation, Exportation and Manufacture of Small Arms and Light Weapons in West Africa has been at the forefront of attempts to curb arms trafficking in West Africa. This legal document, formerly a moratorium, has since become a Convention signed by heads of states and governments on 14 June 2006 in Abuja (Nigeria), making the moratorium a legally binding instrument. Even though there is participation in continental and global instruments, such as the Bamako Declaration, the UN Firearms Protocol and the UN Programme of Action, the ECOWAS Convention provides the foundation for SALW implementation measures in West Africa. The ECOWAS Convention was launched in 1998 to clean up SALW across the region. This effort by West African nations to deal with the challenges of arms trafficking in the region provided a code of conduct which outlined, among other things, the establishment of national commissions (NatComs), the development of a regional arms register, harmonization of legislation, training of security personnel, and the declaration of weapons and ammunition used for peacekeeping operations. Some of these national commissions do not have civil society representation.

However, in countries like Ghana, actors involved in and associated with illegal arms production have their own "code of conduct" and form a close-knit network whereby arms producers swear an oath never to disclose vital information to anybody (Aning 2007: 207). The ban on the manufacture and sale of guns in the country is a known fact, yet these activities continue to take place, in part due to the existence of the close and secretive network.[4]

How can regional and international bodies ensure that state actors comply with these legal instruments? Also of significance is the realization that there is no way to monitor major non-state actors involved in arms sale and production. Identifying and ensuring that these non-state actors (in most cases illegal arms producers) follow international rules and regulations will pose a major challenge. In spite of the legal measures set in place, the question remains as to how to monitor the illegal spread of these weapons. There is still no way to make countries accountable to and compliant with these frameworks, which limits any form of adherence. Arms trafficking therefore cannot be curtailed unless mechanisms of governance obtain the skills, intent, resources and most of all the political will from their members to administer and manage the process. Currently, the institutions and the processes designed to fight illicit trade in arms still remain at a disadvantage when the extent of the problem is taken into account.

The next section will examine more closely the case of Nigeria to understand better the challenges of SALW in West Africa and the options available for change.

Case Study: Nigeria

In spite of the laws and reforms in place at the national, regional and international levels to curb and tackle arms trafficking, they are not sufficient since communities continue to face insecurities. In Jos, Nigeria, 26 mercenaries armed with 22 double-barrelled guns were found around the Gengere/UTC area of the city after the November 2008 clashes in the city. This shows how difficult it is to enforce these laws at the grassroots level, especially with the prevalence of armed groups and vigilantes in these areas. The recent 2010 crisis in Jos and the insecurity that continues to exist is characterized by vigilante groups and organized militia.

Nigeria has experienced numerous conflicts, especially in the Niger Delta region. This is partly due to arms trafficking. The country continues to face the challenge of illicit light weapons dating back to the 1967–70 civil war, when a comprehensive disarmament programme was not carried out (Vines 2005: 353). Arms smuggling to Nigeria increased in the run-up to the presidential elections in 2002 and before the local elections in 2004 (Vines 2005: 353). In 2002, the Nigerian Customs Service reported that it had intercepted small arms and ammunition worth more than 4.3 billion naira (US$34.1 million) between January and June.[5]

In many cases these weapons come from outside the country; for example, weapons from the Great Lakes Conflict are being handed on to the Niger Delta (Onuoha 2006: 111). Sometimes, these weapons are cast off from previous conflicts in countries like Sierra Leone and Liberia. Nigeria's proximity to the Atlantic Ocean has made it easier for the country to be supplied with these weapons. Guns are also easily transferred between Nigeria and other neighbouring countries like Chad, Benin and Niger.

The Niger Delta region of Nigeria, known for constant conflict, has become a hotspot for small arms and light weapons. The impact of SALW in the region has reduced oil production because militant groups are armed and continue to cause havoc in the region, halting production and increasing global oil prices. The availability of SALW has fuelled kidnappings, conflicts among various groups and all forms of violence. Across the country, regular crime has intensified as well as highway banditry.

In 2003, it became evident that there was a shift in the tools used in political violence from machetes, clubs and knives to small arms, such as locally fabricated and imported pistols and a range of assault rifles.[6] More recently in the Delta region, explosives, rocket-propelled grenades and gunboats have been among the weapons dumped from recent disarmament efforts (BBC 2010).

The Delta problem depicts a deeper crisis of the illegal arms network across Africa and around the world. The Delta is part of this network and Nigeria has become a lucrative market for illegal arms. The artificial and porous borders between Nigeria and its neighbouring countries have made for easy arms transfers. Through channels created by political figures, arm dealers and mercenaries, numerous weapons have found their way into the Delta region, to be used by state security forces, private security firms hired by oil companies and armed groups. Military sources in Nigeria claim that pistols can be purchased at very affordable prices, between 3,000 naira (about US$25) and 7,000 naira (about US$58), depending on the type, seller and area of purchase (Ebo 2003: 11). In other parts of Nigeria, this illegal transfer and cheap availability of arms is a major challenge. Many communities do not feel safe. This drives individuals to purchase weapons to ensure their protection from various threats, thus creating a vicious cycle. Most of these weapons are obtained illegally and not registered.

Past national legislation targeting arms trafficking in Nigeria has not been successful. The Firearms Act of 1959, which covered the import and export of firearms and the penalties regarding the violation of the laws, was very hard to implement and it proved especially difficult to prosecute violators. In 2001 the Firearms Act was reviewed after fewer than 50 out of 12,000 individuals were successfully prosecuted in relation to arms trafficking and the illegal possession of arms between 1990 and 1999 (Musah 1999: 132). In July 2000, the government of Olusegun Obasanjo set up a 12-member National Committee on Proliferation and Illicit Trafficking in Small and Light Weapons. Its purpose was to gather information on illegal arms trafficking and to provide recommendations on how to deal with the problem. This committee was not very effective in performing its role, and its findings have not been published; although in the time up to July 2001, it did publicly destroy 428 rifles, 494 imported pistols, 287 locally made pistols and 48 Dane guns seized by security agencies (cited in Vines, 2005: 354), a tiny fraction of the weapons circulating in the country.

Civil society responses

The lack of strong governing and regulatory institutions at the national, regional and international levels has created a space for transnational actors to move and act freely, while making it more difficult for civil society to act. Controlling SALW not only involves action at the top levels of government, but requires a bottom-up approach, especially where weapons are transferred through villages and communities. Civil society is presently targeting international, regional, national and communal levels. How can civil society, as a mobilizing force in the international arena, help to curb uncivil acts such as arms trafficking in Africa? Equally important is exploiting and expanding on how best to employ and merge the positive forces of civil society that globalization has provided to limit the role of growing uncivil acts.

UNPoA Section I, 16 indicates the importance of civil society. Civil society organizations (CSOs) can function as beneficiaries, informal overseers, partners and advocates of reform as well as service providers (OECD-DAC 2007: 224). In this regard, a continued awareness of "briefcase" non-governmental organizations (NGOs),[7] that are not legitimate actors and only look out for their own interests, needs to be created.

Governments must involve civil society at every level when dealing with arms trafficking in Africa. In Sierra Leone, for example, discussion on the Poverty Reduction Strategy Paper of 2005–7 involved a broad engagement with civil society, NGOs and other stakeholders, and their inclusion was evident in a section on "Strengthening national security" in the final document.[8] In South Africa, civil society was actively involved in the Defence Review Work Group and the various subcommittees that helped to develop the Defence White Paper and Defence Act, which has proved to be very effective.

A major propellant for change is the need for policymakers at all levels to understand the impact of civil society involvement in achieving sustainable security sector reform. Without a burgeoning and legitimate civil society and the skills it provides to achieve change, security sector reforms will be ineffective and any efforts by states to curb acts such as arms trafficking will be for naught.

Civil society organizations, in partnership with UN country level offices, are significant entry points through which arms production, sale and trafficking can be curbed. At the local level, civil society participation is essential in creating and sustaining programmes that focus on the collection, management and destruction of small arms. This is especially important during disarmament, demobilization and reintegration (DDR) exercises in post-conflict situations where weapons, if not effectively collected and destroyed, could be recycled in future conflicts.

In cases where the production, sale and transfer of arms are a means to sustain livelihoods, civil society in partnership with local governments and communities can work to develop other income-generating alternatives. Training programmes should provide these individuals with new skills. Skills development in information technology, carpentry and electrical engineering are some of the options available. This might involve carrying out a needs-based assessment in various communities to see what services they require and, through that, determining what occupations and skills are necessary to provide those services. For ex-combatants, these programmes should focus on how to provide them with legitimate sources of livelihood to reintegrate them into their societies. In effect, this will make it easier for them to give up their arms. These processes will require government support.

The "buy-back process" (when guns are handed in, in exchange for money) could be encouraged by civil society working with local communities. Communities that have taken part in weapons collection programmes have been offered water wells, the building of schools, agricultural tools and other development aid in return (OECD-DAC 2007: 106–7).

Civil society can also bring awareness to states and communities about the legal instruments that focus on arms trafficking. This can be done through nationwide mass campaigns. West African countries have carried out mass campaigns in the past on HIV/AIDS, among other issues. Civic education can be used to strengthen local capacity and local involvement in public education programmes that focus on issues such as human rights and small arms proliferation. The message of non-violence and peace-building is also key for young people who can be easily pulled into these trafficking activities.

By closely examining the concept of SSR programmes, civil society is an important tool in ensuring that there is broad local ownership and civilian oversight. Through the media, print and verbal communication, local groups with the support and assistance of civil society can own the process and spread the word about the negative impact of arms trafficking.

At the regional level, partnerships can be established between bordering countries to address arms trafficking. Discussions among peer security services such as the police and the military on how to address arms production and arms trafficking should be encouraged. This can be enhanced through the sharing of information, skills and personnel. Bilateral and multilateral partnerships should be explored among countries that share common borders in West Africa. Suitable training of border officials is vital. These officials should also be held accountable in enforcing the legislation regarding arms trafficking. Measures must be set in place to deal with corrupt officials.

Civil society, with support from governments, should be given the opportunity to train its law enforcement agencies to adequately prepare them as they deal with various individuals and situations in the field. Skills in negotiation, mediation, communication and conflict analysis are critical and will assist them in their work.

Lobbying for and promoting arms non-proliferation must be taken on by civil society. By informing the government of the ills of arms trafficking, civil society can push for more action. Political leaders must be pressured and reminded of their legal commitments to address arms trafficking. Civil society can also act as a check and a monitor on government activities by promoting transparency and accountability regarding small arms and light weapons. South Africa is the only country on the continent to have provided a national arms export report in recent years.[9]

Civil society can encourage the registration of locally made guns and firearms especially in large arms producing countries like Ghana. In this case, governments can explore and promote gun registration. Civil society can work closely with the government on creating options and opportunities to legalize production.

More avenues of cooperation between local arms producers should be explored. An example is the meeting on 13 May 2003 convened by the Accra-based African Security and Dialogue Research, which brought together local producers of arms, senior police officers, the Armed Forces, Members of Parliament, the Ministry of the Interior, the Ministry of Justice, civil society groups and members of the diplomatic corps. Its purpose was to gain the trust of the local producers and build mutual trust and confidence between the different actors (Agboton-Johnson, Ebo and Mazal 2004). Local producers admitted to having the capacity to employ their skills to focus on the manufacture of agricultural tools, while proposing that the government guarantee them ready markets for the tools (Agboton-Johnson, Ebo and Mazal 2004).

Logistical and financial support is key to developing weak local civil society organizations. International actors can help by enhancing their skills, developing their internal accountability and building sound management procedures and effective monitoring and evaluation (OECD-DAC 2007: 224). Established international NGOs should work together with and assist local CSOs in accomplishing their goals and programmes.

Platforms for collaboration should be explored through training, research and workshops where ideas and information can be exchanged. At the regional level, CSOs specializing in the illicit arms trade should be linked to share information and explore together the various ways of addressing this challenge.

At the global level, leaders of both developed and developing countries must work together to combat arms trafficking. Tackling transnational organized crime was high on the agenda for the United Kingdom's presidency of the G8 industrialized nations and the European Union in 2005, and this should continue to be the case for arms trafficking as well (Vines 2005: 2). The role of ECOWAS is key and legislation should focus on laying down stringent rules and regulations to deal with international arms traffickers, brokers and others involved in illicit arms transfers. There must be room for the ECOWAS moratorium to be reviewed and changed to meet the emerging challenges of arms trafficking within the region. The need for advanced technology is also critical to assist with identifying, tracking and tracing these arms.

Notes

1. As Garth le Pere and Brendan Vickers's contribution to this volume details (chapter 3), the dynamics and various manifestations of arms trafficking, transnational organized crime and terrorism, as they play out in the African environment, are inextricably linked to the permissive spaces opened up by globalization.
2. This cycle of supply and demand of weapons has taken place among non-state actors in Burkina Faso, Ghana, Guinea, Ivory Coast, Nigeria, Sierra Leone and Liberia.
3. Chapter 11 below by Luk Van Langenhove and Tiziana Scaramagli details the utility of interactions and regional integrations, such as ECOWAS, between neighbour states facing the same challenges as a method of coping with the accelerating positive and negative forces of globalization.
4. As William Coleman concludes (chapter 1 above), globalization has directly produced networked society and has indirectly produced new forms of violence and networks of uncivil society in opposition and contradistinction to civil society and networks.
5. These arms were intercepted at the border of Benin and Nigeria and some from smaller boats coming in from Niger, Chad and Cameroon (Vines 2005: 354).
6. In one of Nigeria's 36 states (Cross River State), the police recovered 54 guns in 2002, 16 in the possession of politicians and another 8 connected to politically motivated murders. In Edo State a gubernatorial aspirant (Lucky Imaseun) was arrested in possession of arms. In Bayelsa State, 11 people were killed in a shoot-out by politicians contesting councillorship elections (Vines 2005: 354).
7. These are also known as one-man NGOs.
8. This section focused on the importance of developing the capacity of security institutions and partnerships with non-security actors.
9. Although South Africa reported for the period 2000–2, it has reported nothing since 2003 (Berman 2007: 12).

REFERENCES

Agboton-Johnson, Christiane, Adedji Ebo and Laura Mazal (2004) "Ghana", in *Small Arms Control in Ghana, Nigeria and Senegal*, West Africa Series No. 2 (English Version). London: International Alert, pp. 11–19.

Aning, Kwesi (2007) "Are there emerging West African criminal networks? The case of Ghana", *Global Crime*, 8(3): 192–212.

Aning, Kwesi et al. (2005) "Small arms proliferation in Ghana: A baseline assessment", Report for the Government of Ghana and United Nations Development Programme with the support of Small Arms Survey (SAS), Geneva.

Berman, Eric G. (2007) "Illicit trafficking of small arms in Africa: Increasingly a home-grown problem", Small Arms Survey presentation at the GTZ-OECD-UN Economic Commission for Africa Expert Consultation of the Africa Partnership Form, Addis Ababa, 14 Mar.

Duffield, Caroline (2009a) "Hope and rusty guns in Niger Delta", BBC report, 5 Sept. At <http://news.bbc.co.uk/2/hi/programmes/from_our_own_correspondent/8237742.stm> (accessed Aug. 2010).

Duffield, Caroline (2009b) "Will amnesty bring peace to Niger Delta?", BBC report, 5 Oct. At <http://news.bbc.co.uk/2/hi/africa/8291336.stm> (accessed Aug. 2010).

Ebo, Adedeji (2003) *Small Arms Control in West Africa*, West Africa Series No. 1 (English Version). London: International Alert.

Human Rights Watch (2007) *Criminal Politics: Violence, "Godfathers" and Corruption in Nigeria*. New York: Human Rights Watch.

IRIN (Integrated Regional Information Network) (2006) "GLOBAL: Small arms: The real weapons of mass destruction", in *Guns Out of Control: The Continuing Threat of Small Arms*, United Nations Office for the Coordination of Humanitarian Affairs, pp. 3–7.

Musah, Abdel-Fatau (1999) "Small arms and conflict transformation in West Africa", in Abdel-Fatau Musah and Niobe Thompson, eds, *Over a Barrel: Light Weapons and Human Rights in the Commonwealth*, London: Institute of Commonwealth Studies, pp. 109–40.

Musah, Abdel-Fatau (2002) "Privatization of security, arms proliferation and the process of state collapse in Africa", *Development and Change*, 33(5): 911–33.

OECD-DAC (Organisation for Economic Co-operation and Development/ Development Assistance Committee) (2007) *OECD-DAC Handbook on Security System Reform: Supporting Security and Justice*. Paris: OECD.

Onuoha, Godwin (2006) "Contextualising the proliferation of small arms and light weapons in Nigeria's Niger Delta: Local and global intersections", *African Security Review*, 15(2): 108–14.

Vines, Alex (2005) "Combating light weapons proliferation in West Africa", *International Affairs*, 81(2): 341–60.

5

Organized crime in Southern Africa

Charles Goredema

Globalization is associated with benefits and challenges in almost equal measure.[1] It manifests itself in more opportunities for the movement of people, commodities, capital and ideas across the world. A common assumption is that this should result in easier and more frequent trade and investment, and enhanced integration of economies, cultures and policies. However, globalization impacts on people, commodities, capital and ideas operating in the same context as transnational organized crime. A decade ago Louise Shelley (1999) observed:

> Transnational organizations are as diverse as multilateral businesses. While legitimate multinational corporations are based almost exclusively in the developed countries, the majority of transnational criminal organizations are based in third world countries. Multinational corporations market their products in industrialized countries and also have significant market share in many developing countries. Many transnational criminal organizations make enormous profits by marketing their illicit products such as drugs and trafficked human beings in developed countries. They represent large and successful examples of entrepreneurship in many parts of the world where third world entrepreneurs are not able to compete in the legitimate international economy.

While it is tempting to dismiss Professor Shelley's remarks as somewhat simplistic, one should bear in mind that they were informed by empirical evidence on the nature, global incidence and distribution of organized crime at that time.

As with proponents of globalization, transnational criminals experience the benefits, costs and risks of doing business that are associated with greater integration. It is important to note that increases in organized crime in countries such as those in Southern Africa preceded globalization, but processes precipitated by globalization have a bearing on patterns of crime. It has been argued, as William Coleman does in chapter 1 of this volume, that globalization does not just resemble colonialism, but is its extension. Both globalization and colonialism share a context populated by, and concerned with resources, economic activity and markets.

Perhaps the clearest manifestation of globalization is the accelerated expansion of technology. Recent observations point to certain spheres of criminal activity as being connected to this expansion. These include fraudulent transactions which are facilitated by the use and manipulation of computers; fraudulent transactions facilitated by and disguised by increased trade using transfer pricing as a symptomatic case study; fraudulent transnational investment transactions; and other transactions to evade taxation. Beyond these activities that can be connected to the abuse of innovations in technology and banking, globalization can also be linked to the influx of counterfeit commodities; escalation of trafficking in drugs; escalation of illegal migration; escalation of trafficking in precious resources; and the collusion of public officials to facilitate or conceal criminal activity.

This chapter assesses the state of affairs in Southern Africa – a small, but resource-rich region of the world – in the past decade. It reviews the implications and impact of globalization on patterns and trends of transnational crime using the Southern Africa region as a case study. It examines developments in spheres of crime most visibly impacted by globalization and the related financial turmoil, on account of opportunities yielded or closed. This chapter profiles some of the recurrent crime types in Southern Africa, and in order to provide context and description for the relationship between organized crime and globalization, it considers each type in terms of its nature, apparent causal and catalysing factors, main perpetrators and the markets that sustain it.

Fraud and technology

The use of technology to "forge documents or to create/manipulate data and information" (Savona and Mignone 2004) is rampant in Southern Africa, as in other parts of the world. Savona and Mignone highlight the increased use of new information and communication technologies as instruments which amplify the capacity to commit financial crime through fraud. The range of computer-facilitated fraud is very broad, including various guises of the ubiquitous 419 scams associated with West African syndicates; the use of fictitious companies to defraud importers, which is common in import-dependent countries such as Zimbabwe and Lesotho; the use of fictitious companies to defraud revenue-collecting authorities in countries such as South Africa, Namibia and Malawi. Criminals have been able to take advantage of the demand for imported products such as pharmaceuticals[2] and motor vehicle spare parts to delude legitimate businesses into paying for substandard products. In some cases no products are forthcoming at all.

In the case of revenue fraud, fictitious companies are used in making fraudulent claims for refunds of value added tax (VAT). South Africa has experienced a flurry of fraudulent claims emanating from fictitious subsidiary companies located in neighbouring countries that purport to have imported manufactured goods from South Africa and paid duty on them. As these claims appear to have subsided, with the enhancement of the detection capacity of the South African Revenue Service, copycat versions are sprouting up on the border between Namibia and Angola. Fraudulent VAT refund claims continue to occur with respect to transactions conducted through Katitwe, Oshikango and Oshivambo. Chinese retail businesses, of which there are 133 in Oshikango, have been implicated in this type of activity, revolving around trade in goods with customers from Angola who come into Namibia to buy directly from retailers and pay VAT on purchases. Two sets of VAT refund claim documents are prepared. One set is handed to the customer to facilitate the refund. Retailers then connive with customs officers at the borders to securely achieve a "secondary" refund, as if the goods were exported by the business rather than directly collected by the customer. This practice thrives on corruption among customs officers. However, British Crown Agents working on the Angolan side recording import goods have been helpful in detecting some cases.

There has been an evident upsurge in fraud committed by means of credit cards. This report from a credit card company manager represents the reality in the area of fraud facilitated by credit cards perceived in South Africa. He reported that:

> [it] is now common – and making use of technology that can often be purchased off the shelf – for data from genuine cards to be compromised in one country in the morning, counterfeit cards produced using the stolen data in then [sic] afternoon in a second country, then purchases made that evening in a third country. These countries may not even be on the same continent. (Cited in Costa 2004)

Credit card cloning is a common method by which these offences are committed. Along with capturing vital data using rogue websites, centres of tourism in the region are regularly targeted as data sources. For example, South African tourist destinations reported a 47 per cent increase in credit card fraud between June 2007 and June 2008; the level of losses each year has escalated to more than 500 million rand (about US$70 million).

A comprehensive profiling of the syndicates behind the spike in credit card fraud does not yet exist, but there are anecdotal indications of their composition. It is known that the criminal networks involved include lowly paid waiters, who have been implicated in data harvesting at some outlets. Wealthy operatives, who are likely to be the syndicate bosses, are also involved. Between the two levels are the technical experts who perform the cloning and card production. Whatever the case may have been in the past, it is evident that technical cloning skills are now located in the region. Prominent countries in this regard are South Africa, Zambia, the Democratic Republic of the Congo and Mauritius. The involvement of nationals of countries such as China, India, Taiwan and Bulgaria suggests that these skills have been imported into the region.

Fraud in trade

Transfer pricing involves artificial price management and is essentially a crude form of corporate smuggling. Transfer pricing is usually described by reference to the context in which it occurs, as:

> the pricing of goods and services within a multi-divisional organization, particularly in regard to cross-border transactions. For example, goods from the production division may be sold to the marketing division, or goods from a parent company may be sold to a foreign subsidiary, with the choice of the transfer price affecting the division of the total profit among the parts of the company.[3]

In that sense, it can also be considered a form of corporate organized crime.

Multinational companies (MNCs) justify it as a method of profit maximization by taking advantage of differences in taxation levels. Statistics are admittedly difficult to come by, but surveys show that transfer pricing has become common and is set to continue. Only South Africa and Botswana have transfer-pricing regulation in Southern Africa.[4] The rest of the region resorts to tax avoidance regulations. Even then, authorities in different countries focus on particular kinds of transfers, with no universal approach. Some pay more attention to intercompany sales, while others focus on management services and others on royalties and financing transactions. This enables MNCs to play them off against each other in dangling investment possibilities. It also enables the MNCs to forum-hop even after establishing enterprises in any one country.

The United Nations Conference on Trade and Development (UNCTAD) has recognized transfer pricing as an issue of concern since the 1990s. MNCs justify fund transfers between related companies in different countries in any of the following situations:

- where one company raises charges on another for administrative or management services;
- in the form of royalties and other charges for intangibles;
- where one company charges another for supplying goods for resale;
- in financing transactions;
- and, as charges for technical services. (Turner 1996)

The practice of outsourcing management services to external subsidiaries has also become a frequent occurrence and may be subject to abuse. Instances have come to light in the last decade involving transnational trading between Zimbabwe and Botswana as well as South Africa and Zimbabwe. For example, fund transfers occur between holding companies set up in Zimbabwe and subsidiaries established in Botswana, and in South Africa "siphoned" funds from Zimbabwe are transferred to the ultimate prejudice of Zimbabwean investors.

Concessionary arrangements ostensibly intent on encouraging exploitation of mineral resources have been a source of criminal conduct in the subregion since the 1980s. A common form of such arrangements is the permission to export unprocessed commodities, such as emeralds or rough diamonds, without paying tax or duty, for quality evaluation (assaying). Abuses consist of the understatement of volumes exported, which facilitates the excess volume of exports to be sold and the proceeds to be retained abroad.

Fraud in investments

Transaction-based fraud is becoming a method of organized crime often turned to. The United Kingdom's *Crime Threat Assessment Report* for 2008–9 notes:

> There are a number of reasons why serious organized criminals are attracted to non-fiscal frauds. These include the high profits and low risks, an awareness of opportunities to commit frauds derived from experience of money laundering by opening false bank accounts, purchasing property and cashing in mortgages, loans and insurance policies early, and ready access to the necessary capabilities,

> for example multiple identities, front businesses, international contacts, and low-level criminals to take "hands-on" risks. (SOCA 2008)

The last decade has witnessed the development of transnational pyramid schemes, whose complexity demands the involvement of multiskilled crime syndicates. Recent pyramid schemes have even used falsified documents to create the facade of a sound basis for investments. In one case, the originators of the scheme created false orders and invoices to give investors the impression that returns would be generated by legitimate trading transactions. The underlying lucrative business supporting the enterprise into which investment was being attracted was presented as pharmaceutical products for the management of HIV/AIDS.[5] Misleading orders and invoices generated by computers induced massive investments from individual high net worth clients and pension fund brokers. As the largest economy in the region, South Africa hosts its largest pyramid schemes, whose activities have radiated as far afield as the United Kingdom and continental Europe.

Southern African countries have long been familiar with the so-called pyramid investment or "Ponzi" scheme. Ponzi schemes are fraudulent schemes disguised as legitimate shrewd asset management and investment schemes. They are characterized by the use of new members or "investors" in the lower levels of a pyramid-like structure to fund the payment of "returns" to longer standing investors in the upper levels of the pyramid.

Tax evasion

Trade involving the region, both internally and externally, has continued to grow simultaneously with progress towards greater economic integration. The Southern Africa Development Community, which traces its roots to the mid-1970s, now comprises 14 members of varying size and levels of development.[6] It aspires to becoming a free trade area. The defining characteristics of the region include the central position of South Africa as a hub of trade and industry, particularly after 1994; the importance of the coastal countries to the management of trade and the regulation of smuggling; and the significance of natural resources to economies and to crime.

South Africa is an important source and transit country for commodities destined for the rest of the region. Smuggling syndicates cannot avoid channelling commodities through its ports and territory. They tend to exploit South Africa's position by marketing commodities declared to be in transit (and therefore not subject to import tax) within South Africa. When they cannot take advantage of South African markets in this way, criminals exploit adjacent markets in Zimbabwe or Namibia. Commodities passing through South African ports have evaded import duty on the pretence that they are destined for the northern parts of Mozambique or for Malawi. The goods are thereafter offloaded in Zimbabwe, with the paperwork completed at the exit borders. Sometimes, bribed officials of the Zimbabwe Revenue Authority (ZIMRA) process the paperwork in Harare. The complicity of ZIMRA officials in smuggling rackets is a source of concern for revenue authorities. As such, arrests tend to be few and far between.

Trafficking

The eight coastal countries in Southern Africa – Angola, Namibia, South Africa, Mauritius, Madagascar, Mozambique, the Seychelles and Tanzania – have lengthy maritime frontiers. The illicit exploitation of marine resources off the shores of Southern Africa has a long history. Monitoring activities in the adjacent waters and traffic movement along the coast presents monumental challenges. Both the coastal shelves and coastal borders bristle with the kinds of opportunities that organized crime networks feed upon. More recently, Southern Africa's connection with the trafficking of narcotics, particularly in South Africa, dates back to the 1990s (Steinberg 2005).

The drug trade

Steinberg highlights the critical factors that have contributed to the flourishing but illicit predatory trade in abalone and drugs between South Africa and parts of South East Asia:

> The first was the weakening of the rand against the US dollar that began in the early 1990s and continued steadily for the following decade. The second factor was the pre-existing presence in South Africa of a large and highly efficient Chinese organised crime network ... The third factor is the immense difficulty South Africa has had, and continues to have, in devising and executing an efficient border control function. Fourth, and with little doubt the most interesting and important, is the mutation in the socio-political identities of the coloured fishing communities on the abalone-rich shoreline during South Africa's transition to democracy; it was, above all, the evolution of a distinctive political consciousness that animated the taking of the perlemoen stock from the water. (Steinberg 2005)

The impact of fluctuations in the exchange value of currency on the incidence of illicit harvesting of perlemoen, or abalone, and drug trafficking was palpable. In less than a decade, perlemoen was almost poached into extinction, and the quantity of narcotics on the streets of South Africa, especially methaqualone (mandrax) and methamphetamine (tik), dramatically increased.

Transactions in which abalones poached from the southern Cape coast are exchanged for mandrax and heroin (eliminating the need for money) from South East Asia continue to be part of the drug trafficking trade in South Africa. Similarly, recent trends show an increase in the exploitation of other forms of marine life off the coast of Tanzania and Namibia – namely the poaching of tuna fish. The underlying backdrop to the current scenario is summed up by Andre Standing thus:

> While historically North America, Europe and Asia have managed to consume a large quantity of fish from their own waters, overfishing and population growth has led, quite rapidly, to a dependence on fish imports from further afield. The European Union (EU) for example, has seen several of its key commercial fishing stocks severely depleted by overfishing since the 1970s and now imports over 60 per cent of fish from beyond its borders, primarily from Africa. Yet, despite dwindling fish supplies, the industrial fishing fleets of developed nations have failed to shrink accordingly. Indeed, there is now widespread agreement that the international fishing fleet is suffering from chronic overcapacity, with subsidies being blamed for a large part of the problem. Thus, with dwindling fish stocks back home, a bloated fishing industry that supports thousands of jobs, and the growing popularity of fish as a healthy food option, the importation of fish from developing countries has become critical for the global North and far East. (2009: 324)

The Environmental Investigation Agency in the UK highlights the growing importance of environmental crime to organized crime networks (see Banks et al. 2008). Crime networks illegally barter fish in exchange for narcotics if money is not available or to avoid issues of money laundering.

The patterns of trade in narcotics affecting Southern Africa have not changed much over the past 20 years. Of note in that period is perhaps the greater prominence of Angola as a transit and destination country. A common modus operandi involves trips by Angolan nationals to South America, ostensibly to procure clothing and other apparel to sell in street markets of major towns. On the return journeys, the traders double as drug mules, ingesting condoms of cocaine and importing the drug into the region.

The markets which sustain the drug trafficking trade in Southern Africa are mostly in the major urban centres of South Africa, Namibia and

Angola. Markets in Europe have also retained their significance on account of the higher returns. An escalation in the production of narcotics in the early 2000s, especially in South Africa, prompted visible responses from the police, with some successes. The narcotics laboratories in South Africa and Tanzania have, however, proved to be resilient.

Mineral resources

Organized crime is also active in the sphere of mineral resources, particularly those that have a small consumer market in the region. Strong global linkages have long existed between production/extraction centres in Southern Africa, refining/beneficiation centres elsewhere and the ultimate markets. Producing countries continue to struggle to monitor activities at their end of the line. Multinational initiatives such as the Kimberley Process Certification Scheme (KPCS), established in 2000, reflect part of the response.

The capacity of the KPCS to address issues of non-compliance, smuggling, human rights violations and money laundering in diamond production areas continues to be questioned. A study by Human Rights Watch on rudimentary diamond mining in eastern Zimbabwe documented the activities of smuggling syndicates controlled by police officers: "Groups of between two and five police officers would partner with a large group of local miners under a loose arrangement where police provided the local miners security and escort in the fields in return for a share of the proceeds from selling any diamonds the local miners found" (2009: 25). The scenario mirrors activities in an earlier period in the Lunda provinces of Angola, where informal miners or *garimpeiros* were subjected to exploitation by public officials. Some of the rough diamonds originating from Zimbabwe are sold through third countries. Diamond buyers based in South Africa have been implicated in the trade in diamonds from Zimbabwe. An investigating team from the KPCS conducted an inspection in Zimbabwe at the beginning of July 2009. It noted some human rights violations and recommended that the army be removed from the diamond fields. Trading in Marange diamonds was to be suspended pending this action.[7]

At a more sophisticated level, the imprint of organized crime is seen in the theft of more valuable copper concentrate and mining equipment. Copper concentrate and mining equipment are stolen in transit to loading points, repackaging points or during export. Truck drivers stop over at buyers' delivery points, but they later claim to have been hijacked or simply dump the truck and run away. Drivers also divert trucks of copper ore or empty the high-grade ore and reload with low grade ore or plain earth.

Local entrepreneurs buy copper ore, while the buying of concentrate and anodes appears to be dominated by Chinese buyers, who own smelters in the industrial areas of Kitwe and Ndola where the concentrate and anodes are rebranded. They are then exported, mostly to China. In a recent case, a mining company lost a truck of concentrate, which was diverted by a driver while in transit for export packaging. It was sold to a Zambian buyer, who in turn sold it to a group of Chinese traders. The Chinese had already sent the ore to Johannesburg en route to China by the time the police investigations led to them. The ore was impounded by Interpol in Johannesburg and was in transit back to Zambia in March 2009. This case is still in court.

Mostly, illegal miners sell the ore directly to buyers who are licensed traders in copper ore. There are a few Zambian kingpins among the buyers. They own legitimate mining businesses, but have mines which are either fronts or lack sufficient capacity to supply large mines. They therefore depend upon alternatively sourced ore to meet the demand. The businesses are then used to absorb the stolen ores. The kingpins are seasoned criminals in the province who will not hesitate to cause harm to anyone crossing their path. They are also known to resolve conflicts openly and violently.

Ore is also sold to Chinese traders who are found all over the copper belt, and, in a few instances, to Indian buyers. The Chinese buyers keep a low profile and act under the front of being bona fide investors. They stick to themselves and work in groups of their own, seldom involving the services of locals. They are also buyers of stolen non-ferrous products, such as electric cables.

Research findings show that police officials collaborate in the commission of illegal mining operations rather than stop them. Their collaboration takes many forms, from receiving bribes during anti-crime operations to being on the payroll of the kingpins. Police also conduct raids, especially on Chinese pilling and smelting points, to seek cash bribes. Even more complex and difficult to pin down are relationships between politicians, high-ranking police officials and master buyers. Politicians, both personally and through their campaign organizers, pursue these master buyers to demand campaign money.

Ivory

The global trade in ivory, which has been tightly regulated since the early 1990s, continues in Southern Africa, largely through the activities of syndicates that are aided and abetted by small-scale poachers. The high water mark in the last decade was probably the transaction which came to light in June 2002 with the seizure of 6.2 tonnes of ivory aboard a ship that had docked in Singapore, en route to Japan. The ship originated in South Africa, although its cargo came from the hinterland. As reported by the UK's Environmental Investigation Agency:

> Investigations into the Singapore seizure revealed a well established syndicate of South East Asian and African nationals, operating across at least five borders and spanning two continents. Recovered documentation showed that the syndicate had been active for at least eight years prior to the seizure, and had dispatched 19 similar sized shipments since 1994. Such a formidable record of activity represents literally thousands of poached elephants and black market ivory worth hundreds of millions of dollars.
>
> Sourced largely from elephants in Zambia, the ivory was transported to Malawi for packing and inspection by potential buyers, before being taken by road to Mozambique. From there it was shipped to South Africa, and on to Japan via Singapore. The modus operandi employed to avoid detection included the use of personal and company pseudonyms, laying false trails, mis-declaration of goods, bribing customs officials, fake documentation and multiple trans-shipments. (Banks et al. 2007: 5)[8]

Since the demand for ivory has not abated, so trade continues too. The lawlessness that persists in Zimbabwe renders that country a ready source of illicitly procured ivory.

Counterfeit commodities

A large proportion of counterfeit commodities is introduced into the region through the coastal countries, but significant amounts also come in by air. A smaller, but growing percentage is produced within the region. Stretched borders, most of which are poorly controlled, facilitate the transnational influx and distribution of counterfeit commodities once they have landed in the region.

In 2007, the International Chamber of Commerce estimated that the value of the global industry in counterfeit commodities was US$650 billion, while the World Customs Organisation then estimated it to be worth 7 per cent of global commerce. The message behind these figures is that counterfeiting and related piracy are issues of significant global concern. Over the last decade, every country in the region has encountered counterfeiting and piracy of digital media, computer software, pharmaceuticals, clothing, cigarettes and spare parts for motor vehicles. The production and circulation of counterfeit currency continues in a few countries – particularly the Democratic Republic of the Congo, Zambia and South Africa.

The market for counterfeit consumer commodities is larger than that for narcotics, with the result that the volume of trade is significantly larger. As poverty levels impact on commodities, so too does the attraction and marketability of counterfeit products. Zimbabwe presents classic proof of this proposition: the economic implosion since 2000 has led to a proliferation of retailers and black market dealers peddling pirated commodities of all descriptions at bargain prices. While the initial consignments could be traced to China and India, these sources have been overtaken by Zambia, South Africa and the Democratic Republic of the Congo. South African commerce and industry is in turn constantly besieged by counterfeit commodities from China, South East Asia and from other African countries.

Counterfeit cigarettes in particular emanate from China and Zimbabwe. Most of the piracy related to clothing pertains to sportswear – which is in high demand around the time of major sporting events. The syndicates behind the supply of counterfeit commodities, which were very active during the football tournaments in Angola (January 2010) and South Africa (June and July 2010), include some politically connected individuals.

Stolen motor vehicles

Motor vehicle theft has a long history in Southern Africa. The hub of the illicit markets is South Africa, where most stolen vehicles originate: 50 per cent of vehicles stolen in South Africa are intended to be disposed of as complete vehicles in the South African market, 30 per cent are intended to be sold in neighbouring countries, and 20 per cent are broken up for spare parts. The spare parts are in turn disposed of locally and in neighbouring countries.[9] Four-wheel drive and pickup vehicles are usually intended for external markets in the region, while sedans and minibuses feed the domestic market.

Case studies show that most vehicle theft cases are committed by organized crime networks. The virtually symbiotic linkages between vehicle theft and other kinds of predatory crime such as robberies of cash, house burglaries and business robberies continue to be a feature of organized crime in the region.

Trends of illegal migration

The scope of this chapter is not broad enough to go beyond examining the impact of globalization on the "pull factors" to illegal migration.[10] These factors are mainly prompted by changes in the strength of economies of different countries as they try to cope with internal developments and respond to fluctuations in global market prices of the commodities on whose trade they depend. A major negative impact of globalization in this area is visible in countries affected by deindustrialization or massive retrenchment. This has yielded increased insecurity, making populations more susceptible to involuntary migration, exploitation and trafficking. Even though not all countries which have experienced negative impacts of this nature are in Southern Africa, the region has not been spared from being used by nationals from further afield as a transit region or springboard for illegal migration.

The comparative rates of unemployment in the region have had a significant effect on migration trends. Five countries have experienced exceptionally high rates of unemployment: Malawi, Mozambique, Swaziland and Zambia each average 45 per cent, while Zimbabwe has more than 80 per cent. Major intraregional migration is understandably dominated by Zimbabwean nationals, who have moved out of the country en masse in virtually all directions. South Africa is the main destination, to which at least 2 million moved illegally between 1995 and 2008. However, the proportion of that number trafficked is indeterminate. It is important to note that there has been a marked increase in child trafficking to South Africa over the last two years.[11]

Botswana and Tanzania present case studies of migration trends between the region and the world at large. There is evidence of "assisted migration" of Pakistani nationals to the United Kingdom through Botswana. Entry is through the main airport or by land across the Okavango Delta. Migrants each pay between US$5,000 and US$6,000 to a facilitator, normally a Pakistani national resident in Botswana. The latter is tasked with "organizing" entry visas and work permits for the migrants. The migrants are usually employed by this facilitator for some time in Botswana before applying for visas to the UK and the United States. Similarly, Tanzania is regularly used as a staging post by Somali nationals en route to South Africa through Zambia or Malawi.

Money laundering

Money laundering is an inevitable ancillary activity to organized crime. This chapter does not purport to quantify the scale of proceeds emanating from the lines of activity discussed. Suffice it to say that in comparative terms, fraud schemes account for the greater volumes of funds laundered within and from Southern African countries.

Noticeable trends have emerged over the last decade in Southern Africa. First, the utilization of sponsorship of sporting teams to obscure money laundering. In South Africa, football teams, on account of their cash-generating tendency, provide an avenue for mingling proceeds of crime with income from the league, from matches, and from successful tournaments. Illicit income associated with sports sponsorship is derived from drug trafficking, pension fund fraud and extortion rackets. A second trend is the prominence of the role of entertainment outlets in facilitating dealings in drugs and obscuring money laundering. The final trend is the greater use of offshore trusts to invest the proceeds of tax evasion.

Conclusion

The picture that has emerged since Professor Shelley's observations quoted at the beginning of this chapter is more complex than may have been evident then. In contrast, Jenni Irish-Qhobosheane observes:

> as is the case with most forms of organized crime, a dramatic upsurge has occurred since the 1990s. The established networks appear to have expanded, and new groups involved in cross-border crime have mushroomed. A number of commentators have noted the porosity of the borders between the countries of the Southern African Development Community (SADC), and the increase of economic trade and regional integration, and suggested that together these provide a possible explanation for the proliferation of organized crime across the region . . . [Southern Africa has] become both a target and a source of criminal organizations. (2007: 147–8)

The past decade has shown that transnational crime syndicates based in both the developing and the developed countries regard Southern Africa as fertile territory. It appears that the major driving force to which an upsurge in organized crime can be attributed over the last decade is the huge demand in affluent societies for resources and commodities. Most of these commodities are located in the less affluent parts of the world. In that period, the flow of resources in the direction of the wealthier countries has been accompanied by ever escalating trends of unregulated migration in the same direction.

Notes

1. See the definition of globalization on the Australian website <http://www.globaleducation.edna.edu.au/globaled/go/pid/178> (accessed June 2009).
2. Medical drugs such as haemoglobin B12 and vitamin complex B12 have been offered through fraudulent advertisements.
3. Adapted from the Wikipedia encyclopaedia definition. At <http://en.wikipedia.org/wiki/Transfer_pricing> (accessed June 2010).
4. This was the finding of a survey of Anglophone African countries in 2004 by Ernst & Young.
5. The scheme, which collapsed in June 2009, revolved around the exploits of Barry Tannenbaum's Frankel Investments.

6. The member states are Angola, Botswana, the Democratic Republic of the Congo, Lesotho, Madagascar, Malawi, Mozambique, Namibia, Seychelles, South Africa, Swaziland, Tanzania, Zambia and Zimbabwe.
7. As reported on the Voice of America News, 6 July 2009. An interim report was delivered to the Minister of Mines for Zimbabwe on 4 July 2009.
8. Also, see Human Rights Watch 2009.
9. These statistics are derived from the South African Insurance Crime Bureau newsletter, June 2009.
10. For more on the activities and actors involved in human trafficking see chapter 14 by Kirsten Foot in this volume.
11. In one instance reported in May 2009, two trucks carrying children of both sexes which originated in Zimbabwe were intercepted in Botswana en route to the Ramotswa border post with South Africa. There have been reported cases of children being brought to South Africa on the pretext that they were to be reunited with their parents who had illegally migrated to the UK. In a few cases, these children end up stranded in South Africa, awaiting visas and suffering exploitation.

REFERENCES

Banks, Debbie, Justin Gosling, Julian Newman, Rachel Noble and Mary Rice (2007) *Upholding the Law: The Challenge of Effective Enforcement*, Environmental Investigation Agency Briefing. At <http://www.eia-international.org/files/reports163-1.pdf> (accessed Sept. 2010).

Banks, Debbie, Charlotte Davies, Justin Gosling, Julian Newman, Mary Rice, Jago Wadley and Fionnuala Walravens (2008) *Environmental Crime: A Threat to our Future*, Environmental Investigation Agency Report. London. At <http://www.illegal-fishing.info/uploads/EIAEnvironmentalCrimereport.pdf> (accessed June 2010).

Costa, Antonio M. (2004) "Emerging challenges", in Ernesto U. Savona, ed., *Crime and Technology: New Frontiers for Regulation, Law Enforcement and Research*, New York: Springer, pp. 1–5.

Human Rights Watch (2009) *Diamonds in the Rough: Human Rights Abuses in the Marange Diamond Fields of Zimbabwe*. At <http://www.hrw.org/en/reports/2009/06/26/diamonds-rough-0> (accessed June 2010).

Irish-Qhobosheane, Jenni (2007) *Gentlemen or Villains: Thugs or Heroes – the Social Economy of Organised Crime in South Africa*. Johannesburg: South African Institute of International Affairs.

SAICB (South African Insurance Crime Bureau) (2009) Newsletter, issue 4 (June), South African Insurance Crime Bureau, Johannesburg. At <http://www.saicb.co.za/images/stories/documents/SaicbJune2009.pdf> (accessed June 2010).

Savona, Ernesto U. and Mara Mignone (2004) "The fox and the hunters: How IC technologies change the crime race", in Ernesto U. Savona, ed., *Crime and Technology: New Frontiers for Regulation, Law Enforcement and Research*, New York: Springer, pp. 7–28.

Shelley, Louise (1999) "Identifying, counting and categorizing transnational criminal organizations", *Transnational Organized Crime*, 5(1) (Spring): 1–18.

SOCA (Serious Organised Crime Agency) (2008) *The United Kingdom Threat Assessment of Serious Organised Crime 2008–09*. At <http://www.soca.gov.uk/assessPublications/downloads/UKTA2008-9NPM.pdf>.

Standing, Andre (2009) "The European Union and the scramble for African fish", in Roger Southall and Henning Melbers, eds, *A New Scramble for Africa: Imperialism, Investment and Development in Africa*, Scotsville, South Africa: UKZN Press, pp. 324–56.

Steinberg, Jonny (2005) "The illicit abalone trade in South Africa", Occasional Paper 105 (Apr.), Institute for Security Studies, Pretoria.

Turner, Robert (1996) *A Study on Transfer Pricing*. Toronto: Ernst & Young.

6

Maoism in a globalizing India

Ajay K. Mehra

The persistence of "Naxalism",[1] the Maoist "revolutionary" politics, in India after over six decades of parliamentary politics is a visible paradox in a democratic "socialist"[2] India. Inheriting pre-independence "revolutionary" politics situated in a feudal-colonial context, India "resolved" it by 1951 with political, military and civil society initiatives. However, the socioeconomic conditions that aided the Communist Party of India to launch a Russian and Chinese inspired revolution in Telangana[3] in 1946 persisted and aided the China-inspired communist faction to launch another "revolution" from Naxalbari, in West Bengal, in 1967. The Indian state suppressed the movement within five years, leaving the basic issues, land reforms and rural deprivation, which had inspired the two experiments with Marxist-Leninist-Maoist (henceforth Naxalism) unresolved.

Despite the reemergence, consolidation and expansion of Naxalism, India's democratic politics and republican state have failed to resolve this violent brand of politics. India has come into the twenty-first century with a decade of departure from the Nehruvian socialism to a free-market, rapidly globalizing economy, which has created new dynamics (and pockets) of deprivation along with economic growth. Thus the same set of issues, particularly those related to land, continue to fuel protest politics, violent agitator politics, as well as armed rebellion.

What has led to the persistence and consolidation of Naxalism in India? Are government and political parties in India able to grasp the socioeconomic dynamics encouraging these politics, or are they stuck with a security-oriented approach that further fuels them?

The situation

The complexities of this variety of politics are rooted as much in the economic realities of the country as in its stratified social structure. Indeed, the Constitution of India has attempted social and economic "upliftment" of the sections known as the Scheduled Castes (SCs) (also known as *dalit* or oppressed) and the Scheduled Tribes (STs) (also known as *adivasis* or *girijans* – literally, the aborigines or the hill people), incorporating provisions related to fundamental rights, ensuring liberty and equality as well as affirmative action (reservation in public employment and so on). Entrenched feudal structures, emerging commercial interests, new alliances and the nexus between the entrenched order, new interests, political elites and the bureaucracy, and deficient public infrastructure and facilities, perpetuate exploitation. The resulting miseries have made these sections of the population vulnerable to calls for revolutionary politics.

Aware of pervasive poverty in the country at the time of independence and its long-term debilitating impact on society and polity, Nehru stressed the need for reducing India's poverty: to "insure an irreducible minimum standard for everybody, the national income had to be greatly increased ..." (cited in Bhagwati 2004: 53). India has achieved success in poverty alleviation since independence. A whopping 56.7 per cent of Indians lived below the poverty line in the mid-1960s; only a quarter of the Indian population are in that state now, but 26 per cent of a billion in absolute numbers is still a staggering figure.[4] The World Bank's *World Development Report 2000/2001* placed India (at $755 or less GNP per capita in 1999) among the countries with low income; after two decades of its market economy, India simultaneously claims overflowing foreign exchange reserves, a 7–8 per cent growth rate and a place among low income countries. In the Human Development Index 2007, published by the United Nations, India is two places down from 2004 at 128 (out of 177 countries). Deficient in most of the public infrastructure for human development such as health, education, housing, gender equity and so on, cash-strapped governments at the centre and in states are either fumbling or withdrawing from these areas on the sly. Naturally, those on the margins are vulnerable to calls for a "revolution" that would give them a chance both to avenge their exploitation and to transform the social, political and economic order.

India's development dichotomy has also had a destabilizing impact on people's settled lives. For decades, the Indian state has failed to provide alternative livelihoods to those displaced by developmental projects. According to an estimate, between 1951 and 1990, 8.5 million members of STs were displaced by developmental projects. Representing over 40 per cent of all the displaced persons, only 25 per cent of them were rehabilitated (Fernandes 1994: 22–32). Another review of 32 major dam projects across the country shows that most of the displaced have been from either STs or SCs (Patwardhan 1997). Of the 12 states where dam-related displacements took place, 10 have been affected with Naxalism, and in the other two Maoist groups have recently been active (Mehra 2006).

Although there are no definitive data, Dalits and Adivasis have been reported to form a large proportion of the Maoists' foot soldiers.[5] Aside from the displacement–rehabilitation hiatus compelling them into rebellion, atrocities against them have also been committed. A study of atrocities against these two sections of society reveals correspondence between the prevalence and spread of Naxalism and the geographical location of atrocities (Mehra 2006).

The susceptibility of the vulnerable continues under the new emerging context of the liberalization, marketization and globalization of the Indian economy, which have added new dominance structures to the existing ones. Both the centre and the states are competing with each other to invite domestic and foreign direct investment (FDI). To facilitate this and attract investors, Special Economic Zones (SEZ) are being set up. Acquisition of land for SEZs as well as for industrial projects is increasingly becoming contentious, leading to protests and violence.

The lineage

The factors behind current Maoist revolutionary politics, particularly the participation of the Dalits and Adivasis/Girijans, their political-ideological roots and the impact of globalization, are best understood in a historical perspective.

The Telangana movement

The Telangana (erstwhile Hyderabad state) peasant uprising in 1944 was rooted in resentment and anger against the oppressive domination of the *deshmukh*s, originally revenue collectors with magisterial powers, who survived regime changes to be entrenched as landlords (*dora*) with near complete control over their *pargana*s (administrative unit) and *praja* (subjects). Revenue collection, paid in cash to the state, gave the landlords unlimited powers vis-à-vis their *praja*. They also took on the role of merchants and usurers, perpetuating the practice of servile labour, reducing a vast majority of sharecroppers and landless labourers to a life of slavery (Thirumali 1992: 477–81). The Dalits – washer men, cobblers, potters, etc. – had to offer free service to them, and others sent one male member daily for household work under the *vetti* (forced labour) system, even women for "pleasure" (Ranga Rao 1979: 152; Sundarayya 1972: 11). Inflation and food crises in the wake of the Second World War created indebtedness. Taking advantage, the *dora*s seized land, aggravating landlessness.[6]

The Communist Party of India (CPI) infiltrated the Andhra Mahasabha – founded in 1928 to oppose domination of the Telugus by the Urdu-speaking Muslim elite and the Marathis in the Nizam-ruled Hyderabad state – gradually taking control of it and transforming it into a radical organization. The grain levy campaign against the Nizam's regime, which it launched in 1941, galvanized the rural masses. The movement turned violent in 1946 when the people of Jangaon Taluka resisted the attempt by the *deshmukh* to seize the harvest of a member, which led to a militant mass struggle for local control: "the peasantry in about 3000 villages, covering roughly a population of three million in an area of about 16,000 square miles . . . had succeeded in setting up gram raj, on the basis of fighting village panchayats" (Sundarayya 1972: 4). A powerful militia comprising 10,000 village squad members and 2,000 regular guerrilla squads organized in defence of the peasantry drove out the landlords and seized and redistributed 1 million acres of land; the daily wages of agricultural labourers were increased and a minimum wage was enforced (Sundarayya 1972: 4).

After the accession of Hyderabad to India in 1948 and the consequent support of the landlords and rich peasants, the army severely suppressed the communists. Dwindling popular support after Gandhi's disciple Acharya Vinoba Bhave launched the *bhoodan* (land-gift) movement in Telangana in 1951,[7] the abolition of the *jagirdari* land tenancy system by the government, land reforms and internal contradictions within the CPI made the party unsustainable. Eventually, Soviet advice resulted in withdrawal of the movement in 1951 (Ram 1971: 52; Sundarayya 1972: 308; Banerjee 1984: 66–7).

Naxalbari and the spring thunder over India

The tribal-peasant uprising in Naxalbari, in West Bengal's northern frontier district Darjeeling on 3 March 1967, also reflected the existence of mass discontent (Mohanty 1977: 31). Mobilization, indoctrination and arming of the tribes and peasants by the CPI/CPM (Communist Party of India (Marxist)) had been going on for a decade when an attack on the granary of a *jotedar*[8] flared up after clashes with the police in Naxalbari, Phansideva and Kharibari police stations of the Siliguri subdivision.

Unrest in the Darjeeling district reflected the lack of implementation of the land reforms enacted in the 1950s.[9] The ceiling provisions of the

1954 Act made 17,000 acres available for redistribution, of which only 7,500 acres had been redistributed by 1967, leaving over 50 per cent of the cultivators in the area holding 1–5 acres of land. Most such cultivators ended up as sharecroppers, cultivating Jotedars' land on a year-to-year basis and dividing the harvest with them. But whereas the West Bengal Estates Act of 1954 provided that the cultivator-sharecropper should get two-thirds of the harvest, in reality, the produce was being equally divided. Since he received his share only in kind (*paddy*), which was insufficient, the cultivator was forced to borrow both grain and money from the Jotedar, at high rates of interest, for living, seeds, fertilizers, festivals and other special occasions, keeping the sharecroppers in a state of serfdom.

The leaders mobilized people against exploitation and led agitations against exploitative policies, despite a ban on the CPI since 1950. Kanu Sanyal outlines the evolution of the Naxalbari movement:

1 1951–4: the organizational stage in which "the peasantry of Naxalbari, advanced through clashes to get them organised";
2 1953–7: the period of worker–peasant alliance and "a united class of workers and peasants";
3 1955–62: a very significant stage – when, responding to the call given by the West Bengal Kisan Sabha (Peasants' Organization) "to regain the possession of *benami*[10] land", the subdivisional Kisan Samiti (peasants' council) in Naxalbari "gave a call to confiscate the entire produce of *jotedar's* land", unless the Jotedar could furnish proof of his ownership before the peasant committee. A call was also made to the peasants to arm themselves to protect their crop from the Jotedars and the police;
4 1962–4: despite the India–China war, the peasants refused to embrace chauvinism. (Sanyal 1974: 21–7)

The two major splits in the Communist movement in India, in 1964 and 1969, were consequences of the radicalization of the splitting unit; each split resulted in the parent unit being accused of "revisionism", of making compromises for the sake of power.[11] Even though the CPM painstakingly organized peasants in the area, there were sharp differences in the party leadership over the strategy to be adopted. First, the vanguard leaders Charu Mazumdar and Kanu Sanyal agreed that the "Chinese path is the path of liberation in India; [and] agrarian revolution can be completed through armed struggle", but they disagreed regarding strategy, as discussed by Charu Mazumdar (Sanyal 1974: 21–7; Mukherji 1979: 42–5). Later, consensus advocated seizure of land from the Jotedars, the cultivation of the land and the sharing of half of the product from the plantation workers' land.

The unanticipated windfall of power in 1967 had a section of the CPM feeling that India was not ripe for revolution and witnessed the CPM-in-government – Home Minister Jyoti Basu and Land Revenue Minister Hare Krishna Konar (earlier an advocate of armed struggle) – negotiating with the CPM-in-revolution – the Mazumdar-Sanyal group (Mukherji 1979: 42–57). The Konar-led cabinet mission to talk to Charu Mazumdar and Kanu Sanyal in May 1967 failed. Jyoti Basu's instructions to the police not to enter the rebel strongholds were criticized. The movement took a violent turn, inviting retaliation from the police. The Naxalites ignored three appeals by the state cabinet to surrender by 4 July 1967; their key leaders were arrested, and by September the situation had been "brought under control" (Mohanty 1977: 44–5). Consequently, the administration decided to take up immediately "those aspects of land reforms which could be tackled 'completely and quickly' and thereby restore confidence among the panic-stricken people in the affected areas" (Mehra 2002). By September, the government claimed to have distributed 984.22 acres of land among 686 persons (Mukherji 1979: 57). But the land distribution by the bureaucratic machinery created a number of fresh anomalies (Mukherji 1979: 57–61).

The CPM split in 1969. The newly born CPI(ML) (Communist Party of India (Marxist-Leninist)) resumed the movement in December 1969, when it turned conspiratorial and violent, relied increasingly on terror by its guerrilla squads, neglected mass mobilization of the peasants and focused on agrarian issues. The government retaliated strongly, crushing it by mid-1972 (Mukherji 1979: 62–73).

The Srikakulam movement

The revival of the tribal-peasant movement in Srikakulam, the northernmost district in Andhra Pradesh, in 1959, with the formation of the Girijan Sangham (Hill People's Association), indicated the persistence of the issues of the 1946 movement. In 1965, the Sangham organized a meeting of 300 representatives of the agricultural workers from the area, educating them about their rights. In 1967, a schoolteacher, Vempatapu Satynarayana, organized the Girijans of Parvathipuram taluk of the Srikakulam district to launch non-violent struggles against exploitation. Andhra Communists then persuaded the schoolteacher to join the CPI. After a decade, the organized violence by the landlords and the complicity of the state administration and the police turned him to violent action. He was eventually killed in a police "encounter" in 1970 (Calman 1985: 45–8).

In the Srikakulam district, 43.1 per cent of the total population were either cultivators or agricultural labour; the non-working population amounted to nearly half of the total population (1961 census). An increase in agricultural labour in proportion to the cultivators indicated that big farmers were grabbing the land that belonged to small cultivators, reducing them to labourers on their own land and their annual per capita income to (1968) 135 rupees ($18). Worse still, the tribals were continuously losing their land to the plains people, who were moving to the hills to grab land, forcing the Girijans into indebtedness. Legislation failed to prevent indebtedness. From 1952, the tribals also suffered from the limits and rules imposed by the government on tribal access to forest land.

The death of a tribesman on 31 October 1967 at the hands of a landlord eventually provided the spark:

> between early 1968 and late 1970 the revolutionaries had mobilized almost the entire tribal population in the Srikakulam Agency Area [and] carried out numerous attacks resulting in the death of at least 34 landlords. In ... July 1969, the revolutionaries controlled nearly 300 villages out of the 518 in the Agency. The ... Ryotanga Sangram Samithis ruled over the region, tried the money-lenders in Praja Courts (People's Courts), annulled debt agreements, redistributed land and conducted military training among the people. (Mohanty 1977: 53)

In a concerted action, the police declared Srikakulam a disturbed area and succeeded in killing and arresting a number of Naxalites; by the mid-1970s, the movement had lost its punch. The Maoists' annihilation tactics boomeranged in the plains where they were organizationally weak. In the hills, aside from *dalams* (armed groups), hundreds of Girijans participated in brutal killings (Calman 1985: 79). The movement had nonetheless succeeded in setting the social agenda in the area. Aside from trying to give immediate relief to the *girijans* and introducing developmental schemes, the government addressed the landlessness among the *girijans*. Even the restoration of the cultivable land benefited wealthier vested interests (Calman 1985: 99–125). By the late 1970s, the peasant labour associations (Ryotu Coolie Sangham) with the CPI(ML) launched a movement for redistribution of land and for wasteland illegally occupied by the landlords (Bergman 1984: 116–17). During the emergency (1975–7), the Naxalite movement was crushed.

After their release in 1977, many of Charu Mazumdar's colleagues left the party and formed their own groups. Two groups, led by K. Seetharamaiah and C. P. Reddy, were from Andhra Pradesh. The third group, led by Vinod Mishra, and Reddy's group were active in Bihar (Mohanty 1991: 30–1). In fact, on 22 April 1980, K. Seetharamaiah, the founder of the People's War Group, gave Maoism new life when he discarded Charu Mazumdar's "total annihilation of class enemies" line as the only form of struggle and laid stress on floating mass organizations and taking up economic struggles to spread the movement (Das 2000).

Paradigmatic shift

Naxalism has gone through an ideological, organizational and strategic paradigm shift in the new millennium, as the persisting issues are magnified and complicated by globalization. The merger of several Maoist groups, but still with separate identities, during 1999 and 2003 has been the most salient development in the expansion and consolidation of the Maoist movement in recent times, bringing greater organizational cohesion, more concerted action and an apparent ideological clarity (Mohanty 2006a). The process of mergers and consolidation during 2003–4 resulted in the emergence of three major Maoist groups: CPI(Maoist), CPI(ML)-Liberation and CPI(ML), aside from several smaller ones operating independently. The merger on 21 September 2004 of the two extreme militant groups – CPI-ML(People's War) and the Maoist Communist Centre of India – into CPI(Maoist), currently the largest and most powerful group, has been the most noteworthy development in recent times. With the formation of the People's Liberation Guerrilla Army, 3,500-strong and equipped with sophisticated arms and a well-designed organizational structure, the CPI(Maoist) has developed an edge, controlling, according to a Ministry of Home Affairs report in 2007–8, 361 (out of 10,027) police stations in 13 states.[12] The party takes forward the Charu Mazumdar line of rejecting parliamentary politics, describing the current stage as "New Democratic Revolution" (a variant of the "people's democratic revolution" of the 1970 programme), aimed at achieving agrarian revolution with a strategy to liberate "the rural areas first and then having expanded the base areas – the centre of democratic power in rural areas – advance towards countrywide victory through encircling and capturing the cities" (Banerjee 2006: 3160). It enjoys considerable support among the tribal and peasant populations in many states.

The CPI(ML)-Liberation, on the other hand, began in 1977 in central Bihar and focused on mass organization; it expanded by supporting the Indian People's Front during the 1980s and 1990s. It has participated in electoral processes, successfully in some cases, and also from time to time launched mass trade union, peasant, women's and students' organizations.

The CPI(ML) is led by Kanu Sanyal. His Communist Organization of India(ML) merged with CPI(ML) Unity Initiative, the Unity Centre, CPI(ML) Janashakti, and some groups of Andhra Pradesh, Maharashtra and Kerala to create a stronger organization following the theory of "mass revolutionary trend", developed by T. Nagi Reddy and Chandra Pulla Reddy, which was aimed at keeping revolutionary politics conjoined with mainstream parliamentary politics. Other mass organizations attached to it are Raitu Coolie Sangham, Andhra Pradesh Federation of Trade Unions, People's Democratic Students Union and Sthree Vimukti

Sangathana (Women's Liberation Organization) and their news organ *Class Struggle*. Along with its support organizations, such as the Indian Federation of Trade Unions and All India Kisan Mazdoor Sabha, which have been active in several states, the CPI(ML) has continued to be a significant force, both underground and in issue-based mainstream political mobilization (Mohanty 2006a; Ramana 2006).

Indeed, the mergers and consolidations, significant from the perspective of organizing and strengthening Maoist politics, have sorted out the prevailing ideological incoherence that had splintered the movement. This made coordination possible, as was reflected in the Fifth Regional Conference of South Asian revolutionary parties organized in 2003.[13] Since the two groups do not reject parliamentary politics, they have been able to coordinate their activities. However, as some Maoist groups are still active under different names, despite the shift in focus from personalities to ideologies, issues and methods, personality-based outfits persist, thus confusing India's revolutionary collage. This puts a question mark over the cohesiveness of the Coastal Regulation Zone and a red corridor from Nepal to the south of India, despite the large number of areas in this stretch under the control of various Maoist groups.

The pre-organizational character of the Maoists is due to the underground nature of the parties. Ideological parallelism and revolutionary strategy are reflected in violent actions by *dalam*s (at times while being pursued by the paramilitary forces), actions which are later regretted by the central leadership. This reflects the prevailing perplexity and mystification in organizational, ideological and strategic aspects of the Maoist movement, despite its impressive expansion since 2000. Recently the Maoist movement has been marred by acts of extortion and ruthless killing of innocent people suspected of being police informers (Banerjee 2006: 3159).

Globalization and revolution

Organizational consolidation and ideological and strategic cohesion have given the Maoists greater punch in battling the Indian state and facilitated their expansion and consolidation.[14] The Naxal expansion to 16 states (table 6.1) shows that the issues responsible for the origin of Maoism persist and are finding more areas for expansion than ever before.

There was Naxal influence in 2007 in 194 districts (nearly one-third of the 612 districts in the country) in 16 states, in various degrees: 65 (14 per cent) of the affected districts were highly affected. Not only has the intensity of the violence increased in most of the affected states, as Operation Greenhunt was launched near the beginning of 2010 to tame the

Table 6.1 Districts affected by Naxalism in 2007, with degree of intensity

States affected (no. districts in state)	Highly affected districts	Moderately affected districts	Marginally affected districts	No. districts affected	% districts affected
Andhra Pradesh (23)	12	7	4	23	100.00
Bihar (39)	16	3	13	32	82.00
Jharkhand (24)	14	4	5	23	95.83
Chhattisgarh (18)	7	1	6	14	77.70
Orissa (30)	8	5	9	22	73.33
West Bengal (18)	4	3	10	17	94.44
Maharashtra (35)	2	4	1	7	20.00
Karnataka (27)	1	9	2	12	44.44
Madhya Pradesh (48)	–	2	4	6	12.5
Uttar Pradesh (70)	1	2	3	6	8.57
Tamil Nadu (29)	–	2	6	8	27.58
Kerala (14)	–	–	3	3	21.42
Uttarakhand (13)	–	5	4	9	69.23
Haryana (20)	–	2	5	7	35.00
Rajasthan (32)	–	3	–	3	09.38
Gujarat (25)	–	–	2	2	08.00
16 (465)	65	52	77	194	41.72

Total of all districts = 612; 31.7% of all districts are affected.
Source: Institute of Conflict Management, New Delhi (updated 31 October 2007).

Maoist challenge, the Government of India has admitted that 20 states, 223 districts (out of 626) and 2,000 police stations are affected with Naxal violence across the country (Mehra 2009). The 65 highly affected districts in 2007 were spread over 9 of the 16 affected states. Even if we consider that some states use Maoism as a ploy to get more funds from the Union government and we consider the methodology of the Institute of Conflict Management data in table 6.1 with some circumspection, the spread is ominous. Chhattisgarh, rich in natural resources (and with 43.7 per cent forest and 31.75 per cent tribal population), is projected to be nearly 60 per cent under the Naxalite control in 2010 at the present rate of their expansion.

The key to Maoist success in the affected states is the population suffering deprivation such as the STs and the SCs (Expert Group 2008). Both the Telangana and Naxalbari movements began in similar ways with the peasants and tribals being mobilized against exploitation, enslavement, indebtedness, deprivation and humiliation in two backward rural areas.[15] The Maoist spread since the mid-1980s, in a pattern along a group of states, which has allowed organizational consolidation as well as coordination, shows that these factors facilitating their growth continue to exist. Maoism remains a rural product; the countryside is where the greatest exploitation of and the most cases of atrocities against the Dalits, Adivasis/Girijans and other marginalized sections of the population take place.

The official figures on atrocities against the SCs and STs over the years show correspondence between high rates of targeted violence (which can be taken as an indicator of exploitation that goes beyond physical atrocities) and Naxalism. Most of the states affected with Naxalism have a high rate of atrocities on Dalits, though a direct correlation between the two needs to be worked out methodically. The frustrations of the Dalits and lower Other Backward Classes is exacerbated by the fact that they do not get redress from the system; not only is the machinery of law and order biased against them, judicial pronouncements, particularly in the lower courts, also display caste bias (Shukla 2006). Indeed, Dalits have used mainstream political participation to obtain a share in power, restricting Dalits from joining extremist politics. However, discriminatory and exploitative social structures, as well as the inadequacies of mainstream political mobilization (Mehrotra 2006), lead a section of them to succumb to Maoist politics.

Similarly, the Scheduled Tribes, referred to in the present context as the Adivasis (indigenous people) and Girijans (hill people), described as "the last frontier of human rights", have also been at the receiving end of violence by the dominant castes/classes for centuries (Dhagamwar 2006: 11). Given that the British subjugated the tribal population with the former legal system – incomprehensible to the STs – it is not surprising that there are increasing atrocities against them (Dhagamwar 2006: 41–3).[16]

India's development dichotomy, which has created over the years a wide displacement–rehabilitation hiatus due to governmental apathy and corruption, as well as established exploitative structures, continues to create pockets of disaffection. The hiatus is visible in Maoism-affected states. This dichotomy is as old as independent India's developmental history; it has acquired new dimensions in a globalized economy. The displacement of 8.5 million Adivasis between 1951 and 1990, representing 41 per cent of all the displaced, in projects related to dams, mines, industries, wildlife, etc., of whom only 25 per cent were resettled, leaving 6.4 million who were dispossessed of their hearth, home and livelihood without proper resettlement measures, creates a huge pocket of discontent (table 6.2).

The Hindu (31 March 2007) pointed out that of the 22,141 families displaced by the Hirakud dam in Orissa in 1957, only 2,185 were resettled by 2007. Not surprisingly, the Adivasis would be receptive to arguments

Table 6.2 Conservative estimate of persons and tribals displaced by development projects, 1951–1990 (in hundreds of thousands)

Types of project	All DPs	Percentage of DPs	DPs resettled (lakhs)	Percentage of resettled DPs	Backlog (lakhs)	Backlog (per cent)	Tribals displaced (lakhs)	Tribals as percentage of all DPs	Tribals DPs and resettled (lakhs)	Percentage of tribal DPs resettled	Backlog of tribal DPs	Backlog of tribal DPs (per cent)
Dam	164.0	77.0	41.00	25.0	123.00	75.0	63.21	38.5	15.81	25.00	47.40	75.0
Mines	25.5	12.0	6.30	24.7	19.20	75.3	13.30	52.20	3.30	25.00	10.00	75.0
Industries	12.5	5.9	3.75	30.0	8.75	70.0	3.13	25.0	0.80	25.0	2.33	75.0
Wildlife	6.0	2.8	1.25	20.8	4.75	79.2	4.5	75.0	1.00	22.0	3.50	78.0
Others	5.0	2.3	1.50	30.0	3.50	70.0	1.25	25.0	0.25	20.2	1.00	80.0
Total	213	100	53.80	25.0	159.20	75.0	85.39	40.9	21.16	25.0	64.23	75.0

1 lakh = 100,000; DP denotes displaced person.
Source: Fernandes 1994: 22–32.

about the bias of the ruling classes against them. Various studies, including one by the World Bank and the World Commission on Dams (2000), point out that the Government of India has not factored into the projects displacements and the socioeconomic costs of rehabilitation, or the impact of failed resettlement on social unrest. As the World Commission on Dams report put it:

> Large dams have had serious impacts on the lives, livelihoods, cultures and spiritual existence of indigenous and tribal peoples. Due to neglect and lack of capacity to secure justice because of structural inequities, cultural dissonance, discrimination and economic and political marginalisation, indigenous and tribal peoples have suffered disproportionately from the negative impacts of large dams, while often being excluded from sharing in the benefits ... (I)n India, 40–50% of those displaced by development projects were tribal people ... (2000: 110)

Walter Fernandes, who has studied the displacement–rehabilitation hiatus since independence, points out that 40 per cent of the displaced between 1947 and 2000 have been tribals, and 20 per cent each Dalits and backward castes. That 80 per cent of those displaced are voiceless may explain the poor rates of rehabilitation (2007: 203).[17]

Another study of the people displaced by 32 large dams across the country since independence shows that mostly tribals, Dalits and backward castes in nine states (including undivided Bihar, Uttar Pradesh and Madhya Pradesh) were affected and the resettlement rate was low (table 6.3). The states in bold in the table are Naxal-affected, and if we add Jharkhand, Uttarakhand and Chhattisgarh to that list, 11 Naxal-affected states show the displacement–rehabilitation hiatus. Considering that Orissa, West Bengal, Jharkhand and Chhattisgarh are facing major displacement-related discontent and spontaneous and non-party agitation, it should be evident that a pocket of frustration is waiting to be seized on by the Maoists.

The tussle for forest rights, which also concerns the tribal population and is virtually as old as the displacement conundrum, is currently the focus of an intensive social and political debate in India, and is an area that deserves careful handling, particularly in the context of land acquisitions for industrialization and the setting up of SEZs. This process has caused major turmoil in Orissa, West Bengal and Jharkhand. In Jharkhand, for example, several people's organizations have been protesting since 2005, fearing displacement by industrial projects that are in the pipeline with promised FDI. A large part of Jharkhand, 21 out of 22 districts, are already affected by Naxalism and any insensitive handling of the situation will only add to the support base and the ranks of the Maoist groups (Hebbar 2006: 4953).

Table 6.3 Percentage of tribal people affected by some large dams in India

Project	State	Total no. displaced	% of tribals displaced	SC/Others
Hirakud	**Orissa**	110,000	18.34	n.a
Bhakra	HP	36,000	34.76	n.a.
Pong	HP	80,000	56.25	n.a.
Ukai	Gujarat	52,000	18.92	n.a.
Lalpur	Gujarat	11,300	83.20	n.a.
Daman Ganga	Gujarat	8,700	48.70	n.a.
Karjan	Gujarat	11,600	100	n.a.
Icha	**Orissa**	30,800	80	n.a.
Manas	**Bihar**	3,700	31	n.a.
Chandil	**Bihar**	37,600	87.92	n.a
Povalam	**MP, Andhra Pradesh**	150,000	52.90	n.a.
Tittuli	**Maharashtra**	13,600	51.61	n.a.
Upper Indravati	**Orissa**	20,000	43.76	13
Machkunda	**Orissa**	16,200	51.1	10.21
Subarnarekha	**Bihar**	64,000	67.29	27
Kabini	**Karnataka**	20,000	30	n.a.
Mandira	**Orissa**	n.a.	68.18	n.a.
Masanjor	**Bihar**	16,000	Mostly tribal	n.a.
Bansagar	**MP**	142,000	75	n.a.
Mahi Bajaj Sagar	Rajasthan, **MP**	35,000	76.24	2.13
Kadana	Rajasthan, Gujarat	30,000	100	n.a.
Bisalpur	Rajasthan	70,000	70 (SC + ST)	
Bargi	**MP**	35,000	43	10 SC, 19 OBC
Maithan and Pachet	**Bihar, West Bengal**	93,874	53.46	n.a.
Nagarjun Sagar	**Andhra Pradesh**	25,490	36	7 SC, 45 OBC
Srisailam	**Andhra Pradesh**	100,000	81 (SC + ST)	
Rihand	**UP, MP**	47,500	Mostly tribal	n.a.
Upper Kolab	**Orissa**	50,771	52	17
Narmada Sagar	**MP**	170,000	20	14
Sardar Sarovar	Guj., **Maha., MP**	200,000	56	9
Kulku	**Orissa**	14,000	Mostly tribal	
Surya	**Maharashtra**	7,290	100	

SC = Scheduled Castes; ST = Scheduled Tribes; OBC = Other Backward Class.
HP = Himachal Pradesh; MP = Madhya Pradesh; UP = Uttar Pradesh.
The states appearing in bold are Naxalite-affected: they were not in bold in the original table, which did not include a proposition about a causal link between displacement and Naxalism.
Source: Patwardhan 1997, one of 126 contributing papers to the World Commission on Dams.

Considering that their expansion in the present rural bastions over the past six decades has not been easy, the Maoists appear both circumspect and devoted to planning their "urban" task ahead. An 85-page document prepared by a pool of experts and adopted by the Maoists at their Ninth Congress in 2001 surveys the emerging urban India and the socio-economic disparities and dichotomies emerging out of migration, the conditions of workers in the organized and unorganized sectors, and prevailing frictions, if not conflict, that could help to build their movement:

> Work in the urban areas has a special importance in our revolutionary work ... in our revolution ... From the beginning we will have to concentrate on the organization of the working class, which being the leadership of our revolution has to directly participate and lead the agrarian revolution and the people's war and on building a revolutionary workers movement. Moreover, on the basis of revolutionary workers movement we will be able to mobilize millions of urban oppressed masses and build struggles against imperialism and feudalism ... Building up of a strong urban revolutionary movement means that our Party should build a struggle network capable of waging struggle consistently, by sustaining itself until the protracted people's war reaches the stage of strategic offensive ... (Maoist Documents 2001)

Given the fact that globalization has increased the rate of industrialization and urbanization, swelling the labour force, the Maoists appear ready for an urban thrust.

Furthermore, since the liberalization of the Indian economy and its interaction with the processes of globalization, the rural market has been integrated with urban commerce, producing "new structures of power based on land and capital" (Mohanty 2006a: 3164) which have the potential to further marginalize the rural poor. This has also combined with the rapid expansion of national and global capital and their quest for investment opportunities in industry and trade, and the creation of new SEZs. This process has begun to threaten the marginal farmers and peasants with dispossession and displacement from their only source of livelihood, land. This cannot be compensated with money for the simple reason that farming is the only skill the displaced communities have. The promise by the government and the companies to guarantee employment to at least one person from each family has proved hollow.

Villagers have put up stiff resistance, braving bullets in Kalinganagar (Jajpur district of Orissa on India's east coast) against the Indian industrial giant Tata's proposed steel plant, fearing displacement. The disruption has been on for three years. Analysts argue that there is a dangerous drift because "the rulers have ignored the people's demand for an alternative development strategy" (Mohanty 2006b).

In Singur (West Bengal), because of the projected new small car factory of the Tatas, and in Nandigram, because of the West Bengal government's SEZ project, there has been popular resistance since 2006.[18] Incidentally, West Bengal has seen unbroken rule by the CPM since 1977. The state, which witnessed the second Maoist revolutionary movement since independence (1967–72), has experienced the resurfacing of Maoism in recent years. During these two popular protests, while CPM cadres attacked the protesters like organized gangs, the Maoists mingled with the people. Several citizens' initiatives and intellectuals criticized the CPM-led West Bengal government. While historian Sumit Sarkar bemoaned lack of transparency, economist Amit Bhaduri called it "developmental terrorism" (Chakravartty 2007; Bhaduri 2007). Bhaduri passionately argued that a "strategy under which the state allies with corporations to dispossess people of their livelihoods is nothing but developmental terrorism, irrespective of the political label of the political parties in office. We must chart out an alternative path of development; such possibilities, although limited, exist in the present situation" (2007: 552).

Among the rapidly growing urban middle class, the corporate world is in a hurry to expand its manufacturing capacity. That means more land for manufacturing and trading. The peasants and the tribals are the natural victims of acquisitions and displacements. The expanded mining activities encroach upon the forest domain of the Naxalites. Infrastructure development needs more steel, cement and energy. In steel alone, India has to almost double capacity from 60 million tons a year now to 110 million tons. India has plenty of iron ore and coal. Lacking public sector capacities, the income-poor but resource-rich states of eastern India are awarding mining and land rights to Indian and multinational companies.

Most of these deposits lie in territory inhabited by poor tribals and that is where the Naxals operate. Chhattisgarh, a state in eastern India, has 23 per cent of India's iron ore deposits and abundant coal. It has signed memoranda of understanding and other agreements worth billions with Tata Steel and ArcelorMittal, De Beers Consolidated Mines, BHP Billiton and Rio Tinto. Other states inviting big business and FDI have made similar deals. US companies like Caterpillar want to sell equipment to the mining companies now digging in eastern India. The appearance of mining crews, construction workers and truckers in the forest has seriously alarmed the tribals who have lived in these regions from time immemorial. The Naxalites, however, know the tribals well and have recruited from their ranks for decades (Kripalani 2008).

In the wake of the expanding influence of Naxalism, the Indian government has realized the anomalies in the Indian Forest Act of 1927, largely based on previous Indian Forest Acts, particularly that of 1878, implemented under the British. After intense and acrimonious debate, the Scheduled Tribes and Other Traditional Forest Dwellers (Recognition of Forest Rights) Act 2006 was enacted to ensure justice to the tribals in the onward march of development. But controversies and debates have only been compounded since then. Development-induced displacement and politics in the process of rehabilitation are the major issues that remain unresolved and create fractious dichotomies that the Naxals exploit (see Oliver-Smith 2001).

The Land Acquisition Act of 1894 is the legal instrument that has been used for acquiring land for developmental projects. Realizing that this antiquated colonial Act has caused a displacement–rehabilitation hiatus over the years, the United Progressive Alliance (UPA) coalition government was in a hurry to enact a new land acquisition act and rehabilitation and resettlement policy before the fourteenth Lok Sabha (House of the People) completed its term and the election of April 2009. Promising to bring in generous, humane rehabilitation and resettlement for land evictees, the UPA's proposed Land Acquisition (Amendment) Bill 2007 was passed by the Lok Sabha, but could not go through the Rajya Sabha (Council of States). The Bill promised rehabilitation before acquisition, eliminating displacement in the process.

However, the Bill's amended reintroduction in July 2009 ran into both internal and external resistance. In the cabinet, Railway Minister Mamata Banerjee, the All-India Trinamul Congress leader from West Bengal who stopped the powerful Tatas from setting up the cheap car (Nano) enterprise in Singur, opposed the Bill because it included "private" purpose in it, implying that corporate and private commercial interests are synonymous with "public" purpose. This also led to protests by prominent human rights activists (see Srivastava 2009) in Delhi. As and when this Bill is passed by the Indian Parliament to become an Act, along with the Scheduled Tribes and Other Traditional Forest Dwellers (Recognition of Forest Rights) Act 2006, it will become one of the main legal instruments in the era of globalization to attempt to ensure development without discontent and rebellion. It remains to be seen whether it will blunt the Maoist offensive on the Indian state.

Conclusion

Globalization has added further fuel to the fire of India's Maoist revolutionary politics by creating zones of prosperity and conspicuous consumption, on the one hand, and extreme deprivation, on the other. Indeed, despite pervading socialist rhetoric, competitive politics has given a chance to many from the margins to rise in the power zone; affirmative action and welfare programmes have allowed a section of the poor to improve their socioeconomic condition. Thus both opportunities and inequality have increased in twenty-first century India, presenting new challenges to the Naxalite movement.

Notes

1. The name is derived from the village of Naxalbari in West Bengal state in eastern India.
2. Adopting the establishment of a "socialistic pattern of society" as a goal of the Indian National Congress in the Avadi Congress on 14–15 August 1957, Jawaharlal Nehru, an avowed socialist, said: "I am a socialist and a republican and am no believer in kings or princes or in the order which produces the modern kings of industry, who have greater power over the lives and fortunes of man than even the kings of old, and whose methods are as predatory as those of the old feudal aristocracy . . ." Indira Gandhi used socialist rhetoric and inserted "socialism" into the Preamble of the Constitution of India in 1976 through the 42nd constitutional amendment.
3. Then a part of the princely state of Hyderabad ruled by the Nizam, now a part of the south-eastern coastal state of Andhra Pradesh.
4. India's poverty ratio was 45.3 per cent (47.4 per cent rural and 35.5 per cent urban) in 1951–2, climbing to 56.7 per cent (57.6 per cent rural and 52.9 per cent urban) in 1965–6. This ratio continued till 1978 and began declining in 1983. The Planning Commission computed India's poverty ratio in 2004–5 at 28.3 per cent (29.2 per cent rural and 26 per cent urban), a rise from 26.1 per cent in 1999–2000 (27.1 per cent rural and 23.6 per cent urban), showing that between one-quarter and one-third of the Indian population still live in penury (Datt 1998). Despite the reduction of poverty from around half to near a quarter, the number of poor, both rural and urban, is still disconcertingly high and the income disparity between rich and poor is widening.
5. A study commissioned by the Planning Commission said, "The main support for the Naxalite movement comes from Dalits and Adivasis . . . High levels of rural poverty, therefore, are likely to indicate high distress among SCs and STs . . . While there is no simple correspondence between the areas under Naxalite influence and the proportion of Dalits and Adivasis in the population, it is the case that these areas generally have relatively high Dalit and Adivasi concentration" (Expert Group 2008: 3).
6. In 1951–2 in Telangana, in a village in the region, 1 family owned 800 acres, 8 others approximately 100 acres each, 20 more about 40 acres, and another 169 no more than 5 acres each. One holding of 4 acres of dry land and 6 acres of wet land was in fact being shared, and cultivated jointly, by 7 families. As many as 110 out of 380 families were landless (Dube 1955: 72).
7. A *Sarvodaya* (upliftment of all) leader, Bhave was invited to Telangana by a colleague. His request for a contribution of 100 acres of land in a village was met forthwith. The internationally acclaimed *bhoodan* movement of the 1950s and 1960s was thus born.
8. Jotedars were landowners who had been leased out lands for specific periods by the British government under the Acts of 1859 and 1879.
9. According to Mohanty (1977), "The 1954 Estates Act of West Bengal had prescribed a ceiling of 25 acres of land for each household. But the loopholes in the Act were large enough for the big landowners to escape the ceiling provisions." With 99 per cent of Darjeeling district being rural, having the lowest density of population in the state, it had 58.59 per cent tribal population in 1971. In each of the three police station areas in 1971, a very small number of Jotedars cultivated more than 15 acres of land. The

number of those with larger holdings was even smaller, with a high number of landless and nearly 60 per cent of the population being non-workers. Further, 10 per cent of the population of the Siliguri subdivision was wage-labour in tea plantations, mining, forestry, etc. They formed an important part of the Naxalite movement. The Communists had cleverly built a strong peasant–worker bond through the Bonus Struggle of 1955 (1977: 32–7).

10. *Benami*, literally "without name", refers to the reaction of the landlords to the Land Ceiling Act, whereby they transferred "surplus" into the name of family members, into a fictitious name, or even into the name of a pet.
11. The social base of the party also split, which explains the involvement of the CPM in revolutionary politics since 1964. The CPI retained the intellectuals, the so-called "fellow travellers", and trade unions, particularly in the organized sector and the professions; the CPM took away the organizations of the poor peasantry and agricultural labour (see Sinha 1963).
12. According to a report from the Ministry of Home Affairs in 2005–6, they controlled nearly 76 districts in 9 states.
13. Originally at <http://www.awtw.org/back_issues/fifth_South_Asia_Regional.htm>.
14. In chapter 1 above, William Coleman supports the argument that, compared to long-standing vertical social forms, network societies, as new social structures, have become more efficient due to their flexibility, their scalability and their survivability.
15. Comparatively, Edgardo Lander characterizes the broad historical problems in reference to Latin American debates and experiences related to democracy, citizenship and civil society.
16. The National Crime Records Bureau publishes figures of crime against SCs and STs in its annual publication on crime in India. For the 2007 figures for the SCs see <http://ncrb.nic.in/cii2007/cii-2007/Table%207.1.pdf> and for the STs see <http://ncrb.nic.in/cii2007/cii-2007/Table%207.9.pdf> (both accessed June 2010). Over the years, these figures are similar, with some variations. For an analysis of 2006 figures with implications for Naxalism see Mehra 2008.
17. Also see a study of displacement caused by the Indira Sagar dam by Betwa Sharma, who concludes: "The displaced at the Narmada valley are running out of survival options as their living conditions swiftly deteriorate" (2006: 5224–5).
18. See *Mainstream* 2007.

REFERENCES

Balagopal, K. (1982) "Peasant struggle and repression in Pedapally", *Economic and Political Weekly*, 15 May, p. 815.

Balagopal, K. (2005) "Have we heard the last of the peace talks?", *Economic and Political Weekly*, 26 Mar., pp. 1323–9.

Balagopal, K. (2006) "Maoist movement in Andhra Pradesh", *Economic and Political Weekly*, 22 July, pp. 3183–7.

Bandyopadhyay, D. (2006) "A visit to two 'flaming fields' of Bihar", *Economic and Political Weekly*, 30 Dec., pp. 5302–4.

Bandyopadhyay, D. (2007) "Land of the overlords: A field trip to Katihar and Purnea", *Mainstream*, 10 Mar.

Banerjee, Sumanta (1984) *India's Simmering Revolution*. New Delhi: Select Book Syndicate.

Banerjee, Sumanta (2006) "Beyond Naxalbari", *Economic and Political Weekly*, 22 July, pp. 3159–63.

Bergmann, Theodore (1984) *Agrarian Reforms in India*. New Delhi: Agricole Publishing Academy.

Bhaduri, Amit (2007) "Development or developmental terrorism", *Economic and Political Weekly*, 17 Feb., pp. 552–3.

Bhagwati, Jagdish (2004) *In Defense of Globalization*. New Delhi: Oxford University Press.

Bhatia, Bela (2006) "On armed resistance", *Economic and Political Weekly*, 22 July, pp. 3179–83.

Calman, Leslie J. (1985) *Protest in Democratic India: Authority's Response to Challenge*. Boulder, CO: Westview Press.

Chakravartty, Sumit (2007) "Singur: The resistance continues", *Mainstream*, 26 Jan., pp. 45–7.

Das, Ashok (2000) "Naxalism: Y2K problem sans solution", *Hindustan Times*, 10 Feb.

Datt, Gaurav (1998) "Poverty in India and Indian states: An update", *Indian Journal of Labour Economics*, 41(2).

Dhagamwar, Vasudha (2006) *Role and Image of Law in India: The Tribal Experience*. New Delhi: Sage.

Dube, S. C. (1955) *Indian Village*. London: Oxford University Press.

Expert Group (2008) *Developmental Challenges in Extremist Affected Areas: Report of an Expert Group to Planning Commission*. New Delhi: Planning Commission, Government of India.

Fernandes, Walter (1994) "An activist process around the draft national rehabilitation policy", *Social Action*, 45 (July–Sept.): 277–98.

Fernandes, Walter (2004) "Rehabilitation policy for the displaced", *Economic and Political Weekly*, 20 Mar., pp. 1191–3.

Fernandes, Walter (2007) "Singur and the displacement scenario", *Economic and Political Weekly*, 20 Jan., pp. 203–6.

Gallantar, Marc (1996) "The aborted restoration of indigenous law", in N. Jayaraman and Satish Saberwal, eds, *Social Conflict*, New Delhi: Oxford University Press.

Hebbar, Ritambhara (2006) "Forest Bill 2005 and tribal areas: A case of Jharkhand", *Economic and Political Weekly*, 7 Jan., pp. 4952–5.

Independent Citizens' Initiative (2006) "Open letter to Government and Maoists", *Economic and Political Weekly*, 8 July, pp. 2977–9.

Kripalani, Manjeet (2008) "In India, death to global business: How a violent – and spreading – Maoist insurgency threatens the country's runaway growth", *Business Week*, 7 May. At <http://www.businessweek.com/magazine/content/08_20/b4084044908374.htm> (accessed June 2010).

Mainstream (2007) "Nandigram: Naked terror and massacre of democracy", Editorial, *Mainstream*, 17 Mar.

Maoist Documents (2001) *Urban Perspective: Our Work in Urban Areas*. At <http://www.satp.org/satporgtp/countries/india/maoist/documents/papers/Urbanperspective.htm> (accessed June 2010).

Mehra, Ajay K. (2000) "Caste conflict in India", in K. M. de Silva, ed., *Conflict and Violence in South Asia*, Kandy, Sri Lanka: International Centre for Ethnic Studies, pp. 131–78.

Mehra, Ajay K. (2002) "Revolution resurgent", *The Hindu*, 12 Jan. At <http://www.hindu.com/2002/01/12/stories/2002011201361000.htm> (accessed June 2010).

Mehra, Ajay K. (2006) "India's nowhere revolution: Riddles, mysteries and enigmas", *Mainstream*, 12 Aug., pp. 31–8.

Mehra, Ajay K. (2008) "India's experiment with revolution", Working Paper No. 40, Heidelberg Papers in South Asian and Comparative Politics, South Asia Institute, University of Heidelberg, Sept. At <http://archiv.ub.uni-heidelberg.de/volltextserver/volltexte/2008/8710/pdf/Heidelberg_Paper_Mehra.pdf> (accessed June 2010).

Mehra, Ajay K. (2009) "A nowhere approach to India's nowhere revolution", *Mainstream*, 31 Oct., pp. 11–17.

Mehrotra, Santosh (2006) "Well being and caste in Uttar Pradesh: Why UP is not like Tamil Nadu", *Economic and Political Weekly*, 7 Oct., pp. 4261–80.

Mohanty, Manoranjan (1977) *Revolutionary Violence: A Study of the Maoist Movement in India*. New Delhi: Sterling.

Mohanty, Manoranjan (1991) "Chinese revolution and the Indian Communist movement", *China Report*, 27(1): 30–1.

Mohanty, Manoranjan (2006a) "Challenges of revolutionary violence: The Naxalite movement in perspective", *Economic and Political Weekly*, 22 July, pp. 3163–8.

Mohanty, Manoranjan (2006b) "KBK to Kalinganagar: A dangerous drift for Orissa and India", *Mainstream*, 14 Oct., pp. 23–30.

Mukherji, Partha N. (1979) "Naxalbari movement and the peasant revolt in North Bengal", in M. S. A. Rao, ed., *Social Movements in India*, vol. 1, New Delhi: Manohar.

Nayyar, Deepak, ed. (2002) *Governing Globalization: Issues and Institutions*. New Delhi: Oxford University Press.

Oliver-Smith, Anthony (2001) *Displacement, Resistance and the Critique of Development: From the Grass Roots to the Global*, Final Report for ESCOR R7644 and the Research Programme on Development Induced Displacement and Resettlement, Refugee Studies Centre, University of Oxford, July.

Patwardhan, Amrita (1997) "Dams and tribal people in India", Paper to the World Commission on Dams, for Thematic Review I.2: Dams, Indigenous People and Vulnerable Ethnic Minorities. At <http://www.dams.org/docs/kbase/contrib/soc207.pdf> (accessed June 2010).

Pavier, Barry (1981) *The Telangana Movement 1944–1951*. New Delhi: Vikas.

Ram, Mohan (1971) *Maoism in India*. New Delhi: Vikas.

Ramana, P. V. (2006) "Naxalism: Trends and government response", *Dialogue*, 8(2): 58–69.

Ranga Rao, K. (1979) "Peasant movements in Telangana", in M. S. A. Rao, ed., *Social Movements in India*, vol. 1, New Delhi: Manohar.

Sanyal, Kanu (1974) "More about Naxalbari", *Proletarian Path*, 2(4–5): 21–7.

Sharma, Betwa (2006) “Death knell in the Narmada Valley”, *Economic and Political Weekly*, 23 Dec., pp. 5224–5.

Shukla, Rakesh (2006) “Judicial pronouncements and caste”, *Economic and Political Weekly*, 21–27 Oct., pp. 4411–14.

Sinha, D. P. (1963) *The India China Border Dispute and the Communist Party of India*. New Delhi: Community Party of India.

Srivastava, Mihir (2009) “Land Acquisition, Rehabilitation and Resettlement Bills face opposition”, *India Today*, 24 July. At <http://indiatoday.intoday.in/index.php?issueid=115&id=53329&option=com_content&task=view&sectionid=4> (accessed June 2010).

Sundar, Nandini (2006) “Bastar, Maoism and Salwa Judum”, *Economic and Political Weekly*, 22 July, pp. 3187–92.

Sundarayya, P. (1972) *Telengana People’s Struggle and Its Lessons*. Calcutta: Communist Party of India (Marxist).

Thirumali, I. (1992) “Dora and Gadi: Manifestations of landlord domination in Telangana”, *Economic and Political Weekly*, 19 Feb., pp. 477–82.

Williamson, John and Roberto Zagha (2002) “From the Hindu rate of growth to the Hindu rate of reform”, Working Paper No. 144, Center for Research on Economic Development and Policy Reform, Stanford University. At <http://www.stanford.edu/group/siepr/cgi-bin/siepr/?q=system/files/shared/pubs/papers/pdf/credpr144.pdf> (accessed Aug. 2010).

World Commission on Dams (2000) *Dams and Development: A New Framework for Decision-Making*. At <http://www.dams.org/report/> (accessed Aug. 2010).

7

Globalization and South Asian insurgencies

S. D. Muni

Introduction

Globalization has been unfolding for centuries. The spice trade, the Silk Road, colonialism and unregulated migration were all part of it. However, globalization, as understood in contemporary international relations studies, is only a few decades old. South Asian insurgencies, in this sense, are older than the emergence of contemporary globalization.

Insurgencies can be grouped into three categories: religious, ethnic and systemic. South Asia has witnessed all of them. Among religious insurgencies we find the Shia–Sunni conflict in Pakistan and the Islamic extremism à *la* Al Qaeda and Taliban terrorism in Pakistan and Afghanistan.[1] Prominent among the ethnic insurgencies are the Sikh (Khalistan) and North East insurgencies of India, the Baloch uprising in Pakistan, the Chakma revolt in Bangladesh, the Nepali conflict in Bhutan and the Tamil insurgency in Sri Lanka. Among the systemic insurgencies, the Maoists' insurgency in Nepal and other democratic uprisings in Nepal and Pakistan and the Naxal revolt in India claim a prominent place.[2]

Many of the present-day insurgencies in South Asia and elsewhere in the developing world are described as terrorist movements. Terror is no doubt used as a method, sometimes a principal method, in waging these insurgencies, but most of them have specific goals, political as well as socioeconomic, and also use other methods in addition to the unleashing of terror on innocent civilians. Terrorism is also deployed because these conflicts are unequal, asymmetric and unstructured.

Globalization has influenced and impacted insurgencies in many different ways. To begin with, the globalized approach to development, based on intensive exploitation of natural resources and unequal distribution of the benefits of growth, has helped to generate "uncivil" societies. Those left out and deprived of the developmental process have become ready recruits of these "uncivil" societies.

Globalization has also directly affected both the means and the ends of insurgencies and terrorism (Kurth Cronin 2002–3; Lia 2005). Insurgencies have greatly enhanced their fighting methods through the use of new technologies, easy access to transnational movements of people and goods and newer sources of support, all facilitated by globalization. In terms of the ends "foreign intrusions and growing awareness of shrinking global space have created incentives to use ideal asymmetrical weapons, terrorism, for more ambitious purposes" (Kurth Cronin 2002–3: 51).

Limited ethnic and political objectives have been enhanced to alter regional and global power structures. Globalization has "increased interconnectedness, inter-dependence and de-territorialisation". Accordingly, there is "increased flow of capital and commodities, people and ideas across borders", and the effects of all of these on the overall "operating environment" have been harnessed by the insurgent and terrorist groups to their considerable advantage (Lia 2005: 17–38; also see Jones 2004; Mason 2003; Adamson 2005; Romano and Sandbrook 2004).

These groups have also taken advantage of what Brecher and others describe as "globalization from below", with various non-state and societal groups, ranging from professional non-governmental organizations (NGOs) to terrorists, insurgents and criminal groups, establishing networks to promote their respective causes (Brecher, Costello and Smith 2000).

To look at the impact of globalization on insurgencies, two South Asian insurgencies have been chosen here: the ethnic insurgency in Sri Lanka by the Liberation Tigers of Tamil Eelam (LTTE), and the Maoists of Nepal, a systemic one.[3] Sri Lanka's Tamil insurgency began in 1983 at the height of the Cold War and was militarily crushed with the killing of its supreme leader Velupillai Prabhakaran in May 2009. However, the structures of the LTTE's spread in terms of leadership, linkages and material stakes (offices, agents, commercial links, fixed and liquid resources and assets) outside Sri Lanka are still intact. It remains to be seen what will happen in future as the possibility of a revival of Tamil resistance in some form or other (violent or peaceful) will depend upon the political solution of the Tamil question by the Sri Lankan state and the nature of that solution.

The Nepal Maoists are a post-Cold War development. The most interesting contrast between the two cases is that while globalization has induced a drastic shift in ends and means by the Nepal Maoists' insurgency – to abandoning violence and seeking democratic transformation – globalization reinforced the aim of the LTTE to stick to its objective of a separate state secured through violence and war. The Maoists may not admit it, but a major shift in their strategic and ideological formulations started under the thrust of the "global war on terror" (post 9/11), making them realize that the international community would resist any military victory on their part. This chapter will look at the differences between the impacts of globalization on these two insurgencies in the concluding section.

Various dimensions of globalization interact with the dynamics of insurgencies. The focus here is on three areas: the role of diasporas, the transnational linkages/operations, and the use of information and communication technologies.[4] These areas encompass most of the newer developments in insurgency movements. The impact of globalization in these three areas has also changed the character of insurgencies in South Asia.

Diasporas

Diasporas have come to play an important role in international politics as a part of postmodern developments that take into account people's migration across borders. The presence of diasporas in a host country raises the issues of identity and assimilation; the diasporas' groups also become easy instruments, as well as targets, of propaganda, lobbying and other foreign policy purposes of the home country (Shain and Barth 2003). The diasporas also have a very significant economic role as a source of remittances that contribute to foreign exchange reserves and meeting economic needs in many of the developing countries. There are countries like China, and of late even India, that have developed specific policies addressed to their diasporas.

The economic, as well as political, role of the diasporas is not confined to state entities. Many non-state entities, including insurgencies and terrorist groups, also benefit from the political and economic role of diasporas. A RAND Corporation study argues that after the end of the Cold War, the role of rival states has declined in supporting insurgencies and the vacuum created in this respect has been filled, to a considerable extent, by the diasporas (Rabasa et al. 2004; see also Bunker 2002). The role played by the diasporas in sustaining many insurgencies in the developing countries has become decisive (Demmers 2007).

The role of diasporas depends upon their size, composition, place and identity in the host country. These factors will determine the diasporas' "nationalism", which may be viewed as an asset by the home state. The diasporas can also relate to the ethnic and political/ideological identity of the given insurgency/conflict back home. Depending on the specific nature of their identity, diasporas relate either to the state or to the insurgent movement at home. For instance, in the case of Sri Lanka, a Sinhalese diaspora will generally relate to the Sri Lankan state and a Tamil diaspora to Tamil militancy. In the case of Nepal, sections of diasporas looking for democratic transformation will identify with the Maoist cause, but those who prefer stability and disapprove of violence and the ideological extremism of the Maoists will support the monarchy. The diaspora will not be active if it does not identify with the cause in question. The efficacy and impact of its role will, however, depend upon its organization and leadership in the host country.[5]

Tamil Tigers

All of the South Asian insurgencies have made use of diasporas, but the most effective and rewarding use has been made by the Tamil Tigers. Tamil diasporas have existed for a long time, but their organization and political consciousness were shaped in the context of the ethnic conflict in Sri Lanka that flared up in July 1983. All of the Tamil militant groups of Sri Lanka helped in organizing and engaging politically with the Tamil diasporas, but after 1987, when all of the other Tamil militant groups laid down their arms except the LTTE, it was the LTTE which made the most of diasporic support.

Estimates of the size of Tamil diasporas range from 750,000 to 800,000 strong. The largest concentration is in Canada, with an estimated 250,000. Diasporas number 150,000 in India, 110,000 in the United Kingdom, about 50,000 in Germany, and 30,000 each in Australia, Switzerland and France (Falksohn and Rao 2008). In smaller numbers, Tamil diasporas may be present in 40 other countries, including the United States, where despite its smaller size the diaspora is politically very active and supportive of the Tamil cause.

The LTTE has worked hard to organize the Tamil diasporic community to serve its political cause. The organizational structure is federal, with local Tamil associations linked to national associations. There are at least seven well-known national federations of Tamil associations in Australia, Switzerland, France, Canada, the US, Norway and the UK. There are occasional political and ideological conflicts and rivalries between and within these associations, but the LTTE has generally managed to use them all. The LTTE has also successfully used the World Tamil Federation, which has many Indian Tamil associates as well, in pursuance of its objectives. With offices in these countries and many more, 54 in all according to some estimates, including in countries like Botswana, Laos, Myanmar, Qatar and South Africa, the interests of the LTTE have been more varied and wider than simply engaging the diasporas.

The LTTE has generally used these linkages for three purposes: fundraising; publicity, propaganda and lobbying; and networking for its other commercial activities, arms procurement and shipping. The most profitable and vital of these purposes has been fundraising. There is often an overlap between these three activities, where the same organizations and volunteers are motivated to deliver different tasks at different times, but fundraising has remained the principal goal of the LTTE's activities in relation to the diaspora groups.

According to a World Bank assessment, the LTTE raised an average of US$480 million per year during the 1990s. Recent estimates vary from $200 million to $300 million per year. In an address delivered at the International Institute for Strategic Studies Shangri-La Dialogue, Singapore, Sri Lanka's Foreign Minister Rohitha Bogollagama quoted *Jane's Intelligence Review* as describing the LTTE "as second only to Colombia's FARC terrorist group in its income and has documented that it raises $200–300 million a year for arms procurement among others". "The former UN Secretary General Kofi Annan", he continued, "once described terrorist groups, which capitalise on the nexus between drug trafficking and arms smuggling, as representing a supranational subversive threat to the humanity. Today, the LTTE has established a presence in the arms black market and has been servicing several other terrorist groups as well" (Bogollagama 2008).

The funds raised by the LTTE covered approximately 50–60 per cent of its overall expenditure.[6] Money was sourced both through voluntary contributions and forced collections or extortions. Voluntary contributions were mobilized through the diaspora associations with the help of committed workers. The amount collected was transferred by diverse means ranging from personal baggage to legal bank and illegal hawala transactions.[7] Often the funds collected were paid directly for arms procurement or other purchases needed for the LTTE's varied operations. The LTTE's "Hero's Day" functions were used annually for special fundraising.

In many places, contributions by diasporas to LTTE funds were institutionalized. In Norway, during the early 1990s, every Sri Lankan Tamil living and working there was expected to contribute at least 100 Norwegian krones (approximately US$12) every month. There were about 6,000 to 7,000 Sri Lankan Tamils living and working in Norway at that time.[8] Funds were also raised on special occasions and for specific causes. For instance, the LTTE raised a considerable amount of money in the name of tsunami humanitarian relief during 2004–5. Strong emotions of ethnic nationalism were invoked to maximize contributions, though there are reports that very little from these contributions has actually reached the affected people. Explaining the LTTE's power to control the diaspora, Demmers writes: "Indeed a large share of the LTTE's power to control Tamil population both at home and in the disapora lies in their successful rhetoric. The organization combines revolutionary messages of self-determination with a rejection of both Tamil tradition and ethnic pluralism and Western cosmopolitanism, giving expression to feelings of exclusion and negative attitudes . . ." (2007: 20).

Reluctant members of the diasporas have also been coerced by the LTTE's strong-arm methods for raising funds. Many members of Tamil diasporas have close family relations living in Tamil-dominated areas in Sri Lanka. Their safety and well-being depend upon the LTTE's goodwill; thus "goodwill" has been exploited to raise money. The LTTE also engages in human trafficking; transporting people from Sri Lanka to distant countries in search of peace, jobs, studies and better careers. Money is extracted from such migrants when they exit Sri Lanka and also when they revisit Sri Lanka. Intimidation, threats and violence used by the LTTE to extract money were detailed in a Human Rights Watch report released in March 2006 (Human Rights Watch 2006: 48). Specific case studies of extortion have been presented to substantiate the point that Tamil expatriates visiting Sri Lanka have been victims of such extortion.

The World Tamil Movement has been involved in collecting the proceeds of extortion on behalf of the LTTE.[9] It denies doing so, but admits:

> We are sympathetic to our cause there and because the LTTE is fighting for our rights and in the vanguard we have always campaigned to help them . . . We don't raise funds but we canvas and advise people to help our people there [in Sri Lanka] for rehabilitation from the war and tsunami . . . we ask them to give it to the TRO [Tamil Rehabilitation Organization] or SEDAT [Social and Economic Development Association of Tamils]. Some give to the TRO branch here, or some give bank-to-bank transactions. People do it individually in their own way. (Human Rights Watch 2006: section 5)

The common method used is to collect money from those visiting Sri Lanka or to secure commitments to pay on a regular basis following a return to the host country. In securing such commitments, passports can be confiscated and, on the basis of information collected during visits, individuals are systematically pursued later for payments.

The Sri Lankan government started working to curb the flow of funding from the diasporas to the LTTE towards the end of the 1990s. The process, initiated by the former Sri Lankan Foreign Minister Lakshman Kadirgamar (who was assassinated by the LTTE in 2005), has been carried further by the present regime. As a result, Western governments are gradually putting restraints on the raising and transfer of such funds. Thus the flow of funds declined, but in no way did it completely stop. The LTTE made extensive use of informal and covert banking channels, as well as humanitarian organizations, in moving these funds.

Besides raising funds, the LTTE employed established and elite sections of the diasporas in lobbying for their cause in host countries. Influential lawyers and community activists have worked with their local members of parliament to promote the Tamil cause in Sri Lanka. These sections of Tamil diasporas have also pleaded in parliamentary committees dealing with Sri Lankan issues in host countries. Local parliamentarians in the host countries have issued statements, pressured the Sri Lankan government and tried to influence the policies of their governments towards Sri Lanka.[10] On many occasions, the Sri Lankan government's military actions have been condemned by the diaspora lobbyists by emphasizing violations of human rights.

The diasporas openly supported the LTTE during its last days of war by raising the question of "humanitarian catastrophe" and "genocide"; they asked for a ceasefire to save trapped and innocent people. There were demonstrations in various countries such as Canada, Norway, the UK, the US and Australia against the Sri Lankan army's "ruthless" operations.[11] The pressure thus built up by the diaspora communities influenced a number of European countries and the US, which raised the question in the United Nations Human Rights Council and at the Security Council. There were also threats from the international community to investigate the Sri Lankan government for "crimes against humanity". There were also even demands for direct international intervention to stop the war under the provisions of the "responsibility to protect". The United Nations Secretary-General sent a representative and also visited Sri Lanka himself to take stock of the humanitarian situation (UNIC Colombo 2009). The Sri Lankan government rubbished these attempts as efforts to save the LTTE (ColomboPage 2009).

Nepal Maoists

The Nepali diaspora is also, like the Tamil diaspora, quite sizeable and widely distributed.[12] The largest concentration of the Nepalese (non-Indian) diaspora is in India. More than 1 million Nepalese are estimated to be scattered in and around New Delhi and the National Capital Region alone, covering parts of the states of Haryana and Uttar Pradesh (UP). The total number of Nepalese in India may be somewhere between 8 and 10 million and this number keeps on fluctuating depending on conditions in Nepal. In recent years, the rise in violence and instability resulting from the Maoists' insurgency and popular uprisings induced thousands of Nepalese to migrate to India. There is an estimated presence of about 1.7–2 million Nepalese in the rest of the world, mostly in West Asia, particularly in Qatar, Saudi Arabia and the United Arab Emirates. The Nepalese are also scattered in South East Asia (Hong Kong, Malaysia, Singapore and Thailand), Britain, the US (150,000) and Europe. In all, there are at least 25 countries where Nepali diasporas are present.

The diasporas are organized locally and also along ethnic lines. In 2000, an umbrella organization called Non-Resident Nepalese (NRN) was established. It is believed that the NRN sent about 100 billion Nepali rupees as remittances during 2002–3, and this went on growing at a rate of 30 per cent (Sarup 2004). NRN opened chapters in 24 countries and were planning to do so in another 30 countries.

Due to a number of constraints, Nepal Maoists have been able to make only a limited use of the diasporas in pursuance of their political objectives. First, the cause being fought for by the Maoists from the beginning, of carrying out a people's war to establish a "New Democracy", wrapped in extremist leftist ideological jargon, was not popular with people settled abroad and identifying with the Nepali state. This changed with the redefinition of the Maoists' goals and the recasting of their political strategy. The establishment of a republic and a democratic system are not as motivating as ethnic nationalism, evident in the case of Sri Lanka. The Maoists also launched their people's war in 1996, and it was escalated in 2001. The Nepalese settled in India were always factored into the working out of the Maoists' strategy for revolution, but perhaps they did not have the time, or even the links, to focus their attention on diasporas elsewhere to obtain their political and material support. The Nepali diasporas, except those in developed countries, were generally made up of poor people, in labour-intensive and menial jobs, where they did not have much awareness, or money or the confidence necessary to support a home-based insurgency.

The only places where some of these factors did not apply were India and the developed West. In India, the Maoist leader Dr Baburam Bhattarai had organized Nepali students and workers since his student days in Jawaharlal Nehru University. The All Nepal National Free Students' Union was established in 1965, but it went through various splits and political/ideological regroupings. The organization affiliated with the Maoists' insurgency was called the All Nepal Free Students' Union (Revolutionary) (ANFSU(R)). This was rechristened as the All Nepal National Independent Students' Union (Revolutionary) (ANNISU(R)). This organization has been used by the Maoists for publicity and propaganda purposes and also for securing logistic support in the cause of the insurgency. There is no reliable evidence, but it was believed that the

Maoists also raised funds through some of the diaspora organizations and individuals in India and elsewhere.

The Nepali diasporas were divided on political lines between the king, the Maoists and other mainstream political parties. The Maoists only received class-based support from the poorer sections of the Nepalese living abroad. However, after 2002 and particularly after 2005, when the king made autocratic moves, opinion within the diasporas moved in favour of democracy. The conclusion of the 12 Point Agreement between the Maoists and the Seven Party Alliance also blurred the ideological unacceptability of the Maoists as the struggle turned into one between the king and the "people".

When the Jan Andolan-II (People's Movement-II) emerged in 2006, a large majority of the diasporas had become sympathetic to the cause of a republican Nepal. This strengthened the Maoists and the anti-monarchy movement of the political parties. Nepali migrants held rallies and demonstrations in India, the US, the UK, Hong Kong and Australia, where the king's "regressive" moves were criticized and strong demands for peace and democracy were raised. Since the victory of the Jan Andolan-II, the Maoists have started appealing to the NRN and other diaspora members to come forward to help the reconstruction of the country. Political party leaders, such as Girija Prasad Koirala, Sushil Koirala, Sujata Koirala and Madhav Kumar Nepal, have been hosted by diaspora associations in the US in support of establishing a democratic republic in Nepal.

The LTTE and the Nepal Maoists have also used the issues of democracy, freedom of expression and human rights to mobilize diasporic support. These issues now constitute a robust part of the global ideological consensus, particularly in the context of the post-Cold War perception of "New World Order" and the post-9/11 focus on spreading awareness of these values at a global level. This context helped the two insurgencies to build pressure from the international community on the states they confronted at home. International and local human rights organizations and NGOs, including Amnesty International, facilitated the task of these insurgencies in this respect. International human rights organizations now make hardly any distinction between the human rights of terrorist cadres and innocent people.

Transnational linkages

Globalization has provided great impetus to commercial and human movements across boundaries. It has also facilitated networking and engagements where interests converge, be they related to trading in material goods or ideological and intellectual ideas. The transnational linkages thus created have been exploited not only by legitimate entities of states and business communities, but also by uncivil groups and organizations. "The increased permeability of the international system has also enhanced the ability of non-state terrorist organizations" to promote their interests (Kurth Cronin 2002–3). Terrorist organizations have established and nursed transnational links for building financial resources, procuring arms and establishing ideological networks and support bases. South Asian insurgencies have not lagged behind in this respect.

Tamil Tigers

The LTTE was known for running elaborate commercial operations that included shipping, money laundering, trafficking in people, arms and drugs, etc. The LTTE started building its commercial establishment and network from the early 1980s. Velvettiturai port in Jaffna was a traditional hub for trading and smuggling networks even before the outbreak of ethnic conflict in Sri Lanka. Being born and brought up in Velvettiturai, the LTTE chief Prabhakaran had a natural instinct to work through this network. He started his commercial operations "like a good merchant capitalist by registering a company in Singapore for buying radio sets, invested in Malaysia, started a shipping company in Cyprus and played the share market in London" (Davis 1996). Yangon (Myanmar) was one of the early ports of call for LTTE freighters because Prabhakaran's grandfather had property there. The LTTE's commercial establishment was expanded and reinforced with a fleet of vessels registered in Panama, Honduras and Liberia by Prabhakaran's trusted comrade Selvarasa Padmanathan, popularly known as KP in the LTTE circles, with the help of Pratima Das, a Bombay shipping magnet (Davis 1996).

By 1991, the LTTE's commercial *cum* arms procurement operations had expanded sufficiently. In a confession to the Indian intelligence agencies, one of the LTTE operatives disclosed:

> KP has been dealing not only with the financial transactions of the LTTE but also in procuring arms and ammunition, communication equipments, fibre-glass boats and engines and other essential electronic gadgets for his organization. Most of the arms and ammunition required by the Tigers are purchased through the underworld arms dealers operating in various European countries such as the UK, West Germany, Yugoslavia, Belgium, France, Austria and Cyprus . . . KP has been in this line since 1986 . . . The LTTE has been purchasing arms and ammunition worth three to four million US dollars per annum . . . (Sakhuja 2006, quoting from the report of the Jain Commission set up by the Government of India to inquire into Rajiv Gandhi's assassination)

In these operations, goods were ferried first to Indian ports, and then taken to Sri Lanka in smaller fishing boats. The advantage to the LTTE of the Indian access in this respect came under increasing pressure during the operation of the Indian Peacekeeping Force (IPKF) in Sri Lanka in the 1980s, and in the aftermath of the assassination of the former Indian prime minister Rajiv Gandhi in 1991 by the LTTE. This led the LTTE to shift its operations to South East Asia, particularly Thailand and Singapore. The convenience of Thailand for the LTTE was inherent in its shorter distance of only 2,200 kilometres from the northern Sri Lankan coast and the easy availability of weapons from the former conflict areas of Cambodia, Laos and Myanmar.[13] In addition, "brand-new weapons are also freely available, either smuggled from China or obtained openly from legal manufacturers. There are more than 10,000 trawlers and other vessels roaming the Thai seas. This makes it difficult to strictly monitor weapons smuggling activities" (Spur Australia 2009a; see also Spur Australia 2009b). LTTE ships did not indulge in arms smuggling all of the time. Most of the time, the LTTE vessels "engage[d] in transporting a variety of general cargo like timber, cement, flour, sugar, salt, steel, etc. The LTTE vessels also engage[d] in drug smuggling and gunrunning, human smuggling and transporting LTTE cadres" (Sakhuja 2006). In only 10–15 per cent of its operations, the LTTE vessels carried contraband goods like arms and drugs, and that also along with the normal cargo, to avoid being detected.

The LTTE's merchant fleet, comprising an estimated 11 ships, was separate from the vessels and smaller boats of its Sea Tigers. Even the command and control of the two operations was supposed to be kept separate. There were around 150 personnel engaged in the merchant navy operations. Most of these people were trained LTTE cadres, though the possibility that the LTTE hired sailors and navigators from other countries like the Philippines, Indonesia and some East European countries cannot be ruled out.

In international shipping business, the changing of the identity of ships is not uncommon and the LTTE also made good use of this practice to protect its illegal operations and the identity of its merchant vessels. In almost every respect, the LTTE merchant navy operations were as globalized as any other shipping line could claim. Besides South East Asia, the LTTE navy also had trading links with South Africa and Latin America in terms of generating funds through the transportation of cargo and for ferrying arms.

In addition to running a well-developed merchant navy, the LTTE's transnational linkages also involved dealings with a large number of insurgent and terrorist organizations. Among the Islamic terrorist groups, the LTTE had close contacts with Palestinian groups, Kurdish groups based in Europe, Taliban and Al Qaeda affiliates in Afghanistan and Eritrea, and the Abu Sayyaf group in the Philippines (Jayasekara 2008). Some of these contacts started much before 9/11 when the LTTE was looking for arms and training during the initial phase of its struggle. Subsequently, these links developed commercial and arms procurement interests as well. In South Asia, the LTTE had links with almost all of the insurgents groups in India's North East, and also the Naxal groups in Andhra Pradesh. The Maoists of Nepal also initially established contacts with the LTTE, but did not pursue them to any length, largely to avoid possible Indian displeasure.

The LTTE's relations with these transnational groups were geared towards a mix of political and commercial objectives. Though ethnic nationalism was a common factor between the LTTE and similarly based insurgent groups like United Liberation Front of Assam (ULFA) and other North East insurgency groups in India or the Karens of Myanmar, there was no convergence of their specific political interests with those of the LTTE. The LTTE dealt with them for commercial purposes, to provide training and to procure as well as supply arms. After 1987, a strategic dimension to these commercial links developed as the LTTE faced the IPKF and decided to support India's insurgent groups in order to weaken India internally. There have been twists and turns in the LTTE's approach towards India, influencing its dealings with the Indian insurgent groups. The LTTE was also cautious in handling its relations with Islamist terrorist groups like Al Qaeda so as to avoid any retaliation from the US and its Western allies, particularly after 9/11.

The LTTE carried on fairly elaborate international relations of its own, in pursuance of its political objective. At the grassroots level, these relations were maintained by about 54 LTTE offices in various countries, but the top leadership of the LTTE also interacted with high diplomatic officials. The thrust of these relations was to secure the support of the West and India and also to secure LTTE's diverse commercial, political and organizational interests. The attitude of the US and the European Union became somewhat indifferent and uncooperative towards the LTTE over the course of five years or so, but Norway and Australia remained sympathetic and showed understanding towards the LTTE.

In a so-called balanced observation, the Australian Parliamentary Joint Committee on Intelligence and Security argued against proscribing the LTTE. The basis of this argument was that the LTTE, as a self-determination organization, enjoyed public support and the Tamil diasporas may have helped move the LTTE towards peace and democracy. The report said on 1 June 2007:

> The LTTE poses no direct threat to Australia or the Australian interests … we have to ensure we have a genuine understanding of the political situation in

the country in which we choose to intervene. But this is often difficult. If a struggle for self-determination has persisted for a long time, this persistence is a strong indicator that both sides of the conflict enjoy significant support; many support the government but many also support the non-state actor seeking self-determination. Therefore it is important that Australian law keep the interests of both in mind when publicly declaring a stance.

> A legal intervention that criminalizes the LTTE is likely to prevent the Tamil Diaspora from continuing to engage the LTTE in a direction of peace, development and democracy. Currently there are various private individuals and Diaspora think tanks that are considering the best possible ways of engaging the LTTE in a direction of peace, but criminalizing them will outlaw this activity.

Norway's sympathy and support for the LTTE has been indicative in the LTTE's demand for Norway to play the role of peacemaker between it and the Sri Lankan government.[14] There were allegations by the Sri Lankan government that Norway clandestinely supplied radio and broadcasting equipment to the LTTE in December 2002, besides other favours. Then Sri Lankan President Chandrika Kumaratunga protested to the Norwegian Prime Minister in writing at violation of Sri Lankan laws and the Vienna Convention on diplomatic practices.[15]

In relation to India, the LTTE had a complex love–hate relationship, but it realized that its linkages and bases of support in India would be critical to the success of its struggle. The sympathies of a number of Western countries towards the LTTE had come out into the open in the past, as noted earlier. India, however, continued to keep the LTTE at a distance and refused to intervene, despite considerable internal and international pressure, to halt the war that eventually eliminated the LTTE leadership.

Nepal Maoists

The Maoist insurgents of Nepal had no major commercial operations. They collected most of their funds through bank robberies, extraction and taxes in their areas of dominance, including from foreign tourists coming to Nepal for mountaineering and tracking expeditions. Some estimates put Maoists' collections at more than $100 million (Kumar 2003: 184).

In addition, there have been reports that the Maoists traded in cannabis, the plant from which marijuana and hashish are prepared, because this plant grew in abundance in the areas where the Maoists had been in full control, namely Rukum, Dolpa, Rolpa, Salyan and Pyuthun (Ramachandran 2004). There has, however, been no hard or reliable evidence to suggest deep involvement of the Maoists either in the cultivation or trafficking of drugs. The Maoists did make money out of the sale of another rare herb called Yarcha Gumba (Codryceps Sinesis), which is used in Chinese potency medicines. This herb is available in the Himalayas and the Maoists have been selling it off to the Chinese to raise resources (Kantipur Online 2008). The Maoists claim to encourage commercial use of this herb in Nepal's national interest.

The transnational relations of the Maoists have been limited mostly to their ideological groups. These relations fall in two categories, one in the West and another with India and in South Asia. The Nepal Maoists were the founding members of the Revolutionary International Movement (RIM), established in 1984. Through this organization, they came in contact with the Colombian and Peruvian communists and also the Revolutionary Communist Party of the US. In his report to the Second National Conference, the Maoists' leader Prachanda (Pushpa Kamal Dahal) accepted the critical role played by these contacts in advancing the Nepalese struggle. He said:

> [the] RIM committee kept on playing important role in synthesizing experiences of the world ... Among all of them, those of people's war in Peru, led by Comrade Gonzalo had been the highest and most important. Also, the documents and articles written by the Revolutionary Communist Party of the USA, and its Chairman Bob Avakin played an important role in lifting the debate to a new height. At the same time, positive and negative experiences of armed struggles in various countries, including Turkey, India, the Philippines, Bangladesh, Iran, had been on the agenda for direct debates and interactions. (Communist Party of Nepal (Maoist) 2002)

RIM welcomed the launching of the People's War in Nepal in 1996. Since the Nepal Maoists were the only group among RIM members to launch a People's War, they have even aspired to take the leadership of RIM and make it a "Third World" dominated organization. To that end, even after the success of the Jan Andolan-II, the Maoists organized a RIM meeting in December 2006 (International Crisis Group 2007: 16–17).

As a regional chapter of RIM in South Asia, the Maoists took the initiative in establishing a Coordinating Committee of Maoist Parties and Organizations of South Asia in July 2001. The Maoist groups from India, Bangladesh, Nepal, Bhutan and Sri Lanka joined in this initiative and have been holding annual meetings to talk about their respective strategies of struggle.

However, operationally, the most useful linkages of the Nepal Maoists have been with the Indian Naxal groups. It is believed that the Nepal Maoists played a key role in bridging differences among these groups and their leaders, particularly between the Maoists' Community Centre and the People's War Group, both in the Indian state of Andhra Pradesh. The Maoists also established operational linkages with other Indian insurgent groups in the North East, like ULFA, Bodo and the Kamtapur Liberation Organization. These linkages have been used by the Maoists for logistic support in several areas: the procurement of arms; health and educational help for the relatives of their cadres; movement, shelter and rescue; and training and transport, etc.

After 2005, Nepal Maoists were careful to avoid any offence to India by way of their linkages with the Indian Naxalites. The Indian Naxalites have not endorsed the Nepal Maoists' deviation from the radical path by joining hands with other mainstream parties. There have been harsh words between the erstwhile comrades. The Government of India also officially toned down its criticism of Nepal Maoists for their alleged operational links with the Indian Naxal groups.

The Nepal Maoists have developed their own strategy to deal with new challenges and have changed their overall political approach. They have proved to be more resilient and innovative, something reflected in their success in reaching power and having their leader, Prachanda, become, however briefly, Prime Minister of Nepal.

Assessment

Globalization has facilitated and reinforced South Asian insurgencies. The use of information technology (IT) by the South Asian insurgencies has enhanced their mobility and communication strategies and abilities. The LTTE, a close-knit organization with elaborate and extensive diasporas and commercial interests, could not have managed without an effective use of IT.

Regarding the Nepal Maoists, the difficult terrain and the communication situation in Nepal could be overcome through satellite cell-phones and FM radios. The radios became very forceful instruments of propaganda as well as a communication network for the Maoist cadres. The Maoists' leaders had access to satellite telephony to keep in close contact with each other, the regional commanders, grassroots cadres and international contacts. The king, when he took over direct power and vowed to fight the Maoists in February 2005, ordered the disabling of the mobile telephone network and FM radio stations as a first step. That step in itself, however, did not succeed in paralysing the communication network of the Maoists, and in addition contributed to the build-up of popular resentment against the monarchy.

Two positive aspects of the insurgency–globalization linkage need to be taken into account. One is that if the state, or the counterinsurgency operations, work systematically, they can erode and contain, if not completely eliminate, the spillover of globalization. The Sri Lankan government, from the late 1990s, moved to curb the LTTE's diaspora funding sources and the supply of arms from old war zones like Cambodia, Laos and Myanmar. Then Foreign Minister Lakshman Kadirgamar and his successor from 2005, Rohitha Bogollagama, worked hard to sensitize the countries concerned and mobilize support among them to ensure restraint on undesirable diasporic activities and clandestine flows of arms. To a considerable extent they succeeded. This has been helped to a large extent by the anti-terrorism atmosphere created in the aftermath of 9/11. But there surely is a need to strengthen such efforts at the regional as well as global levels. Bilateral measures can only work to a limited extent.

The Sri Lankan government's deft manipulation of international political fault-lines was also evident during the final phase of the ethnic war that eliminated the LTTE in Sri Lanka. Colombo refused international advice or pressure to relent in its ultimate goal of eliminating the LTTE. Given India's refusal to sell arms to Sri Lanka, China, Pakistan and Ukraine were approached. China emerged as the biggest arms supplier to Sri Lanka (Pubby 2008).[16] The continued support from China, Russia, Pakistan and India helped Sri Lanka in its war against the LTTE, even at a time when international pressures were building up against the war. These countries were also mobilized to counter any resolution against Sri Lanka in the UN Human Rights Council in Geneva on 19 May 2009.

The other positive aspect of globalization is inherent in the transformation of insurgency goals. The Nepal Maoists, through their various transnational links with similar ideological groups, also realized that dogmatism was a barrier to the success of revolutionary struggles. This is where the Nepal Maoists shifted from the path of "new democracy" to "competitive socialism". The global consensus against terrorism was certainly one of the important factors in inducing a rethink. This led the Maoists to revise their grand strategy from a "people's war" to a "united front" and democratic mobilization in achieving the goals of a republic. The dramatic change in Nepal's internal conflict would not have taken place and the Jan Andolan-II would not have happened without the Maoists shifting from the path of violence and in favour of democratic mobilization.

The role of the international community and the coordination of its efforts have been critical in helping the Maoists undertake these changes. Once the Maoists realized that without India's support they could not advance in their political goals, they quickly changed their stance towards India. The criticism of India as an "expansionist power" was toned down and channels of communication were established with New Delhi. This greatly helped them to operate in Indian territory and also to forge a united front with the Nepali mainstream political parties. Any deviation from this path of constructive engagement between the insurgency and the forces of globalization has the potential of reversing the transformation to the disadvantage of the Nepali people, regional peace and stability and the interests of international community. Any attempt to isolate the Maoists and marginalize them in building the new republic would force the Maoists back to the path of violence and destruction.

Signs of this reversal have emerged following the Maoists' short-lived participation in power after their strong showing in the Constitutional Assembly elections of April 2008. The Maoist prime minister Prachanda resigned after his failure to sack the chief of the Nepal Army.[17] The impatience shown by the Maoists towards changing the critical institutions of state power gave rise to fears among other political actors and the mainstream parties, as well as the international community, including India, that the Maoists were aiming to control the state. The Maoists did not realize that the non-Maoist political forces were feeling frustrated and insecure after their poor performance in the electoral battle and were thus waiting for any occasion to isolate the Maoists. On their part, the Maoists had not been sincere in their commitment to the peace process. The "Prachanda tapes" reveal the Maoist leader inflating the numbers of his People's Liberation Army for integration into the Nepal Army, exposing the insincerity of the commitment.[18] The Maoists also failed to learn to operate the levers of state power in a democratic political structure. If the unfortunate breakdown of the political consensus among the Maoists and the Nepali political parties persists, as it seems it will, the Nepal peace process may break down.

Globalization has impacted these two South Asian insurgencies very differently. While the Maoists of Nepal changed their strategy, deviated from the path of "people's war" and collaborated with political parties and the international community, the Sri Lankan Tigers' thrust for war and towards a separate state was reinforced. The LTTE has been militarily crushed. Its political fate and the possibility of the revival in some form of Tamil resistance will depend upon the way Colombo approaches a resolution of the ethnic conflict, as noted earlier.

These differing impacts of globalization can be explained by the inherent characteristics of the struggle that has been waged by these insurgent groups and the respective way in which the globalization processes impinged upon them. To begin with, the LTTE emerged as the wronged group, a victim of ethnic discrimination and violence by the majority Sinhalese community. The hardcore ethnic stance of the Sri Lankan state and the failure of the Sinhalese leadership to evolve a broad-based consensus to meet the legitimate Tamil grievances facilitated the Tamil militancy's image as an aggrieved group. As such, the LTTE received global sympathy and generous support, helping it to consolidate and reinforce its goals and strategies. In contrast, the Nepal Maoists emerged as an ideologically aggressive organization. They were ideologically incompatible with the tenets of globalization and accordingly found themselves at odds with the currents of globalization. As we have noted, they also did not get much financial or political support from the diasporas. Globalization also exposed the Maoists to diverse ideological currents and the failure of "Communist" movements elsewhere in the world. This forced them to review, rethink and revise their approach, their goals and strategies, particularly in the short and medium terms.

While the LTTE's top leadership, especially Prabhakaran, had no global exposure – he remained caught in his conflict environment and tunnel thinking – some of his associates, like Anton Balasingham, Kittu (Sathasivam Krishnakumar) and Mahatya (Gopalaswamy Mahendirarajah), had extensive global exposure, but on critical matters they did not have a final say. The Maoist leadership, on the other hand, in their search for victory and success interacted with diverse global currents and thus became amenable to change. The ethnic struggle of the Tamils was highly emotional and its intensity was enhanced by the LTTE's induction to self-sacrifice, through the cyanide capsule, which every LTTE cadre carried. This also led to the LTTE's suicide terrorism. This emotive intensity and the cult of sacrifice for the chosen cause also made the LTTE rigid in sticking to its ends and means. The Nepal Maoists had no such suicide streak. They ran their revolutionary struggle on logical lines, however dogmatic their logic may have been. They were trained to take life in their perceived fight for justice, rather than sacrifice their own lives. With a pragmatic leadership, this made the Maoists' struggle resilient and thus amenable to both the negative and the positive influences of globalization.

The point that emerges from this comparison is clear. There are both negative and positive impulses in globalization processes for insurgencies. The impact of these impulses will, however, depend upon the character of the membership and the way these impulses are absorbed. It may be erroneous to surmise that globalization has either universally softened or hardened insurgencies.

Notes

1. Some scholars have a tendency to club the Kashmir conflict in India as a part of religious insurgency, but that would be misleading in view of the complex nature of the Kashmir issue, which has strong historical and transnational dimensions.
2. For a more detailed analysis of the Naxal revolt in India, please see chapter 6 above by Ajay Mehra.
3. A religious insurgency has not been taken for comparative analysis as considerable literature is already available on Al Qaeda and Taliban terrorism in Afghanistan and Pakistan.

4. Diasporas can be covered under transnational linkages; however the significance of the role of diasporas has increased considerably and there are separate studies on this role by itself.
5. See, for instance, An-Na'im 2002. Also see Khagram, Riker and Sikkink 2002.
6. The LTTE runs efficient commercial enterprises and gets its funding through other sources. The LTTE's funding was analysed in detail by *Jane's Defence Weekly*, 25 Aug. 2007.
7. The Hawala system relies entirely on trust (Weiner 2001).
8. This is based on the author's own interviews and study in Oslo. Also see Fuglerud 1999.
9. See "Priya's story" detailed in Human Rights Watch 2006: section 6.
10. The author personally witnessed such lobbying by Tamil diaspora members in the US House Committee hearings in 1986, where the lobbyists were willing to promise naval facilities and access rights in the proposed Tamil Eelam if the US were to support the creation of such a separate Tamil state in Sri Lanka.
11. The UK House of Commons discussed the Sri Lankan situation on 29 April 2009; see, for example, <http://www.readmyday.co.uk/maryreid/archive/2009/05/11/tamil-demonstration-outside-parliament.html> (accessed June 2010). Also see *Economist* 2009.
12. There are currently no figures that accurately represent the total size of the diaspora.
13. Author's interview with the Cambodian Home Minister in July 2005. The former Sri Lankan Foreign Minister Lakshman Kadirgamar had mentioned to the author in personal interviews in Laos the details about the LTTE's illegal operations linked to Cambodia and Laos, during his official visit to Laos in 1999.
14. For an account of Norway's support to the LTTE see Jansz 1998.
15. The text of the letter, written on 31 Dec. 2002, appeared on the official website of the Sri Lankan government, <http://www.priu.gov.lk>.
16. China was also engaged in some of Sri Lanka's strategically important developmental projects like the exploration of oil and gas in the "gulf of Mannar" and the development of Hambantota port on the southern coast.
17. For a discussion of the issues involved, see Muni 2009.
18. For more on the "Prachanda tapes", see Mishar 2009 and *Nepali Times* 2009.

REFERENCES

Adamson, Fiona B. (2005) "Globalization, transnational political mobilisation and networks of violence", *Cambridge Review of International Affairs*, 18(1): 31–49.

An-Na'im, Abdullahi (2002) "Religion and global civil society: Inherent incompatibility of synergy and inter-dependence", in M. Glasius, H. Anheier and M. Kaldor, eds, *Global Civil Society 2002*, Oxford: Oxford University Press, pp. 55–76.

Bogollagama, Hon. Rohitha (2008) "How successful is counter terrorism in the Asia-Pacific? Sri Lanka's experience", speech given by the Minister of Foreign Affairs of Sri Lanka at the International Institute for Strategic Studies Shangri-La Dialogue, Singapore, 31 May.

Brecher, Jeremy, Tim Costello and Brendan Smith (2000) *Globalization from Below: The Power of Solidarity*. Cambridge, UK: South End Press.

Bunker, Robert J., ed. (2002) *Non-State Threats and Future Wars*. Basingstoke: Taylor and Francis.

ColomboPage (2009) "International community tried to save LTTE chief at the last moment, Sri Lanka government says", news report, 24 May. At <http://www.colombopage.com/archive_091/May1243178591CH.html> (accessed June 2010).

Communist Party of Nepal (Maoist) (2002) Issue of *The Worker*, No. 7 (Jan.): 44.

Davis, Anthony (1996) "Tiger international", *Asia Week*, 26 July.

Demmers, Jolle (2007) "New wars and diasporas: Suggestions for research and policy", *Journal of Peace, Conflict and Development*, 11: 1–26.

Economist (2009) "Sri Lanka: The coming battle", *Economist,* 27 Apr.

Falksohn, Rüdiger and Padma Rao (2008) "Tamil Tigers exploit exiles abroad to fund insurgency", *Spiegel Online,* 14 Feb. At <http://www.spiegel.de/international/world/0,1518,535316,00.html> (accessed June 2010).

Fuglerud, Oivind (1999) *Life on the Outside: The Tamil Diaspora and Long Distance Nationalism.* London: Pluto Press.

Human Rights Watch (2006) "Funding the 'final war'; LTTE intimidation and extortion in the Tamil diaspora", Human Rights Watch, New York, Mar.

International Crisis Group (2007) "Nepal's Maoists: Purists or pragmatists?", Asia Report No. 132, Katmandu/Brussels, 18 May.

Jansz, Fedrica (1998) "The LTTE rides high in Norway while Lanka gets torn apart". At <http://www.sinhaya.com/norway.htm> (accessed June 2010).

Jayasekara, Shanaka (2008) "Tamil Tiger links with Islamist terrorist groups", *Asian Tribune*, 4 Mar.

Jones, David Martin, ed. (2004) *Globalization and the New Terror: The Asia Pacific Dimension*. London: Edward Elgar.

Kantipur Online (2008) "Yarcha rules spark protest", 5 May. At <http://www.kantipuronline.com/kolnews.php?&nid=146061>.

Khagram, Sanjeev, James V. Riker and Kathryn Sikkink (2002) *Restructuring World Politics: Transnational Social Movements, Networks, Norms*. Minneapolis: University of Minnesota Press.

Kumar, Dhruba (2003) "Consequences of the militarized conflict and the cost of violence in Nepal", *Contributions to Nepalese Studies*, 30(2): 167–216.

Kurth Cronin, Audrey (2002–3) "Behind the curve: Globalization and international terrorism", *International Studies*, 27(3): 30–58.

Lia, Brynjar (2005) *Globalization and the Future of Terrorism: Pattern and Predictions*. London: Routledge.

Mason, T. David (2003) "Globalization, democratization and the prospects for civil war in the new millennium", *International Studies Review*, 5(4): 19–35.

Mishar, Pramod (2009) "Reading the tapes", *Kathmandu Post*, 13 May.

Muni, S. D. (2009) "The civil-military crisis in Nepal", *The Hindu*, 6 May. At <http://www.hindu.com/2009/05/06/stories/2009050655151100.htm> (accessed June 2010).

Nepali Times (2009) "Maoists tricked UNMIN", *Nepali Times*, 6 May.

Pubby, Manu (2008) "China emerging as main source of arms to N-E rebels: Jane's Review", *Indian Express*, 22 May. At <http://www.indianexpress.com/news/china-emerging-as-main-source-of-arms-to-ne-rebels-janes-review/312894/0> (accessed June 2010).

Rabasa, Angel, Cheryl Benard, Christine Fair, Theodar Karaski, Rollie Lal, Ian Lesser and David Thaler (2004) *The Muslim World after 9/11*. Santa Monica: RAND Corporation.

Ramachandran, Sudha (2004) "Nepal cashes in on cannabis", *Asia Times*, 21 Apr. At <http://www.atimes.com/atimes/South_Asia/FD21Df05.html> (accessed June 2010).

Romano, David and Richard Sandbrook (2004) "Globalization, extremism and violence in poor countries", *Third World Quarterly*, 25(6): 1007–30.

Sakhuja, Vijay (2006) "The dynamics of LTTE's commercial maritime infrastructure", Occasional Paper, Observer Research Foundation, New Delhi, Apr.

Sarup, Kamala (2004) "Interview: Upendra Mahato", *Nepal Digest*, 29 Oct., pp. 3–5. At <http://www.thenepaldigest.org/pdf/TND_102904.pdf>.

Shain, Yossi and Aharon Barth (2003) "Diasporas and international relations theory", *International Organization*, 57(3): 449–79.

SPUR Australia (2009a) "Why LTTE and Thailand", Society for Peace, Unity and Human Rights for Sri Lanka. At <http://www.spur.asn.au/thaicurrentnews.htm> (accessed 2009).

SPUR Australia (2009b) "LTTE Tamil Tiger terrorist activities in Thailand", Society for Peace, Unity and Human Rights for Sri Lanka. At <http://www.spur.asn.au/ThaiCurrentNews.htm> (accessed 22 July 2009).

UNIC Colombo (2009) "Ban asks Sri Lanka to heed calls for accountability, transparency", UNIC/PRESS RELEASE/79-2009, United Nations Information Centre, Colombo, 8 June.

Weiner, Roger G. (2001) "Financing of international terrorism", Criminal Division, US Department of Justice, Oct.

8

Terrorism and political movement in Kashmir

Rekha Chowdhary

Terrorism has come to be defined against the background of the terrorist attacks on the United States on 11 September 2001: since that time, "9/11" has become the basis for defining the global response.

Security analysts, strategic experts and political decision-makers all over the world have been swayed by the particular understanding of terrorism offered by the US government. As defined by the US Department of Defense and the Federal Bureau of Investigation (FBI), terrorism is "the unlawful use of force or violence against persons or property to intimidate or coerce a government, the civilian population or any segment thereof, in furtherance of political or social objectives" (US Department of Justice 2005: iv). It has been framed purely as a criminal activity, justifying not only an action by the state after the terrorist incident, but also an action for its prevention.[1] It was in accordance with this definition that the US State Department identified 45 terrorist groups and 8 "rogue states" supporting terrorism.[2] Washington appropriated for itself the leadership role in dealing with these groups and states, declaring a global war against them.

Given the way that 9/11 has redefined terrorism, as per American logic, it has not only obscured the alternative meanings of terrorism, but has also transformed it into an autonomous ahistorical phenomenon. "Abstracted from time and history", it is seen as "uncaused original evil", an evil which is neither preceded nor caused by anything (Nuzzo 2004: 338). "9/11 is presented", argues Nuzzo, "as the Nietzschean 'monument' that has lost any connection with its causal explanation – a monument placed outside any causal chain of explanation, a hypostatized event placed outside history" (2004: 337).

> From the outset, the logic of the Bush administration has aimed at presenting 9/11 as an event with no cause, certainly not as an effect of some (hidden or yet unknown but still discoverable) cause. By uncovering the conceptual structure that supports the official definition of terrorism insistently circulated by the media, we discover that terrorism is presented as that which has no ground and is beyond all law. Terrorism is not the effect of a cause; it is not grounded in a ground. And 9/11 is the cause of all evil that, in turn, has no cause and stands at the origin of the causal chain with no possible explanation. (2004: 337)

This ahistorical approach to terrorism has made it into a "politically charged" term that has been used to raise mass emotions against a "designated enemy". To quote Gates (2001), "the concept of terrorism is a rhetoric device used for condemning one's enemies rather than a scientifically definable category". Few people, according to him, "can speak of terrorism without a degree of emotional involvement, and there is a strong tendency on the part of potential victims to associate the technique only with enemies who might use it against them". Often, it becomes a term to brand an "identified group" as associated with terrorist activities or as sympathizers of terrorism, and in the process the world is seen in binary terms – as comprising those people who are associated in one way or the other with terrorism and those who are victimized by terrorism. A new hierarchy is therefore created between the Western world that is victimized by terrorism and the non-Western world, specifically Islamic countries and groups, seen as the principal propagators of terrorist activities.

Terrorism has thus become a geostrategic term used to justify intervention in the internal affairs of countries. Terrorism, it is argued by many, has been a convenient tool for the US to label any threat to its interests. By using the label "terrorist", it has sought to justify its proactive interventions, which range from regime change to war.[3] The usage itself remains selective and obscures US-sponsored terrorist activities, or for that matter activities of any state that claims to be a part of the "global war against terror". Domestically, in the name of tackling the terrorist challenge, the state can also assume unrestrained power over its own citizens and erode their civil liberties. Reference can be made to the Patriot Act of the USA enacted in 2001, which gave new powers to the law enforcement authorities against "terrorist" individuals and groups (Coen 2001).

The contemporary usage of the term terrorism has also obviated the relations between terrorism and resistance. By isolating it from its historical context and by holding groups and individuals responsible for it, terrorist linkages with the politics of resistance have been camouflaged.

Until as late as the 1980s, terrorism was seen as a part of the resistance movement and therefore had some positive connotations. The very origin of the term during the Terror phase of the French Revolution was based on its positive and normative meaning. Terrorism, in the modern period, continued to have a normative basis through its connection with the politics of resistance, especially with reference to decolonization.

After the Second World War, terrorism as a tool for revolutionary struggle was used as a matter of course by national liberation struggles. Referring to the twentieth century as an era of national movements, in places like Algeria, South Africa, Israel and Vietnam, Cronin (2002) argues that struggles for separate power became "a catalyst for terrorism, especially aimed at the objective of gaining independence or autonomy from established colonial powers". The birth of many new states after these struggles further legitimized the use of terrorist violence. Terrorists, at that time and place, were seen as "freedom fighters" fighting for a "just cause".[4]

In the later period as well, especially during the 1970s and 1980s when terrorism acquired an international character, it was still seen in terms of a "just war" against imperialism. As Cronin (2002) argues, this phase of terrorism captured the imaginations of many young people. Cronin notes:

> Sometimes the lowest common denominator among the groups was the forces against which they were reacting – e.g., "imperialism" – rather than the specific goals that were sought. But a notable innovation was the increasing commonality of the international connections among the groups. Especially after the 1972 Munich Olympics massacre, for example, the Palestinian Liberation Organization (PLO) captured the imaginations of many young radicals. In Lebanon and elsewhere, it also provided practical training in the preferred techniques of mid-twentieth century terrorism such as airline hijacking, hostage-taking and, of course, bombing.

As Oberschall argues, terrorism is not the act of a madman or of political and religious sociopaths, it is an act of political agents, be they ethnonational, religious or ideological, who choose covert, violent means to achieve political goals (2004: 27). Terrorist acts cannot be explained only with reference to violent individuals or collectives, or in terms of cultural values of certain groups or communities. As Black argues, "No individual or collectivity is violent in all settings at all times, and neither individualistic nor collectivistic theories predict and explain precisely how violence occurs ... Violence occurs when the social geometry of a conflict – the conflict structure – is violent" (2004: 15). Terrorism, therefore, is "an extreme, violent response to a failed political process engaging political regimes and ethnic and ideological adversaries over fundamental governance issues" (Oberschall 2004: 26).

Terrorism breeds in a situation of wide-ranging discontent. To understand it one has to go beyond the act of terrorism and ask the question: what is the historical or political context in which this act is taking place? It is important to note that terrorism is not the first method adopted to express discontent. When other methods of resolving conflict and addressing issues of political importance do not seem to be working, only then are terrorist methods adopted. Bird, Blomberg and Hess (2008) note:

> Broadly speaking, they feel that there is no superior alternative. This will be the case where the relevant political system is undemocratic. In a national setting, the government may be autocratic and may seek to suppress opposition views through banning free speech and rights of assembly and association. In a global setting, perpetrators of terrorism may feel that their own governments are not representing their views in global organisations, or it may be that they feel that the global organisations are themselves undemocratic, marginalising the views of poor countries, that nonetheless account for a large proportion of the world's population.

It is in the context of the paradigmatic shift in the conceptualization of terrorism and its isolation from the politics of resistance that this chapter is written. Elaborating upon the case study of Kashmir, it argues that terrorism is not an autonomous phenomenon and does not exist in isolation from the resistance movement. By contextualizing terrorism in Kashmir with its historical and political background, and by linking it with popular discontent, this chapter seeks to contest the contemporary understanding of terrorism as an "original evil" and locate it in the context of resistance politics. It also seeks to explore the basis of legitimization of terrorist acts and emphasize that terrorism cannot operate in isolation from the wide support of people in whose name these movements take place.

Terrorism in Jammu and Kashmir

Terrorism (hereafter referred to as armed militancy) came to define political responses in Kashmir in 1989. At the beginning, it was a small indigenous group of Kashmiris who initiated the era of militancy under the banner of the Jammu and Kashmir Liberation Front (JKLF).[5] The JKLF was initially supported by Pakistan, but was later on abandoned in favour of a newly launched organization, Hizb-ul-Mujahideen (Hizb).[6] Hizb, like the JKLF, was manned by local Kashmiri youth, but its ultimate objectives were quite different from those of the JKLF. While the JKLF aimed at complete independence of the erstwhile state of Jammu and Kashmir as it stood before October 1947, the Hizb aimed at a merger of the state with Pakistan. Devoid of financial and other kinds of support from Pakistan and facing elimination of its cadre by the Hizb, the JKLF was forced to declare a ceasefire in 1994 and began to operate as a political, rather than a militant, group.

By this time, militancy in Kashmir had acquired a more violent and brutal form. In the name of Islamic Jihad (Jehad), outfits manned by mercenaries from Afghanistan, Pakistan and other countries started operating here. The three major organizations operating through foreign Jihadi elements were Harkat-ul Mujahideen,[7] Lashkar-e-Toiba[8] and Jaish-e-Mohammad.[9] Apart from these major groups, there were numerous smaller outfits which operated in Kashmir. Most of these outfits were either associated with the bigger outfits, or were front organizations launched in the wake of the ban imposed on some organizations.

Having gone through various phases, militancy in Kashmir has, at present, both an indigenous and a foreign face. Hizb remains the most active indigenous militant organization, while the three above-mentioned foreign organizations, along with many others, operate either directly or through their front organizations.

For two decades now, Jammu and Kashmir has been affected by armed militancy. Large numbers of people have been killed in terrorist incidents and other incidents of violence perpetrated by security forces or by the counter-insurgency groups. Although the brunt of this militancy has been felt in the Valley of Kashmir, as well as the militancy-infested areas of Jammu, the Kashmiri militancy has made its impact beyond the state of Jammu and Kashmir and there have been a number of attacks in other parts of India, especially in the capital city of Delhi. Of these, the one on the Parliament of India, in December 2001, was the most notable.[10]

One of the intended consequences of militancy has been the internationalization of the conflict. Although for a long time India continued to take the official position of terming the militancy as a "proxy war of Pakistan", it began gradually to take cognizance of the conflict by making overt and covert efforts to deal with it. In 2003, the Government of India initiated a comprehensive peace process and started dialogue with Pakistan as well as with separatists in Kashmir. It will take time to reach a resolution of the conflict to the satisfaction of all the parties involved.

The conflict situation and the politics of resistance

External dimensions of conflict

The context of this militancy has to be located in the politics of resistance in Jammu and Kashmir. This conflict can be traced to the moment of decolonization, the Partition of India and the emergence of two sovereign states – India and Pakistan.[11] More than 500 princely states of erstwhile British-controlled India were given the option to join either of the two states, though demography and politics played a major role in the exercise of such an option. Since Pakistan was created in response to the demand to carve a Muslim Homeland, it was considered inevitable that the Muslim majority areas, like Jammu and Kashmir, would join this new state. However, neither the Hindu ruler who was given the legal right to make the choice nor the Kashmiri Muslim leadership representing the majority of people of the state were keen on joining Pakistan. While the ruler, looking for ways to sustain his control over power, explored the possibility of remaining independent, the Muslim leadership organized under the banner of National Conference was keen on maintaining the distinct Kashmiri identity, and therefore preferred negotiation with plural and secular India rather than facing the risk of getting assimilated within all-Muslim Pakistan. The Accession issue itself created the problem – with Pakistan claiming Kashmir on the basis of its Muslim-majority population, and the princely ruler remaining indecisive about the issue even two months after the transfer of power from the British to the Indian and Pakistani states.

The Accession of Kashmir to India ultimately took place under the extraordinary circumstances created by the invasion of its territories by the tribals supported by Pakistan, The princely ruler signed Accession with India, but Kashmir, which was partitioned across the Line of Control between Pakistan and India, became a bone of contention between India and Pakistan. While India took the issue of the invasion of Kashmir to the United Nations, hostility between India and Pakistan continued and increased over time.

Internal dimensions of the conflict situation: resistance politics

The conflict situation in Kashmir, however, extends beyond the contestation between India and Pakistan.[12] It also has an internal dimension: Kashmiri identity. It is around the latter that the politics of resistance has taken shape. The present phase of resistance politics that was started in 1989 was preceded by two earlier phases of resistance: from the early 1930s to 1947, and from 1953 to 1975.

It was during the first phase of resistance politics that the contours of identity politics took shape around the question of alien control of political power, on the one hand, and the exploitative structure of economy, on the other. The extreme poverty and backwardness of the Kashmiris, in the context of the oppressive nature of the political power controlled by "outsiders" since the sixteenth century, was the dominant discourse of the movement led by the National Conference and its charismatic leader, Sheikh Mohammad Abdullah.[13] The "Quit Kashmir movement" of the 1940s, therefore, was organized around the demand for the abolition of the monarchy and transfer of power to people, a reorganization of the agrarian structure and the right of the people to decide the question of the future of Kashmir and its accession to India or Pakistan. It was during this phase that the people of Kashmir developed a sense of political community, seeking to control their own political destiny and demanding an autonomous space for their political expression.

It was due to the successful culmination of the first phase of resistance politics that the political leadership of Kashmir, subsequent to the abolition of the monarchy, could negotiate autonomy for Kashmir within the government and a special constitutional status under Article 370 of the Indian Constitution. Unlike the other states of India, Jammu and Kashmir was to have its own constitution and was to decide its own terms of constitutional integration with India.

However, the constitutional autonomy of the state could not be sustained for long as it came to be perceived as contrary to the "national interest". In a country recently partitioned on a religious basis, the idea of constitutional and federal asymmetry could not be accommodated within the predominant discourse of nationalism, and its logic at that time of "unity with uniformity". A plea was was made for the "constitutional integration" of Jammu and Kashmir to bring it into par with the rest of the states of India in terms of its relationship with the central government.

A second phase of resistance politics was initiated in the wake of the systematic erosion of the constitutional autonomy of the state. Soon after Sheikh Abdullah, the popular leader of Kashmir, was ousted from power in 1953 (and kept in detention) and the process of "constitutional integration" of the state with the centre was initiated. Meanwhile, in the name of the "national interest", democratic norms were compromised – elections were manipulated and governments sponsored by the centre were imposed on this state. It was against this background that the Plebiscite Front, led by colleagues and sympathizers of Sheikh Abdullah, contested the finality of the accession of Kashmir to India and demanded the right of Kashmiris to decide their own political fate. The Plebiscite Front dominated the political scene in Kashmir for two decades. It was in 1975, when Sheikh Abdullah joined political power, that the Plebiscite Front was dissolved.

It is against the background of the earlier two phases of resistance politics that the present phase of militancy and political movements, since 1989, must be analysed. The present phase arose from the accumulated discontent of the Kashmiri political community over the existing political arrangement, given the absence of democratic channels for political expression, intrusion by the centre into the politics of the state and the lack of autonomy for local politics. However, one can trace its continuity with the earlier two phases of resistance. The logic of the politics of resistance, as in the earlier two phases, is defined by the urge for an autonomous space for the expression of Kashmiri identity. The reason as to why the militancy erupted in 1989 lies in the resentment and popular perception that Kashmiri identity had not been allowed to express and assert itself.

Accumulated discontent, mass response and terrorism

The immediate context of the militancy is provided by three political events that took place during a short span of five years, 1984–9. The first was the dismissal of the legitimately elected National Conference government, led by Farooq Abdullah, in 1984.[14] This led to substantial resentment in the Valley. It not only reminded the Kashmiris of the ousting of Sheikh Abdullah from power (and his prolonged detention) at the behest of the central government, but also brought to the fore the logic that no government, however democratically elected, could function in the state unless it was supported by the ruling party at the centre. It was in acknowledgement of this logic that Farooq Abdullah subsequently decided in favour of an alliance with the Congress Party. Commonly known as the Rajiv-Farooq accord, this alliance, formalized in 1986, was the second political event that not only generated anger against the centre, but also caused substantial damage to the credibility of the National Conference. Farooq Abdullah was blamed for being a political opportunist who had compromised Kashmiri dignity and identity.

The Assembly election of 1987, perceived to be rigged, was the third and the final event leading to massive popular reaction. The National Conference-Congress combination swept the election, while the Muslim United Front that had come into existence to counter the National Conference-Congress failed to win the expected number of seats. The coalition government formed after this election was confronted with a crisis of governance right from the beginning.

However, the feeling of alienation has deeper roots that go far beyond these events. It lies in the cumulative discontent simmering in the Valley since the early 1950s. It is a response of the majority of Kashmiris who feel that their basic urge for an independent political space has remained unmet and that they have been forced to experience an ever-intrusive politics. In the common perception, there has been an erosion of the political dignity of the people of Kashmir.

It is in this context of alienation that armed militancy came to the surface. Soon after the 1987 Assembly elections, the young Kashmiris under the banner of the JKLF decided to launch an armed struggle.[15] Apart from the JKLF, there were a number of other militant groups, whose presence in Kashmir was marked by targeted killings (of agents of the state, including police informers and intelligence officers); bomb blasts; attacks on government offices and government property; and kidnapping.[16] Militancy incapacitated the political structures and rendered the agencies of political mediation irrelevant. By 1989, most of the political actors had been made ineffectual and there was a political vacuum. There was an erosion of political authority and the Indian state had to use its coercive apparatus to prop it up.

Militancy and popular support

Militancy received massive popular support. The first generation of militants, many of whom had participated in the 1987 electoral process in various roles (as candidates, election agents or campaigners), were adopted by the people as "our boys" working for "the cause". Militancy, at that time, was seen to be a desperate response of the people of Kashmir who had become "convinced" after the Assembly elections that there was no political channel for the expression of their political urges. Militant violence was seen as the last resort to focus national and international attention on the political frustration of Kashmiris.

This militancy was not isolated, backed as it was by the popular response. There was very spirited support from people moved by the sentiment of *Azadi* (freedom). By 1990, this response had acquired the form of a mass movement. Huge processions of Kashmiris took place almost on daily basis. To show their anger against the Indian state, thousands of Kashmiris thronged the streets of Srinagar chanting the slogans of *Azadi*.[17]

Throughout 1989–90, there were numerous more or less spontaneous demonstrations against India. On any issue, people would find a reason to come out to express their sentiment. For instance, a demonstration against Salman Rushdie's *Satanic Verses*, in February 1989, became a week-long anti-India demonstration. The political response of the people at that time was so intense that the government had to impose indefinite curfews. People violated the curfew and joined huge processions. (However, they remained indoors on the call of *Hartal* (strike) by the militants. This phenomenon came to be known as *civil curfew*.) By early 1990, there was mass insurgency. Describing this situation Schofield notes:

> At the end of February an estimated 400,000 Kashmiris marched on the offices of the United Nations Military Observer Group to hand in petitions demanding the implementation of the UN resolutions. It was reported as the largest demonstration the Kashmir valley has seen ... Nearly every day a procession

of lawyers, women, teachers, doctors marched through the streets of Srinagar. (2004: 150)

The mass response not only led to the collapse of the political order, but also to the withdrawal of the political parties from the scene. So intense was the expression of popular resentment that it forced the central government to dissolve the state's Assembly in January 1990.

Indigenous militancy

The armed militancy that emerged at that point of time was indigenous and rooted in mass politics. Not only was the first generation of militants made up of local Kashmiris, but the logic of militancy was also purely local: "Young men aged between sixteen and twenty five, they came from the towns of Srinagar, Anantnag, Pulwama, Kupwara and Baramula ... majority were well-educated – doctors, engineers, teachers, policemen – who had become alienated by Indian government policies in New Delhi and lack of job opportunities" (Schofield 2004: 146).

It was at a later stage that foreign militants started operating and militancy reflected international linkages. Although Pakistan got involved in militancy right from the beginning – since the cadre of the JKLF sought its material support – recruitment remained local. Even at a later period, when Pakistan sought to control the militancy through the creation of Hizb-ul-Mujahideen, it did so through the involvement of local Jamaat-e-Islami. The Hizb, which remains one of the most visible militant organizations in the state, is manned by Kashmiris.

The reason why the militancy could sustain itself during the initial period was that it was rooted in the indigenous political movement. The militants enjoyed strong legitimacy during this time, and there was a total identification of Kashmiri society with them. The gun-wielding militants roamed freely and were celebrated. They were seen to be doing heroic things and were called *Mujahids* (freedom fighters). Those killed in encounters with security forces were known as *Shaheeds* (martyrs).

Delegitimization of violence and terrorism

However, during the second phase the character of this militancy changed and it lost much of its popularity. At least three reasons were behind this. First, unlike the first generation of militants who had joined militancy for reasons of ideology and commitment to the Kashmiri cause, the second generation of militants had many other extraneous reasons for doing so – including money and power. With the gun assuming ascendancy over political means, it was often used to silence dissent, eliminate competitors and gain control over resources.

Second, militancy lost much of its sheen when it became an internal war for supremacy between the JKLF and the Hizb-ul-Mujahideen. With most of the cadre of the JKLF eliminated at the hands of Hizb, Kashmir faced its first disconnect between militancy and the movement. By 1994, the JKLF had declared a ceasefire and withdrawn from armed action.

Third, and most important, was externalization in the context of Jihadis or the mercenary militants fighting in the name of Islam. At the beginning the Jihadis were welcomed and their role in the movement was appreciated. Yet their continued presence generated tensions within the movement. This had serious implications for the legitimacy of Jihadis and for the armed militancy as a whole. The Jihadi phase of militancy, which began in 1993, generated a twofold tension within the movement – based on its external basis and its underlying logic of pan-Islamism.

There was always a difference in the popular response towards the indigenous militants, who were seen as part of the movement, and the Jihadis, who were seen as "guests". The cultural difference between the Jihadis and the local people, specifically in terms of their approach towards religion, brought out the distinctively external element of the Jihadis. Islam in Kashmir, as Khan argues, "became the religion of the great majority of rural Kashmir ... largely because, through the Rishis, it allowed the main configuration of pre-existing Kashmiri popular religion to adapt itself to the wider Islamic framework" (2002: 178). Muslim Rishis and their shrines, therefore, became the symbol of Kashmiri Muslim identity. Numerous local practices and rituals associated with the Rishis and shrines bring out the cultural feature of Islam which is unique to Kashmir.[18]

The irreverence of the Jihadis towards the shrines and the local rituals and practices generated a negative response towards them. This became evident during the siege and later burning of Chrar-e-Sharief, one of the most revered shrines of Kashmir by Mast Gul, a Harkat-ul-Ansar Jihadi trained in Afghanistan.[19]

The pan-Islamic agenda of Jihadis has also been problematic. The Jihadis operating in Kashmir consider religion as the logic of the movement and see it in the context of the pan-Islamic agenda. This does not reflect the ground reality of Kashmir and does not go down well with the local imagination. For most of the Kashmiris, the conflict has a purely political basis and has nothing to do with pan-Islamism.[20]

Delegitimization of violence and armed militancy

The Jihadis could thus not sustain the legitimacy enjoyed by the militants in Kashmir during the earlier period. By the mid-1990s, a clear-cut societal response had emerged in Kashmir against militancy and violence. Thus, Abdul Gani Lone, one of the senior separatist leaders, asserted in the late 1990s that these "guest militants" were no longer welcome in Kashmir: "They are not for azadi. They are for international jehad and they have their own global agenda." Their presence earlier had been required as they had come to help and support the Kashmiris in their struggle, but in the process they had transcended their role as "supporters" and assumed the role of the "owners" of the movement. This was objectionable because they were not only giving the local movement an external dimension, but were also being insensitive to the local responses (Chowdhary 2002).

Lone did not stop at suggesting the exit of the non-Kashmir Jihadi elements from Kashmir, he also asked the local Kashmiris to lay down their arms. This, in his opinion, was essential for creating a political environment in which the problems could be resolved through dialogue and negotiation. He said that the phase of armed militancy was over and there was now a need to shift the direction of the movement towards more peaceful methods. In 2001 he urged militants to "help in solving the Kashmir problem" by not resorting to violence (quoted in *South Asia Monitor* 2001). Since militancy was no longer rooted in local political responses, it had lost popular support.[21]

The impact of 9/11

One of the major impacts of 9/11 was the delegitimization of armed militancy at the global level. Yet militancy had been delegitimized in Kashmir long before. In the mid-1990s the political discourse had already begun to change and the movement had started to shift from the politics of violence to the politics of dialogue.

However, 9/11 accelerated this. First, armed militancy lost international support. Thus the movement had to change its strategy. Meanwhile, 9/11 put pressure on Pakistan to change its position vis-à-vis armed militancy in Kashmir. Although it did not take an immediate U-turn towards militancy in Kashmir, a gradual change in its position has been visible since this episode. The decline of militancy in Kashmir in recent years is evidence of Pakistani restraint.

The most significant implication of 9/11 has been that South Asia has become a region of strategic interest for the US. Significant pressure has thus been put upon India and Pakistan to enter into dialogue and resolve the Kashmir conflict. As a result of such pressure, a comprehensive peace process was initiated between the two countries from 2003. Efforts were also made by the Indian government to initiate dialogue with separatists in Kashmir.

Within Kashmir, the politics of resistance entered a new phase – a phase of political mechanisms. In this new phase, the mass response towards militancy has changed. Despite this change, there is some linkage between militancy and the movement. This linkage can be seen in two ways. First, since armed militancy served the crucial purpose of taking the movement to a stage where it attained international visibility and equipped the Kashmiris to regain the negotiability of their political future, the role of the armed militants in the final resolution is important. There is a feeling among separatists in Kashmir that the militants need to be brought to the table for the sustainability of any long-term peace process. However, this feeling is reserved only for the Hizb-ul-Mujahideen and not for the foreign militants.

Second, though militancy does not enjoy the kind of legitimacy it did in the initial period, the people of Kashmir still identify with the militants, especially the local militants. Although there is a strong antipathy towards militant violence, the local militants are still owned by and are seen to be serving the cause of the movement. The death of a local militant becomes an occasion to show identification with the militancy. Invariably huge crowds join the funeral procession of the slain militants.

The support for militancy will continue in Kashmir, despite its delegitimization, as people still feel that the basic issue underlying the conflict remains unaddressed.

Conclusion

This chapter has sought to show the relationship between armed militancy and political movements. It has argued that the armed militancy which arose in Kashmir in 1989 was rooted in the political movement. The movement had preceded the militancy and had already passed through various phases. The phase of militancy manifested not only mass discontent accumulated over time, but also a frustration with the political process. Armed militancy, thus, was not the first response of the Kashmiris; other methods of resistance had been pursued earlier.

The chapter has also argued that armed militancy needs the support of the masses in whose name it uses violence. Such support is made available only if the militancy enjoys legitimacy. In the case of Kashmir, the militancy enjoyed a very high level of legitimacy in the initial period through its link with the movement. As the militancy became autonomous and developed a logic of its own, it lost this legitimacy.

A distinction has been drawn between the indigenous logic of the militancy, and the logic imposed from above. The indigenous logic must remain valid for the militancy to retain the support of people. The failure of the Jihadi politics to redefine militancy as a part of pan-Islamism or global Jihad reflects this very clearly.

Armed militancy in Kashmir shows that terrorism is neither an isolated development, nor an ahistorical event. It is very much a part of a wider political resistance and is merely one of the varied expressions of that resistance. Resort to armed militancy is an extreme act of desperation and of frustration, resulting from accumulated discontent and the unavailability of other means of having this resentment recognized.

Notes

1. The FBI makes a distinction between two types of terrorist related activity: a terrorist incident and a terrorism prevention. A terrorist incident is a violent act or an act dangerous to human life, in violation of the criminal laws of the United States, or of any state, to intimidate or coerce a government, the civilian population, or any segment thereof, in furtherance of political or social objectives. A terrorism prevention is a documented instance in which a violent act by a known or suspected terrorist group or individual with the means and a proven propensity for violence is successfully interdicted through investigative activity. See US Department of Justice 2005.
2. These eight states included Iraq, Iran, Syria, Libya, Sudan, North Korea, Cuba and Afghanistan.
3. To quote Nuzzo (2004), "terrorism is construed by the official definition of the Bush administration as a phenomenon lying outside and beyond any law – civil law as well as moral law, international law, the law of peace, as well as the law of war. Terrorism terrorizes precisely because it is outside all law and all order. It follows (by the logic to which propaganda forces public opinion) that the only response to terrorism can be war, that is, the total annihilation of the enemy. It follows also that war against terrorism will not abide by any law and will simply consecrate terrorism's absolute lawlessness."
4. In international political practices as well as in political theory, one can find justification for the politics of resistance as well as the use of violence in the resistance politics. Political analysts make reference to Article 51 of the United Nations Charter and to UN General Assembly Resolution 3246 of 1974 as the basis of legitimacy for the right of resistance. In political theory, the necessity of violence for political purposes was conceptualized by Franz Fanon. Fanon not only gives a justification for revolutionary violence but also for terrorism per se. It is only through violence that the liberation of the oppressed people of the colonized world can be possible.
5. The JKLF was originally established in 1964 but became involved in militancy only in 1989. The immediate provocation for initiating the era of militancy in Kashmir was provided by the Assembly elections held in 1987. These elections were perceived to be heavily rigged. Soon after the elections a number of young people crossed the Line of Control in search of financial, armed and other kinds of support for waging an armed struggle in Kashmir. Among those who were the first to cross over to Pakistan for armed training was Mohammad Yosuf Shah, who was a candidate in one of the Assembly seats in the city of Srinagar. He later assumed the name Syed Salahuddin and has been heading the Hizb-ul-Mujahideen, the most important indigenous militant organization of Kashmir. Among others who crossed over at that time for armed training were Yasin Malik, the chief of the JKLF in Kashmir, Abdul Hamid Sheikh, Ashfaq Majid Wani and Javed Ahmad Mir.

6. This was mainly due to a divergence of political objectives between Pakistan and the JKLF. While Pakistan aimed at a merger of Jammu and Kashmir with Pakistan, JKLF aimed at the complete independence of the erstwhile territories of Jammu and Kashmir under the control of India, Pakistan and China.
7. This organization started working in Kashmir in 1993. It was initially named Harkat-ul-Ansar. Harkat, based first in Pakistan and then in Afghanistan, was established in mid-1980s. It was active in terrorist operations in Burma, Tajikistan and Bosnia.
8. Lashkar started its operation in Kashmir in 1994. Lashkar is the military wing of Markaz-ad-Dawa-wal-Irshad, a Pakistan-based religious organization.
9. Jaish is a more recent organization formed by Maulana Masood Azhar, a Pakistani cleric, in 2000.
10. In the attack in Mumbai of 26–29 November 2008, high-profiled hotels and foreign tourists were targeted; 166 people were killed. However, the Mumbai attack was not the handiwork of the militants operating in Kashmir, but rather of Pakistani groups like Lashkar-e-Taiba.
11. In comparison, Edgardo Lander's contribution (chapter 2 above) examines the colonial legacy and the decolonization of Latin American society and current projects of social transformation, democratization and inclusion in South America.
12. The external dimension of the conflict has contributed to the present phase of armed militancy in Jammu and Kashmir; it would have been impossible for the armed militancy to sustain itself in Jammu and Kashmir without the material and political support of Pakistan. However, it is mainly with reference to the politics of resistance around the issue of Kashmiri identity that one can actually trace the basis of the armed militancy in this state. Armed militancy should be seen as one of the recent manifestations of resistance politics.
13. The successive regimes of Mughals, Pathans, Sikhs and Dogras were portrayed as an indignity to the local Kashmiris. However, it was in the very establishment of the Dogra rule in 1846 that the loss of dignity in its extreme form was perceived. The fact that money exchanged hands in the transfer of power from Sikh rulers to the Dogras (the Treaty of Amritsar by which the Dogra rulers came to control Kashmir) made this so.
14. This government had been voted into power in 1983 with a huge mandate within the Valley. However, because of the defections engineered by the Congress (the ruling party at the centre), the National Conference government was reduced to a minority and replaced by a government of defectors led by G. M. Shah. The outside support for this new government was provided by the Congress.
15. Crossing over to Pakistan they received armed training and returned to Kashmir in 1989, initiating a new phase of the politics of resistance.
16. Among the groups operating at that time, Al Barq, Al Fateh, Al Jehad and Allah Tigers may be mentioned.
17. Schofield quotes one of the Kashmiris that she interviewed about the scenario in Kashmir at that time: "There were loudspeakers in the mosques, encouraging people to come out. Everyday, all day people were shouting slogans, 'Azadi, Azadi' was broadcast from the minarets. With extraordinary optimism the people believed they had won their struggle almost before it had begun. Even I was thinking: within ten days, India will have to vacate Kashmir" (2004: 148).
18. Khan argues, "Despite the criticism of the local practices by the Ahl-i-Hadith, a vast majority of villagers celebrate the anniversaries of their saints in the traditional manner. They continue to practise vegetarianism on festive occasions when they invite relatives and friends to taste the modest vegetarian food as a mark of respect to the disciplined soul of Rishis. In certain areas austerity is practised in the true manner of their patron saints; relics of the Rishis such as their dress, wooden clogs, cups, turbans, staff, etc., are

exhibited on festive occasions when devotees invoke the intercession of the Rishis in the presence of these relics" (2002: 234).

19. This fourteenth-century shrine of the patron saint of Kashmir Sheikh Nooruddin Wali was occupied by more than a hundred militants.
20. It is due to the political nature of the movement that the mass of Kashmiris have silently but very forcefully rejected the onslaught of fundamentalism. The societal response to the fringe organization trying to use the space created by the movement for forwarding the "Islamist agenda" of veiling women or enforcing cultural codes has been firm. These organizations have not been allowed to appropriate the movement for "religious" purposes.
21. In the late 1990s the majority of militants came from outside the region. With the entry of Harka-ul-Mujahideen and Jaish-e-Mohammad, the militancy acquired a heavily foreign character. The Jihadi logic pursued by these organizations was unsuited to the sentiments of the ordinary Kashmiris and went against the tradition of Kashmir's politics.

REFERENCES

Bird, Graham, S. Brock Bloomberg and Gregory D. Hess (2008) "International terrorism: Causes, consequences and cures", *World Economy*, 31(2): 255–74.

Black, Donald (2004) "The geometry of terrorism", in "Theories of terrorism: A symposium", ed. Roberta Senechal de la Roche, *Sociological Theory*, 22(1) (Mar.): 14–25.

Chowdhary, Rekha (2002) "Lone's liberal legacy", *Economic and Political Weekly*, 22 June.

Coen, Rachel (2001) "Are you a terrorist? Media passivity enables rollback of civil liberties", *Extra! magazine (FAIR)*, Dec. At <http://www.thirdworldtraveler.com/Terrorism/Are_You_Terrorist.html> (accessed June 2010).

Cronin, Audrey Kurth (2002) "The historical and political conceptualization of the concept of terrorism", SSRC Workshop on Terrorism, Georgetown University, 14–15 Nov.

Gates, John M. (2001) "Understanding terrorism", *Media Monitors Network*, 11 Sept. At <http://www.mediamonitors.net/johnmgates1.html> (accessed June 2010).

Khan, M. Ishaq (2002) *Kashmir's Transition to Islam: The Role of Muslim Rishis*. Delhi: Manohar.

Nuzzo, Angelica (2004) "Reasons for conflict: Political implications of a definition of terrorism", *Metaphilosophy*, 35(3) (Apr.): 330–44.

Oberschall, Anthony (2004) "Explaining terrorism: The contribution of collective action theory", in "Theories of terrorism: A symposium", ed. Roberta Senechal de la Roche, *Sociological Theory*, 22(1) (Mar.): 26–37.

Schofield, Victoria (2004) *Kashmir in Conflict: India, Pakistan and the Unending War*. Delhi: Viva.

South Asia Monitor (2001) "Stepping carefully in Kashmir", *South Asia Monitor,* No. 29 (1 Jan.), Center for Strategic and International Studies, Washington, DC. At <http://csis.org/files/media/csis/pubs/sam29.pdf> (accessed June 2010).

US Department of Justice (2005) *Terrorism: 2002–2005*. Washington, DC: Federal Bureau of Investigation. At <http://www.fbi.gov/publications/terror/terrorism2002_2005.htm> (accessed June 2010).

9

Jihad in the age of globalization

Nasra Hassan

Since globalization cannot be stopped, the focus ... should be on how it is managed and how resources are shared.

Michael Moore, head of World Trade Organization, July 2003

Jihad can never be stopped as it is a Command from Allah.

A leader of Ezzedin Qassam, armed wing of Palestinian Hamas

Jihad is permanent and eternal, jihad has no borders and no limitations, it is universal, global, cosmic.

Head of Pakistan's biggest jihadist group

Introduction

At its best, globalization is envisioned as a world without borders, facilitating the exchange of ideas, goods and systems for the benefit of all. This is similar to jihad, which recognizes no borders on Allah's Earth, and is also, as conceptualized in Islam, aimed at the betterment of the individual, societal, communal and global condition through laws and systems advocated by Islam. Modern jihad – which gained attention as a contemporary threat and global danger following 9/11 – lends itself, then, to the best and worst in globalization, using its tools and techniques to great advantage.

This chapter lays out the various ways in which jihadist movements use the tools of contemporary globalization. The chapter begins with an introduction to the origin and nature of jihad and its associations with globalization discourse. The discussion then moves on to the global reach of jihad by focusing on the various ways that the tools of globalization are utilized, including criminal means of acquiring funds, the maintenance of traditional networks, the transport of goods across maritime routes and the use of cell-based networks. The chapter then explores the similarities between jihadist movements and globalization, including the use of the internet and network technologies to expand reach.

Jihad and globalization: Tangled together

In the words of a Pakistani lawyer trained in constitutional law and Islamic law, with experience in applying both in court cases in defence of his clients from religion-based parties: "Actually, Islam introduced globalization fourteen centuries ago. Our religion exploded beyond the Arabian peninsula, into other continents. It demolished borders and 'national' rule, it did away with inequality and exploitation."[1] From this perspective, Islam and globalization have a long and storied history. By extension, so do jihad and globalization. In personal interviews, Sheikh Ahmed Yassin, founder and head of Palestinian Hamas who was killed in a targeted Israeli air strike in 2004, spent much time explaining the concept of Palestine as an Islamic trust, the conditions for jihad and "martyrdom operations", which in the view of Hamas and other religion-based parties are not "suicide operations".

The martyr aspect of jihad has strong religious associations and is well respected by those in the cause:

> "Just as Allah mandated jihad to protect Islam and Muslims, martyrdom was mandated to protect the jihad. Although the concept existed before Islam, Allah bestowed a very high honour on the martyrs, second only to that of the prophets. But it must be emphasized that the status of martyr is achieved only when the sacrifice of one's life is in Allah's cause, an intention and outcome that is judged and accorded only by Allah."[2]

This explains why in many "lands of jihad" – territories where jihad is obligatory or where Islamists have decreed it be introduced – the honorific of *shaheed* (he who has sacrificed his life) is followed by the supplication *Inshallah*, i.e. "if Allah so wills".

Under fundamentalist Islamic interpretations, ideas of national sovereignty are not seen to be compatible with religious doctrine. Many "do not recognize governments or states which arrogate for themselves the quality of 'sovereignty'. We recognize no laws made by man, no institution created by men and run by them, no rules and regulations which can be made, cancelled and remade at will."[3] Within this interpretation only the will of Allah is regarded to have authority, authority which is not constrained within national borders or boundaries.[4] The primacy of Allah and the spread of Islam therefore entails that "globalization is the natural order of things, under divine guidance. Of course man does evil, this is why Islam was revealed to show us how to live perfect lives. And for this to happen, we need jihad."[5]

There is, however, a contrasting and non-Islamic rationalization for globalization:

> Globalization cannot be stopped. It is a "megatrend" of world history. However, it is not a fated natural event but the result of an intentional political strategy called neoliberalism, which was devised in the control centres of world economic and political power. All that can therefore be done is to set up social and ecological fences to pen in and tame this particular horse before it gallops away: in other words, to influence globalization by political means. (Nuscheler 2002)

One could respond that this view is flawed if it is assumed that only the Islamic way of looking at phenomena has permanent validity; the secular analysis of globalization is marred by temporary applicability.

The dark side of globalization has spawned and facilitated ideas, goods, services and systems which threaten to crush and destroy civil society. These include, but are not limited to, transnational crime groups[6] and illegal weapons trafficking,[7] as well as the questionable business and ethical practices of transnational corporations. The resources required to counter the misuse and its consequences – whether unintentional or deliberate – are massive. The profits and advantages generated by illegal, illegitimate, unethical and immoral transactions and usages are so vast, concrete and often immediate that the war against them cannot be definitively won. It is more likely that there will be a constant battles here and there, as regulators, government and authorities attempt to curb their growth.

While contemporary jihadist groups are not the major users or abusers of globalization, they have been quick and innovative. They adopt and adapt those areas of activity in which globalization and its tools can help them circumvent laws and controls. Their businesses in white, grey and black areas feed and support each other.

Since jihad is not limited to non-Muslim states, there are no exemptions for Islamic or Muslim-majority countries. Even states with a constitution based on Islamic principles are prone to jihad if the regime is declared "un-Islamic", if it does not implement Sharia law in its entirety, is oppressive to its Muslim citizens or allied to *kuffar* (non-Muslim) states, or seeks to suppress jihad. In an interview with the author, a senior jihadi cleric and leader explained:

> Jihad is undertaken not simply to bring Islam to non-Muslims. Its ultimate objective is Allah's rule over His entire creation, the globe and the skies. Therefore, jihad must lead to a change in the nature of the state and its institutions. And territory by territory, land by land, continent by continent, Allah's Word will blanket the globe.[8]

Interlocutors interviewed for this research, in many parts of the Islamic world, state the importance of jihad as the sole correct manner of liberating an occupied Islamic territory, restoring Islam to an area formerly under Muslim rule or introducing Islam to a "land of jihad". This is an essential condition for these jihadist movements – elections and referenda are not adequate, because the manner of introducing or restoring Islam determines the nature of the state which results; hence the means are as important as the end. The best guarantee of a truly Islamic entity is liberation via jihad.

The views and positions of these interlocutors invariably display a two-track time and space schemata in the context of jihad, a constant shuffle between the global and eternal on the one hand, and the here and now on the other. The unwavering long-term objective of bringing about Allah's Rule over the entire globe, maybe in hundreds of years (numerology based on the Qur'an yields dates for certain territories), is balanced by the need for jihad in the contemporary instance: for example in Afghanistan, Chechnya, Iraq, Pakistan, Palestine and elsewhere.

Armed with belief and patience, determination and tenacity, the possibility of immediate action as well as an eternal promise, every jihadi is destined to be either a *ghazi* (conquerer, victor) or a *shaheed*. As jihadis have disclosed in interviews, "so ours is the victory, in each and every case".

The Islamic concept of "sacred space" is interpreted differently by jihadis: for them, a "land of jihad" is sacred space since it is a jihad battlefield – as are the spaces where Muslims congregate. In this sense a town or neighbourhood in the West that is largely populated by Muslims is considered "sacred space", to be protected and defended by jihad. The processes of globalization offer jihadis another "sacred space" which they will defend as robustly as they do terrestrial jihad.

Global jihad

Globalization cannot function without localization. That relationship is asymmetric, without shared values and an equitable distribution of resources. It results in an unequal exchange of benefits and advantages, to the detriment of the poorer parts of the world. These unbalanced flows enable uncivil socioeconomic and political norms to flourish. Since the jihadis cannot simply undertake a virtual jihad, they parallel that asymmetry to wage their own asymmetric warfare.

Traditional defensive jihad was fought in a local area; offensive jihad (considered a priori defensive jihad) was fought in distant "lands of jihad". There are numerous rulings on taking the initiative: "This means pursuing the kuffar in their lands and calling them to Islam and fighting them if they do not agree to submit to the rule of Islam. This type of jihad is a communal obligation upon the Muslims" (al-Munajjid 2007). The classic concept aside, it is the tactic of "hit them where it hurts" that drives modern jihadism, as it does the "war on terror".

The internationalization of jihad through "foreign" jihadis (referring to non-locals, or Muslims born and/or raised in the West, or converts) is a huge benefit to these movements. More than just the expertise brought over by veterans, imported jihadis act as a link to groups elsewhere, in particular in their home countries. Recently, the salient example of an internationalized or globalized jihad was Bosnia. Jihadis from across the Islamic world, as well as from the West, made their way – either singly or in small groups, organized or on their own – to fight for Islam in Europe.

Violent jihad

As a result of primary research on many continents, the following characteristics can be indentified as essential for militant and violent jihad and suicide operations, whether in the home territory, in the overseas territory of migration, or elsewhere:

1 A cause that resonates naturally and deeply (Islam), the grievances growing stronger with actual or perceived attacks or violations.
2 A charismatic figure who attracts, encourages and guides, making direct participation desirable (e.g. an imam, teacher or local figurehead who incorporates an idealized distant figure, such as Osama bin Laden).
3 A local cell (for practical arrangements to execute operations).
4 A plan which translates the yearning for jihad into implementation (e.g. dispatching recruits for training or to the battlefield in a "land of jihad", or organizing suicide bombers, arms and materiel).
5 A network whose tentacles spread wide and deep into the Islamic ummah (community) on many continents (metanetwork and networks of networks).

Criminality

For a grouping that swears by the Sharia, jihadis have a peculiar attitude to legality and criminality: since only Allah's Laws are to be obeyed, the laws and legal institutions of non-Sharia states range from the irrelevant to the sinful. An extrapolation from this position is that whereas using drugs and narcotics is forbidden, trafficking in these illicit products is not a sin – provided the activity and the earnings serve Allah's Cause, such as jihad, charity and other good works for the Muslim community.

Hence, cultivating narcotic drugs, turning opium into heroin, trafficking in illegal substances, smuggling, criminal and other anti-social behaviours such as abduction, kidnapping, extortion, robbery, bank hold-ups, counterfeiting, piracy, money laundering, etc., are all permissible in order to generate the funds required to support a higher mission. Taliban figures have verified: "We provide desperately needed jobs with which our cadres and supporters can feed their families."

Where there is doubt, jihadis have a like-minded cleric issue a *fatwa* (edict) which provides precedence, justification and a religion-based cover for the activity. A fatwa is enough to overcome hesitation and encourage emulation.[9]

Verifiable hard data on the value of financial flows from transnational illegal activity are difficult to compute accurately. Most organizations such as the World Bank use a complex system of extrapolation to arrive at figures and amounts. For example, in the case of Afghanistan, the United Nations Office on Drugs and Crime (UNODC) puts the export value for Afghan traffickers of opium, morphine and heroin at border prices in neighbouring countries at US$4 billion in 2007, US$3.4 billion in 2008, and US$2.8 billion in 2009. Tapping into and facilitating this illicit trade provides jihadist groups with ample funding for their enterprise – for example, UNODC calculates that the Taliban makes US$125 million in annual profits from opiates alone. When supply outstrips demand, leading to a fall in prices, the Taliban appears to manipulate the opium market through hoarding and taking a passive attitude towards drug cultivation instead of actively promoting it, to reduce the fall in prices (UNODC 2008; 2009).

The big drug money from Afghan narcotics, however, is made in Europe, with the street value of the opiates priced at US$2.8 billion (for Afghan producers), translating into over US$55 billion globally – greater than the GDP of many small countries. Along the delivery routes towards Europe there are increases in price between countries, and at different borders. For example, the price at the Afghan–Iran border is lower than that at the Iran–Turkish border. In general, the farther the contraband moves away from its point of origin, the higher the price – whose most important determinant is the risk factor. The smuggling routes run northwards through central Asia and westwards into Europe; eastwards through Iran and into Turkey, via maritime routes to the Gulf; from Turkey into Western Europe, via Central Asia or the Balkans. Another route runs southwards into Pakistan, and from there to the Gulf, and on to Europe.

Along with the trade in illegal narcotics, jihadist organizations also exploit the illegal trade in tobacco products. At a World Health Organization meeting in Geneva, participants were informed that cigarette and tobacco smuggling were financing militant or extremist groups such as the Taliban and sapping approximately US$40 billion per year from government budgets in lost revenue. Researchers also alleged that "half a dozen terrorist" or militant groups, including the Taliban, Al Qaeda in the Islamic Maghreb, Hezbollah, left-wing FARC (Revolutionary Armed Forces of Colombia) rebels in Colombia and the Real IRA (Irish Republican Army) in Northern Ireland, relied on black market tobacco for revenue. David Kaplan, editorial director of the US-based Centre for Public Integrity, argues: "We believe that tobacco has been second only to drugs as a source of finance to the Pakistani Taliban" (*Dawn* 2009).

Revival of traditional networks

Jihadis as well as smugglers are reviving historical, regional and local cultural practices – predating modern globalization – to support and carry out jihad and to introduce, regionalize and globalize the phenomenon.

Traffickers and smugglers transfer and trade using connections based on family, clan, and tribal and organizational networks. These follow age-old patterns of seasonal nomadic migration and historical trade patterns and pathways such as the silk routes across Central Asia. Traditional markets have been resuscitated in recent times (e.g. sites of ancient slave auctions have turned into arms bazaars). Reviving former networks, no matter how old or dilapidated, is easier than creating new ones. Well after the fall of the Saddam Hussein regime in Iraq, an international entity discovered that a flooding of the black market with drugs, arms and other contraband was facilitated by the activation of smuggling networks set up by the former regime to circumvent the crippling sanctions of the preceding decade.[10]

The waters referred to as the Gulf of Oman have historically supported one of history's busiest trading and shipping networks. This geopolitical commercial area covers the Arabian Sea from Pakistan in the east, along the Gulf to the Shatt al-Arab river and the Red Sea in the west, the Horn of Africa, along the Somali coast and even down to Zanzibar and the Kenyan coast to the south.

While water routes have carried people and goods throughout history, the imposition of tighter air transport controls have led insurgents, jihadis, terrorists, smugglers and traffickers to revert to the use of the maritime environment – or a mix of marine and land routes – to transport personnel, cash, high-value commodities, arms, explosives and equipment and supplies.

Methods and practices designed for regular innocuous activity have been adapted for criminal or terrorist use thousands of miles away. Breath-holding techniques developed over centuries for deep-sea pearl diving in the Gulf are practised by jihadis in rivers and lakes in Pakistan and Afghanistan to evade detection or capture. A jihadi recounted to me how he had once escaped from detention by floating across a river on an empty clay pitcher – the idea came to him when a less fundamentalist fellow detainee sang an ancient Punjabi love song in which the beloved, using a jar to get to a tryst with her lover, drowns.

Another maritime hub is the Straits of Malacca in South East Asia, where local jihadist groups engage in activities and use techniques which parallel those in the Oman waters; while the exchange of ideas, views, funds, trainers and material among these networks is nothing new, their magnitude and scope is. Also fairly new are links between maritime and land-based networks, which collaborate in developing the easiest, simplest and most efficient ways to move people and goods.[11]

Global enterprise, global cell

The following example shows how the basic principles of globalization were used by a 19-member global smuggling enterprise engaged in both legal and illegal activities. The cell was arrested and tried for smuggling drugs from Pakistan to the Netherlands, with planning and financing organized out of the United Arab Emirates (UAE). The drugs were hidden in towels in Faisalabad (a major textile manufacturing centre in Pakistan), repackaged in cartons and trucked to Karachi, where they were placed in a container for shipment. The consignment left Karachi for Sri Lanka, where the cargo was routed on another vessel sailing to Southampton, in the UK, from where the drug-towels were trucked to Antwerp, in Belgium. The cargo was impounded by Belgian police just before it reached the Dutch border.

In this example, a self-sufficient "global" cell formed around the technical expertise and infrastructure required for major illegal activity. The majority of its members were Pakistani. A British citizen of Pakistani origin, resident in the UAE and a wealthy owner of a number of legitimate businesses, was the main planner and financier.[12] His partners in the deal were other British citizens of Pakistani origin or Pakistanis: those based in the UAE owned legitimate businesses dealing with export-import, trading, information technology, money exchange, hotels, cyber cafés and auto sales; one was an economics professor, another had the task of using the fax machine at the place where he worked to communicate with other members. They also ran parallel illegitimate businesses: the owner of the auto showroom, a Pakistani with residency in Japan but living in the UAE, dealt in drugs and stolen cars from overseas and was also a financier of the deal.

The smugglers based in Pakistan had a similar range of activities: one owned the licence for an airline company and coordinated with shipping companies, another was in charge of receiving and disbursing the funds and developing future smuggling projects; a key figure was a port official who cleared the cargo against payment; another UK national of Pakistani origin, with expertise in customs clearace and complex shipping, acted as consultant in exchange for a percentage of the profits – he also imported and exported stolen and expired goods. Adding to the globalized nature of such cells, many Pakistani businessmen, as well as smugglers and criminals who work in the Gulf, provide huge sums to jihadist groups as well as to charities; it is not easy to trace the origin or end use of the donations.[13]

Of the three native Europeans, one was a Dutchman who partnered in a UAE company and was considered one of the biggest drug dealers in Europe – his company was the consignee for the shipment; one was a Belgian living in the UAE whose role was as recipient of the consignment in Belgium; and the third was another Dutchman who was the main buyer of the smuggled drugs.

Transfer of funds

A preferred method of transferring funds is the popular informal and alternative system which is difficult to detect or trace and far cheaper than modern financial instruments, institutions or channels. This parallel banking is done via a chain of known personal contacts and is based on absolute trust. The best-known system is *hawala* (Arabic for "change" or "transform", hence a promissory note) or *hundi* (Sanskrit root, meaning "collect", an ancient South Asian credit instrument) – the words are often used interchangeably. National and international authorities have been unable to make even a dent in this traditional system, which has been used since time immemorial in Africa, Asia and the Middle East.

Migrant communities brought it to the West. Simply put, a person hands over the cash at one location and receives a name, telephone number and sometimes a code word; anyone in possession of these three items of information can receive the cash at the other end.

Despite the intricate cash-exchange arrangements of these networks it is false to believe that they are rooted purely in creating wealth. "It is a fallacy that our lifeblood, our oxygen, is cash," a Punjabi mid-level organizer of jihadist activity told me. "We need jihad to live, to survive – everything else is logistics. Of course cash is important, but it is neither the starting point nor the most essential in our work." The small to modest sums required for major operations complement these activities. During interviews, jihadis have quoted the low amounts necessary for their operations and explained that "Allah and His people ensure we receive enough to carry out our work".[14]

On occasion, gold or other commodities are traded instead of cash. Depending upon circumstances, the trading may not involve a physical transfer of goods. Handing over the commodity at one end and receiving cash at the other, or vice versa, is also popular. For a marriage in an extended jihadist family with members spread over Pakistan, the Gulf, Germany, the United Kingdom and the United States, cash and/or high-value goods were handed over to a *hawaladar* (hawala operator) in 13 locations. A few days later, cash, gold for jewellery, a TV set, household electric gadgets and a car were handed over to the family of the bride and groom – who were cousins – in their home town.[15]

Throughout history, parallel banking has been part of the international financial system and – except in countries where laws penalizing this system have been enacted – perfectly legal. Even where it is not, people continue to use the system – because it is quick, cheap and efficient.

For Muslims, hawala is compliant with the Sharia; for non-Muslims, it offers compliance with practices which are based on tradition, honour and a high comfort level. Non-Muslims make as much use of the hawala transfer as do Muslims. Nor is the system restricted to hawala or hundi – a variation is the "flying money" used by Chinese communities.

No one can accurately compute the amounts which criss-cross the globe annually via the hawala or hundi system. Estimates for 2008 range between tens and hundreds of US$ billions. These rough estimates are extrapolated from a matrix of socioeconomic data covering formal remittances, earnings, cost of living and cultural patterns. From time to time, in the case of jihadist groups, a rise in bank heists corresponds to a temporary curtailment in funding inflows from overseas as well as to the requirement of larger amounts for complex and high-tech terrorist operations.

For the jihadis, money laundering is a barter system, without negative or illegal connotations; it is simply one more method of acquiring, transfering or using cash, goods or services – both to support themselves and to finance the jihad.

Actors

Substate or non-state actors – whether revolutionaries, rebels, insurgents, jihadis, terrorists, mercenaries or criminals – behave similarly, though the rhetoric and discourse may differ. These actors exploit grey areas offered by weak states with rampant corruption and no rule of law; they correctly assume that national, regional or international intelligence systems do not have the capacity, resources, interest or political will to track their activities across borders; they adapt in ways that make tracking them difficult; they network, overlap and function in a national or subregional environment of failing states and collapsing structures; and they often deliver what the state cannot or will not – speedy justice, a livelihood, basic services, an identity and power based on affiliation – counting on the sympathy and support of those in far-flung communities. If any of the latter were done in a positive context, they would be consistent with the definitions and expectations of true globalists.

Adopting new technology

The need for the world-wide web arose "'from the geographical dispersion of large collaborations, and the fast turnover of fellows, students, and visiting scientists,' who had to get 'up to speed on projects and leave a lasting contribution before leaving'" (quoted in Zeltser 1995). From its origins in the 1960s, when the US initiated research on the development and use of computer networks for military application, to the development of the web, nothing has enabled globalization as much as the almost "free" use of borderless, uncontrolled cyberspace to connect people and ideas, set up metanetworks across the globe, communicate in real time, exchange vast quantities of information, report events, store and retrieve data, teach, convince, recruit, plan – and help to execute jihad beyond borders.

Jihadist "software" – ideas, concepts, practices, traditions, techniques, enthusiasm, zeal, tenacity, patience – is even more easily globalized than its "hardware" – the trade and transfers of supplies and equipment as well as the exchanges of clerics, commanders and trainers. In the Islamic world, or wherever there are Muslim communities, the easiest recruitment for jihad traditionally takes place in the mosque or the *madrassa* (Islamic school attached to the mosque). Now, the internet and email as well as various platforms, websites, blogs and other means facilitate the quick spread of the call. Jihadist literature is dispatched all over the world via cyberspace. Enthusiastic jihadis set up and administer websites in many languages and translate and post jihadist news.

These sites seem to attract jihadis who crave action on the battlefield and attach themselves – in person and in cyberspace – to clerics who advocate violence. "We want action, not rhetoric," jihadis tell me. This is partly why fatwas issued in favour of suicide operations are more powerful and find greater resonance than those against. Through the web, jihadis research and exchange fatwas and positions that support their brand of jihad.

Some websites focus on local jihad, others cover a region or a theme, while some attempt to span the globe. Websites which carry inflammatory material (explicit hate literature) or incite to violence are often hacked or shut down, but quickly resurface with another internet provider address. Although jihadist literature is still printed in as great numbers as before, for local consumption, the internet allows jihad-sponsoring groups to circumvent censorship and other controls. Desktop publishing based on global feeds ensure easy dissemination via CDs or compressed files when jihadist printing houses are forced to shut down.

The immediacy of news, and visuals in particular, plays a major role in fuelling outrage and anger in the Islamic world, and in increasing anger and grievances even among those who do not engage in militant jihad. Mobile internet has turned the ubiquitous cellphone into an instant delivery system. Jihadist internet aficionados attack anti-jihad websites. In mid-2009, the self-styled "Cyber Unit of the Ansar" sent a note to Kavkaz Center boasting that it had shut down a number of Russian websites through cyber attacks.[16]

In view of the geographic dispersion of the jihadis and the "lands of jihad", requirement for speed, and the desirability of making a lasting contribution before departing this life, the web immeasurably facilitates the work of cross-border jihad.

Conclusion

Globalization will not go away. Neither, for now, will militant Islamism or jihad: its adherents will remain in search of perpetual jihad. However, there are pressing issues which need redress irrespective of their link to violence, such as poverty, marginalization, alienation, an unremitting lack of basic services, of employable skills, jobs, good governance, democracy, rule of law, access to justice, protection of human rights, and the possibility of a future – of, simply, a decent life.

If economic refugees and asylum seekers stayed home because conditions were better – if conditions were acceptable in their own area – would jihadis continue to migrate seeking "lands of jihad"? I posed this question to a senior cleric-commander. He responded, "Some may remain, but pure mujahids are not swayed by economic or financial gains. They do jihad because they are jihadis. Until death."

However, another view, perhaps even more important, is also articulated with passion. In a wide-ranging discussion with a group of young tribal jihadis, all from a middle-class background with no prior association with extremism, who had collectively decided to leave university in Peshawar without completing their Master's degrees and to join jihad, they had this to say:

> Our state has sold out, our rulers are corrupt. We have no hope of improvement in our lives, our land does not produce enough to feed us, our natural resources are stolen from us, our education does not guarantee us employment, our people die like flies when death rains from the skies; and "international law" is selective and exclusionary. First and foremost, we want justice. We do not want charity. If we have justice as a right, and if our laws are just, we can get jobs, we can finance decent lives. Our jihad is for justice, for a better world for our children, for a better world for everyone.

Notes

This chapter is based on material from the author's work in progress covering *inter alia* Muslim suicide bombers, martyrdom, jihadist militancy, jihad Sharia and rule of law. The second and third epigraphs to the chapter are from author interviews, January 2009 and March 1998.

1. Author interview, Karachi, 2005.
2. From one of the author's interviews in the Gaza Strip, 1997–9.
3. Author interview with university-educated jihadist commander, Pakistan–Afghanistan border, 2007.
4. Ibid.
5. Ibid.
6. For more on this, see Charles Goredema, chapter 5 in this volume.
7. Dorcas Ettang discusses this above (chapter 8).
8. Author interviews, the Punjab, Pakistan, 1999–2009.
9. Author collection of fatwas on jihad, martyrdom and related themes.
10. Author research, Central Asia, 2003; re Iraq, information from source based in Baghdad, 2005.
11. Author research on traditional methods and routes, 2003–8, as part of a larger research project.
12. After the trial, US authorities froze the assets of 9 suspects and 13 enterprises with ties to him.
13. Author research, the Gulf, background information from security officials, 2007–8.
14. Author interview, Gujranwala, Pakistan, May 2005.

15. Author visit to jihadist family home, Faisalabad, Pakistan, May 2005.
16. Author interview with the head of one of Pakistan's most hard-core jihadist groups, the Punjab, Pakistan, December 2008.

REFERENCES

Al-Munajjid, Muhammad Saleh (2007) "Ruling on physical jihad", KavkazCenter.com, 24 Aug. At <http://www.kavkazcenter.net/eng/content/2007/08/24/9652.shtml> (accessed June 2010).

Dawn (2009) "Cigarette smuggling funding terrorists", Dawn.com, 20 June. At <http://www.dawn.com/wps/wcm/connect/dawn-content-library/dawn/the-newspaper/front-page/cigarette-smuggling-funding-terrorists-069> (accessed June 2010).

Nuscheler, Franz (2002) "Globalization: Is the South losing touch?", *Adult Education and Development*, 58. At <http://www.iiz-dvv.de/index.php?article_id=420&clang=1> (accessed June 2010).

UNODC (2008) "Drugs finance Taliban war machine, says UN drug czar", United Nations Office on Drugs and Crime, 27 Nov. At <http://www.unodc.org/unodc/en/press/releases/2008-11-27.html> (accessed June 2010).

UNODC (2009) "Addiction, crime and insurgency: The transnational threat of Afghan opium", United Nations Office on Drugs and Crime, Oct. At <www.unodc.org/unodc/en/data-and-analysis/addiction-crime-and-insurgency.html> (accessed June 2010).

UNODC (2010) *The Globalization of Crime: Transnational Organized Crime Threat Assessment.* New York: United Nations Office on Drugs and Crime.

Zeltser, Larry (1995) "The world-wide web: Origins and beyond", Zeltser.com. At <http://www.zeltser.com/web-history/> (accessed June 2010).

10

Security challenges in a unipolar globalized world

M. J. Akbar

It has been, historically, easier to protect an empire than to establish it. The axiom holds in a post-empire age, when a superpower protects its interests through alliances, or, to use the term favoured by its antagonists, neo-colonies. A superpower, by definition, has a global presence and power, which it preserves because the challenge is, almost always, regional. The superpower can, consequently, mobilize its assets from across the globe to subdue a regional challenge.

The shift in the twenty-first century is that the challenge is also being orchestrated through a global network, fragmenting the response of the superpower and weakening its ability to strike back. The epicentre of the confrontation between America and its antagonists is the region between Palestine-Iraq and Afghanistan-Pakistan, now in near-perpetual warfare provoked by cause and effect. There are wide differences of cause, interest and objective between the many forces that seek to eliminate the American presence from their midst, and mutual antagonisms may be as bitter as their dislike of America, but this is of little comfort to Washington and the Pentagon. The wars provoked by 9/11, in Afghanistan and Iraq, have weakened America militarily and politically, reducing its ability to influence events (at least for the moment) even in crucial trouble spots like Israel-Palestine and potentially game-changing nations like Iran.

Iraq and Afghanistan are separated by Iran. The history of US–Iran, US–Afghan and US–Iraq relations runs along parallel grooves, one bilateral groove and the other interrelated. In 1979 America's military intervention in Iran, after its diplomats were taken hostage, ended in humiliation due to uncharacteristically indecisive leadership. The Soviet occupation of Afghanistan the same year changed the geopolitical dynamic; America chose the Afghanistan–Pakistan border as its preferred battleground, and encouraged Saddam Hussein's Iraq to go to war with Iran. A war-impoverished Saddam thought he had similar licence in Kuwait, forcing not only the first Gulf War, but also creating conditions for Al Qaeda to turn against America. Eventually, the only sanctuary that Osama bin Laden found was in Afghanistan, from where he launched 9/11.

America's response in Afghanistan was inevitable; in fact, America had little option but to destroy the Taliban. Its move against Saddam Hussein was more opaque, and hence open to more interpretations. Seven years after 2003, questions linger about the reasons for the military intervention. It seems that President George W. Bush invaded Iraq to destroy Saddam Hussein, dismantle an actual or potential nuclear infrastructure, introduce democracy and regain American influence over an oil-rich nation. Framed through this lens, the US was exploiting post 9/11 goodwill to solidify its influence in an oil-rich and turbulent region.

But Bush's success has led to unintended consequences, including the unlikely strengthening of Iran as a regional power. The long war has exacted a strategic price that is being paid[1] by Bush's successor, Barack Obama, as the US leadership of the world comes under severe strain. Despite the defeat of Saddam Hussein in Iraq, security challenges in the Middle East have become increasingly complicated, signalling that the US's venture has proved pointless, if not completely fruitless. This chapter uses the US intervention in Iraq to demonstrate how the interconnected nature of globalization makes it difficult for a dominant unipolar actor to assert its own national interests. In this instance, the fall of Hussein resulted in the inadvertent strengthening of Iran, further complicating the US situation. This chapter begins by placing the nature of US relations in the Middle East in a historical context before surveying the various contemporary concerns that influence American foreign policy in the region. The chapter then focuses on the nuclear security situation as it relates to Iran–US relations. As is evident from the US intervention in Iraq, the increasing speed of globalization has meant that old models of foreign relations no longer hold. By attempting to assert its military and strategic primacy the US has now altered the geopolitical situation in the Middle East, creating new realities that are at least as dangerous to America as the ones they replaced.

American foreign relations and the Middle East

The Islamic revolution of 1979 left Iran friendless and vulnerable. To the west, in Iraq, Saddam Hussein, who had a working relationship with the deposed Shah of Iran, was concerned about an Iran-inspired Shia insurgency. To the south, Saudi Arabia was provoked by an open challenge from the Ayatollah Khomeini, who lamented that the holiest cities of Islam had gone under the control of a regime loyal to America. To Iran's east, leftists beholden to the Soviet Union, described by Khomeini as the "lesser Satan", but a Satan nevertheless, ruled Afghanistan.

America, upset at the fall of the Shah, waited cautiously to see what the Ayatollahs would do once they had exhausted their rhetoric. Immature bravado destroyed any possibility of rapprochement. In November 1979, university students seized 52 Americans working in the Tehran embassy and held them hostage for 444 days.[2] In December, Soviet troops marched into Kabul to prop up their loyalists, and America's attention shifted from a problem to an opportunity. Washington challenged the Soviets on the battlefields of Afghanistan, managing the war from the safe haven of Pakistan. This was done principally through the office of a delighted Pakistani president, General Zia ul Huq, and the interservices intelligence agency that reported directly to him, the ISI. In the meantime, Washington outsourced the conflict with Iran to an unacknowledged proxy, Iraq.[3]

Saddam Hussein, encouraged from the shadows, tested Tehran in 1981 with an invasion, but Iran proved less brittle than he had estimated. Over eight years, war drained both nations until Khomeini accepted a ceasefire. The Ayatollah died in 1989 from old age. Famously, former US Secretary of State Henry Kissinger had wanted both sides to lose in this war, and he proved prophetic. Following the Iran–Iraq war, an inflamed, self-obsessed, debt-ridden Hussein overreached and occupied Kuwait in 1990.

The Al Qaeda turning point

The early 1990s constituted the high point of American triumph and goodwill across the world: the fall of the Berlin wall, Soviet defeat and disintegration, the military victory over Hussein in Kuwait, and a domestic economic boom. Iran seemed little more than a pesky fly that could be swatted when someone had the time to do so. However, as the decade progressed, Afghanistan had become a hopeless mess, and American Senators avoided a radically changed country rather than chasing its soil to pose for pictures with the mujahedin. President Bill Clinton, wrapped up mainly in domestic concerns, let the region drift along its own dangerous currents. Afghanistan descended from confusion to chaos.

In the winter of 1994, Pakistan intervened unilaterally. It armed and financed a group of students, led by a then-unknown Mullah Omar, who took swift advantage of the disarray and established a Taliban government. A Sunni theocracy had fought its way to power adjacent to a Shia theocracy, but that is where the comparison ended. The state structure and polity of Afghanistan were primitive compared to Iran. Relations between the Taliban and Iran were frozen and hostile. Through the years of Taliban rule the region seemed locked in an arid impasse. The only plant that flourished in the Pak-Taliban wasteland was a poisonous growth called Al Qaeda.

It was this group that would trigger seismic change by launching an attack on US soil. Washington's immediate response to attacks against the World Trade Center and Pentagon on 11 September 2001 was unequivocal. When the Taliban refused to hand over Osama bin Laden, American and British forces invaded and forced the Taliban from power. President Bush's second war, in 2003, was more controversial in both origin and consequence. Iran could not have received a more generous gift; it had been liberated from two implacable foes that had blocked its regional flexibility. In both Iraq and Afghanistan, American intervention inspired armed resistance movements, providing Iran a further opportunity to weaken America.

The tea leaves were easy to decipher in Tehran because the Pentagon made no secret of its problems. General Richard A. Cody, the Army Vice Chief of Staff, testified to the Senate Armed Services Committee that the Army had gone "out of balance". He admitted: "The current demand for our forces in Iraq and Afghanistan exceeds the sustainable supply, and limits our ability to provide ready forces for other contingencies . . . our readiness is being consumed as fast as we build it" (Cody 2008). In 2006, the US Army was granting "moral waivers" to thousands of new recruits, meaning that a criminal record was not necessarily a hindrance to their joining the Armed forces.

Iran helped the Iraqi resistance until it achieved a vital Iranian objective: the announcement of the withdrawal of American troops. America had done Iran a historic favour by removing Saddam. But the continued presence of permanent American bases in Iraq constituted a direct threat to Iran, particularly when American politicians were competing in their belligerence towards Tehran. The Iraqi insurgency became Iran's first line of defence, and continued until there was recognition in Washington that a long-term presence in Iraq was untenable.

Simultaneously, a message went out to the Coalition in Baghdad, and was understood, that America's interests in the region could not override Iran's. When the agreement on the withdrawal of American troops was signed in 2008, there was no provision for a permanent American military base.

By altering the power balance, America's intervention in Iraq has helped to make the region safer for Iran. The Pentagon made a strategic error in 2003: while it had the correct measure of Hussein's forces, it underestimated the formidable striking power of shadow armies, a multitude of insurgent groups working under different, and sometimes mutually hostile, banners, but temporarily united by a common enemy. In retrospect, it can be argued that Bush invaded the wrong country in 2003. In Iran, the US would have found a nuclear infrastructure, thus satisfying the limited needs of public opinion. In Iraq, the Bush administration used a "weapons of mass destruction" thesis that was exposed as a lie. Bush was seriously hampered by lack of credibility in his confrontation with Iran.

In fact, by the end of Bush's second term, America had all but admitted that any form of political or military stability in Iraq was impossible without Iran's cooperation.[4] In return, Iran extracted a slow and measured compensation, the pace of which has been accelerated in the post-Bush era. Despite its effective nuclear programme, Iran received a good-character certificate from America's National Intelligence Estimate (NIE) in 2007. Iran's president, Mahmoud Ahmadinejad, called the NIE assessment a "declaration of surrender" (Dahl 2007).

A safer place for Iran

An effective "Shia space" now extends from Herat in west Afghanistan to the border of Syria and the northern, Shia-dense districts of Saudi Arabia. The Sunni counterweight has been lightened considerably and the region has been adapting for a while. Relations between Saudi Arabia and Iran are at least lukewarm if not warm. Smaller Arab states try to take out whatever insurance policies are on the anvil. In 2007, the Gulf States invited Ahmadinejad to speak at their annual meetings in Manama and Bahrain – home port of the American fleet in the Gulf – and suggested an expansion of relations with Tehran. In 2008, Saudi Foreign Minister Saud al-Faisal told an Iran–Saudi parliamentary friendship meeting in Riyadh that all efforts should be made to solidify Saudi-Iranian relations, and both should "stand vigilantly against all conspiracies" (quoted in Cherian 2008).

King Abdullah of Saudi Arabia raised the bar when he invited Ahmadinejad to join the 2007 Haj as his personal guest; the invitation was accepted. During Bush's visit to Saudi Arabia in January 2008, *New York Times* columnist Maureen Dowd, travelling with the President, quoted an unnamed "insider at the Saudi royal court" as saying, "We don't need America to dictate our enemies to us, especially when it's our neighbour." Though given anonymously, there is little doubt that the comment was not given accidentally.

On 2 and 3 March 2008, Baghdad received its first state visit from a Middle East nation. Ahmadinejad drove in calmly from the airport, making an ostentatious display of the fact that he did not need the heavy security of Bush, Blair or Brown – the three principal architects of the Iraq invasion. He only briefly entered the Green Zone (the secure area within which American officials and the government operate), to call on the Prime Minister Nuri Kamal al-Maliki, and instead spent more time outside the security area. Maliki described the talks as "friendly, positive and full of trust". Iraq's Kurdish President, Jalal Talabani, who speaks Farsi, asked Ahmadinejad to call him "Uncle" (quoted in Scheer 2008). The implication drawn from Ahmadinejad's visit was that he was safer outside the Green Zone than the Iraqi government was within it.

In Baghdad, Ahmadinejad equated Hussein with America, saying "dictators and foreigners have tried to tarnish and undermine the emotional relations between two states [Iran and Iraq]" (quoted in Akbar 2008). On the second day of his visit he was quoted as saying that the foreign presence in Iraq "was an insult to the regional nations and a humiliation ... We believe that the major powers who have come to the region from thousands of kilometers away should respect the will of nations and leave this region" (Tran 2008). He told a news conference on 2 March: "Six years ago, there were no terrorists in our region. As soon as others landed in this country and this region, we witnessed their arrival and their presence" (Associated Press 2008). On 3 March, CNN reported that Ahmadinejad travelled quite freely in Baghdad, and assessed that the only winner of the invasion and occupation of Iraq seemed to be Iran. It quoted senior Iraqi officials, speaking on the condition of anonymity, that they consistently heard two points being made in talks: Iran was a neighbour and on the way to becoming a nuclear power; America was thousands of miles away. Iran offered Iraq a billion dollar loan before Ahmadinejad returned home.

Far less ostentatiously, Iran began to send the occasional feeler to Washington. Ayatollah Ali Khamenei declared that he was not permanently opposed to ties with the United States. The departure of Donald Rumsfeld from the Bush cabinet became the starting point of a graded implementation of the Baker-Hamilton recommendation of a dialogue with Tehran without any dilution in the policy of eliminating its weapons capability.

On 13 January 2008, the head of the Iranian Revolutionary Guard Corps

> slipped into the green zone of Baghdad last month [December 2007] to press Tehran's hard-line position over the terms of the current talks with American officials, it was claimed last week. Iraqi government sources say that Major

> General Mohammed Ali Jafari, 50, travelled secretly from Tehran. Jafari appeared to have passed through checkpoints on his way into the fortified enclave that contains the American embassy and Iraqi ministries, even though he is on Washington's "most wanted" list. Last year Washington condemned the Revolutionary Guard Corps as a "foreign terrorist organization" and imposed sanctions on it. (Colvin 2008)

The Corps had been accused of supplying rockets, mortars and roadside bombs known as explosively formed projectiles (EFPs) to Shia militias in Iraq through the Quds Force, one of its units. Jafari's mission was to broaden the scope of talks between Ryan Crocker, the American ambassador to Iraq, and Hassan Kazemi Qomi, his Iranian counterpart, to include the release of Iranian diplomats being held in Baghdad by the Americans. There is speculation that Saudi Arabia had helped facilitate US–Iran contacts.

It is apparent that the Pentagon also reached some form of understanding with the most militant of the pro-Iranian Iraqi Shia clerics, Moqtada al-Sadr, before General David Petraeus's "Surge" in 2007 that wound down the war. Sadr pole-vaulted from most-wanted in 2005 to most-helpful in 2007, when he announced a "ceasefire". *The Economist* (2008) reported that Petraeus had praised Sadr as "responsible". Ironically, up until 2006, Sadr and his Mahdi Army were considered the greatest threat to Iraq's future. It is possible that America now recognizes Sadr as part of Iraq's future.

Sadr used this "ceasefire" to go back to school[5] at the famous seminary at Qom, in Iran, an alma mater of Imam Khomeini. It is likely that Sadr probably sees himself as the future Khamanei of Iraq. But Iraq cannot be another Iran, if only because the population is not homogeneous, but Shias will be in effective control of Baghdad. That, in essence, has been Bush's gift to the Shia community. Iraq and Iran are, and are likely to remain, allies. It has been reported that when a major American oil company showed interest in some Iraqi oil fields, it was told by the oil ministry in Baghdad that it might be worthwhile to get Tehran's approval for the deal.

During Israel's widely condemned air-and-land attacks on Gaza in January 2009, Ahmadinejad wrote to King Abdullah daring him to prove that he was worthy of the claim, in his capacity as Custodian of the Two Holy Places, of being leader of the Muslim world. On 22 January the *Financial Times* published an article by Prince Turki Al-Faisal (2009), former director of Saudi intelligence, former ambassador to Britain and America, and now chairman of the King Faisal Centre for Research and Islamic Studies in Riyadh:

> Last week, President Mahmoud Ahmadi-Nejad [sic] of Iran wrote a letter to King Abdullah, explicitly recognizing Saudi Arabia as the leader of the Arab and Muslim worlds and calling on him to take a more confrontational role over "this obvious atrocity and killing of your own children" in Gaza. The communiqué is significant because the de facto recognition of the kingdom's primacy from one of its most ardent foes reveals the extent that the war has united an entire region, both Shia and Sunni. Further, Mr Ahmadi-Najad's call for Saudi Arabia to lead a jihad against Israel would, if pursued, create unprecedented chaos and bloodshed in the region.

Prince Turki used phrases more reminiscent of an intelligence chief than an ambassador:

> America is not innocent in this calamity. Not only has the Bush administration left a sickening legacy in the region – from the death of hundreds of thousands of Iraqis to the humiliation and torture at Abu Ghraib – but it has also, through an arrogant attitude about the butchery in Gaza, contributed to the slaughter of innocents. If the US wants to continue playing a leadership in the Middle East and keep its strategic alliances intact – especially its "special relationship" with Saudi Arabia – it will have to drastically revise its policies vis à vis Israel and Palestine. (Al-Faisal 2009)

A warning rarely comes in sharper language. As for the jihad against Israel:

> So far, the kingdom has resisted these calls, but every day this restraint becomes more difficult to maintain. When Israel deliberately kills Palestinians, appropriates their lands, destroys their homes, uproots their farms and imposes an inhuman blockade on them; and as the world laments once again the suffering of the Palestinians, people of conscience from every corner of the world are clamouring for action. Eventually, the kingdom will not be able to prevent its citizens from joining the worldwide revolt against Israel. (Al-Faisal 2009)

Iran had made remarkable progress, with the right mix of deference and diplomacy, in co-opting powerful members of the Saudi establishment towards its own agenda.

Eight days after this piece was published, the Associated Press (2009b) put out a story that quoted General John Craddock, the American who is NATO's supreme allied commander, as saying that "NATO would not oppose individual member nations making deals with Iran to supply their forces in Afghanistan as an alternative to using increasingly risky routes from Pakistan". A few days earlier, NATO's secretary general, Jaap de Hoop Scheffer, had urged members, including the United States, to "engage with Iran to combat Taliban militants in Afghanistan" (Associated

Press 2009b). The Pentagon and NATO had concluded that the war in Afghanistan needed Iran's active assistance as well.

Reassessing US-Iranian relations

President Barack Obama spoke of conciliation with Iran in his inaugural address on 20 January 2009, and followed it up in an interview to the television channel Al Arabiya, saying that "if countries like Iran are willing to unclench their fist, they will find an extended hand from us" (CBS News 2009). Ahmadinejad, who offered a carrot in the form of a congratulatory message to the new President, could not resist fiddling with a stick as well. He demanded that America should apologize for 60 years of bad behaviour.

Tehran's formal response came at a symbolic moment, during the televised rally marking the thirtieth anniversary of the Islamic revolution. Ahmadinejad's language was comparatively warm, even if some sentences had the feel of bureaucratic vetting: "The new US administration has said that it wants change and it wants to hold talks with Iran. It is clear that change should be fundamental, not tactical, and our people welcome real changes. Our nation is ready to hold talks based on mutual respect and in a fair atmosphere" (quoted in Fathi 2009).

It then addressed the most important concern of the United States: "The Iranian nation is the biggest victim of terrorism ... If you really want to uproot terrorism, let's cooperate to find the initiators of the recent wars in the Middle East and the Persian Gulf region, try them and punish them" (quoted in Fathi 2009). If Ahmadinejad meant George Bush and Tony Blair, which he did – "Bush and his allies should be tried and punished" (quoted in Fathi 2009) – the Obama administration was not going to lose any sleep over this unlikely prospect.

A Stratfor report identified the next step:

> The foreign ministers of NATO states gathered Thursday in Brussels to discuss the pressing geopolitical topics of the day: Russia, Afghanistan and Iran. For some, it was a summit filled with hope; for others, intense fear; for all, groundbreaking change. At the summit, US Secretary of State Hillary Clinton first leaked – and then openly announced – that she would like to invite Iran to an international conference on 31 March to map out a strategy for Afghanistan. This was the first real sign from the Obama administration that it intends to follow through with its pledge to extend a hand to Iran, should Tehran "unclench its fist" – beginning with a multilateral setting in which Iran's regional influence would be recognized. (Stratfor Global Intelligence 2009)

On 20 March, the Persian New Year, Obama made a gesture of some significance to Tehran. He offered Iran a "partnership", and invited it to "take its rightful place in the community of nations" (quoted in Spetalnick and Hafezi 2009). He did not make any reference to Iran's nuclear programme. Most important, he referred to the nation as the "Islamic Republic of Iran", thereby recognizing the legitimacy of the regime that had taken American diplomats hostage three decades before. Supreme leader Ayatollah Ali Khamenei chose to respond. Amid the usual finger-wagging lay a hint of the real response: it would be based on reason, not emotion.

A few days before the 31 March conference, Iran announced that it would attend the conference to discuss Afghanistan at The Hague. From this, it can be assumed that there will be a gradual escalation of cooperation between Iran and the US-led NATO forces in Afghanistan.

However, in the aftermath of the 2009 Iranian presidential elections, it remains to be seen how the US and Iran will move forward. The Obama administration has hinted that the political situation in Iran could harm the prospects for cooperation. Secretary of State Hillary Clinton, speaking at the Council for Foreign Relations, said: "Neither the president nor I have any illusions that dialogue with the Islamic Republic will guarantee success of any kind, and the prospects have certainly shifted in the weeks following the election" (quoted in CNN 2009).

The nuclear power game

There is little doubt, however, that Iran has achieved recognition as a regional power. Iran's priority now is to obtain tacit recognition of its nuclear programme as the counterpoint to Israel, much in the way that the United States accepted Pakistan's right to respond to India's nuclear weapons capability.

There are currently three levels in the hierarchy of nuclear states. At the top, the five victors of the Second World War – the US, Russia, the UK, France and China – have maintained their lock on the postwar world by arrogating the right to legal nuclear weapons and a veto in the United Nations Security Council. Following them, the Middle Three – Israel, India and Pakistan – have been permitted a status between legitimacy and untouchability. Two of the Middle Three are America's strategic allies and India is on its way to becoming one. And at the bottom there are a number of countries on the cusp. It is widely believed that Japan and South Korea are virtual nuclear states; and Iran has made no secret of the fact that it is on the way to an indigenous capability, however comparatively unsophisticated it might be. North Korea is the outcast.

Official American policy since Dwight Eisenhower is a world free of nuclear weapons. But Britain and the United States have set aside proliferation concerns to quietly help allies, whether Israel or Pakistan. Now that the group of unauthorized nuclear states might include Iran, serious thought is being given in some quarters to disarmament.

Henry Kissinger (2009) published a persuasive essay on the need to check the exploding growth of nuclear weapons. He argued, "Efforts to develop a more nuanced application [of nuclear power] have never succeeded, from the doctrine of a geographically limited nuclear war of the 1950s and 1960s to the mutual assured destruction theory of general nuclear war of the 1970s." The new war zones of ideology and regional conflict, rogue states and non-state actors, he continued, constituted a very real threat of a bomb being used by stealth. The possibility of preventing such a catastrophe would "prove increasingly remote unless the emerging nuclear weapons program in Iran and the existing one in North Korea are overcome".

But the history of nuclear status is linked back to the cause-and-effect chain. Iran points a finger at Israel; Pakistan could not remain indifferent to India; India was compelled by China; China asserted itself as a nuclear equal of the Soviet Union and America; and the Soviet Union felt bound to achieve parity with America. The chain began at the top and the unravelling, if there is to be any, must also start with the top.

Kissinger was clear-headed about where the process needs to restart. America and Russia control 90 per cent of the world's weapons, with America having a clear advantage in the numbers game. A strong, rarely expressed, motivation for proliferation is the view that nuclear weapons are the only guarantee of independence during a resurgence of neocolonization. Iran has watched America invade nations to its right and left, and threaten it on a regular basis. There is a double paradox operating. The West might argue that the nuclear programme makes Iran vulnerable; Tehran believes that its security can only be guaranteed by nuclear weapons, and that even the process is a deterrent. The potential of radioactive fallout from the bombing of Natanz or Busheyr has to be taken into consideration.

The dismantling of nuclear weapons cannot be symmetrical. Smaller powers will not easily surrender their limited ability to suit the arithmetic of larger powers. A key to de-escalation is some form of guarantee against superpower intervention, but there is no foolproof insurance available.

There has been a quiet revival of defunct departments of nuclear energy, in the name of peaceful power, even as India's track record of responsible behaviour has been rewarded by worldwide acceptance of its nuclear assets. French President Nicolas Sarkozy, who took office in May

2007, has signed deals worth billions of dollars for nuclear power plants or technical advice with Morocco, Libya, Algeria, Qatar and the United Arab Emirates.[6] China opened a nuclear counter, if not a shop, during its Africa summit in 2007. Egypt was among those interested.[7]

Regional governments cannot rule out the possibility that America's equation with Iran may shift from the Axis of Evil to the Axis of Equals.

Conclusion: The war in Iraq is "over" and Iran has won

The 2003 Iraq War has dented the post-Cold War perception of American invincibility, leading to significant shifts in the geopolitics of the Middle East, the most combustible region in the world. The move to democracy in Iraq has irreversibly changed political equations within the country in favour of the majority community, the Shia, which, while being Arab and nationalist, is far closer to Iran than America – many Iraqi Shias are more sympathetic to the values of the Islamic revolution of Ayatollah Khomeini than to the principles of George Washington.

Notes

1. The high price of the war includes a total financial cost that some estimates say will surpass US$1 trillion (Belasco 2009) as well as, at the time of writing, the lives of 4,327 US military personnel (Associated Press 2009a).
2. For more, see Ramazani 2005.
3. For a good description of US operations regarding Afghanistan, see Prados 2002.
4. For more on how cooperation between the United States and Iran could be mutually beneficial see Jahanbegloo 2009.
5. The Shia religious hierarchy begins from *talebeh*, student, from whence the word *taliban*, to *alim*, teacher, *masalegu*, one who can explain problems, *vaez*, preacher, *mojtahed*, interpreter of the law, and then to Ayatollah, a rank equivalent to *marja-e-taqlid*, one worthy of emulation.
6. The estimated cost of a new nuclear unit in 2008 was 5–7 billion dollars; not the best money-for-value investment in an area overflowing with oil if peaceful energy is all they want.
7. For more, see Watts 2006.

REFERENCES

Akbar, M. J. (2008) "Arc of turbulence, axis of equals", *Strategic Culture Foundation*, 1 Apr. At <http://en.fondsk.ru/article.php?id=1321> (accessed June 2010).

Al-Faisal, Turki (2009) "Saudi Arabia's patience is running out", *Financial Times*, 22 Jan. At <http://www.ft.com/cms/s/0/a11a77b0-e8ef-11dd-a4d0-0000779fd2ac.html>.

Associated Press (2008) "Ahmadinejad: US fueling Iraqi violence", news report, 2 Mar. At <http://www.thefreelibrary.com/Ahmadinejad:+US+fueling+Iraqi+violence-a01611472902> (accessed June 2010).
Associated Press (2009a) "US military deaths in Iraq war: 4,324", *ABC News*, 16 July. At <http://abcnews.go.com/International/wireStory?id=8105211> (accessed June 2010).
Associated Press (2009b) "NATO: Members may use Iran for easier routes to Afghanistan", FoxNews.com, 3 Feb. At <http://www.foxnews.com/story/0,2933,487445,00.html> (accessed June 2010).
Belasco, Amy (2009) "The cost of the Iraq, Afghanistan, and other global war on terror operations since 9/11", Congressional Research Service Report for Congress, 28 Sept. At <http://fas.org/sgp/crs/natsec/RL33110.pdf> (accessed June 2010).
CBS News (2009) "Obama appeals directly to Iranian people," 20 Mar. At <http://www.cbsnews.com/stories/2009/03/20/politics/100days/worldaffairs/main4878320.shtml> (accessed June 2010).
Cherian, John (2008) "Building bridges", *The Hindu*, 25(7). At <http://www.hinduonnet.com/thehindu/thscrip/print.pl?file=20080411250706300.htm&date=fl2507/&prd=fline&> (accessed June 2010).
CNN (2009) "Iran crackdown 'shifted' prospects for US talks, Clinton says", CNN.com, 15 July. At <http://www.cnn.com/2009/POLITICS/07/15/clinton.speech/> (accessed June 2010).
Cody, General Richard A. (2008) "On the readiness of the United States Army", Statement before the Senate Armed Services Committee Subcommittee on readiness and management support, 13 Mar. At <http://armed-services.senate.gov/statemnt/2008/April/Cody%2004-01-08.pdf> (accessed June 2010).
Colvin, Marie (2008) "Iran's Revolutionary Guard in secret Iraq talks with the US", TimesOnline, 13 Jan. At <http://www.timesonline.co.uk/tol/news/world/iraq/article3177705.ece> (accessed June 2010).
Dahl, Fredrik (2007) "Iran says US report a 'declaration of surrender'", Reuters, 16 Dec. At <http://www.reuters.com/article/politicsNews/idUSDAH66861820071216?feedType=RSS&feedName=politicsNews&rpc=22&sp=true> (accessed June 2010).
Dowd, Maureen (2008) "Faith, freedom and bling in the Middle East", *New York Times*, 16 Jan. At <http://query.nytimes.com/gst/fullpage.html?res=9806E0D9153AF935A25752C0A96E9C8B63&sec=&spon=&pagewanted=2> (accessed June 2010).
Economist (2008) "The enigma of Muqtada al-Sadr: Choices for Iraq's Muqtada al-Sadr", *The Economist*, 16 Feb.
Fathi, Nazila (2009) "Iran offers 'dialogue with respect' with US", *New York Times*, 11 Feb. At <http://www.nytimes.com/2009/02/11/world/africa/11iht-11iran.20096101.html> (accessed June 2010).
Jahanbegloo, Ramin (2009) "The Obama administration and Iran: Towards a constructive dialogue", CIGI Working Paper No. 43 (June), Centre for International Governance Innovation, Waterloo, Canada.

Kissinger, Henry A. (2009) "Containing the fire of the gods", *New York Times*, 6 Feb. At <http://www.nytimes.com/2009/02/06/opinion/06iht-edkissinger.1.19991669.html> (accessed June 2010).

Prados, John (2002) "Notes on the CIA's secret war in Afghanistan", *Journal of American History*, 89(2) (Sept.): 466–71.

Ramazani, Rouhollah K. (2005) "Iran's hostage crisis: International legitimacy matters", *Comparative Studies of South Asia, Africa and the Middle East*, 25(2): 273–8.

Scheer, Robert (2008) "The 'Great Satan' strike out", Daily Muslims.com, 8 Mar. At <http://www.dailymuslims.com/print/1033.html> (accessed June 2010).

Spetalnick, Matt and Parisa Hafezi (2009) "Obama offers new start with Iran", Reuters, 20 Mar. At <http://www.reuters.com/article/newsOne/idUSTRE52J0O020090320> (accessed June 2010).

Stratfor Global Intelligence (2009) "Geopolitical diary: Change in US foreign policy", Stratfor Global Intelligence, 6 Mar.

Tran, Mark (2008) "Iran demands withdrawal of foreign troops from Iraq", *Guardian*, 3 Mar. At <http://www.guardian.co.uk/world/2008/mar/03/iran.iraq> (accessed June 2010).

Watts, Jonathan (2006) "The savannah comes to Beijing as China hosts its new empire", *Guardian*, 4 Nov. At <http://www.guardian.co.uk/world/2006/nov/04/china.jonathanwatts> (accessed June 2010).

Part III

Responses

11

Regional integration as a response to globalization

Luk Van Langenhove and Tiziana Scaramagli

Introduction

The Westphalian world order originated when the world was not yet as globalized as today. The related treaty and the consequent birth of the sovereign state represented a good answer to the deep social, political and economic changes that ended feudalism (Spruyt 1994). Today, we are facing new societal transformations that challenge the capacities of the Westphalian world order to provide efficient and effective governance. As the world becomes more globalized, so does uncivil society, and individual states seem ill-equipped to tackle it. However, states are trying different avenues to cope with the accelerating positive and negative forces of globalization. One such avenue is the partial transfer of classical state functions and powers to supranational levels of regional governance (Van Langenhove 2008). This occurs via regional integration, a process of complex social transformation in the interactions between neighbouring states. This can be particularly useful when states are facing the same problems, such as, for instance, cross-border illegal activities.

With globalization, we have seen an increasing growth of both legal and illegal cross-border networks, because flows of communication, trade and individuals have become exponentially more immediate. Regional integration can represent an important means through which states can better deal with globalized uncivil society. Transferring a number of government prerogatives to the supranational level allows states to share expertise, institutions, tools, policies, personnel and funds, in order to better deal with cross-border illegal activities.

Regional integration can be studied from three angles. First, there are the integration *projects*: the normative ideals and goals put forward by region builders as the telos of what needs to be achieved by integration. Second, there are the integration *processes*: the actual step-by-step transformations that lead to integration. Third, there are the *products* of integration: the institutions, policies and practices that emerge as outcomes of the process (Morgan 2005: 4). In this chapter, the focus will be on the integration projects, as this will allow a better understanding of the varieties in processes and products.

Regional integration is always linked to certain policy domains of states, according to which varieties of integration are possible. Consider the following three broad policy domains that together define a state's "actorness": first, economic policy (every state is a single market with its own economic policy); second, the institutional framework associated with the delivery of public goods (every state has an executive, legislative and judicial power); and third, the capacity to provide security (a fundamental element of state sovereignty is the protection of the citizens).

Each of these three domains can fall subject to the projects and processes of regional integration. And, in principle, the possible end-result each time could be total integration, whereby what once functioned at the level of an individual state now operates at the supranational regional level. In other words, there exists a different telos for the integration of each policy domain. Suppose that such a total integration would occur simultaneously in all three domains, then a new state would be created; but such total integration hardly exists. What does exist is partial integration in each of the three domains.

Accordingly, one can identify three major types of actions that lead to regional integration: first, the act of removing economic obstacles to integration; second, the act of building adequate institutions or regulations that favour the delivery of regional public goods; and third, the act of integrating a region to acquire the capabilities to face common security threats. In each of these areas, the aim of responding to the growing challenges of uncivil society is evident.

This chapter will be devoted to a vertical and horizontal discussion: on the one hand, to an analysis of the three types of integration acts as different degrees of response to uncivil society and, on the other hand, to the study of some cases (European Union, Economic Community of West African States, Association of Southeast Asian Nations, Pacific Islands Forum, Andean Community and Organization of American States), in order to highlight how they are progressively strengthening their mandates to include the fight against illegal cross-border activities. Different examples of regional organizations' policies aimed at combating cross-border criminal networks will be analysed in order to demonstrate that these challenges are shaping the new agenda of regional organizations and to show how these organizations are facing the negative forces deriving from globalization.[1]

Different degrees of integration as responses to uncivil society

The emergence of a supranational region is hindered by several obstacles. The most significant obstacle is the concept of sovereignty, as it limits – *de jure* – the possibility of "interference" in the internal affairs of each of the concerned states. Similarly, fixed boundaries can be used to control and limit the flow of goods, people and money across borders. This results in states more or less being islands; within a given state, travel and trade are easy, but crossing the borders is difficult, if not impossible (especially with regard to entering a foreign country). Feelings of traditional identity and nationalism can also be a major obstacle as they – *de facto* – limit the urge towards integration.

The acts of removing economic obstacles, building adequate institutions or regulations, and integrating a region to promote security follow their own trajectories and can remain insulated within one dimension of governance or, alternatively, spill over. These different types, or "generations", of regional integration can emerge in a single organization, evolve from one to the other, or be totally separate, according to the mandate agreed upon by the member states (Van Langenhove and Marchesi 2008; Costea and Van Langenhove 2007). As this chapter aims to demonstrate, the driver that pushes for a further degree of integration is often linked to the emergence of new problems created by cross-border uncivil society.

Integration by removing economic obstacles

The first generation of regional integration is based upon the idea of a linear sequential process of economic integration involving the merging of separate (national) economic spaces into larger supranational economic regions (Balassa 1961). This process begins with a *free trade area*, in which states agree to remove all custom duties and quotas on trade passing between them, while keeping the right to unilaterally determine the level of custom duties on imports coming from outside the region. The next stage is the *customs union*, where a common level of duty on external trade arrangements is applied. This common external tariff is negotiated and allows for the conduct of a common commercial policy, as if the states of the customs union have one single border together with their neighbouring countries. The subsequent stage is the *common market*, where free movement of goods and factors of production are added. As such, a "single market" is created for goods, services, investment and people, allowing for free movement between the participating countries. Finally, during the *economic union* stage, a common market is installed and there is a complete unification of monetary and fiscal policy. In the case of a complete *monetary union*, there is a single currency backed by a common monetary policy instituted in a common central bank. A full economic union involves such a large number of common policies that one can speak of a *political union*.

The main driver of the regional integration process is the expansion of markets. State boundaries have always limited markets and cross-border trade but, as argued by Mattli, new technologies have increased the scope of markets between the boundaries of a single state (1999: 46). So, those who expect to gain from wider markets "will seek to change an existing governance structure in order to realise these gains to the fullest extent" (Mattli 1999: 46). Globalization, as well as developments in transport, has undoubtedly contributed to an increased demand for such regional economic integration. First generation integration is a response of states to the challenges of globalization. It is the reaction of states to the risk of remaining isolated by the economic benefits of globalization and a way of trying to enlarge markets, while keeping some national sovereignty. As Ahearne and von Hagen have argued, such regionalism is a natural response to the diversity in the world of economy (2006: 22).

Furthermore, states may choose to integrate their markets in order to respond more efficiently to cross-border economic or financial illegal activities. By doing this, they decrease the probability of being victims of globalization's isolation and of the consequent risk of having their markets too weak to counter illegal economic, financial or trade activities.

Finally, security considerations may also be a driving force towards economic integration. States can go to war with each other, but to the extent that they form a single economic space, the likelihood of such wars decreases. Creating a single economic space might thus contribute to preventing war. But it is of course no guarantee of that.

Integration by building institutions and regulations

Second generation regional integration, or "new regionalism", can occur independently of the above-described sequencing of economic integration, which does not represent the only possible driver for building a supranational region. There are other domains in which states may wish to cooperate in order to facilitate dealing with common problems or to create win-win situations. In principle, there is not a single aspect of the social realm that cannot be subject to integration processes. Integration can potentially be initiated by any kind of actor. This implies that not only state-driven integration is possible, but also integration from below (when the initiative comes from citizens). Of course much citizen-driven integration can only occur to the extent that states allow such integration to occur.

However, second generation regional integration can also follow directly from first generation regionalism as a way to ensure that economic integration is fully realized. The step from first to second generation integration can also be conditioned by problems encountered in realizing first generation integration. Aside from the previously described conflicts between the national interests of individual states and their willingness to integrate, one can identify three phenomena upon which states need to come to an agreement. First, there is the issue of geographical limits of the process: which countries can or cannot join an existing agreement? Not only economic, but also political considerations will be of importance in deciding upon the widening. This opens possibilities for second generation integration. Second, there is the so-called "spillover": where will economic integration stop? If, for instance, one wants to create a competitive economic union, this implies achieving a good innovation system; and this is in turn linked to research and development. Third, there is the question of integration towards a common policy that remains intergovernmental, as opposed to integration causing the transfer of a part of the national sovereignty to a supranational instance, which can act autonomously and where the decision structure is not based upon national delegates. To the extent that it involves only a partial transfer of sovereignty, one can describe this as "halfway integration", defined as "giving nations full or nearly full autonomy in some important matters while providing full or nearly full control to a supranational authority on other important matters" (Etzioni 2001: xxv). Such halfway integration can be considered to be the most important characteristic of the second generation of regional integration. Most regional trade arrangements do not have any supranational structures and have institutional support that remains rather limited. While the economic integration *stricto sensu* is mostly a story of lifting obstacles, the non-economic integration involves specific institution building or regulations that promote or facilitate integration in fields such as justice, security, culture, education, etc.

At the same time, second generation regionalism is more extroverted than first generation. Due to globalization, the line between purely internal and external policies is becoming blurred. What affects a country has consequences for its neighbours, and the case of uncivil society here is particularly evident. Competences related to foreign policy formulation in fields such as trade and development tend to migrate, even if partially, to the regional level. Additionally, according to Hettne, new regionalism has the potential to promote certain "world values", such as security, development and ecological sustainability, better than globalism (Hettne 1999: xvi).

In other words, while first generation regional integration is introverted and protectionist in nature, exclusively focusing on the creation of economic benefits for its members, the second generation brings in a more extroverted form of regionalism, opening integration to new domains, although the focus is still mainly on the consolidation of internal political integration. While first generation regional integration is generally a top-down process led by national governments and elites, with a strong emphasis on the process of government, the second generation is characterized by the multiplication of actors involved in regional integration building, including national and regional civil society actors in a bottom-up process focusing on regional governance. Second generation regionalism in Europe, and to some extent elsewhere in the world, is related to a transformation of the nation-state and "the dispersion of authoritative decision-making across multiple territorial levels" (Hooghe and Marks 2001: xi).

More importantly, second generation regional integration often occurs when states belonging to a first generation integration scheme realize that the interdependence of their economies can weaken their markets and financial systems. Opening markets and increasing economic interdependence expose states to a series of illegal activities that being locked into their own borders would not produce. The ease brought by globalization in encouraging investments in a foreign country, in emigrating to work in another state, in trading across borders without many restrictions has induced impressive economic growth, but has also encouraged the spread of illegal cross-border activities and reinforced international uncivil society networks. If the economic integration is not regulated and does not possess ad hoc institutions aimed at ensuring political control over the economic dynamics, first generation regional integration, in a globalized world, can hardly be sustainable.

Integration by promoting security

The third evolution of regional integration reflects what is happening now in some regional organizations, whose mandates are progressively broadening in order to respond to growing cross-border threats derived from the interdependence generated by the first two degrees of integration. When a regional organization is economically and politically integrated, the member states are often willing to rely on it also for security-related issues. Such a form of regional integration is difficult to achieve, as it jeopardizes one of the main principles of state sovereignty: security policy. However, the concepts of sovereignty and non-interference now seem valid only for national problems, such as, for instance, discrimination against minorities, executions, violations of freedom of expression, coups d'état or political persecution. At the same time, for threats normally related to globalized uncivil networks, such as drug and arms trafficking, money laundering and people smuggling, states are willing to share their efforts to combat these activities regionally. Recently, most regional organizations have developed some kind of co-operation in security-related domains involving illegal problems with a specific regional dimension.

Security provisions within a regional organization's territory normally do not imply the existence of regional armed forces or war technologies. More commonly, regional security is promoted at the third degree through common policies and institutions, aiming at defining rules, ensuring their respect, coordinating member states' efforts, developing expertise and creating common instruments of prevention, control and reaction in relation to cross-border illegal activities. The development of deeper forms of cooperation, like common personnel for border control, soldiers, joint mechanisms or operational structures, requires a much higher level of competence transferred from the national to the supranational level. Therefore it represents quite a limited example.

A further step in the development of this degree of regional integration is the enlargement of the instruments used in combating cross-border uncivil society, including soldiers, technologies, judicial and police cooperation, the establishment of regional courts for dispute settlement or joint efforts in the promotion of international conventions on transnational crime. This implies a further transfer of sovereignty from the member states, which is mostly jeopardized by the reluctance of many governments to trust authorities other than the national ones and to have confidence in supranational institutions over which they cannot exercise full control.

Finally, the most developed step of this third degree is the ability and expertise of regional organizations to get involved externally in combating transnational organized crime and uncivil networks outside their borders. This implies helping other regional organizations in dealing with ad hoc problems, or directly engaging in a state unable to face a particular security threat alone, by deploying political and technical instruments, personnel and sometimes armed forces in order to prevent conflicts. This step in pushing forward regional integration implies a geopolitical and foreign policy identity, very sensitive and controversial features of state sovereignty. This is the reason why so far only the European Union (EU) has shown a strong – although in its case sometimes fragmented – commitment in promoting security outside its borders.

This first part of the chapter aimed to analyse different degrees of regional integration, in response to different challenges from uncivil networks. The next part will now focus on various regional organizations, in order to highlight concrete examples of regional solutions to illegal globalized activities.

Regional organizations' responses to uncivil society

On what basis is it possible to affirm that regional integration is an important tool in jointly faced cross-border criminality? What are the concrete examples of this recent trend in developing instruments for fighting illegal activities? How are different regions in the world dealing with global uncivil society? Are there common areas of regional interaction?

The scenario of regional organizations with their mandates, institutions, policies and aims is incredibly heterogeneous. This section will try to give an overview of the different instruments regionally developed in combating illegal activities.

The European Union

The EU is the exemplar case of an economic regionalization that has broadened towards other areas of society. Because it is believed that a true economic integration cannot be achieved if trade and economy are isolated from the rest of society, the EU has "deepened" integration beyond economic issues and, in some policy domains, the EU is even close to a "supranational state", but in many other domains, co-operation – not to say integration – is still very weak or even non-existent.

The European Union is a political model that challenges conventional assumptions about governance all over the world. European integration is a "polity-creating process in which authority and policy-making influence are shared across multiple levels of government – subnational, national, and supranational" (Hooghe and Marks 2001: 2). The multilevel model reveals a shift of authority in several key areas of policy-making, from national states up to European-level institutions, together with the devolution of political authority from the national level down to the subnational level of government.

A main characteristic of second generation regional integration, as developed in Europe, is a strong institutional framework. In a long development process, from 1957 to the Maastricht Treaty in 1992, European governments have been giving the EU a unique and complex institutional architecture.[2] The so-called "three pillars" formed the base of this architecture. The first pillar consists of the European Community, together with a series of procedures and accompanying institutions or arrangements, such as the co-decision procedure with the European Parliament, a consultative Committee of the Regions and a programme of monetary integration. This pillar can be regarded as supranational. The second pillar deals with the Common Foreign and Security Policy (CFSP) and it is basically intergovernmental. The same holds for the third pillar: Police and Judicial Co-operation in Criminal Matters, originally named Justice and Home Affairs. The three pillars share the same institutions, although they play different roles in each of them.

Internally, it is in the third pillar that activities related to cross-border uncivil society are implemented. In this framework, some bodies have been created in order to deal with cross-border illegal activities within EU territory. Europol, the European Law Enforcement Organisation, was established in the Treaty of Maastricht. It is based in The Hague, and started in 1994 as Europol Drugs Unit. Europol started its full activities in 1999 and its mandate was progressively broadened to include immigration networks, terrorism, forgery of money, trafficking in human beings, illicit vehicle trafficking and money laundering.[3] Eurojust is a body established in 2002 to improve the coordination and competence of national authorities when they are dealing with combating cross-border illegal activities. It helps the member states to cooperate legally and to implement extradition requests.[4] Frontex, an EU agency based in Warsaw, deals with improving cooperation among the member states on border security. Its main tasks are to assess the risk at EU borders, coordinate member states' efforts in border management, train personnel from the member states and support their joint operations.[5]

The EU is the only regional actor able to intervene beyond its borders in promoting the fight against terrorism, human smuggling, illicit trafficking and criminal networks, together with a strong emphasis on conflict prevention and management. Its external policies cover a wide array of non-military and military areas: economy, development aid, regional co-operation and conflict prevention, allowing Christopher Piening to speak of a "global Europe" while referring to "the EU's external role as partner, trader, competitor, benefactor, investor and paradigm for countries and emerging regional groupings throughout the world" (Hänsch 1997). Since the Treaty of Maastricht, the EU has developed a strong external dimension in combating uncivil society, in particular through its Common Foreign and Security Policy and its political instruments, the European Security and Defence Policy (ESDP) – with growing numbers of civilian and military missions in almost every continent – and the European Neighbourhood Policy, aimed at stabilizing EU neighbouring states.

The achievements of the treaties of Maastricht and Amsterdam aspired to give Europe the opportunity to become a strong security actor, designing new institutional tools and legal instruments of foreign policy, such as the creation of a High-Representative for CFSP, the definition of the Petersberg Tasks and the path towards the creation of a unified defence policy.[6] But this was not an easy task and the EU was confronted with a "capabilities–expectations gap" brought about by the lack of valid military capabilities to support its policy goals.[7] Though the Cologne and Helsinki summits have drawn the main lines for the achievement of the "headline goal" of creating a European Rapid Reaction Force, the emerging ESDP has been confronted with several problems, such as the problem of resources, the lack of cooperation between the European defence industries, the need to avoid duplication, and, most of all, the need to clarify the relationship with NATO (Schmitt 2000).[8]

The difficulties in efficiently using the complex mechanisms of the CFSP and the lack of necessary defence capabilities maintained the perception of the EU as a still predominantly "civilian power", a "payer" rather than a "player" in global peace and security (Ginsberg 2001). Although the EU has so far been unable to exert strong military power when conflicts are rising, it has been rather successful when working in peace-building and stabilization after war. There were promising results in the first Rapid Reaction Force missions, such as in the Former Yugoslav Republic of Macedonia and Operation Artemis in Congo, but the existence of a strong and unified European "hard security" arm is still a long way away.

The EU, since its creation, has gone through all of the different degrees of regional integration and has actually developed a strong commitment in combating illegal networks within and outside its borders. This happened because its member states became aware of the fact that they were unable to face alone the consequences of globalization and of the opening of their borders to goods, services, persons and capital. Therefore, they have been willing to increase their cooperation in combating globalization's negative forces together while taking advantage of its economic development side. However, the case of the EU does not represent the only example of regional policies aimed at combating global uncivil networks.

Economic Community of West African States

The Economic Community of West African States (ECOWAS) is composed of 15 member states and was created in 1975 with the adoption of the ECOWAS Treaty to promote economic growth through the establishment of an economic and monetary union. It is in its Department of

Gender Development, Youth/Sports, Civil Society, Employment and Drug Control that activities related to the fight against cross-border trafficking are inserted. The programme on drug control develops policies dealing with coordination, information sharing and involvement with the stakeholders in strengthening drug control in the region. The main activity is to promote regional meetings at the ministerial level among member states to draw a common strategy towards drug control and money laundering. The organization has also created the Inter-Governmental Action Group against Money Laundering in West Africa (GIABA) to protect ECOWAS economic and financial systems against money laundering. In January 2006, the statutes of GIABA were revised to reflect the growing link between money laundering and terrorist financing, following the 11 September 2001 terrorist attacks on the United States.[9]

There are attempts within ECOWAS to design and implement regional policies against uncivil networks. But, as is often the case with African regional integration schemes, there is still little evidence of the effectiveness of such policies. This is related both to the institutional weakness of the regional integration organizations, and to the problems of mobilizing African states to fully endorse and execute what has been decided at regional level. As recently noted by Ninsin and Tlon:

> delays at the numerous checkpoints and corruption among customs and immigration personnel tend to negate the ECOWAS effort to promote the free movement of people, goods and services. Many are concerned that illicit activities (such as rising levels of armed robbery, drug trafficking and other criminal activity) have compromised the security of residents and the spirit of ECOWAS. (2009: 17)

Association of Southeast Asian Nations

The Association of Southeast Asian Nations (ASEAN) was established in 1967 with the mandate of enhancing economic growth, social progress and cultural development and improving regional stability through the promotion of the rule of law (UNDP and UNU-CRIS 2009: 60). One of its most developed areas is the fight against transnational crime and terrorism and drugs. In this framework, ASEAN has developed a regional approach to illegal drug trafficking. In 1984, the ASEAN Drug Experts Meeting approved an ASEAN Regional Policy and Strategy in the Prevention and Control of Drug Abuse and Illicit Trafficking. In 1998, ASEAN foreign ministers signed the Joint Declaration for a Drug-Free ASEAN by 2020, asking the member states to commit themselves to eradicating the production, processing, trafficking and use of illicit drugs in South East Asia by the year 2020. The ASEAN anti-drug effort involves various bodies in shaping strategies, elaborating policies and starting activities against illicit drug trafficking, which, in the context of ASEAN cooperation, comes under the broader framework of transnational crime. The ASEAN Ministerial Meeting on Transnational Crime adopted in 1999 the ASEAN Plan of Action to Combat Transnational Crime, which has established mechanisms and activities to coordinate ASEAN member countries' policies to combat transnational crime, with a particular focus on drug trafficking at the regional level. The strategy includes information sharing, legal cooperation, capacity building, training and extraregional cooperation. ASEAN Senior Officials on Drug Matters (ASOD) aims at enhancing the implementation of the ASEAN Declaration of Principles to Combat the Drug Problem of 1976. It foresaw the strengthening of joint efforts in the control and prevention of drug trafficking in the region.[10]

Pacific Islands Forum

The Pacific Islands Forum (PIF) started as an international agreement in 1971 as the South Pacific Forum. It was only in 2000 that it became a full-fledged regional organization following the creation of its Secretariat. This agreement represented the will of the member states to engage more at the regional level, in order to improve cooperation and coordination among them. The region faces increased problems with transnational organized crime and remains confronted by the global security challenge of terrorism. The region has experienced an increase in transnational criminal activity:

> Globalization, improved communications and information technologies, greater mobility of people, goods and services, and the emergence of the globalised economy has shifted criminal activity from its traditional domestic base. Consequently the Pacific region has been targeted for the illegal movement of people and goods, illicit financial transactions, and as a base of operations for criminal organisations and entities. (Pacific Islands Forum Secretariat 2009)

This shows the deep awareness of the organization on what represents new security threats and on globalization's controversial effects.

In this framework, the PIF has started to build the capacity of law enforcement agencies to combat transnational crime with border management, data exchange and anti-money laundering monitoring. In relation to transnational security, the PIF has developed a programme assessing the nature and level of transnational criminal activities in the Pacific and providing an annual study of these threats to inform its member states.

Andean Community

The Andean Community was created in 1969, with the Cartagena Agreement signed by five South American countries (Bolivia, Chile, Colombia, Ecuador and Peru), in order jointly to improve their peoples' standard of living through integrated, economic and social cooperation. Despite its relatively small dimension, different areas of cooperation have been developed, in particular for security-related issues. In this framework, in 2003, the member states adopted a cooperation plan to fight illegal weapons traffic. This plan represents a comprehensive strategy to fight illicit trafficking in small arms and light weapons, in particular linked to terrorism, corruption and drugs. The Andean Community's initiatives in this direction respond to the support of United Nations programmes in this domain:

> The Andean Community Member Countries, as they have proclaimed in several international forums, consider that illegal drug production, trafficking and consumption, asset laundering, diversion and smuggling of chemical precursors, and arms trafficking seriously undermine their development and security. (Andean Community 2009)

The Andean Community strategy encompasses initiatives that can be taken more efficiently jointly than individually, in such areas as information exchange, improved coordination among competent authorities, the training of national officials in anti-drug measures, agreement on legal assistance on criminal matters and the negotiation of trade preference programmes that support illegal drug control.

Organization of American States

The Organization of American States (OAS) brings together 34 states to strengthen cooperation on democratic values, defend common interests and create a forum of discussion. Its main focuses are strengthening democracy, promoting human rights and the fight against poverty, terrorism, illegal drugs and corruption. In this framework, the OAS has created the Inter-American Drug Abuse Control Commission (CICAD). The fight against drug trafficking is pursued in parallel with involvement against arms trafficking through the Inter-American Convention against the Illicit Manufacturing of and Trafficking in Firearms, Ammunition, Explosives, and other Related Materials of 1997. Human smuggling represents a domain of initiatives since 2006, with the first Meeting of National Authorities on Trafficking in Persons, which aimed at studying ways to strengthen cooperation and develop regional policies and strategies of prevention.

Conclusions

This chapter has analysed the repercussions of globalized uncivil society, both on the degrees of regional integration and on the already existing regional organizations. States have used and continue to use different vertical levels of integration with their neighbours to react to the negative forces of globalization. Almost every regional organization is now developing mechanisms to face transnational illegal activities, which cannot be fought by individual states with national policies, but have to be faced with the joint efforts of interdependent states. As such, there has been a recent diffusion of regional instruments to respond to transnational organized crime in the framework of pre-existing regional organizations.

But regional integration comes in different varieties, developing from an introverted trade-based first generation regionalism, to a second generation concerned with institution-building and regulation frameworks, and to what could be a kind of third generation, where the regional organization has the responsibility of providing security for its members. The EU's internal and external security dimensions, presented as the best reflection of this evolution, has been considerably developed during the transition from first to second generation regionalism, with the aspiration to become a "global actor".

The essence of a third degree of regionalism is thus that a region is given the mandate to protect its citizens with a wide range of means, from purely political instruments to armed forces common to its member states. This trend can potentially reach the point where a regional organization is able to project itself externally, in order to promote security beyond its borders. This implies that the region claims a position similar to that of a state in the multilateral organs. It also implies that a region engages in "bilateral" relations with other regions or states, again much as any other state would do.

The cases of the EU, ECOWAS, ASEAN, PIF, the Andean Community and OAS have shown how far all of these regional organizations are going in the fight against globalized uncivil society. Drug and arms trafficking and money laundering are the threats most addressed regionally. Their links with terrorist networks are now starting to be inserted into the agenda of regional processes. The EU, following these domains, is the organization which has the broadest range of areas of competence and the largest number of institutions and instruments created for dealing with cross-border illegal activities.

In moving from a first to second and third degrees of regionalism, regional organizations can become strong actors in combating transnational uncivil society. Globalization has brought transnational criminal activities as new priorities on the international agenda through the growing economic, political and social interdependence among states, the increased possibilities of movement across borders and the explosion of communication opportunities. In this context, cross-border uncivil society can trigger or enhance regional integration; the latter being a necessary, but insufficient step in this direction if not complemented by consistency and coherence between the different levels of governance. It is for these reasons that regional integration can be seen as a possible taming driver of the uncivil side of globalization (UNU-CRIS 2008).

Notes

1. By contrast, in chapter 12 Marisa von Bülow analyses how non-government organizations create cross-border linkages, organizations and frames (increased levels of transnationalization) while rooted at local or national levels.
2. For a history of European foreign policy cooperation, see Regelsberger, de Schoutheete and Wessels 1997; Nuttall 2000.
3. For a profile of Europol see <http://www.europol.europa.eu/index.asp?page=facts>.
4. See more from the Eurojust website at <http://www.eurojust.europa.eu/index.htm> (accessed June 2010).
5. See Frontex "Tasks" at <http://www.frontex.europa.eu/origin_and_tasks/tasks/> (accessed June 2010).
6. For a useful basis for the theoretical conceptualization of EU's global actorness, see Sjöstedt 1976; Allen and Smith 1990; 1991; Bretherton and Vogler 1999; Ginsberg 2001. See also Costea 2005.
7. See Hill 1993; 1998.
8. See for instance Howorth 2000.
9. See more about the Inter-Governmental Action Group against Money Laundering in West Africa (GIABA) at <http://www.giaba.org/index.php?type=a&id=193> (accessed June 2010).
10. See ASEAN, "Drug matters" at <http://www.aseansec.org/4967.htm> (accessed 2009).

REFERENCES

Ahearne, Alan and Jürgen von Hagen (2006) "European perspectives on global imbalances", *Bruegel Working Papers*, 2006/01.

Allen, David, and Michael Smith (1990) "Western Europe's presence in the contemporary international arena", *Review of International Affairs*, 16(1): 19–37.

Allen, David and Michael Smith (1991) "Western Europe's presence in the international system", in Martin Holland, ed., *The Future of European Political Cooperation*, London: Macmillan, pp. 95–120.

Andean Community (2009) "Drug control effort". At <http://www.comunidadandina.org/ingles/Exterior/drug_control.htm> (accessed June 2010).

Balassa, Bela (1961) *The Theory of Economic Integration*. London: Richard D. Irwin.

Bretherton, Charlotte and John Vogler (1999) *The European Union as a Global Actor.* London: Routledge.

Costea, Ana-Cristina (2005) "The European Union as global and regional security actor, setting the scene", *Romanian Journal of International Studies*, 1: 78–98.

Costea, Ana-Cristina and Luk Van Langenhove (2007) "EU's foreign policy identity: From 'new regionalism' to third generation regionalism?", in Jessica Bain and Martin Holland, eds, *European Union Identity*, Baden-Baden: Nomos, pp. 86–104.

Etzioni, Amitai (2001) *Political Unification Revisited: On Building Supranational Communities*. Lanham, MD: Lexington Books.

Ginsberg, Roy H. (2001) *The European Union in International Politics: Baptism by Fire*. Lanham, MD: Rowman and Littlefield.

Hänsch, Klaus (1997) "Foreword", in Christopher Piening, *Global Europe: The European Union in World Affairs*, Boulder, CO: Lynne Rienner, p. ix.

Hettne, Björn (1999) "Globalisation and the new regionalism: The second great transformation", in Björn Hettne, Andras Inotai and Osvaldo Sunkel, eds, *Globalism and the New Regionalism*, Basingstoke: Macmillan, pp. 7–11.

Hill, Christopher (1993) "The capability–expectations gap, or conceptualizing Europe's international role", *Journal of Common Market Studies*, 31(3): 305–28.

Hill, Christopher (1998) "Closing the capabilities–expectations gap?", in John Peterson and Helen Sjursen, eds, *A Common Foreign Policy for Europe? Competing Visions of the CFSP*, London: Routledge, pp. 18–39.

Hooghe, Liesbeth and Gary Marks (2001) *Multi-level Governance and European Integration*. Lanham, MD: Rowman and Littlefield.

Howorth, Jolyon (2000) *European Integration and Defence: The Ultimate Challenge?* Chaillot Paper No. 43. Paris: Institute for Security Studies.

Mattli, Walter (1999) *The Logic of Regional Integration: Europe and Beyond*. Cambridge: Cambridge University Press.

Morgan, Glyn (2005) *The Idea of a European Superstate: Public Justification and European Integration*, Princeton: Princeton University Press.

Ninsin, Kwame A. and Tlon, L. (2009) "Implementing the ECOWAS idea in Ghana: Taming the state, empowering the people", in Kwame A. Ninsin, ed., *Nation-States and the Challenges of Regional Integration in West Africa: The Case of Ghana*, Paris: Kathala, pp. 11–18.

Nuttall, Simon J. (2000) *European Foreign Policy*. Oxford: Oxford University Press.

Pacific Islands Forum Secretariat (2009) "Security". At <http://www.forumsec.org.fj/pages.cfm/political-governance-security/security/> (accessed Aug. 2010).

Regelsberger, Elfriede, Philippe de Schoutheete de Tervarent, and Wolfgang Wessels (1997) *Foreign Policy of the European Union: From EPC to CFSP and Beyond*, London: Lynne Rienner.

Schmitt, Burkard (2000) *From Cooperation to Integration: Defence and Aerospace Industries in Europe*, Chaillot Paper No. 40. Paris: Institute for Security Studies.

Sjöstedt, Gunnar (1976) *The External Role of the European Community*. London: Saxon House.

Smith, Michael (1998) "Does the flag follow trade? Politicisation and the emergence of a European foreign policy", in John Peterson and Helene Sjursen, eds, *A Common Foreign Policy for Europe? Competing Visions on the CFSP*, London: Routledge.

Spruyt, Hendrik (1994) *The Sovereign State and Its Competitors: An Analysis of Systems Change*. Princeton: Princeton University Press.

UNDP and UNU-CRIS (2009) *Delivering Human Security through Multi-level Governance*. Brussels: United Nations Development Programme and United Nations University – Comparative Regional Integration Studies. At <http://www.undp.org/eu/documents/hsbooklet.pdf> (accessed June 2010).

UNODC (2008) *Drug-Free ASEAN 2015: Status and Recommendations*. Bangkok: United Nations Office on Drugs and Crime, Regional Centre for East Asia and the Pacific.

UNU-CRIS (2008) "Deepening the social dimensions of regional integration", ILO Discussion Paper No. 188, International Institute for Labour Studies, Geneva.

Van Langenhove, Luk (2008) "Transforming the Westphalian world order into a world of regions", in Anđelko Milardović, Davor Pauković and Davorka Vidović, eds, *Globalization of Politics*, Zagreb: Political Science Research Centre Zagreb, pp. 107–27.

Van Langenhove, Luk and Daniele Marchesi (2008) "The Lisbon Treaty and the emergence of third generation regional integration", *Jean Monnet/Robert Schuman Paper Series*, 8(9) (June).

12

Civil society and trade protests in the Americas

Marisa von Bülow

Introduction

Civil society organizations (CSOs) are political actors independent of political parties and the state, that seek to shape the rules (formal and informal) that govern social life.[1] When CSOs enter the international realm, they do so in different ways. While some focus on protesting in the streets, others struggle to come up with alternative proposals and ideas to influence the outcome of decision-making processes, and still others engage in both direct action and the generation of alternatives. These strategies may be targeted at various actors at different levels: at allies beyond national boundaries through campaigns and the creation of coalitions, or by lobbying domestic institutions. They may focus on influencing states' behaviour, or alternately seek to influence public opinion, international organization officials or other civil society actors. Thus the CSOs studied here are not inherently benign or malicious forces in the international arena.

The growth of civil society from domestic to global has not been steady. What I call "pathways to transnationality" are the multiple, and sometimes intersecting, routes used by CSOs to link domestic and international arenas. These pathways may be temporary or sustained, but are not unidirectional. How do CSOs create cross-border linkages, organizations and frames (increased levels of transnationalization) while rooted at local or national levels?[2] The multiple pathways to transnationality that CSOs take are, in part, the result of an absence of a consensus about what collective action in a globalizing world should look like.

Trade, as a negotiating arena, offers the possibility of studying the dynamics of interaction among a heterogeneous set of actors who have struggled to find common strategies and frames in the domestic and international arenas. In the past 20 years, debates about trade policies have shifted considerably in terms of the actors that participate in them, ranging from labour federations with millions of members to tiny, issue-specific non-governmental organizations (NGOs). The goal of this chapter is to address the apparent paradox that is the increased relevance of transnational collective action on the one hand, and the persistence of claims to the preservation of national sovereignty and the strengthening of nation-states on the other. This paradox is illustrated by an analysis of the goals and strategies of CSOs that have challenged free trade negotiations in the Americas since the beginning of the 1990s.

As part of broader research focusing on the interactions among CSOs that have challenged free trade agreement negotiations in the Americas, from the North American Free Trade Agreement (NAFTA) to the Free Trade Area of the Americas (FTAA), this analysis is based on field research undertaken mostly in four countries: Brazil, Chile, Mexico and the United States.[3] CSOs from these countries have been among the key building blocks of the emerging trade protest networks of the past 20 years. The issues raised by challengers of trade negotiations touch on the decision-making processes, the agenda of negotiations and the impacts of the implementation of agreements.

This chapter presents the analytical approach used and its relevance to current theoretical debates on transnational collective action. It then applies this approach to the study of how trade challengers in the Americas have struggled to come up with a set of common alternatives to the agenda of trade negotiations. It focuses mostly on the experience of a group of CSOs that created the Hemispheric Social Alliance (HSA), a multisectoral coalition launched in 1997 that brought together NGOs and social movement organizations from the entire hemisphere.

Multiple pathways to transnationality

The literature on transnationalism of the past four decades has demonstrated the increased relevance of CSOs in the international arena. However, most analyses have focused on understanding why these actors have become so important – the problem of origin – and what kinds of impacts they have had – the problem of outcome. Insufficient attention has been paid to understanding how actors decide with whom to build ties, the sustainability or fragility of transnational ties, and the complex relationship between domestic and transnational activism. One critical issue is the endurance of the relevance of domestic arenas in transnational collective action.

The resilience of the national in the transnational

An important question in the transnationalism literature is: where is mobilization likely to be most effective? For some, given the weakening of the authority and power of nation-states, the global level has become more relevant. In this perspective, even if CSOs were to focus on national sovereignty claims, this would be a mistake.[4] For others, states still hold considerable power, and thus actions at the national and local levels are most likely to succeed (Halperin and Laxer 2003; Akça 2003). By structuring the debate in either/or terms, however, both sides remain unaware of the dilemma of travelling *across* levels.

CSOs are not necessarily willing to declare the end of the sovereign nation-state.[5] However, often civil society actors from the North, as well as from the South, feel that they defend their country's sovereignty and the general interest better than their own governments.[6] Their ultimate goal is to strengthen national states, not to weaken them. But many NGOs, social movements and labour unions look with mistrust at any attempt to create global civil society arenas that would undermine their own autonomy and flexibility.

An approach that minimizes or excludes the national from the transnational runs the risk of falling into an inverted version of "the territorial trap". John Agnew coined this phrase in his critique of the ontological presumption in international relations theories that social, economic and political activities are contained within the territorial boundaries of states, in contradistinction to processes going on outside state boundaries (Agnew 1994: 62). The global civil society literature tends to do the opposite, thinking in terms of the "outside", or the global level, as the privileged space for the civil, or "the pursuit of justice and virtue", as Agnew put it.

The analytical framework proposed builds on contributions from various scholars who have attempted to understand the complex intertwining processes of collective action that take place across levels. Some of the main research topics that address this challenge have been: the relationships between domestic and global opportunity structures and the tactics deployed by actors;[7] the new organizations created to coordinate action across levels;[8] changes in the repertoires of contention;[9] the emergence of new forms of "transnational citizenship" (Fox 2005);[10] and the impacts of global issues on locally rooted organizations.[11] This literature

Table 12.1 Four pathways to transnationality

		DURATION	
		Intermittent	Sustained
SITE	Domestic	Periodic domestication	Sustained domestication
	International	Periodic transnationalization	Sustained transnationalization

represents a sustained effort to understand how actors sometimes "domesticate" international grievances and issues and/or "externalize" them (Imig and Tarrow 2001; Rootes 2005; Tarrow 2005).

The expression "pathways to transnationality" helps capture the different routes taken by CSOs in a context of uncertainty as they participate in debates, coalitions, and events. Table 12.1 differentiates schematically among four possible pathways, according to two key dimensions of these responses: the site of activism and its sustainability. By differentiating between the sites privileged by actors, this typology incorporates Sidney Tarrow's argument that "not all activism that is relevant to transnational politics takes place in the international arena" (Tarrow 2005: 30). Temporal variation relates to the degree to which action at each of these sites is more or less intermittent or sustained. As Kathryn Sikkink has argued, many actors privilege domestic political change, but often maintain transnational activism as a complementary and compensatory option that is used intermittently (2005: 165).

This typology does not imply that choices of pathways are fixed. On the contrary, whether action develops mostly at the domestic or the international site, and whether it is intermittent or sustained, is a matter of permanent debate among actors. Choices, thus, are "contingently reconstructed by actors in ongoing dialogue with unfolding situations" (Emirbayer and Mische 1998: 966). More specifically, they can change because of lessons learned or through negotiated interactions with other actors, and are impacted by perceived changes in the political environment, as new opportunities may open for collective action.[12] Furthermore, the four possible pathways are not necessarily in contradiction with one another. CSOs may use more than one at a time, depending on the issue at stake.

Ideational pathways

A key challenge in transnational collective action is the search for common frames, policies and ideas, or ideational pathways. Creating common frames is a classic collective action challenge. CSOs have increasingly felt pressure to present specific alternative proposals and demands to

Table 12.2 Ideational pathways to transnationality

		DURATION	
		Intermittent	Sustained
SITE	Domestic	Claims oriented primarily to the domestic arena	Projects oriented primarily to the domestic arena
	International	Claims oriented primarily to the international area	Projects oriented primarily to the international area

negotiators. The pressure comes from parliamentarians, government officials, the media, and from other civil society actors, and has led to contentious debates among allies that often, as in the case of trade debates, come from different countries and have different interests.

In the 1980s, David Snow and his colleagues introduced the concept of "framing" into the study of social movements to understand how organizers present ideas in order to attract supporters and convey their messages (Snow et al. 1986; Snow and Benford 1988). In general terms, transnational framing has been easier under campaigns that rally opposition to a specific multilateral agreement than in cases when CSOs try to explain what they stand for and come up with alternative proposals.

The ideational pathways shown in table 12.2 represent, in a schematic way, the different degrees to which actors participate in the debates about ideas along the two dimensions defined above: place and time. As emphasized above, these are not fixed choices and actors may take more than one pathway. Often, the results of multilevel interactions among heterogeneous sets of actors have been transnational frames that are inherently provisional, unstable and ambiguous. Specificity coexists – however uneasily – with broad compromises, and non-negotiable issues are dealt with in different ways, but they persist.

It is important to understand that CSOs do not always operate at various sites identically.[13] Different ideational pathways have specific political consequences. Claims-making implies finding common ground on specific issues, directed at the short term. Project-making implies negotiating and constructing common values, interests and beliefs among what are usually very heterogeneous sets of actors. In sum, multiple pathways to transnationality do not coexist harmoniously. Choices made are impacted by each organization's political identity and history, but the pathway prioritized at a given point in time is also the result of the relational and political embeddedness of actors. Thus choices and their impacts are not totally predictable.

However, it is possible to differentiate among three main types of relational mechanisms that help to analyse choices and how actors move from one pathway to another.[14] These mechanisms are especially important in transnational coalitions that rely on the rule of consensus for decision-making, as is the case of the Hemispheric Social Alliance.[15]

The first relational mechanism is the *extension*, or amplification, of coalition-building strategies and agendas, achieved by adding new allies and/or by incorporating other actors' grievances to one's claims or projects. It implies the coexistence of issues and tactics, but not necessarily a construction of enduring consensus or a transformation of previous interests. It allows actors to broaden their networks and do "multiple targeting", that is, aim at different audiences and adversaries at the same time (Mische 2003). Second, the *suppression* of allies, topics, goals or tactics: "We agree to disagree"; when actors maintain their alliances, but refuse to discuss specific topics. It implies the construction of a minimum common denominator. Third, the *transformation* of coalition-building strategies and/or the content of claims and projects: this is the least common result of interactions, because it implies not only an adaptation, but a change in the perception of agendas, goals and self-interests, and the incorporation of new visions that were not present for the actors before. Extension, suppression, diffusion and transformation can be seen through coalition-building strategies, tactics implemented, and the ways in which CSOs frame their grievances and proposals.

The typology proposed is an outcome of efforts by a group of people to fashion shared understandings of the world. However, negotiated changes do not cancel out conflicts or the asymmetries of power among actors, nor do they erase all differences in all relational contexts. Organizations still belong to multiple networks at different sites and social contexts, and these do not necessarily reinforce each other; sometimes they are contradictory pressures.[16]

Debates about ideational pathways go well beyond the case of trade mobilizations. The largest global gathering of civil society actors, the World Social Forum (WSF), offers a good example. Most of the Forum's organizers have been against launching final declarations and drafting a common agenda or list of demands. The main argument in favour of this vision is that it is too hard to construct common ground in such a heterogeneous setting; trying to do so would only generate fragmentation (Whitaker 2005). According to this perspective, having no blueprints is a good sign, and attempts to find one would lead the WSF to reproduce the old model of the Internationals (Klein 2003; Adamovsky 2006). Thus, it is argued, it is best to maintain the Forum as a decentred space for debate and encounters, not speaking with one voice on any single issue. Both claims and projects are to be constructed by participants, but not by the whole Forum. This issue remains open, however, as some of the participants question the Forum's efficacy solely as a convener of movements and individuals. Proposals have been put forward for the Forum to establish a "minimum platform" which "would provide meaning and design for alternatives to neoliberal proposals" and escape the destiny "of becoming a showpiece for civil society" (Ramonet 2006).

The search for alternatives

Civil society challengers of trade agreements have often been confronted with the question: if not this trade agreement, then what? Given the ideological heterogeneity and the organizational fragmentation that characterize this arena of collective action, it is not surprising that there is no single answer. It has been easier to find common agreement to oppose negotiations, as the Continental Campaign against the FTAA did. Perceptions of self-interest vary among actors belonging to the same types of organizations and countries, but these visions are amenable to changes in their interaction with other actors. Furthermore, as the literature on the role of ideas has emphasized, especially in situations of uncertainty, actors engage in efforts to understand the challenges they face, and the way actors perceive their interests and how to achieve them are more amenable to change.[17]

This approach sees the development of alternatives as the product of processes of negotiation among actors.[18] The interaction mechanisms identified before – extension, suppression, diffusion and transformation – are in play in the process of thinking about ideational pathways. Variation in how CSOs approach the problem of searching for alternatives is related, in part, to the institutional and political context in which they act at the domestic level, or their political embeddedness.

Case study: The Hemispheric Social Alliance and alternatives for the Americas

The HSA is a transnational coalition of CSOs from the Americas. It was defined by its members as an "open space", a "forum of progressive social movements and organizations of the Americas, created to exchange information, define strategies and promote common actions, directed at finding an alternative and democratic development model".[19]

However, even at the height of mobilizations against the FTAA, at the end of the 1990s and the first years of the 2000s, the HSA did not unite the whole universe of CSOs that had been challenging trade negotiations. However, it did bring together some of the main actors in the associational milieu of the transnational field of trade.[20] Most of its members were located somewhere on the centre-to-left of the ideological spectrum, united by a common critique of free trade policies and a negative assessment of the consequences of trade agreements. The hemispheric – and not Latin American – character of the HSA is, in itself, a novelty in terms of transnational relations in the region. As one of the participants argued:

> There is a rupture with the Latin Americanist vision that we cannot make an alliance with Northern movements, and this is very important, it is a contribution of the Hemispheric Social Alliance ... we are in a different era, it is not anymore "the ones in the South fight, those in the North show solidarity". The fight is now on both sides ...[21]

While there are many instances of transnational collaboration among these actors, the HSA was innovative as a plural organization that sought to be a sustained coalition based on common goals and principles. It incorporated organizations and coalitions through their participation in national HSA chapters and/or in regional organizations (many of these existed prior to the HSA's creation). Because of its broad membership, reaching across various civil society sectoral domains as well as the North–South divide, it has been considered an example of "the possibility of broader alliances built around the larger issue of democratising economic governance" (Anner and Evans 2004: 40).

The HSA did not collect fees from its members, but, instead, raised funds from international foundations and NGOs to pay for a small organizational structure and for publications.[22] On the one hand, this avoided criticism of bureaucratization, and diminished the dependence on members with more access to financial resources; on the other hand, it limited the amount of activities that the HSA Secretariat could perform and it created dependence on actors from outside the coalition.[23]

The HSA did not conceive itself "as an organization with structures and hierarchies of any type, but as an ongoing process under construction", but it endorsed the creation of "minimum and flexible coordination instances at the hemispheric, regional, national, local, sectoral levels" (Alianza Social Continental 2006). It did not have its own office spaces, nor did it have permanent staff. It had a rotating Secretariat, a Coordination Committee and, most importantly in terms of decision-making, a Hemispheric Council.[24] Its decision-making was by consensus among all participants.

In spite of the emphasis on horizontality and consensus, the HSA was not an "open space" accessible to all. Its dual affiliation rule generated greater flexibility than more hierarchical organizations, but it did separate those who could become members from those who could not. Individuals and single organizations could not directly apply for membership, and thus actors that were not members of regional coalitions and/or did not wish to become members of national chapters are in practice excluded. Of the 123 CSOs interviewed in Brazil, Chile, Mexico and the US between 2004 and 2005, 55 – almost 45 per cent – did not participate in the HSA. Although this was not a representative sample, it did indicate that an important part of the field of trade challengers remained outside the HSA.

The document *Alternatives for the Americas* represents a rare example of an effort at building a common project at the transnational level within a heterogeneous coalition. Written by the Hemispheric Social Alliance between 1998 and 2005, it was seen as a "living document" that, in its various editions, put into writing alternative visions and proposals related to the debates about trade agreements, regional integration, and development. Although there is no necessary tendency for actors to go from making specific claims to building common projects, when a transnational alliance attempts to do so scholars have a window of opportunity to look into the mechanisms through which actors try to achieve common ground in the long term, as well as their limits.

This document represents a unique effort by a diverse range of CSOs to craft a common alternative platform at the hemispheric level.[25] In its first edition, the authors defined it as "more than an economic doctrine. It is a way to achieve a social integration . . . The priority was the establishment of the basis of an inclusive alliance" (HSA 1998: 6, 10). *Alternatives for the Americas* was simultaneously an internal attempt to create an ideational platform for the members of the Hemispheric Social Alliance and an effort to construct a common frame for outsiders.[26] By writing such a foundation for collective action, members sought to build a collective identity within the coalition, and at the same time foster their external credibility. The five editions of the document offer a good illustration of the mechanisms by which the members of the Alliance have attempted progressively to construct agreement on common alternative proposals.

When compared to the first version, the 120-page long document published in 2005 shows the progressive extension of topics, proposals and demands. Most notably, the later *Alternatives* incorporated specific chapters on education, communications, gender and services. To work against free trade negotiations is defined as an ethical imperative. By presenting the issue as a moral one and as part of a broader crusade against neoliberalism, the authors present their ideas as going far beyond specific trade negotiations.

Having been written by many hands, different editions of *Alternatives* have contradictions within and among them. However, the goal was less to create a thoroughly consistent document than to engage members in a process of construction of provisional agreements that were taken a bit farther in each round. In this sense, the ambiguities in the document are also part of the efforts to create consensus.

Absent in the various editions, for example, is a common position on existing South–South processes of integration. In spite of the critical support given by labour federations of the Southern Cone to MERCOSUR (the Southern Common Market), and of the active participation of some of these in the HSA, the topic is not mentioned. This suppression occurs because there is no common agreement among members, and actors such as CUT-Brazil, a confederation of Brazilian trade unions, refuse to open an internal debate that might question labour's position. Also absent are references to more recent South–South processes, such as the creation of a South American Community of Nations, the Peoples' Trade Agreements, and the Bolivarian Alternative for the Americas proposed by the governments of Cuba and Venezuela in December 2004. Their suppression from the agenda allows actors to "agree to disagree" on this topic.

Finally, the document presents several examples of how demands have been transformed through time. Along with a greater emphasis on the rejection of neoliberalism in general, recent versions make more references to the threats posed by trade agreements to national sovereignty. These are exemplified most often through references to the impacts of NAFTA's Chapter 11 on domestic environmental laws. The demands put forward in *Alternatives* are not anti-capitalist.[27]

Most importantly, it is not an "anti-globalization" programme. In all its editions, the authors emphasize that their goal is not to re-establish protectionist barriers, or demand the implementation of isolationist trade policies.[28] It is, however, a revolutionary document in the sense that based on its critique of free trade policies it presents a non-negotiable denial of neoliberalism, the call for an alternative model and the creation of "a new society". This upward "generality shifting" provides a broader justification for the continuing existence of the Hemispheric Social Alliance than the one provided by the cycles of free trade agreement negotiations.[29] In its 2005 version, the move towards a longer-term and broader agenda, in which neoliberalism became the central target, was made more explicit: "The HSA rejects any agreement based on the neoliberal model . . . The ultimate goal is a new non-neoliberal society" (HSA 2005: 5, author's translation).

Although it is unclear what neoliberalism would be replaced by, the document consistently demands a rebalancing between regulation (domestic and international) and private initiative, with a strong emphasis on the role of national states as the main actors in international relations, and national populations as the ultimate guarantors of popular sovereignty through participatory democracy (HSA 2001: 42).

The sovereignty dilemma

The focus on threats to national sovereignty as an outcome of trade negotiations crosses North–South boundaries, as well as the left–right divide in the ideological spectrum. However, an understanding of the sources of these threats and the most appropriate responses varies considerably along these two axes. In the US, some of the most vociferous critics of trade negotiations are conservative groups that understand these negotiations as undermining the national interest. For these actors, the US should only participate in the multilateral trade system under its own rules. As one of the members of the United States Business and Industrial Council (USBIC) Educational Foundation argued:

> We certainly are not opposed to liberal laws on trade where it serves US nationalism, but we do not believe that they always serve US national interests . . . I want the American government to set the terms of doing business with the United States unilaterally, and if other countries do not agree then they do not have to do business with us . . . I don't believe in a rules-based trade system, because I think there will never be any meaningful consensus on what's fair . . .[30]

The focus is on the growing US trade deficit, the costs of creating new international organizations and bureaucracies, and the possibility of jobs lost to other countries.[31] Other conservative strands of US politics also criticize the limitations imposed by trade negotiations on national sovereignty, focusing on the transfer of power from national to international institutions created by these negotiations, and the potential for increased flows of migrants to the US under new worker visa rules. As one article published in the *New American* argues, "the internationalist architects of the FTAA intend to transform the nation-states of the Western Hemisphere – including the United States – into mere administrative units of the supranational FTAA" (Jasper 2002).

The partial overlap between the arguments on sovereignty and democracy presented by US nationalist conservatives and more progressive trade agreement challengers led to controversial short-term alliances during the NAFTA debates. As Dreiling explains, centre-to-left CSOs had difficulties differentiating their approach from the conservative nationalist opposition to the agreement, a problem that led to internal fissures in US trade coalitions, and to tensions with their Mexican counterparts (see Dreiling 2001: 77–85). In the years that followed, interaction across the ideological spectrum has been limited to non-public exchanges of information, with occasional meetings and signing of broadly worded joint letters addressed to trade negotiators.[32]

Differences between right and left trade challengers in the US are especially apparent with respect to the location of their activities and claims and the proposals on how to deal with threats to national sovereignty. While the right did not engage in transnational collective action, the left became a part of a multilevel field of collective action. Trade challengers often find themselves pressured to act according to "national interests". One participant from the US Catholic Conference of Bishops put this dilemma clearly:

> [We have to answer] why are the US bishops supporting people in other countries, who are not the negotiators, over and against the United States? ... We would say that [it is about] commutative justice, that the bargain itself should be just, that the US has the responsibility to look at not whether the deal will be good for the US or the US people, but whether it is going to be good for the people that the bishops are concerned about in this [other] country.[33]

The motto of the Brazilian Campaign against the Free Trade Area of the Americas – "Sovereignty, yes! The FTAA, no!" – illustrated the way in which the process of multilateral negotiation was domesticated within a nationalistic frame, and how, in the South, it went hand in hand with an anti-imperialist narrative.[34] While Brazilian organizations have not been troubled by the choice of framing in their campaign, these appeals can also be a potential obstacle to building common ground transnationally.[35] As a representative from the AFL-CIO described, when asked about relationships with Latin American allies: "it is very hard to explain that [anti-imperialist] sentiment to US workers. You show them: 'here's a great picture of an anti-FTAA demonstration in Brazil, see how we are unified against this agreement?', and someone asks: 'Why is that American flag burning?!' Trying to explain that is very difficult."[36]

In the various versions of *Alternatives for the Americas*, the issue of national sovereignty is accepted as a key one for all countries. Four main elements compose the shared view of the authors on this issue: first, national sovereignty is a right and should be preserved; second, it is the nation-states' responsibility to ensure that national sovereignty is protected; third, the ultimate guarantors of sovereignty are the citizens, and thus sovereignty should be understood as "popular sovereignty"; and fourth, national sovereignty is not in contradiction with the establishment of international regulations, as long as these are democratically arrived at, with the explicit consensus of the citizens of each country.

The 2002 version clarified the understanding of national sovereignty implied in the document: "National sovereignty should not be understood as autarchy, isolationism or as a pretext for disguised violations of universal human rights. Sovereignty continues to be a right of nations and a basis for legal equality of states within the universe of nations" (HSA 2002: 53–4). Thus sovereignty claims represent political arguments about the right to self-determination, rather than economic arguments against trade liberalization. In spite of this common understanding, actors remain caught between the emphasis on national capabilities and self-determination, and the presentation of alternatives that, in fact, lead to *more* international regulation and *less* self-determination.

The sections of *Alternatives* on environmental protection, human rights, labour rights, and enforcement and dispute resolution illustrate this dilemma.[37] For example, the authors defend the pre-eminence of international environmental agreements over free trade agreements, at the same time that they demand national sovereignty over the right to restrict investments that have negative environmental impacts.[38] The internationalist position is even stronger in the cases of the human rights and labour sections of *Alternatives*. Not only do the authors demand the ratification by all countries of key international human rights conventions, but they also demand the inclusion of their content in trade agreements, and the strengthening of the Inter-American System of Human Rights. In the case of labour, the two key demands are the incorporation of a labour clause, and the progressive upward harmonization of working laws and conditions among signatories of trade agreements. These general demands presuppose a vision of global governance that is not shared by all, one that accepts international regulations that, in practice, put limits to national sovereignty.

The agreement on labour clauses reached in the 2005 version of *Alternatives* is the result of a contentious debate among challengers of trade agreements, labour and non-labour, on the extent to which it is really advisable to introduce labour clauses with trade sanctions for violators. Given the fear of many that these clauses would harm workers in the South and benefit Northern actors, the consensus reached shows the transformation of positions towards a proposed arrangement with labour clauses that are targeted primarily at businesses (and not at countries, as in the case of NAFTA), and that can only be triggered when expressly requested by organizations representing the workers whose rights have been violated.

It is when actors debate possible sanctions and enforcement rules that consensus is hardest, as the authors of *Alternatives* themselves admit: "During the numerous groups' discussions that led to the creation of this document, it was the issue of enforcement that brought out sentiments of nationalism, regional factions, and concerns about protectionism" (HSA 2001: 74; HSA 2002: 95). Not surprisingly, then, this is one of the sections that is most changed when comparing the first and the fifth editions of *Alternatives*. The 2005 version is different from the 1998 one in several aspects: first, it puts greater emphasis on a system that is based on incentives, instead of coercion; second, as in the case of the labour clause, the perpetrators (and not the countries) should be the ones made accountable for violations; and third, the enforcement process has to be transparent and public, with the participation of CSOs and experts. It accepts the idea of supranational tribunals to investigate violation cases and decide on enforcement, at the same time that it guarantees greater control of decisions by demanding the participation of representatives of those affected.

In a similar way to the cases of environment, human rights and labour, this section is an ambiguous balance between the creation of and compliance with international rules and institutions, and respect for national sovereignty. It is also an example of the impact of greater Southern participation in the field of trade challengers. The disciplinary focus on actors that violate laws, instead of on whole countries, was an early demand of the Mexican Action Network on Free Trade (RMALC) during the NAFTA debates about the labour and environmental side agreements; furthermore, the inclusion of those affected by potential sanctions in the enforcement debates and the emphasis on incentives are attempts to avoid enforcement procedures being used as protectionist tools, and to avoid the unintended consequence that penalties negatively affect the development of the South.

In spite of the dedication of members of the HSA to the development of *Alternatives*, this activity is not seen favourably by all challengers of trade agreements. For some, the internal contradictions and inconsistencies of the document render it useless; for others, it is simply not worth the effort.[39] Here the "alternatives" debate links with "strategy" debates. While the need to have feasible alternative proposals is not questioned, for some the exercise of *Alternatives* is a waste of time, because it is not oriented towards change in the short term. Thus, Washington-based organizations, such as Public Citizen, would rather choose another pathway: spend their resources building alternative proposals that are specifically designed to address US legislators' concerns, framing them in a way that will affect decision-making on trade policies at the domestic level.

Conclusion

The efforts by members of the Hemispheric Social Alliance, analysed through the document *Alternatives for the Americas*, are a key example of the mechanisms used to build a common ideational pathway in a heterogeneous transnational arena. However, the Hemispheric Social Alliance faced a well-known dilemma in its efforts to go beyond the identification of common targets to building a joint programme-focused framework. Within the text of the various versions of *Alternatives for the Americas*, two antagonistic pulling forces seem to be at work. One stresses the limits imposed by trade agreements on the capacity of national states to make decisions, and therefore, their anti-democratic character. The other accepts the need for international institutions with power not only to generate agreements, but also to enforce them. Ultimately, to remain members of the HSA, actors may have to face losing most of their freedom and their ability to use different organizational and ideational pathways to transnationality. So far, members have avoided these problems by keeping *Alternatives for the Americas* as a "living document" that could potentially be changed.

The different pathways to transnationality taken by challengers of free trade agreements in the Americas in the past two decades have not led to a neat division between a "civil" and "uncivil" society. The analysis shows that there are multiple pathways to transnationality taken by actors through time, in terms of their sites of activism and the duration of initiatives. It focuses on the dilemmas faced by actors when these choices relate to the task of generating common proposals and alternatives. Successful campaigns and protests have been organized to oppose multilateral negotiations, but reaching international agreements on what should replace them has been much harder.

Notes

1. This definition is based in part on the one offered by Scholte (2003: 11).
2. By contrast, in chapter 11 above, Luk Van Langenhove and Tiziana Scaramagli focus on how nation-states create cross-border linkages and organizations.
3. This research was conducted between 2004 and 2008. For a more thorough analysis of the building of civil society networks and their pathways to transnationality, see von Bülow 2010.
4. For example, Mary Kaldor et al. have argued: "The price that was paid for national sovereignty was the existence of repressive undemocratic governments" and "to the extent that civil society remains wedded to old fashioned notions of sovereignty, the end result may not be democracy but continuing insecurity" (Kaldor, Anheier and Glasius 2005: 16).
5. See, for example, the argument in favour of "deglobalization" made by the founding director of Focus on the Global South (Bello 2002).
6. Sandra Halperin and Gordon Laxer argue that critics of what they call "globalism" from the North tend to view its antidote as global civil society, while critics from the South tend to see the solution as greater sovereignty, not global civil society (2003, esp. p. 3). In fact, these different reactions to the negative effects of globalization span the North–South divide.
7. One of the first systematic contributions to understanding links created among local actors from different countries was the widely quoted "boomerang pattern", defined as a tactic used by domestic actors who are faced with closed domestic channels and hope to achieve their goals by directly contacting international allies (see Keck and Sikkink 1998: 12–13).
8. There is no consensus on how to name the different forms of transnational coalition-building (see, for example, Fox 2002: 352; Tarrow 2005, esp. ch. 9).

9. The literature has focused on the interaction of local and transnational actors with international institutions (Fox and Brown 1998; O'Brien et al. 2000), on the analysis of international protest events (a small sample of recent work includes Adler and Mittelman 2004; Bédoyan, Van Aelst and Walgrave 2004; della Porta 2005; Kolb 2005), and the organization of transnational campaigns (see, for example, Keck and Sikkink 1998).
10. There is an ample literature on this topic, developed especially by scholars of immigration. See, for example, Aihwa Ong's proposal to speak of "flexible citizenship" (Ong 1999) and Nina Glick Schiller's work on "transmigrants" (Glick Schiller 1997).
11. See the contributions in della Porta and Tarrow 2005.
12. The concept of "political opportunities" was defined by Sidney Tarrow as "consistent – but not necessarily formal or permanent – dimensions of the political environment that provide incentives for collective action by affecting people's expectations for success or failure" (Tarrow 1998: 76–7). The use of the concept here emphasizes the relevance of considering how actors may differ in their interpretations of these opportunities, in agreement with the critique of the often overly structural use of the concept presented by authors such as James Jasper and Jeff Goodwin (for this debate, see Goodwin and Jasper 1999a; 1999b; Tilly 1999; Tarrow 1999).
13. This point is made in contradiction to arguments made by other authors; see Hobsbawm 1988: 13–14; Munck 2002: 359.
14. This is not an exhaustive list that explains all the dynamics of interactions.
15. These mechanisms build partly upon the typology of frame alignment processes proposed by David Snow and his colleagues. According to them, frame alignment is defined as "the linkage of individual and social movement organizations' interpretive orientation, such that some set of individual interests, values and beliefs and social movement organizations' activities, goals and ideology are congruent and complementary" (Snow et al. 1986: 464).
16. In this respect, the typology proposed is close to the one developed by Ann Mische, who defined relational mechanisms "as means by which actors jockey over the multiple dimensions of their memberships, identities, and projects in order to build relations with other actors" (Mische 2003: 269). The difference between the mechanisms presented and the ones proposed by Ann Mische is that whereas Mische focuses her attention on "conversational mechanisms", the ones identified here are seen in a broader perspective, as constitutive of the pathways taken by actors.
17. See Blyth 2002, esp. chs 1 and 2, for an analysis of the impact of ideas in contexts of "Knightian uncertainty".
18. This approach follows Mannheim's argument that ideas are not the result of the isolated inspiration of great geniuses, but are best seen as a product of their embeddedness in social relations; see Mannheim 1936.
19. At <http://www.asc-hsa.org> (accessed 1 Mar. 2006).
20. As will be seen below, important exceptions are those organizations that participate in the Continental Campaign against the FTAA but are not members of the Hemispheric Social Alliance, such as Public Citizen in the United States, or ecumenical organizations in Brazil and the conservative organizations that challenge free trade negotiations but do not participate in these initiatives.
21. Interview with Héctor de la Cueva, Director, Center for Labor Investigation and Consulting, Mexico City, Aug. 2004.
22. For example, the publication of various versions of the document *Alternatives for the Americas*, in Spanish, Portuguese and English, has been funded by the John D. and Catherine T. MacArthur Foundation, the Rockefeller Foundation and the Solidago Foundation.

23. For this criticism by Canadian participants in the HSA, see Koo 2001: 44.
24. Initially, the intention was to create a more sophisticated organization, with hemisphere-wide thematic working groups, but only two have been active: the group in charge of monitoring the FTAA negotiations, and the Gender Committee (interview with Gonzalo Berrón, HSA Secretariat, São Paulo, Apr. 2005).
25. As characterized by Doucet 2005.
26. For example, during a meeting between CSOs and official negotiators held in Miami during the FTAA Ministerial Meeting of 2003, government officials criticized protesters for not presenting alternative proposals. In response, one of the members of the Mexican Action Network on Free Trade (RMALC) argued that ever since the NAFTA negotiations civil society challengers of free trade agreements had been working on alternative proposals, which were consolidated in the document *Alternatives for the Americas*.
27. For example, on the issue of foreign investment, all versions of the document argue that "investment regulation should not mean imposing excessive controls on investors or establishing protections for inefficient industries. Rather, it should involve orienting investment and creating conditions to enable investment to serve national development goals while obtaining reasonable returns."
28. "The issue for us, therefore, is not one of free trade vs. protection or integration vs. isolation, but whose rules will prevail and who will benefit from those rules" (HSA 2002: 2).
29. Generality shifting is defined by Mische as a mechanism by which "speakers slide up or down levels of abstraction in regards to the generality or inclusiveness of identity categories" (2003: 271).
30. Interview with Alan Tonelson, Research Fellow, USBIC, Washington, DC, Feb. 2005.
31. For a more thorough exposition of these arguments, see, for example, Tonelson 2000.
32. For example, on 7 November 2001, a total of 170 CSOs, including the USBIC and various labour unions, NGOs and rural organizations, sent a letter to the Speaker of the House of Representatives in opposition to the "fast track" bill that was being debated there.
33. Interview with Rev. Andrew Small, Policy Advisor, US Conference of Catholic Bishops, Washington, DC, Jan. 2006.
34. The anti-imperialist narrative is further explored by Edgardo Lander in chapter 2 above on the discourse of civil society and current decolonization struggles in South America, although he focuses more directly on the case studies of Venezuela, Bolivia and Ecuador than on Brazil.
35. A specific question was asked about this to the person in charge of the Secretariat of the Campaign against the FTAA, who answered that the issue of whether or not a sovereignty-based frame was appropriate was never raised by participating organizations (interview, São Paulo, Apr. 2005).
36. Interview with a representative of the AFL-CIO (American Federation of Labor and Congress of Industrial Organizations), Washington, DC, Aug. 2004.
37. See Doucet 2005 for a discussion that approaches this tension through a discussion of non-territorial and territorial forms of democracy in *Alternatives*.
38. Chapter 13 below by Ricardo A. Gutiérrez and Gustavo Almeira explores more fully the relationship between international environmental and trade agreements, national sovereignty and civil society protests based on concerns over negative environmental impacts.
39. These critiques were raised during interviews with CSOs that are not members of the Hemispheric Social Alliance.

REFERENCES

Adamovsky, Ezequiel (2006) "The World Social Forum's new project: 'The Network of the World's Social Movements'". At <http://www.nadir.org/nadir/initiativ/agp/free/wsf/newproject.htm> (accessed Aug. 2010).

Adler, Glenn and James H. Mittelman (2004) "Reconstituting 'common-sense' knowledge: Representations of globalization protests", *International Relations*, 18(2): 189–211.

Agnew, John (1994) "The territorial trap: The geographical assumptions of international relations theory", *Review of International Political Economy*, 1(1): 53–80.

Akça, Ismet (2003) "'Globalization' and labour strategy: Towards a social movement unionism", in G. Laxer and S. Halperin, eds, *Global Civil Society and Its Limits*, Basingstoke: Palgrave Macmillan, pp. 210–28.

Alianza Social Continental (2006) At <http://www.asc-hsa.org> (accessed 1 Mar. 2006).

Anner, Mark, and Peter Evans (2004) "Building bridges across a double divide: Alliances between US and Latin American labour and NGOs", *Development in Practice*, 14(1–2): 34–47.

Beck, Ulrich (2003) "The analysis of global inequality: From national to cosmopolitan perspective", in M. Kaldor, Helmut Anheier and Marlies Glasius, eds, *Global Civil Society 2003*, Oxford: Oxford University Press, pp. 45–55.

Bédoyan, Isabelle, Peter Van Aelst and Stefaan Walgrave (2004) "Limitations and possibilities of transnational mobilization: The case of EU Summit protesters in Brussels, 2001", *Mobilization*, 9(1): 39–54.

Bello, Walden (2002) *Deglobalization: Ideas for a New World Economy*. London: Zed Books.

Blyth, Mark (2002) *Great Transformations: Economic Ideas and Political Change in the Twentieth Century*. Cambridge: Cambridge University Press.

Dagnino, Evelina, ed. (2002) *Sociedad civil, esfera pública y democratización en América Latina: Brasil*. Mexico City: Editora UNICAMP and Foro de Cultura Económica.

della Porta, Donatella (2005) "Multiple belongings, tolerant identities, and the construction of 'another politics': Between the European Social Forum and the Local Social Fora", in D. della Porta and S. Tarrow, eds, *Transnational Protest and Global Activism*, Lanham, MD: Rowman and Littlefield, pp. 175–202.

della Porta, Donatella and Sidney Tarrow, eds (2005) *Transnational Protest and Global Activism*. Lanham, MD: Rowman and Littlefield.

Doucet, Marc G. (2005) "Territoriality and the democratic paradox: The Hemispheric Social Alliance and its alternative for the Americas", *Contemporary Political Theory*, 4(3): 275–95.

Dreiling, Michael (2001) *Solidarity and Contention: The Politics of Security and Sustainability in the NAFTA Conflict*. New York: Garland.

Emirbayer, Mustafa and Ann Mische (1998) "What is agency?", *American Journal of Sociology*, 103(4): 962–1023.

Ezzat, Heba Raouf (2005) "Beyond methodological modernism: Towards a multicultural paradigm shift in the social sciences", in H. Anheier, Marlies Glasius and Mary Kaldor, eds, *Global Civil Society 2004/5*, London: Sage, pp. 40–58.

Fox, Jonathan (2002) "Lessons from Mexico–US civil society coalitions", in David Brooks and Jonathan Fox, eds, *Cross-Border Dialogues: US–Mexico Social Movement Networking*, San Diego: Center for US-Mexican Studies at the University of California, pp. 341–418.

Fox, Jonathan (2005) "Unpacking 'transnational citizenship'", *Annual Review of Political Science*, 8: 171–201.

Fox, Jonathan and L. David Brown, eds (1998) *The Struggle for Accountability: The World Bank, NGOs, and Grassroots Movements*. Cambridge, MA: MIT Press.

Glasius, Marlies, Mary Kaldor and Helmut Anheier (2005) "Introduction", in M. Glasius, M. Kaldor and H. Anheier, eds, *Global Civil Society Yearbook 2005/6*, London: Sage, pp. 1–18.

Glick Schiller, Nina (1997) "The situation of transnational studies", *Identities*, 4(2): 155–66.

Goodwin, Jeff and James Jasper (1999a) "Caught in a winding, snarling vine: The structural bias of political process theory", *Sociological Forum*, 14(1): 27–54.

Goodwin, Jeff and James Jasper (1999b) "Trouble in paradigms", *Sociological Forum*, 14(1): 107–25.

Halperin, Sandra and Gordon Laxer (2003) "Effective resistance to corporate globalization", in G. Laxer and S. Halperin, *Global Civil Society and Its Limits*, Basingstoke: Palgrave Macmillan, pp. 1–21.

Hobsbawm, Eric J. (1988) "Working-class internationalism", in F. L. van Holthoon and Marcel van der Linden, *Internationalism in the Labour Movement 1830–1940*, Leiden: Brill, pp. 3–16.

HSA (1998) *Alternatives for the Americas*, 1st edn. Bogotá: Hemispheric Social Alliance.

HSA (2001) *Alternatives for the Americas*, 3rd edn. Bogotá: Hemispheric Social Alliance.

HSA (2002) *Alternatives for the Americas*, 4th edn. Bogotá: Hemispheric Social Alliance.

HSA (2005) *Alternatives for the Americas*, 5th edn. Bogotá: Hemispheric Social Alliance.

Imig, Doug and Sidney Tarrow, eds (2001) *Contentious Europeans: Protest and Politics in an Emerging Polity*. Lanham, MD: Rowman and Littlefield.

Jasper, William F. (2002) "Erasing our borders", *New American*, 6 May.

Kaldor, Mary, Helmut Anheier and Marlies Glasius (2005) "Introduction", in H. Anheier, Marlies Glasius and Mary Kaldor, *Global Civil Society 2004/5*, London: Sage, pp. 1–22.

Keck, Margaret and Kathryn Sikkink (1998) *Activists beyond Borders: Advocacy Networks in International Politics*. Ithaca: Cornell University Press.

Klein, Naomi (2003) "Cut the strings", *Guardian*, 1 Feb. At <http://www.guardian.co.uk/politics/2003/feb/01/greenpolitics.globalisation> (accessed June 2010).

Kolb, Felix (2005) "The impact of transnational protest on social movement organizations: Mass media and the making of ATTAC Germany", in D. della

Porta and S. Tarrow, eds, *Transnational Protest and Global Activism*, Lanham, MD: Rowman and Littlefield, pp. 95–120.

Koo, Jah-Hon (2001) "Maintaining an international social movement coalition: The case of the Hemispheric Social Alliance", Master's thesis, School of Social Work, McGill University, Montreal.

Korzeniewicz, Roberto Patricio and William C. Smith (2003) "Redes transnacionales de la sociedad civil: Entre la protesta y la colaboración", in Diana Tussie and Mercedes Botto, eds, *El ALCA y las Cumbres de las Américas: Una nueva relación público-privada?* Buenos Aires: Editorial Biblos and FLACSO/Argentina, pp. 47–74.

Mannheim, Karl (1936) *Ideology and Utopia: An Introduction to the Sociology of Knowledge* (1929). New York: Harcourt Brace.

Milner, Henry (2003) "Civic literacy in global civil society: Excluding the majority from democratic participation", in G. Laxer and S. Halperin, eds, *Global Civil Society and Its Limits*, Basingstoke: Palgrave Macmillan, pp. 189–209.

Mische, Ann (2003) "Cross-talk in movements: Reconceiving the culture–network link", in M. Diani and D. McAdam, eds, *Social Movements and Networks: Relational Approaches to Collective Action*, Oxford: Oxford University Press, 258–280.

Munck, Ronaldo (2002) "Global civil society: Myths and prospects", *Voluntas*, 13(4): 349–61.

Murillo, Maria Victoria (2001) *Labor Unions, Partisan Coalitions, and Market Reforms in Latin America*. Cambridge: Cambridge University Press.

O'Brien, Robert, Anne Marie Goetz, Jan Aart Scholte and Marc Williams (2000) *Contesting Global Governance: Multilateral Economic Institutions and Global Social Movements*. Cambridge: Cambridge University Press.

Ong, Aihwa (1999) *Flexible Citizenship: The Cultural Logics of Transnationality*. Durham, NC: Duke University Press.

Panfichi, Aldo, ed. (2002) *Sociedad civil, esfera pública y democratización en América Latina: Andes y Cono Sur*, Mexico City: Pontifícia Universidad Católica del Perú and Fondo de Cultura Económica.

Ramonet, Ignacio (2006) "Never give up on that other world", *Le Monde Diplomatique*. At <http://mondediplo.com/2006/01/01giveup> (accessed June 2010).

Rootes, Christopher (2005) "A limited transnationalization? The British environmental movement", in D. della Porta and S. Tarrow, eds, *Transnational Protest and Global Activism*, Lanham, MD: Rowman and Littlefield, pp. 21–43.

Scholte, Jan Aart (2003) *Democratizing the Global Economy: The Role of Civil Society*. Coventry, UK: Centre for the Study of Globalisation and Regionalisation, University of Warwick.

Sikkink, Kathryn (2005) "Patterns of dynamic multilevel governance and the insider–outsider coalition", in D. della Porta and S. Tarrow, eds, *Transnational Protest and Global Activism*, Lanham, MD: Rowman and Littlefield, pp. 151–73.

Snow, David and Robert Benford (1988) "Ideology, frame resonance and participant mobilization", in B. Klandermans, Hanspeter Kriesi and Sidney Tarrow, eds, *International Social Movement Research: From Structure to Action: Comparing Social Movement Research across Cultures*, London: JAI Press, pp. 197–219.

Snow, David, E. Burke Rochford, Steven Worden and Robert Benford (1986) "Frame alignment processes, micromobilization, and movement participation", *American Sociological Review*, 51(4): 464–81.

Tarrow, Sidney (1998) *Power in Movement: Social Movements and Contentious Politics*, 2nd edn. Cambridge: Cambridge University Press.

Tarrow, Sidney (1999) "Paradigm warriors: Regress and progress in the study of contentious politics", *Sociological Forum*, 14(1): 71–7.

Tarrow, Sidney (2005) *The New Transnational Activism*. Cambridge: Cambridge University Press.

Tilly, Charles (1999) "Wise quacks", *Sociological Forum*, 14(1): 55–61.

Tonelson, Alan (2000) *The Race to the Bottom: Why a Worldwide Worker Surplus and Uncontrolled Free Trade Are Sinking American Living Standards*. Boulder, CO: Westview Press.

von Bülow, Marisa (2010) *Building Transnational Networks: Civil Society and the Politics of Trade*. Cambridge: Cambridge University Press.

Walker, R. B. J. (1994) "Social movements/world politics", *Millennium*, 23(3): 669–700.

Whitaker, Chico (2005) *Desafios do Fórum Social Mundial: Um modo de ver*. São Paulo: Fundação Perseu Abramo/Edições Loyola.

13

Global production, local protest and the Uruguay River pulp mills project

Ricardo A. Gutiérrez and Gustavo Almeira

This chapter addresses the clash between the local and the global and the way in which local activists resist economic globalization – what Heine and Thakur identify in the Introduction as "glocalization". Drawing upon literature on environmental contention and civil society-centred approaches to environmental foreign policy (Barkdull and Harris 2009), it shows how local environmental protest in the Argentine province of Entre Ríos forced a change in the national government's environmental foreign policy and translated into a major diplomatic controversy between Argentina and Uruguay.[1]

The Uruguay River is part of the Plata River basin and forms part of the boundary between Argentina and Brazil (upper section) and between Argentina and Uruguay (lower section), separating the Argentine province of Entre Ríos from the western departments of Uruguay. In July 2002, the Spanish firm ENCE requested an environmental permit to build a pulp mill on the shore of the Uruguay River from the Uruguayan government. One year later, the Finnish firm Botnia announced its proposal to build a similar plant and so, in March of 2004, it requested from the Uruguayan government the corresponding environmental permit.

With government approval, both plants were to be built near the small Uruguayan city of Fray Bentos (23,000 inhabitants), located 300 kilometres west of Montevideo (capital of Uruguay) and in front of the small Argentine city of Gualeguaychú (80,000 inhabitants). The ENCE plant was originally projected to produce 400,000 tons per year of pulp from eucalyptus chips, while the Botnia plant was expected to produce 1 million tons per year of pulp (FARN 2006: 1–2). The total investment estimated for building the plants amounted to US$500,000–1 million for the ENCE plant and US$1 million for the Botnia plant (MRREE Uruguay 2006).

Given their geographic location, the pulp mill projects soon provoked the resistance of Argentine local environmental groups. Between the end of 2002 and the beginning of 2005, the Argentine government agreed to a shared monitoring plan without rejecting the construction of the plants; however, environmental resistance grew steadily. Eventually, this forced the Argentine national government to take a more critical position. The Argentine government moved from an initial acquiescence to the projects towards the decision to take Uruguay to the International Court of Justice (ICJ). Replicating the protesters' arguments and demands, in May 2006 Argentina claimed before the ICJ that Uruguay had violated the 1975 bilateral treaty regulating the common use of the Uruguay River, as Uruguay had failed either to discuss with Argentina its decision to build the pulp mills, or to take into account the potential environmental impact on the river.

How to explain such a change in only two years? How was it possible that a local environmental protest escalated into an international dispute between two historically allied countries? Why did the Argentine government take up the protesters' agenda and decide to challenge Uruguay before the ICJ?

To answer these questions, this chapter focuses on the nature of global production projects and their impact on the domestic economy of the recipient country; the peculiarities of the protest and its public salience; and the nature of state institutions in charge of environmental and water policies in Argentina. We argue that social protest-triggered issue salience and weak environmental institutions on the Argentine side combined with Uruguayan resistance to any compromise to explain Argentina's shift in foreign policy priorities.

Uruguay's national interest in global production

Following Heine and Thakur's distinction between the globalization process and the globalization project (in the Introduction to this book), it is easy to see to what extent Uruguay adopted globalization as its own project. The Fray Bentos pulp mill projects are part of a long-term national programme to develop the forestry sector in Uruguay as a way of profiting from the international trend to "globalize" the production of timber and cellulose pulp. Over the past two decades, large-scale industrial tree plantations have grown steadily in the Southern Cone of South

America as part of a movement to transfer the production of timber and cellulose pulp while keeping the less contaminating and higher value-added production of paper in the North (Romero and Tubío 2004). Different factors underlie the transfer of tree plantation and cellulose pulp production to the Southern Cone and other Southern sites. Urbanization, the exhaustion of forests and growing environmental concerns in the North, along with the deforestation of tropical forests and the worldwide increase of paper consumption, led multinationals and Northern firms to seek new business opportunities in the South. The globalization of timber and cellulose pulp production has also been sponsored by international organizations such as the World Bank; following the rationale that tree plantation would favour weather stabilization and natural resources protection as well as the development of new business opportunities, not only for multinationals, but also for Southern countries (Romero and Tubío 2004; Torres Rojo and Fossati 2004).

Uruguay, like other South American countries, envisioned the development of the forestry sector as a way of diversifying the domestic economy and increasing exports. From 1987 on, with the passing of the so-called Forests' Law, the Uruguayan government actively promoted the development of forestry, particularly the planting of eucalyptus and pine trees for industrial consumption (Alvarado 2007). Specific state incentives for the development of the forestry sector (such as tax exemption) were complemented with general mechanisms for investment promotion. Passed in 1998, Law 16906 sets out that foreign investment must not be "discriminated" against in favour of domestic investment and that its admission to the country needs no previous state authorization, while the free international transfer of capital and profits is guaranteed. General and specific incentives for the forestry sector resulted in a mixed (domestic and foreign) composition of forestry firms, with a strong presence of foreign investors (Torres Rojo and Fossati 2004).

The total forested area (both native and planted forests) of Uruguay is 1,350,000 hectares, that is, 7.7 per cent of the country's total area. Roughly half of the forested area corresponds to trees for industrial use (600,000 hectares), most of which were planted after 1988. The growing significance of tree plantation manifests itself in the forestry sector trade balance. Historically, the sector trade balance was negative; with an annual deficit of approximately US$16 million between 1989 and 1996. Yet that tendency changed in 1997. In 1999 exports surpassed imports by US$18 million (Forestal WEB 2008).

As of 2000, the rural sector's participation in the Uruguayan GDP was 10 per cent, but the sector's significance in the economy was (and is) high for it offers raw materials for industrial production and is the largest exporting sector. Between 1988 and 2000, the highest increase within rural exports corresponded to timber products – from US$10 million in 1988 to US$100 million in 2000 (Torres Rojo and Fossati 2004).

To promote such an increase, the Uruguayan state invested (through direct disbursement or tax exemption) US$500 million between 1988 and 2000 (around 4 per cent of GDP) (Zibechi 2005). After actively promoting export-oriented timber production, the Uruguayan government started to develop strategies to attract foreign investment for cellulose pulp production in order to diversify the structure of timber-related products and incorporate higher value-added exports.

As part of this diversification strategy, Uruguay signed an investment treaty with Finland (the world's largest producer of paper products after the United States and Canada) in 2002 (López Echagüe 2006: 96–101). This treaty significantly widened the notion of expropriation so as to include "other direct or indirect measures with effects equivalent to expropriation or nationalization" (Article 5), forcing the Uruguayan government to compensate the expropriated firm even in the case of "indirect" measures. In so doing, the Uruguay government was showing its firm decision to increase Uruguay's participation in the global timber-and-pulp market.[2]

The building of the Fray Bentos pulp mills was the next step in the development strategy that the Uruguayan government had envisioned and had been implementing since the end of the 1980s. The official expectations were that, once fully operational, both plants would contribute 2.5 per cent of GDP, 1 per cent of the national workforce, and 1 per cent of total annual government revenues (MRREE Uruguay 2006). Participation in the world timber-and-pulp market was a major, long-term state policy. Therefore, it is not surprising that Uruguay was reluctant to discuss the Fray Bentos projects with the Argentine government, no matter what the Uruguay River Treaty said or what the environmental protesters from across the river claimed.

Bilateral institutional setting and first Argentine foreign policy choice

In 1975, Argentina and Uruguay signed the Uruguay River Treaty (or Estatuto del Río Uruguay – henceforth, the Estatuto) with the "aim of establishing common mechanisms needed for the rational and optimal management of the Uruguay River" (Article 1). To carry out that goal, the Estatuto created the Uruguay River Administration Commission/ Comisión Administradora del Río Uruguay (CARU), made up of "equal number of delegates for both Parties" (Article 49).

The Estatuto establishes that "the Party that intends ... the realization of whatever works that may affect the river's navigation, hydrological regime, or water quality must inform the CARU, which will determine, in up to thirty days, whether the project may cause a damage to the other Party" (Article 7). Furthermore, Article 13 specifies that the obligation to inform the other party "applies to all works referred to in Article 7, be they national or binational, that either Party intends to realize, within its jurisdiction, on the Uruguay River *outside the section defined as River* and the correspondent areas of influence" (emphasis added). Finally, Article 27 stresses that "each Party's right to use the river's water, within its jurisdiction, with sanitation, industrial, or agricultural purposes will be exerted without escaping the procedure established" by Article 7, when such an intervention may affect the river's regime or the water's quality.

The Estatuto also defines the procedures for the resolution of controversies. Article 58 states that the CARU is the first instance for the consideration of controversies, which can be filed by either Party. If no agreement is reached within the set deadline, "any controversy ... may be presented by either Party before the International Court of Justice" (Article 60).

In November 2002, understanding that Articles 7, 13 and 58 of the Estatuto invested them with the right to do so, Argentine delegates to the CARU requested that the Uruguayan Ministry for the Environment send them the environmental impact project presented by ENCE in July 2002. Instead of doing so, the Uruguayan Ministry for the Environment granted an environmental permit to the ENCE project in October 2003, provoking a formal complaint from the Argentine delegation.

In response, the Uruguayan foreign affairs minister sent the ENCE project to his Argentine counterpart in November 2003. The Argentine foreign affairs minister forwarded the project to the Argentine delegation in the CARU. But the Uruguayan government prevented its delegation from discussing the project within the CARU. The Argentine delegation asked the Argentine National Water Institute (INA) to assess the information sent by the Uruguayan government. In February 2004, the INA submitted a report to the CARU that argued that the Fray Bentos pulp mills would have a "considerable" environmental impact and recommended substituting TCF technology for the ECF technology.[3]

In 2004, in spite of the INA's negative report and the previous complaints from the Argentine delegation, the Argentine government decided to minimize the discussion over the Fray Bentos pulp mills. This was probably due to the low importance assigned to environmental issues by the Néstor Kirchner administration and the fact that the Argentine president wanted to avoid a dispute at the time of the Uruguayan presidential elections. Tabaré Vazquez, from the Frente Amplio coalition, was the frontrunner and Kirchner had already thrown his support behind him.

In June of that year, the foreign affairs ministers of Argentina and Uruguay, somehow bypassing the controversy resolution mechanisms established by the Estatuto, "signed a bilateral agreement ending the controversy over the installation of a pulp mill in Fray Bentos" (JGM Argentina 2005: 107). The core of that agreement consisted in requesting the CARU not to assess the pulp mill projects, but to put together a plan to monitor the water's quality. A "preliminary formulation" of the plan was drawn up in November, while the definition of precise monitoring procedures and standards was scheduled for some time in the near future (MRREE Uruguay 2006).

With that agreement, the Argentine government tried to avoid controversy over the pulp mills, despite the fact that the CARU had never analysed the ENCE and Botnia projects. As a confirmation of the Argentine government's acquiescence, the Argentine Chief of Cabinet declared before the Argentine House of Representatives in March 2005: "there would not be any sensitive environmental impact on the Argentine side; it is thought that such an impact would basically be the bad smell that usually comes from pulp mills" (*Clarín* 2006). Tabaré Vázquez, elected Uruguayan president and a close ally of President Kirchner, took office that month.

Developing an opposition network

While the Argentine government ended up opting for an agreement that did not imply any important concession from the Uruguayan government or the foreign investors, in 2003, Gualeguaychú's environmental resistance to the Fray Bentos pulp mills began to develop a "blocking network" (Hochstetler and Keck 2007). Rather than facilitating "the adoption or implementation of policies that they support (enabling activities)", blocking networks typically mobilize resources "to block policies they oppose (blocking activities)" (Hochstetler and Keck 2007: 19).

In 2003, environmentalists from Gualeguaychú and other Entre Ríos cities began to interact to discuss the pulp mill projects. In September, they held the first demonstration against the pulp mills in Gualeguaychú, expressing "the most absolute opposition to the installation of a pulp mill in Fray Bentos, Republic of Uruguay" and rejecting "the environmental impact studies submitted by the foreign investors, which have already been criticized by non-governmental organizations before the Uruguayan

National Office for the Environment" (quoted in Alcañiz and Gutiérrez 2009: 111).

After this first demonstration, the Gualeguaychú environmentalists continued to interact, build wider support within the city and act to get municipal officials to pay more attention to the issue. In February 2005, they stormed the popular Gualeguaychú Carnival, distributing surgical masks to call attention to the risks of the pulp mills. In the words of one of the protesters, by then they were "no more than 10 nuts distributing surgical masks. Nobody paid much attention to us, we thought that our fight would end up being a failure" (quoted in López Echagüe 2006: 61). A rapid escalation of an environmental protest, without precedent in Argentine history, would start in just a few months.

In March 2005, Gualeguaychú environmentalists held an open meeting in a local club to discuss the pulp mill projects. With an unexpected level of attendance, they decided to demonstrate on the Gualeguaychú–Fray Bentos international bridge on 30 April. As many as 40,000 people marched over the international bridge, blocking transit between the two countries – an extraordinary attendance when compared with Gualeguaychú's population of 80,000 inhabitants. The day marked the creation of a new collective actor which, from then on, would lead the protest against the pulp mills: the Environmental Assembly of the Citizens of Gualeguaychú (or Asamblea Ciudadana Ambiental de Gualeguaychú – henceforth, the Asamblea or Gualeguaychú Asamblea).

The Asamblea organized occasional demonstrations against the pulp mills projects – including road and bridge blockades – throughout 2005. But its activities would intensify in the summer of 2005–6. Argentine visitors are crucial for Uruguayan tourism. Besides air traffic, there are two major access points to Uruguay from Argentina: by ferry from the Buenos Aires port or by land transportation crossing the three international bridges over the Uruguay River. Those bridges connect Uruguay with three Entre Ríos cities: Concordia, Colón and Gualeguaychú.

Just before Christmas Eve 2005, the Asamblea started blocking the Gualeguaychú–Fray Bentos international bridge for a few hours. By then, environmental assemblies had formed in Colón and Concordia following the Gualeguaychú experience. Those assemblies would join the Gualeguaychú Asamblea in its fight against the pulp mills, on some occasions also blocking their cities' international bridges.

In January, blockades were intensified during the peak tourist season, upsetting both Argentine tourists and Uruguayans at large. Throughout 2006, the Asambleas of Gualeguaychú, Colón and Concordia blocked the international bridges on several occasions (sometimes simultaneously). In November, as all bilateral attempts to solve the dispute proved unsuccessful, the Gualeguaychú Asamblea decided to block the bridge to Fray Bentos "indeterminately". The "10 nuts" who had started the street demonstrations in 2005 evolved into an important blocking network, with non-governmental organizations (NGOs) and other neighbours' associations from Entre Ríos and the rest of the country.

In the meantime, the conflict over the pulp mills became a top-priority issue in the media, with daily coverage in most important newspapers and broadcasting networks. Given the increasing salience of the issue, the Argentina government was forced to review its initial acquiescence to the pulp mills projects. In August 2005, President Néstor Kirchner met the Asamblea in Gualeguaychú and stated that the claim against the pulp mills was a "national issue" (Carbone 2005).

Explaining protest escalation and issue salience

Three variables help explain the escalation of the local protest into a strong blocking network and the high public salience of the pulp mills issue: the interjurisdictional nature of water issues; the peculiarities of the protest; and the transboundary dimension of the conflict.

The building of a blocking network was facilitated by the interjurisdictional nature of water issues, which under certain circumstances fosters the formation of multilevel networks and appeals to state actors from different government levels. Water policy, like other environmental policies, involves negotiations and conflicts across different overlapping jurisdictions (Schneider and Scholz 2003). Watercourses do not recognize political borders or the federal division of power. In Argentina, the provinces hold legal dominion over water resources, but water use depends on decisions and policies made by the three levels of government (municipal, provincial and national).

As the Uruguay River forms part of the boundary between Argentina and Uruguay, there is an international jurisdiction in addition to the domestic jurisdictions. Any agreement or controversy over the shared use of international rivers requires the diplomatic intervention of the national governments, hence the importance of the Uruguay River Treaty.

Besides diplomatic implications, overlapping jurisdictions have two important effects. First, they enable the development of networks of environmental activists, which in turn allow for a more effective and democratic sharing of information and resources to solve common problems (Schneider and Scholz 2003; Keck and Sikkink 1998).[4] At the time of the first protests, Uruguayan NGOs shared information with Argentine environmentalists in Entre Ríos (López Echagüe 2006: 60–1). As the conflict progressed, the protests concentrated on the Argentine side carried on with a network of different neighbours' associations and environmental NGOs, such as the Centro de Derechos Humanos y Ambiente/Center for Human Rights and Environment (CEDHA), which provided crucial leadership and legal assistance to the neighbours' groups. Out of that assistance came the proposal to challenge Uruguay before the ICJ, a proposal that the *asambleístas* made their own and pressed the Argentine government to pursue.

Second, as local, provincial and national authorities have legal and political stakes in water policy, environmental advocates can hold them all accountable. The neighbours' associations held the governor of Entre Ríos and the national executive accountable to them in their claims for expected damages. This is consistent with Keck and Sikkink's "accountability politics", by which advocates attempt to pressure political actors from different government levels into closing "the distance between discourse and practice" (1998: 24).

As to the peculiarities of the protest, the building of a strong blocking network around the pulp mills issue and its extensive media coverage was favoured by a combination of middle-class radicalism and socio-environmentalism. The radical tactic of blocking the international bridges between Argentina and Uruguay immediately elevated the profile of the protesters' cause. In adopting this tactic, the *asambleístas* mimicked the *piqueteros*; that is, the organizations of unemployed workers in Argentina that blocked roads in order to force authorities to negotiate their withdrawal from the barriers in exchange for jobs or government subsidies (Alcañiz and Scheier 2007). This tactic, we argue, compelled the national government to address the activists' claim. On the one hand, it led the Uruguay government to log a formal complaint before its Argentine counterpart, demanding the ending of the blockades because they affected the country's trade and tourism. On the other, extensive media coverage made it impossible for the Argentine government to downplay the controversy with Uruguay any longer.

In contrast to the *piqueteros*, however, the *asambleístas* are not organized along class cleavages. The protesting neighbour associations and environmental NGOs show a diverse socioeconomic composition, albeit with a predominance of middle-class elements. The Entre Ríos protesters fit what Cotgrove and Duff call the new "middle-class radicalism". That is: "new social groups ... which cut across traditional class-based alignments and cleavages", endorsing "direct action, and the growth of outside politics, [and] a decline in partisan support for the traditional parties ..." (Cotgrove and Duff 2003, quoted in Gutiérrez and Alcañiz 2007: 7).

Yet unlike the middle-class radicalism depicted by Cotgrove and Duff, the Entre Ríos protesters did not choose radical tactics because they held anti-capitalist views. They did so because they had learnt from recent Argentine history that they would hardly attract extensive media coverage and government attention unless they adopted the radical, media-prone tactics of the *piqueteros*.

Another remarkable characteristic of the protest lies in the activists' ability to combine environmental and economic concerns. A strong connection was established between the perception of an environmental risk and the economic activities that are prevalent in the Gualeguaychú area, resembling the kind of socio-environmentalism described by Hochstetler and Keck (2007: 13), that is, a combination of environmental sustainability and sustainable livelihood. From the onset, the activists argued that the pulp mills would have a negative impact on the regional development model based on environmentally friendly economic activities. While the health effects of pollution, the visual impact and unpleasant smells would affect regional tourism centred on the Uruguay River and its "pristine" waters, the pulp mills would also threaten agricultural activities in two different ways: by substituting forestland for agricultural land, and by depreciating "regional" rural products because of the likely pollution of natural resources. The merging of environmental and economic concerns, along with the non-partisan nature of the claim, allowed the initial environmental protest to become a major issue for Gualeguaychú neighbours at large, something soon shared by organizations and social movements from Entre Ríos and the rest of the country.

If middle-class radicalism secured extensive media coverage, non-partisan socio-environmentalism helped the Asamblea to gain wide social representation, thus explaining the activists' success in building a strong blocking network. It is not difficult to understand why the Argentine government refused to repress the blockades and decided instead to transform the controversy over the pulp mills into a top priority issue. Considering that, as a general policy, the Kirchner administration did not authorize the repression of unemployed workers' *piquetes* and chose to deactivate the protests by co-opting their leaders, it is hard to imagine that it would send in security forces to remove this group of protesters from the road – protesters from a wide variety of social backgrounds, who were not acting under the banner of any particular party and who were fighting for a cause with strong regional support, all in full view of TV cameras and news reporters.

Finally, and related to the overlapping jurisdictions, the transboundary dimension of the conflict made it easier for Argentine actors to blame culprits "from the other side" without confronting strong advocates of pulp mills (or the forestry sector) who came "from within". This is related to the "asymmetric" distribution of risks and benefits between Fray Bentos (Uruguay) and Gualeguaychú (Argentina). While the risks would affect both sides of the river, the benefits would only accrue to Fray Bentos and other Uruguayan locations (Vara 2007). Within Argentina, this would explain the success of the sustained collective mobilization against the Uruguayan pulp mills vis-à-vis other cases in which risks and benefits might be more "symmetrically" distributed.

Unlike Uruguay, where the defence of the pulp mills seemed to have reached the status of an indisputable nationalist cause, in Argentina the pulp mills issue became a top priority on the government agenda, but was far from becoming a nationalist cause (Merlinsky 2008). Missing in Argentina was (and is) any consensus around the pulp mills issue as a nationalist cause. President Kirchner's definition of the conflict as a "national issue" was more to appease the activists and press the Uruguayan government to reach a bilateral solution than the expression of any anti-Uruguayan nationalist sentiment. It is worth stressing that, despite declaring it a "national issue", President Kirchner also tried to circumscribe the controversy as an "environmental issue" (*La Nación* 2006).

Yet the fact that the source of the alleged risks was across the border seemed to have facilitated the strengthening of the claim against the pulp mills within Entre Ríos, as well as the Argentine government's final decision to support it. What would have happened if the pulp mills had been located on "this" side of the river? In that case, even if a local environmental claim had emerged, would it have found as much local and regional support as in the case at hand? How would regional economic interests have reacted to the building of pulp mills? What would have been the strategy of provincial and the national government? The building of a strong blocking network capable of pressing the Argentine government would have been more difficult, we argue, if the source of the risks had been on "this" side of the river. In this regard, it is worth noting how the environmental protest originated in the "exchange" of warnings between Entre Ríos and Uruguay activists about risky projects on both sides of the border. Each party had reached the conclusion that it would be more difficult to oppose the project within its own country and that the chances of preventing the projects from implementation would increase if the resistance came from across the border.

To sum up, the interjurisdictional nature of water issues, middle-class radicalism, socio-environmentalism and the transboundary dimension of the conflict help explain the building of a strong blocking network and the salience of the issue in the media and the public mind. There is a vast literature linking issue salience with policy outcomes (Alcañiz and Gutiérrez 2009). Growing socio-environmental protests supported by a wide range of regional social and political actors, systematically covered by the national media, put pressure on the Kirchner administration (2003–7) to pay more attention to the issue. But that does not explain why the

Argentine government took up the protesters' policy choice. To explain this, we must now turn to the foreign policy alternatives tried by the Argentine government.

Searching for a foreign policy

Despite its initial acquiescence to the pulp mill projects, the Argentine government's stance started changing after the first massive demonstration on the Gualeguaychú–Fray Bentos international bridge and the creation of the Asamblea on 30 March 2005.

In May 2005, the presidents of Argentina and Uruguay met in Buenos Aires and agreed on the creation of a Bilateral High-Level Technical Group (GTAN) for the exchange of information and the formulation of monitoring mechanisms. The GTAN first met in August 2005. By 31 January 2006, however, when the first report was due, the Argentine and the Uruguayan delegations in the GTAN could not come out with a joint report and each delegation announced that separate reports would be presented. Released on 3 February, the Argentine report strongly criticized Uruguay for the lack of accurate studies on the pulp mills' environmental impacts, the lack of serious monitoring plans and the violation of the Uruguay River Treaty (MRECIC Argentina 2006). Two weeks later, the Argentine foreign affairs minister detailed the Uruguayan violations of the Estatuto, referring to the permits granted to the firms without previous consultation: the environmental permits and the authorization to build port facilities.

Given the escalation of the protest, the Argentine government's strategy was twofold. First, the president tried to downgrade the diplomatic conflict by defining it strictly as "an environmental issue" (*La Nación* 2006) and by seeking a bilateral solution confined to technical discussion of the environmental impact. Second, the government, targeting domestic audiences, legitimized the protesters' claims on several occasions and showed no intention of impeding or repressing the blockades, despite numerous requests from the Uruguayan government to do so.

Thus, caught between these opposite strategies, in March 2006 the Argentine president decided to upgrade the controversy over the pulp mills on the government agenda and included it in his 2006 opening speech before the National Congress. After criticizing Uruguay for violating the Estatuto, unilaterally authorizing the construction of the pulp mills and impeding any bilateral negotiation, the Argentine president requested that the construction work be called off for 90 days in order to convene an outside technical commission to assess the pulp mills' environmental impact. In his request, President Kirchner addressed the Uruguayan president as follows: "let us avoid being drawn into nationalisms without content. I beg you, I ask you with the greatest humility" (Vidal 2006). Despite the criticism of the Uruguayan government, that was an appeal to find a diplomatic solution, even though the protesters were demanding that, in compliance with the Estatuto, the dispute be solved before the ICJ.

The Uruguayan government first responded to the Argentine request with the argument that the works would not be called off under any circumstances and no negotiation would be started until the road blockades were stopped. However, a surprise agreement was announced by both presidents in Santiago de Chile at the inauguration of President Michelle Bachelet: the blockades would be stopped and the construction works would be called off for 90 days, during which time a solution to the controversy would be sought – much resembling President Kirchner's request.

At the beginning of 2006, the Argentine government was still focused on finding a diplomatic solution. Two factors prevented it from continuing to minimize the bilateral controversy any longer: the issue's extensive media coverage nationwide and the Uruguayan government's growing intransigency over the redefinition of the pulp mill projects. These factors were stimulated, in turn, by the escalation of the environmental protest in and beyond Entre Ríos, and the crucial intervention of the governor of the province of Entre Ríos at the beginning of 2005. The intervention of the provincial governor (with its impact on the national media and the Uruguayan government) gave a wider national and political scope to Gualeguaychú's environmental protest, thus forcing the national government to take a more active and assertive stance towards Uruguay.

In Uruguay, President Vázquez could not stick to the Santiago agreement. All the opposition forces, which had so far backed the government's policy towards the pulp mills and the Argentine complaints, criticized Vázquez for having announced such an agreement. In addition, Botnia only called off its construction works for 10 days, which was unacceptable to the Argentine government and the Gualeguaychú protesters. Vázquez's immediate reaction was to blame Botnia for the failure of the Santiago agreement, but he soon changed his strategy when the protesters decided to block the Gualeguaychú and Colón bridges again. On 18 April 2006, Uruguay filed a demand before MERCOSUR (Southern Common Market), accusing Argentina of not guaranteeing international land transit and blaming it for the economic losses incurred by the bridge blockades. That marked the end of bilateral attempts and forced the Argentine government to seek international mediation.

The Argentine government's first international tactic was to boycott the World Bank/International Finance Corporation (IFC) credit for the

Botnia plant and to simultaneously pressure the environmental Asambleas into stopping the blockades so as to avoid further complaints from Uruguay. In May 2006, the national government decided to go further and finally filed a demand before the ICJ, accusing Uruguay of having violated the Uruguay River Treaty and requesting a provisional injunction for the construction works to be called off immediately on the grounds that they were already causing irreversible environmental damage.

On 7 July 2006, Romina Picolotti, president of CEDHA and legal adviser to the state of Entre Ríos and the Gualeguaychú Asamblea, took office as Secretary for the Environment. By picking Picolotti for the National Secretariat for the Environment, President Kirchner seemed to be pursuing two different strategies: to neutralize and appease the Entre Ríos environmental protesters, and to prepare the national government for the legal battles to be fought in different international arenas. Both strategies would prove unsuccessful.

The ICJ hearings regarding the provisional measure requested by Argentina were held on 8 and 9 June 2006. On 13 July, the ICJ delivered a somewhat ambiguous ruling: the Argentine argument that the construction works were provoking irreversible environmental damage was denied, but Uruguay was to be held responsible for any pollution effects the pulp mills might have in the future. While each party tried to show that the ICJ rule was favourable to its position, the ICJ did not rule on the substantive matter: the violation of the Uruguay River Treaty.

On 6 September 2006, another legal international battle was ambiguously won (or lost) when the MERCOSUR arbitration tribunal ruled that Argentina had not tried to prevent the blockade of the international bridges (thus partly agreeing with Uruguay's position), but rejected Uruguay's proposal that future blockades be prevented through MERCOSUR mechanisms.

In the middle of the international legal battle, in September 2006, ENCE suddenly announced its intention to relocate its pulp mill, and two months later stated that the plant would be built on the Uruguayan shore of the Plata River. However, this news did not help to appease the protesters or to stop the international battle – the protesters kept on with their non-negotiable goal: "No pulp mills on the Uruguay River."

In October, the World Bank/IFC released its final environmental impact study "showing" that the Fray Bentos pulp mills projects would not have any negative impact on the environment and tourist activities. Secretary Picolotti was in charge of convincing the World Bank board that the credit requested by Botnia be rejected. But she was not successful: in November the World Bank decided to finance the Botnia project.

In November, Uruguay requested the ICJ to rule in favour of a provisional measure to force the Argentine government to prevent the bridge blockades. On 23 January 2007, the court ruled that the blockades were not causing irreparable damage and therefore there was no reason to grant Uruguay's request for the measure.

As a last resort, the Kirchner administration sought the mediation of the Spanish king. After several tough meetings in Buenos Aires, Madrid, Montevideo, New York and Santiago de Chile, Spanish mediation was terminated and Uruguay abruptly authorized Botnia to start its operation in November 2007. Since this last failure, both countries have exclusively concentrated on the ICJ process, while the blocking of the Gualeguaychú–Fray Bentos bridge has never been lifted.

Why the government took up the protesters' policy choice

Why did the Argentine government end up endorsing the protesters' policy choice and filing a demand against Uruguay before the ICJ? Two additional variables must be considered in answering this question: the weakness of environmental institutions and the lack of (domestic and foreign) environmental policy in Argentina; and the reluctance of Uruguay to reach any compromise with Argentina.

The weakness of environmental institutions and the lack of an environmental policy, expressing the low priority of environmental issues in Argentina, facilitated the adoption of the protesters' policy choice (Reboratti 2007). Argentina, like many developing states, lacks a strong, centralized environmental institution. Until very recently, the top domestic institution in environmental policy, an under-secretariat, was part of the Ministry of Health and Sustainable Development. As a result of the Entre Ríos conflict, and indicative of the non-existence of any state policy on the environment, President Néstor Kirchner upgraded the agency to a Secretariat dependent on the Chief of the Cabinet and appointed the head of one of the leading NGOs in the Entre Ríos protests (CEDHA) as the new Secretary for the Environment.

Such a "policy void" enhanced the protesters' power to advance their policy choices, as weak environmental institutions offer little resistance to the policy agenda of protesters. What the Kirchner administration had available as a legal framework was the Estatuto that regulates the common use of the Uruguay River. But the government started to pay more attention to the Estatuto and ended up resorting to it to seek a way out of the conflict only because of the protesters' pressure and after several attempts at bilateral negotiation failed.

Uruguay's reluctance to reach any compromise further pushed the Argentine government towards the protesters' position. The successive failures of the GTAN, the Santiago de Chile agreement and the Spanish mediation showed Uruguay's intransigence towards engaging in any negotiation over the plants' location. Beyond likely nationalist sentiments, the Uruguayan intransigence can be explained in the context of the long-term national policy to insert the country into the world timber-and-pulp market and the important incentives and legal compromises associated with this, as well as the initial acceptance of Argentina.

The Argentine government did not share the protesters' claim that *both* plants had to be relocated away from the Uruguay River. After ENCE suddenly announced its decision to relocate its plant on the shore of the Plata River, the Argentine government, convinced that the Botnia plant could not be relocated, tried to negotiate a bilateral monitoring plan for Botnia in the context of the Spanish mediation – a proposal opposed by the *asambleístas*. The abrupt way in which the Spanish mediation was terminated and Uruguay authorized Botnia to start operations showed yet again Uruguay's resistance to negotiating and the Argentine government's inability to find a middle ground between its decision not to repress the blockades and its desire to achieve an agreement with Uruguay. The Argentine government stuck to the road map given by the Estatuto and focused on the ICJ ruling – perhaps in the hope that the protest would weaken in the meantime.

In sum, devoid of an environmental policy of its own and caught between two intransigencies (that of the protesters and that of the Uruguayan government), the Argentine government ended up opting for international legal dispute settlement to avoid domestic political costs. Allee and Huth argue that national executives "will seek legal dispute settlement in situations where they anticipate sizable domestic political costs should they attempt to settle a dispute through the making of bilateral, negotiated concessions" (2006: 219). Consistently, President Kirchner decided to pursue international legal venues to solve the Entre Ríos conflict precisely for these reasons, that is, in order to avoid dealing directly with the "environmental *piqueteros*", given that he could not use coercion or control media coverage.

Conclusion

This chapter has examined a case of glocalization in which local activists were able to build a strong blocking network to oppose multinational projects "from across the border", attract extensive media coverage and set the issue high on the public agenda. In so doing, it has shown how and why the national government took up the activists' policy choice, thus underlining under what (perhaps exceptional) conditions civil society actors may influence environmental foreign policy (cf. Barkdull and Harris 2009; Alcañiz and Gutiérrez 2009).

We argue that the salience of an issue triggered by social protest and the circumstance of weak environmental institutions on the Argentine side, combined with Uruguayan resistance to any compromise, explain Argentina's foreign policy priorities. In turn, three variables explain the escalation of local protest into a strong blocking network and the high public salience of the pulp mills issue: the interjurisdictional nature of water issues; the peculiarities of the protest (middle-class radicalism and socio-environmentalism); and the transboundary dimension of the conflict. Central to this account were the protest techniques chosen by the activists, enhancing the notion that radical (and not necessarily legal) measures are sometimes required to generate sufficient attention from the authorities.

It is early to determine whether the Gualeguaychú environmental protest will evolve into an *effective* blocking network in terms of its non-negotiable goal (no pulp mills on the Uruguay River) or whether it will ever become an *enabling* network. Despite the ICJ's final ruling in April 2010 in favour of the mill, the blockades continued. In the meantime, a final observation on the glocalization conflict involved can be made.

Two opposing domestic stances regarding globalization appear in the case at hand. On the one hand, there is the Uruguayan government's determined embrace of the *globalization project* – see the Introduction to this book on the distinction between the globalization *process* and the globalization *project*. Uruguay's reluctance to agree to any compromise solution to the conflict must be understood in the light of its long-term national policy to insert the country into the world timber-and-pulp market. As expressed by the Uruguay–Finland investment treaty, Uruguay embraced the globalization project in *asymmetrical* conditions, insofar as its power to negotiate was restricted to accepting or rejecting the terms of the investing party – see the Introduction to this book. Yet, it is also true that Uruguay actively pursued the expansion of the forestry sector as a state policy. It is that determination, along with the asymmetrical terms of the interaction with the investors, that explains Uruguay's reluctance to see any change in the Fray Bentos projects.

On the other hand, there is the *local resistance* to the globalization project. The opposition to the pulp mills projects was framed not as a conservationist issue but as a conflict between two development models. To what they saw as a *global extractive* model, the activists opposed a *local environmentally friendly* model. They managed to combine environmental and economic concerns, establishing a strong connection between the pulp mills' environmental risks and the eventual decline of the economic activities prevalent in the Gualeguaychú area. This merging of environmental and economic concerns was central in the recognition of their claim's legitimacy, even among those who rejected the radical tactics chosen by the activists.

The Argentine government's position fluctuated between these two positions. Regarding the timber-and-paper sector, the Argentine government did not oppose the globalization project as such. But it was not capable of identifying its own long-term participation in the project or of finding a middle-ground solution to the glocalization conflict. That is why in order to avoid political costs the Kirchner government opted for an international legal dispute settlement. Thus far, it seems that more than for any other actor involved in the conflict, for the Argentine government globalization has become a hard-to-cope with and unstoppable process.

Notes

1. Argentina is a federal country with three levels of government: national, provincial and municipal. For the sake of brevity, from now on we will refer to the Argentine national government as the "Argentine government".
2. Yet the terms of the treaty with Finland show that the Uruguayan state intentionally embraced the globalization project in *asymmetrical* conditions, with the power only to accept or reject the terms of the industrialized/investing country, not to impose its own conditions – cf. the Introduction to this volume on the asymmetrical nature of globalization.
3. ECF (elementary chlorine free) technology replaces the use of elementary chlorine with dioxide of chlorine, which is less contaminating. Instead, TCF (totally chlorine free) technology replaces any type of chlorine by less contaminating whiteners such as ozone or peroxide of hydrogen. TCF technology was also recommended by Greenpeace and embraced by the Gualeguaychú Asamblea as the only admissible technology (see Greenpeace Argentina 2006).
4. For a more theoretical perspective on the development of civil society networks, see chapter 1 above by William Coleman.

REFERENCES

Alcañiz, I. and R. A. Gutiérrez (2009) "From local protest to the International Court of Justice: Forging environmental foreign policy in Argentina", in Paul G. Harris, ed., *Environmental Change and Foreign Policy: Theory and Practice*, London: Routledge, pp. 109–20.

Alcañiz, I. and M. Scheier (2007) "New social movements with old party politics: The MTL *piqueteros* and the Communist Party in Argentina", *Latin American Perspectives*, 34(2): 157–71.

Alle, T. L. and P. K. Huth (2006) "Legitimizing dispute settlement: International legal rulings as domestic political cover", *American Political Science Review*, 100(2): 219–34.

Alvarado, Raquel (2007) “Política forestal, plantas de celulosa y debate ambiental: Uruguay tras un nuevo modelo de desarrollo”, in V. Palermo and C. Reboratti, eds, *Del otro lado del río: Ambientalismo y política entre uruguayos y argentinos*, Buenos Aires: Edhasa.

Barkdull, J. and P. G. Harris (2009) “Theories of environmental foreign policy: Power, interests, and ideas”, in P. G. Harris, ed., *Environmental Change and Foreign Policy: Theory and Practice*, London: Routledge, pp. 19–40.

Carbone, Florencia (2005) “Compromiso oficial por las papeleras”, *La Nación*, 24 Aug. At <http://www.lanacion.com.ar/politica/nota.asp?nota_id=732599> (accessed June 2010).

Clarín (2006) “Se declaró incompetente el juez que investiga la denuncia de Busti”, *Clarín*, 11 Feb. At <http://www.clarin.com/diario/2006/02/11/um/m-01140200.htm> (accessed June 2010).

Cotgrove, S. and A. Duff (2003) “Middle-class radicalism and environmentalism”, in J. Goodwin and J. M. Jasper, eds, *The Social Movements Reader: Cases and Concepts*, Oxford: Blackwell.

FARN (2006) *Las plantas de celulosa en el Río Uruguay: El análisis de la normativa para una posible resolución del conflicto*. Buenos Aires: Fundación Argentina para los Recursos Naturales.

Forestal WEB (2008) “Informe forestal”. At <http://www.forestalweb.com/uruguay_forestal.htm> (accessed 30 July 2008).

Greenpeace Argentina (2006) “Plantas de celulosa: Cómo construir una solución sustentable”. At <http://www.greenpeace.org/argentina/> (accessed 1 June 2007).

Gutiérrez, R. A. and I. Alcañiz (2007) “From Gualeguaychú to the World Court: Local environmental protest and foreign policy in Argentina”, paper prepared for the Seventh Internacional CISS Millennium Conference, Buçaco, Portugal, 14–16 June.

Hochstetler, K. and M. E. Keck (2007) *Greening Brazil: Environmental Activism in State and Society*. Durham, NC: Duke University Press.

JGM Argentina (2005) *Memoria anual del estado de la nación*. Buenos Aires: Jefatura de Gabinete de Ministros.

Keck, M. E. and K. Sikkink (1998) *Activists beyond Borders: Advocacy Networks in International Politics*. Ithaca: Cornell University Press.

La Nación (2006) “Para Kirchner, ‘no está mal’ que Uruguay negocie con los EE.UU”, *La Nación*, 20 Jan. At <http://www.lanacion.com.ar/nota.asp?nota_id=773758> (accessed June 2010).

López Echagüe, H. (2006) *Crónica del ocaso: Apuntes sobre las papeleras y la devastación del litoral argentino y uruguayo*. Buenos Aires: Grupo Editorial Norma.

Merlinsky, M. G. (2008) “La gramática de la acción colectiva ambiental en Argentina: Reflexiones en torno al movimiento ciudadano ambiental de Gualeguaychú y su inscripción en el espacio público”, *Revista Temas y Debates*, 15 (Aug.): 35–62.

MRECIC Argentina (2006) “Informe de la Delegación Argentina al Grupo de Trabajo de Alto Nivel”, Ministerio de Relaciones Exteriores, Comercio Internacional y Culto, Buenos Aires, 3 Feb.

MRREE Uruguay (2006) "Informe sobre la instalación de dos plantas de celulosa en el Río Uruguay", Ministerio de Relaciones Exteriores de la República Oriental del Uruguay. At <http://www.mrree.gub.uy/mrree/Asuntos_Politicos/Planta%20Celu/informe.htm> (accessed 31 July 2008).

Reboratti, C. (2007) "Ambientalismo y conflicto ambiental en el Río Uruguay", in V. Palermo and C. Reboratti, eds, *Del otro lado del río: Ambientalismo y política entre uruguayos y argentinos*, Buenos Aires: Edhasa.

Romero, J. and M. Tubío (2004) "Caracterización social de los trabajadores asalariados de la fase agraria del complejo forestal", Centro de Informaciones y Estudios del Uruguay, Montevideo, Nov.

Schneider, M. and J. Scholz (2003) "Building consensual institutions: Networks and the national estuary program", *American Journal of Political Science*, 47(1): 143–58.

Torres Rojo, J. M. and A. Fossati (2004) *Estudio de tendencias y perspectivas del sector forestal en América Latina Documento de Trabajo – Informe Nacional Uruguay*, Report of the Uruguayan Ministry of Agriculture and Fisheries, UN Food and Agriculture Organization, Rome. At <http://www.fao.org/docrep/007/j2807s/j2807s00.htm#TopOfPage> (accessed 31 July 2008).

Vara, A. M. (2007) "Si a la Vida, No a las Papeleras: En torno a una controversia ambiental inédita en América Latina", *Redes – Revista de Estudios Sociales de la Ciencia*, 13(25) (July): 15–49.

Vidal, Armando (2006) "Kirchner pidió a Uruguay que frene por 90 días las papeleras", *Clarín*, 2 Mar. At <http://www.clarin.com/diario/2006/03/02/elpais/p-00301.htm> (accessed June 2010).

Zibechi, R. (2005) "Uruguay: Celulosa y forestación, dos caras de un modelo depredador", International Relations Centre's Americas Program, 24 Oct. At <http://www.rebelion.org/noticia.php?id=20767> (accessed 20 July 2009).

14

Actors and activities in the anti–human trafficking movement

Kirsten Foot

Introduction

As Heine and Thakur explain in their introduction to this volume, human trafficking is arguably the darkest of the dark side of globalization. Although firm data are difficult to collect, studies concur that the number of trafficking victims has risen sharply over the last decade (Laczko 2005; Schauer and Wheaton 2006; US Department of State 2001; 2007). Human trafficking has been described by the Human Rights Center of the American Bar Association as "the fastest-growing and third-largest criminal industry in the world today after the arms and drugs trades, generating billions in profits each year" (Morrissey 2006). To date, efforts to stem the trafficking tide have been ineffective, due in part to a low level of coordination between concerned national and international governmental bodies, law enforcement agencies, non-governmental organizations (NGOs) and community organizations.

The United States is regarded as an international leader in transnational anti-trafficking efforts. In the US, human trafficking issues have received increasing attention from non-governmental and governmental actors over the last decade. The US State Department is mandated by the Trafficking Victims Protection Act of 2000 to submit an annual Trafficking in Persons Report to Congress on the state of human trafficking and efforts to counter it, and organizes conferences on global strategies for preventing and prosecuting human trafficking (e.g. US Department of State 2003). The US departments of Justice and Labor also have anti-trafficking programmes through which domestic and transnational trafficking cases are investigated and prosecuted, and, following the pioneering model of the Washington State Task Force against Trafficking in Persons, state governments are required to develop multi-stakeholder anti-trafficking coalitions. But, despite these efforts, the US government has come under criticism internally for lacking a coordinated anti-trafficking strategy and evaluation plan among government agencies, and between US governmental and non-governmental organizations. The US Government Accountability Office report (2006) makes the charge that this coordination gap is preventing the US from determining the effectiveness of its efforts to combat the trafficking of people from other countries into the US, and undermining its abilities to adjust its efforts to better meet needs.

Awareness of the need for coordination is high in other countries as well. For example, the website of the Organization for Security and Co-operation in Europe (OSCE) states its belief that "the key to sustainable solutions in the fight against trafficking in human beings is co-operation and co-ordination". Towards this end, the OSCE operates the Alliance against Trafficking in Persons:

> a broad international forum which aims at combining the efforts of all relevant interlocutors to prevent and combat human trafficking. The spirit of the Alliance has been to develop effective joint strategies, combine efforts of relevant interlocutors in setting a common agenda, and to provide all the OSCE participating States as well as the Partners for Co-operation with harmonized approaches and decision-making aids. (OSCE 2009a)

In addition to the Alliance against Trafficking in Persons, the OSCE also maintains an Alliance Expert Co-ordination Team (AECT), which it describes as:

> a consultative forum involving leading agencies and experts in the field of combating human trafficking. It aims to develop strategic networking and partnerships among active players, facilitating exchanges of experience, best practices and lessons learned, as well as joint actions across the OSCE region. The AECT has carried out a number of advocacy initiatives that have already shown it to be a viable forum for dialogue and concrete co-operation. (OSCE 2009b)

Cooperative efforts are not limited to governments or intergovernmental organizations.[1] Terre des Femmes, an NGO based in Europe, is one of many NGOs whose websites proclaim their commitment to cooperation with other anti-trafficking actors:

> Co-operative participation in specific projects is an essential part of our activities. Networking enables us to exchange up-to-date information, to plan and realise activities with our partners and to increase our powers of self-assertion by combining specific competencies. We can exchange experiences and broaden our view. (Terre des Femmes 2005)

Another example, Global March, an India-based NGO concerned about trafficking as part of its mission to promote children's rights and education, claims members in 140 countries and partnerships with 2,000 organizations (Global March 2009).

The field of anti-trafficking efforts is complex, with a diverse array of actors, many of whom conduct their activities transnationally. Recent surveys of the literature on human trafficking note that anti-trafficking efforts are not studied enough around the world (Laczko 2005; Mattar 2004; Schauer and Wheaton 2006). Within the small body of social science, legal and policy literature on anti-trafficking efforts that has emerged in the last few years, most publications are evaluations of the efficacy of particular policies and programmes, either individually or in comparative analyses (Adams 2003; UNHCR 2006; Aghatise 2003; DeStefano 2007; Munro 2006; Schuckman 2006; Samarasinghe and Burton 2007). However, a few evaluative studies address interorganization coordination issues, demonstrating that around the world factors contributing to ineffectiveness in anti-trafficking efforts include a lack of clarity in definitions of trafficking, gaps in data collection, problems in the integration of data on trafficking within and between anti-trafficking organizations, poor communication and resistance to cooperation between agencies, and a lack of appropriately designed information systems and information-sharing networks (David 2007; Emmers, Greener-Barcham and Thomas 2006; Goldenkoff 2007; Friesendorf 2006). All of these studies advocate for greater coordination between all types of anti-trafficking actors within communities and between the local, national and international levels.

This chapter aims to help remedy the lack of knowledge about the anti-trafficking movement, by presenting findings from a 2008 survey of the websites of nearly 150 anti-trafficking actors, including national and international governmental bodies, law enforcement agencies, non-governmental organizations and community organizations, operating in every region of the world. Findings include regional and worldwide patterns in the types of actors engaged in anti-trafficking work (e.g. governmental, non-governmental, intergovernmental, etc.), the geographical bases and operational areas of anti-trafficking activity, the dominant types of anti-trafficking activity in each area and the relative robustness of each type of anti-trafficking activity.

Methods

Between November 2007 and March 2008, a team of four research assistants searched the web for sites containing content about anti-trafficking activities. They employed multiple search engines based in different countries and used dozens of different search terms; they also followed links between sites to locate additional anti-trafficking sites. Through these procedures, they identified over 300 websites produced by nine types of anti-trafficking actors: (1) businesses; (2) governments; (3) individuals; (4) labour unions; (5) non-governmental organizations; (6) professional associations; (7) United Nations organizations; (8) other (non-UN) intergovernmental organizations; (9) universities/research institutes.

Research team members were native English speakers, and had some literacy in Spanish, French and German. Many of the websites identified had some content in a language other than English; to be included in the database for this project, each site had to have at least some anti-trafficking content in English. The team found some anti-trafficking groups that do not post English language anti-trafficking content on the web, and there are undoubtedly other groups that do not produce any web materials, so the identified sites do not represent all anti-trafficking actors around the world. But the rigour of the identification procedures ensured that the identified sites are representative of anti-trafficking websites produced at least partially in English by actors based in one or more of 46 countries.

After several weeks of site identification, a set of categories and associated keywords were developed to catalogue the sites systematically. For each site, a record was created in an online database, containing the site producer's name, geographical base, level of anti-trafficking operation, types of activities/programmes, geographical focus of anti-trafficking operations and focal victims. These metadata fields allowed the full pool of identified sites to be searched and clustered according to any combination of characteristics, thus enabling a variety of sampling parameters.

The study presented in this chapter was based on content analysis of a purposive sample of 148 websites drawn from the database of 332 sites identified as relevant to anti-trafficking efforts. The sample was stratified by the geographical regions in which the producers were based, and by the general type of anti-trafficking activities on which they reported on their websites. The sampling frame was weighted to ensure inclusion of all region and activity combinations. Geographical focus was employed in the sampling frame in addition to geographical base, in order to have a greater diversity of activities represented in the sample.

Table 14.1 Geographical base and focus regions in the sampled sites

	Base region	Percentage of websites focusing on region (each actor may have multiple focus regions)
Africa	<1%	32%
Australasia/Pacific Islands	<1%	31%
Caribbean	<1%	17%
Eurasia	<1%	25%
Europe	30%	38%
Latin America	<1%	25%
Middle East	<1%	25%
North America	45%	31%
South America	<1%	25%
South Asia	10%	38%
South East Asia	11%	38%
Other		45% (transregional activities)

N = 148 sites in sample.

Despite the fact that the base regions of the actors identified were clustered in North America, Europe, South Asia and South East Asia, there was a good distribution of focus regions represented in the sample. In each region of the world, except the Caribbean, at least a quarter of the sampled actors were conducting some type of anti-trafficking efforts at the time of this study. Although the majority of sampled actors were based in Europe and North America, South Asia and South East Asia were equal with Europe as the regions in which the greatest proportion of actors operate (38 per cent), followed by Africa, Australasia/Pacific Islands and North America (31–2 per cent). Eurasia, Latin America, the Middle East and South America are focal regions for a quarter of the anti-trafficking actors in the sample; the Caribbean drew 17 per cent. Nearly half (45 per cent) of the actors reported conducting anti-trafficking efforts in at least two regions. See table 14.1 for a comparison of the geographical base and focus regions of the actors in the sample.

Based on exploratory analyses of anti-trafficking efforts reported on actors' websites, a coding scheme was developed around eight general anti-trafficking activities: (1) awareness raising; (2) enforcement of anti-trafficking laws/policies; (3) equipping others to counter trafficking; (4) intervention in trafficking; (5) policy advocacy and development; (6) prevention; (7) rehabilitation of trafficked persons; (8) research on trafficking. Each of these activities was operationalized with a set of four to six specific actions (see table 14.4 below for the actions comprising each activity, and the prevalence of the actions across the sample). The ethos of the operationalization was to be inclusive of any and all anti-trafficking actions; thus an "other" category was employed for actions related to each type of activity that did not fit with established action categories.

Research assistants were instructed to look first for any claim regarding each type of activity on the websites in the sample. If an actor claimed to engage in an activity, the research assistant coded the actor's site positively for that activity, and then documented the region(s) in which the actor engaged in the activity. Next the research assistant searched the site for references to particular actions corresponding with the activity. If no specific actions corresponding with the activity were described, the site was coded positively for just the "other" action category for that activity. The rationale for this protocol was to err on the side of generosity in interpreting the actors' websites, bearing in mind the differences in web production practices across countries and types of anti-trafficking actors, as well as the differences in the political and economic conditions in which actors operate.

Coding for specific actions as well as general types of activities enabled analyses of the robustness or intensity with which actors conduct one activity in relation to other activities, along with the prevalence of the general activity. For example, the website of a community-based NGO in Thailand, the Development and Education Programme for Daughters and Communities, reported conducting rehabilitation of trafficking victims in South East Asia, as did the website of Union Aid Abroad–APHEDA (Australian People for Health, Education and Development Abroad), which is the overseas humanitarian aid agency of the Australian Council of Trade Unions. Both sites contributed equally to the assessment of the frequency of rehabilitation efforts in South East Asia.[2] However, after close examination, evidence of only one rehabilitation-related action was found on the Union Aid Abroad–APHEDA site: vocational training for trafficked persons. In contrast, the website of the Development and Education Programme for Daughters and Communities evidenced four of the six types of actions corresponding with rehabilitation of trafficked persons: providing safe shelter, personal care, and basic education as well as vocational training. Thus the latter website indicated greater robustness in the activity of rehabilitation.

In order to facilitate common data collection practices and ease the merging of coding data generated by multiple research assistants, a web-based survey interface was employed through which research assistants recorded their observations of the presence or absence of each action on the websites in a server-based database. Prior to proceeding with actual coding, research assistants completed several rounds of training and clarification of the coding scheme. After each round, areas of disagreement

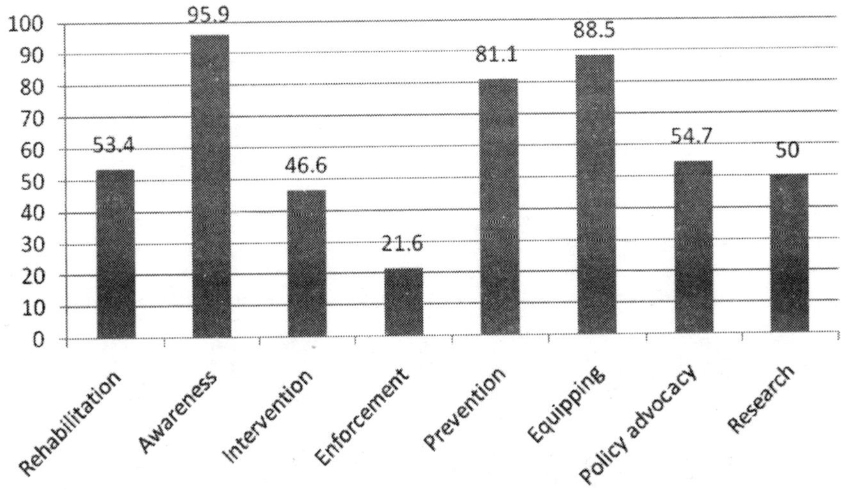

Figure 14.1 Prevalence of anti-trafficking activity (percentage of URLs that engage in activity)

were discussed and the coding scheme was refined for clarity until the inter-coder reliability rate was over 80 per cent for each measure.

Findings

Both the prevalence and robustness of anti-trafficking activities were analysed. As depicted in figure 14.1, awareness-raising was the activity engaged in by the greatest number of anti-trafficking actors (96 per cent), followed by equipping (89 per cent) and prevention (81 per cent). Enforcement was the least prevalent activity among the actors in this sample.

By looking at the sum of the number of actors who engage in each activity in each region, equipping emerges as the activity engaged in most frequently, followed by awareness-raising and prevention (see table 14.2). Again, enforcement is the least frequent activity reported by this sample of actors.

If an actor reported engaging in any one of the actions associated with an activity, their site added to the frequency of the activity. However, as mentioned above, with a range of actions possible for each activity, it is also important to understand the extent to which multiple actions corresponding with an activity are conducted. Therefore, in addition to the

Table 14.2 Cross-site index: Robustness of activity and number of actors by geographic region of activity

Activity	Africa	S. Asia	S. E. Asia	Austral-asia	Caribbean	Eurasia	Europe	Lat. Am.	M. East	N. Am.	S. Am.	Multiple	*N Actions/ Activity*
Rehabilitation	0.45	0.46	0.43	0.52	0.48	0.35	0.34	0.39	0.36	0.36	0.38	0.41	*6*
N Actors	*21*	*26*	*27*	*7*	*7*	*10*	*25*	*9*	*6*	*22*	*4*	*30*	*194*
Awareness	0.51	0.41	0.46	0.48	0.46	0.48	0.44	0.43	0.5	0.47	0.51	0.47	*7*
N Actors	*14*	*26*	*28*	*12*	*8*	*13*	*40*	*8*	*6*	*61*	*7*	*31*	*254*
Intervention	0.27	0.28	0.27	0.25	0.28	0.33	0.32	0.22	0.22	0.27	0.29	0.27	*6*
N Actors	*8*	*15*	*14*	*4*	*3*	*5*	*17*	*6*	*3*	*25*	*4*	*17*	*121*
Enforcement	0.29	0.31	0.3	0.29	0.33	0.39	0.27	0.29	0.17	0.28	0.17	0.3	*6*
N Actors	*8*	*7*	*9*	*4*	*2*	*3*	*10*	*4*	*1*	*10*	*2*	*10*	*70*
Prevention	0.32	0.29	0.36	0.25	0.29	0.29	0.3	0.29	0.28	0.25	0.29	0.32	*6*
N Actors	*19*	*28*	*32*	*8*	*8*	*12*	*26*	*13*	*6*	*21*	*7*	*29*	*209*
Equipping	0.41	0.43	0.43	0.44	0.33	0.38	0.37	0.42	0.4	0.39	0.42	0.31	*6*
N Actors	*20*	*29*	*34*	*14*	*7*	*17*	*42*	*14*	*8*	*52*	*10*	*45*	*292*
Policy advocacy	0.3	0.2	0.27	0.25	0.23	0.29	0.22	0.24	0.26	0.25	0.21	0.3	*7*
N Actors	*12*	*15*	*21*	*8*	*5*	*12*	*34*	*6*	*5*	*33*	*4*	*26*	*181*
Research	0.38	0.38	0.41	0.38	0.38	0.43	0.38	0.36	0.39	0.41	0.39	0.42	*4*
N Actors	*22*	*25*	*26*	*6*	*6*	*14*	*30*	*11*	*11*	*14*	*9*	*32*	*206*

prevalence of each type of activity, the relative robustness of each activity was assessed within and across regions. Robustness was assessed via a cross-site index, in which the number of actions associated with each activity and observed on each actor's site was divided by the number of possible actions for the activity multiplied by the number of websites on which the activity was observed, according to this formula:

$$\frac{\text{Sum of observed actions for an activity}}{(\text{N of possible actions}) \times \begin{matrix}(\text{N of websites on which any action} \\ \text{for the activity was observed})\end{matrix}}$$

The resulting ratio provides a way to compare the number of ways in which each activity was pursued in each region and by each type of actor.

Along with the sum of the actors who reported engaging in each activity, table 14.2 also displays the robustness with which actors engage in each type of anti-trafficking activity across regions. Reading across the top row of each activity reveals the range of robustness for the activity. For example, rehabilitation is most robust in Australasia and least robust in Europe; prevention efforts are most robust in Southeast Asia and least robust in Australasia and North America. Reading down the columns reveals the robustness of each activity within a region. To illustrate, awareness-raising is enacted with nearly twice the robustness of intervention in Africa. Robustness ratios for actors who reported conducting an activity across regions are presented in the "Multiple" column second from the right.

It is striking that almost all of the robustness ratios across regions and activities ranged between 0.25 and 0.5. The highest robustness ratios were just over 0.5 (rehabilitation in Australasia, and awareness-raising in Africa and South America). Robustness ratios under 0.25 were found in intervention in Latin America and the Middle East, enforcement in the Middle East and South America, and policy advocacy in the Caribbean, South America and Europe (the latter may be due to the relatively advanced state of anti-trafficking policies in Europe at this time). The combination of these findings suggests that overall, anti-trafficking actors were taking multiple actions in each type of activity and each region, but that they could expand the range of actions they pursued in each activity if resources were available for them to do so, and if the actions tested for in this study were appropriate and strategic for them. Due to regional differences in the patterns of human trafficking and in political regimes, particular actions may be more or less strategic at this time in a given region.

The sum of the robustness ratios across all regions (not displayed in the table) reveals that awareness-raising is engaged in most robustly,

Table 14.3 Cross-site index: Robustness of activity by actor type

Activity	Business	Govt	Individual(s)	Labour union	NGO	Professional association	UN org.	Other IGO	University/ Institute	*N Actions/ Activity*
Rehabilitation	0	0.15	0	0.17	0.31	0	0.13	0.08	0.04	*6*
Awareness	0.38	0.41	0.43	0.5	0.43	0.29	0.42	0.43	0.43	*7*
Intervention	0.11	0.08	0.06	0.08	0.16	0	0.03	0.06	0.04	*6*
Enforcement	0	0.46	0	0.17	0.04	0	0.08	0.19	0	*6*
Prevention	0.22	0.21	0.08	0.42	0.23	0.17	0.22	0.23	0.13	*6*
Equipping	0.17	0.35	0.31	0.5	0.35	0.08	0.35	0.4	0.17	*6*
Policy advocacy	0	0.14	0	0.07	0.14	0	0.24	0.2	0.11	*7*
Research	0.25	0.34	0	0	0.16	0	0.1	0.25	0.5	*4*
N sites/Actor type	*3*	*8*	*6*	*2*	*93*	*2*	*13*	*8*	*4*	

NGO = non-governmental organization; IGO = intergovernmental organization.

followed by rehabilitation and then by equipping. Policy advocacy, intervention and enforcement are the least robust activities. The sum of the robustness ratios across all activities for each region (not displayed in the table) reveals that anti-trafficking efforts are most robust (with nearly identical levels of robustness) in Africa, South East Asia and Eurasia, and least robust in the Middle East.

Across the sample, actors were more likely to engage in all types of anti-trafficking activities within their base regions than in other regions. However, anti-trafficking activities are transregional to a significant degree. In comparison with actors who engage in an activity within a single region, actors that reported conducting an activity across multiple regions had robustness ratios at the high end of the range in the activities of policy advocacy and research on trafficking. With the exception of enforcement, actors based in the top four regions in this sample (North America, Europe, South Asia and South East Asia) engaged in each activity in multiple regions. Actors based in South Asia had a minimum of three focus regions for each type of activity, actors based in South East Asia had a minimum of four focus regions for each activity, and actors based in Europe and North America reported operating in a minimum of eight regions for each activity.

The robustness ratios for each activity by actor type are presented in table 14.3. The websites of businesses, individuals and professional associations that contained anti-trafficking content were engaged in awareness-raising, prevention and equipping. These actors' sites did not reflect any engagement in rehabilitation, enforcement or research (with the exception of a couple of businesses engaging in a handful of research projects related to trafficking). Sites of government agencies reflected the most robustness in awareness-raising and enforcement, but their ratios for all activities were under 0.5. The highest robustness ratio for United Nations (UN) agencies and other intergovernmental organizations (IGOs) was also in awareness-raising. UN agencies were more robustly engaged in rehabilitation than other IGOs; other IGOs were more robustly engaged in research and enforcement than UN agencies. But the ratios for all IGOs were low for all activities other than awareness-raising. Unsurprisingly, the lowest robustness ratio of NGOs was in enforcement, since enforcement is largely the responsibility of government bodies. The fact that NGOs' robustness ratios for every activity were under 0.5 is a bit surprising since the spectrum of NGOs includes a diverse array of organizations and organizational aims.

Mainly smaller local actors focused on helping local victims conduct rehabilitation. Enforcement is largely left to government agencies, but some NGOs offer online web forms and/or hotline numbers for individuals to report suspicious circumstances or possible perpetrators (e.g. tinystars.org). Activities are aimed at giving victims a safe home and a

Table 14.4 Prevalence of actions within activities across sample

Activity	Action	% of actors reporting action	No. of actors reporting action (N = 148 URLs)
Awareness	General informing	84%	124
	Info/Research dissemination	78%	116
	Conferences	44%	65
	Media artefacts	40%	59
	Campaigning	24%	36
	Offline groups	18%	27
	Awareness – other	3%	5
Enforcement	Investigating traffickers	10%	14
	Arresting or prosecuting	7%	11
	Task Force – cross border	7%	10
	Task Force – in country	6%	9
	Enforcement – other	4%	6
Equipping	Coalition building	73%	108
	Training	51%	75
	Mobilizing	37%	54
	Funding AT projects	22%	33
	Organizing AT action	13%	19
	Equipping – other	4%	6
Intervention	Email to report trafficking	24%	36
	Victim outreach	22%	32
	Ransom rescue	12%	18
	Hotline for trafficked persons	12%	17
	Prayer	8%	12
	Intervention – other	2%	3
Policy	Advising policy writers	42%	62
	Proposing legislation	20%	30
	Advocacy to national govt	16%	24
	Advocacy to international govt	7%	10
	Advocacy to local govt	5%	8
	Advocacy to business	5%	7
	Advocacy to other	2%	3
Prevention	Deterrence	54%	80
	Educate at risk population	40%	59
	Economic development	15%	22
	Fair trade	12%	18
	Prevention – other	8%	12
	Deterrence via economics	2%	3
Rehabilitation	Shelter/Safe space	27%	40
	Basic education	20%	29
	Vocational training	22%	32
	Victim care	46%	68
	Legal assistance	17%	25
	Rehabilitation – other	9%	13
Research	Articles/Reports	43%	63
	Information /Fact sheet	16%	23
	Research – other	10%	15
	Publish journals/books	7%	10

AT = anti-trafficking.

means of rebuilding their future: building shelters/safe havens for victims, education and career training/assistance, giving legal assistance to victims.

Discussion

In sum, the findings from this study indicate that, in general, anti-trafficking actors are taking multiple actions in each type of activity and in each region of the world. However, the relatively low robustness ratios reported above suggest that all types of anti-trafficking actors could expand the range of actions they pursue in each activity, as long as the additional actions are appropriate and strategic in the light of the actors' political and operational contexts.

There may be several reasons why enforcement was the anti-trafficking activity least prevalent worldwide in this study. The mostly governmental and intergovernmental actors engaged in it may be underrepresented in this sample, or less likely to mention their enforcement work on the web. However, the robustness ratio for government agencies in this sample on the activity of enforcement was 0.46; for intergovernmental actors it was 0.19. Both of these indicate room for growth, and perhaps a critical weakness in the anti-trafficking movement. A recent news article reported that although 33 US states now have anti-trafficking laws, there have been very few convictions (Teichroeb 2008). Part of the problem is that most of these laws require prosecutors to prove that traffickers used "force, fraud or coercion", except when the victim is a minor. However, the policy director for the state of Washington's Attorney General claimed that Washington's five-year-old anti-trafficking law has only been put to use once (in a pending case) because prosecutors are not getting referrals from police. According to the reporter's summary of the situation: "The biggest impediment seems to be that police and prosecutors don't recognize trafficking victims when they encounter them, instead seeing victims of other crimes such as sexual assault" (Teichroeb 2008). In a meeting regarding the lack of trafficking convictions, officials from Washington's Attorney General's Office, county prosecutors, police and social service providers agreed that more must be done to educate police and prosecutors. Teichroeb reported:

> "Law enforcement are not necessarily empathetic with the victims," said John Goldman, a former Spokane County sheriff, who trains officers to recognize human trafficking. "They see it as an immigration problem." Prosecutors are more likely to pick "low-hanging fruit" and file charges they know how to handle, rather than risk an untested law, Goldman said. Police and other first responders also need education in how to elicit information from victims, especially those who don't speak English. (2008)

Such problems with enforcement of anti-trafficking laws are likely to be common across the US and in other countries.

Conclusion

Although limited to anti-trafficking organizations that produce a website and that generate some content in English on their sites, the sample of actors whose websites were surveyed had global coverage in their anti-trafficking efforts. Thus the findings from this study are at least suggestive of the state of anti-trafficking efforts worldwide.

The decision to study self-published reports of their activities by anti-trafficking actors on the web had certain drawbacks yet some distinct advantages. Drawbacks included the unevenness of the amount and currency of information presented across websites, and the likelihood that anti-trafficking actors do not report all of their anti-trafficking efforts on their websites. However, since it is also likely that some of the activities reported were proposed rather than actual efforts, or were no longer engaged in at the time of the content analysis, the rate of underreporting may be equivalent to the rate of overreporting. Keeping in mind that the anti-trafficking actors whose activities were studied for this chapter are based in 46 countries and that some work in politically sensitive conditions, key benefits of analysing actor-initiated, self-published reports collected via websites versus soliciting reports through a researcher-initiated survey (i.e. administered via email) were that the risks of insufficient response rates, partial responses, and confidentiality or security concerns were avoided.

The findings from this study evidence a strong transregional prevalence of anti-trafficking efforts. It is possible that the regions in which fewer anti-trafficking efforts are reported have fewer problems as source, transit or destination countries for trafficking victims, or that anti-trafficking efforts in those regions are not represented as well in English-language websites. Still, anti-trafficking actors and analysts may want to look more closely at the dynamics of trafficking and anti-trafficking efforts in these regions.

These findings also indicate that all types of actors could more robustly engage in each type of anti-trafficking activity. For instance, in the area of enforcement, the strategies developed by NGOs such as Tiny Stars and Stop the Traffik for acting as a catalyst for the identification and reporting of traffickers and predators of potentially trafficked persons to the appropriate governmental and intergovernmental agencies could be replicated or adapted by many more NGOs.[3] Tiny Stars, a small US-based organization, presents itself as "dedicated to working with US Federal Law Enforcement to gather evidence against American child predators" regardless of where they exploit children.[4] Acknowledging that many children are trafficked internationally for exploitation by Americans, this organization pursues aims that include funding a global network of undercover agents to collect evidence to be turned over to the US Federal Bureau of Investigation for prosecution, and supporting the enforcement of policies that serve to protect children from predators. Similarly, Stop the Traffik, a web-based coalition with over a thousand member organizations from more than 50 countries, launched a website called Business Travellers against Human Trafficking which both encourages and enables site visitors to report any evidence of trafficking they have witnessed. A list of nine indicators of trafficking for sexual exploitation is provided, along with the following invitation and instructions:

> If you think or know that you have encountered situations of human trafficking (forced prostitution, forced labour), please let us know by filling in the box [web form] below. Business Travellers Against Human Trafficking will investigate the situation. Try to give precise data like: country, city, street name & number, name and first name of victim(s) and all other indications that can help us in investigating the reported situation. (Business Travellers against Human Trafficking 2008)

Such catalytic efforts are needed by many more actors to help increase the prevalence and robustness of enforcement.

As anti-trafficking efforts continue, it will be important to track their development over time and to map them against the evolving dynamics of human trafficking. Future research on anti-trafficking efforts would benefit from a triangulation of web-based data with data collected through other methods that permit identification of anti-trafficking actors who do not have a web presence. It would also be useful to analyse the conditions implicated in the correlations between the prevalence and robustness of particular activities and geographic regions, both because the mere correlation of an activity with a region does not necessarily reflect strategic prioritization of that activity in the region, and in order to learn more about the conditions that catalyse and/or constrain particular activities. Future research should also look more closely at both intra- and interregional anti-trafficking work. Finally, more needs to be learned about how multisectoral collaborations between anti-trafficking actors can be built, optimized, and sustained over time.

Notes

1. In chapter 11 above, Luk Van Langenhove and Tiziana Scaramagli outline intergovernmental and regional cooperative efforts that have been created to better deal with globalized uncivil society and cross-border illegal activities through the sharing of expertise, institutions, tools, policies, personnel and funds; examples include the European Union,

Economic Community of West African States, Association of Southeast Asian Nations, Pacific Islands Forum, Andean Community and Organization of American States.
2. See <http://depdc.org/> and <http://www.apheda.org.au/projects/thaiburma/index.html> respectively (both accessed June 2010).
3. See <http://tinystars.org/>, <http://businesstravellers-org.web26.winsvr.net/> and <http://businesstravellers-org.web26.winsvr.net/Reportwhatyouhaveseen/tabid/54/Default.aspx> (all accessed June 2010).
4. See <http://www.tinystars.org/about.html> (accessed June 2010).

REFERENCES

Adams, N. (2003) "Anti-trafficking legislation: Protection or deportation?" *Feminist Review*, 73(1): 135–9(5).

Aghatise, E. (2003) "Iroko Onlus: Working to combat the trafficking of Nigerian women and girls into Italy", *Canadian Woman Studies,* 22(3–4): 197–9.

Business Travellers against Human Trafficking (2008) "Signs of human trafficking". At <http://businesstravellers-org.web26.winsvr.net/Reportwhatyouhaveseen/tabid/54/Default.aspx> (accessed June 2010).

David, F. (2007) "Asean and trafficking in persons: Using data as a tool to combat trafficking in persons", International Organization for Migration, Geneva.

DeStefano, A. M. (2007) *The War on Human Trafficking: US Policy Assessed*. New Brunswick, NJ: Rutgers University Press.

Emmers, R., B. Greener-Barcham and N. Thomas (2006) "Institutional arrangements to counter human trafficking in the Asia Pacific", *Contemporary Southeast Asia*, 28(3): 490–511.

Friesendorf, Cornelius (2006) "Zuwenig Prävention, Opferschutz und Zusammenarbeit: Strategien gegen den Menschenhandel in Südosteuropa", *Sudosteuropa Mitteilungen*, 46(5–6): 22–35.

Global March (2009) "Global march against child labour: Get involved!" At <http://www.globalmarch.org/joinus/index.php> (accessed June 2010).

Goldenkoff, R. N. (2007) "Human trafficking: A strategic framework could help enhance the interagency collaboration needed to effectively combat trafficking crimes", Washington, DC: United States Government Accountability Office, GAO-07-915, 26 July.

Laczko, F. (2005) "Data and research on human trafficking", *International Migration*, 43(1–2): 5–16.

Mattar, M. Y. (2004) "Trafficking in persons: An annotated legal bibliography", *Law Library Journal*, 96(4): 669–726.

Morrissey, S. (2006) "Sinister industry", *ABA Journal*, 92(3): 59–60.

Munro, V., E. (2006) "Stopping traffic? A comparative study of responses to the trafficking of women for prostitution", *British Journal of Criminology*, 46(2): 318–33.

OSCE (2009a) "Alliance against Trafficking in Persons", Secretariat, Office of the Special Representative and Co-ordinator for Combating Trafficking in Human Beings, Organization for Security and Co-operation in Europe. At <http://www.osce.org/cthb/13413.html> (accessed July 2010).

OSCE (2009b) "The Alliance expert co-ordination team", Secretariat, Office of the Special Representative and Co-ordinator for Combating Trafficking in Human Beings, Organization for Security and Co-operation in Europe. At <http://www.osce.org/cthb/23860.html> (accessed July 2010).

Samarasinghe, V. and B. Burton (2007) "Strategising prevention: A critical review of local initiatives to prevent female sex trafficking", *Development in Practice*, 17(1): 51–74.

Schauer, E. J. and E. M. Wheaton (2006) "Sex trafficking into the United States: A literature review", *Criminal Justice Review*, 31(2): 146–69.

Schuckman, Emily E. (2006) "Antitrafficking policies in Asia and the Russian Far East: A comparative perspective", *Demokratizatsiya*, 14(1): 85–102.

Teichroeb, R. (2008) "State's human trafficking law fails to snag a conviction: After five years on books, only one charge filed", *Seattle Post-Intelligencer*, 22 July. At <http://www.seattlepi.com/local/371716_law22.html> (accessed June 2010).

Terre des Femmes (2005) "Die Kampagne 'Gewalt gegen Frauen ist Alltag' nimmit weiter Fahrt auf". At <http://www.terre-des-femmes.de/>.

UNHCR (UN Refugee Agency) (2006) "Guidelines for international protection: The application of Article 1a(2) of the 1951 Convention and/or 1967 Protocol Relating to the Status of Refugees to Victims of Trafficking and Persons at Risk of Being Trafficked", UNHCR, HCR/GIP/06/07, Geneva, 7 Apr.

US Department of State (2001) "Victims of Trafficking and Violence Protection Act of 2000: Trafficking in persons report", Office of the Under Secretary for Democracy and Global Affairs and Bureau of Public Affairs, United States Department of State, Washington, DC, July.

US Department of State (2003) "Pathbreaking strategies in the global fight against sex trafficking: Prevention, protection, prosecution; Conference recommendations", Conference on Pathbreaking Strategies in the Global Fight against Sex Trafficking, Washington, DC, 23–26 Feb.

US Department of State (2007) "Trafficking in persons report," Office of the Under Secretary for Democracy and Global Affairs and Bureau of Public Affairs, United States Department of State, Washington, DC, June.

US Government Accountability Office (2006) "Human trafficking: Better data, strategy, and reporting needed to enhance US anti-trafficking efforts abroad", *Trends in Organized Crime*, 10(1): 16–38.

Conclusions: A bumpy ride to globalization, Google and jihad

Jorge Heine and Ramesh Thakur

The conflicts of our time are fought by networked social actors aiming to reach their constituencies and larger audiences through the decisive switch to multimedia communications networks.

Manuel Castells, *Communication Power*

A convenient date for marking the transition from one epoch to another remains 1945, for three reasons: the end of the Second World War; the establishment of the United Nations as a universal organization to maintain international peace and security, protect human rights and promote human welfare and development; and the inauguration of the atomic age. Today's global environment is vastly more challenging, complex and demanding than the world of 1945. Just consider the vocabulary and metaphors of the new age, every one of which would have mystified the 1945 generation: Srebrenica, Rwanda, Kosovo, East Timor, Darfur; child soldiers, ethnic cleansing, blood diamonds, 9/11, regime change, HIV/AIDS, global warming; Microsoft, Google, iPod, Blackberry, Facebook, Twitter, YouTube. All of them both symbolize and result from the age of globalization. Moreover, they all empower both forces for good and forces of evil.

One of the most influential "global public intellectuals" is the award-winning *New York Times* columnist Tom Friedman. He may not possess the scholarly accoutrements of an Ivy Leaguer nor exhibit the deep learning and scholarship of an Oxbridge professor. He more than makes up for that with a genius for capturing in bumper-sticker metaphors many important changes driving human history. Thus in *The Lexus and the Olive Tree* (Friedman 1999), he explained how the human drive for enrichment (symbolized by the aspiration to own the luxury Lexus car made by Toyota) confronts the equally powerful human need for locally rooted identity and community (symbolized by the olive tree). Risk-taking nations and individuals alike can exploit the limitless opportunity of globalization to seek material advancement and prosperity but, if they are not careful, they could risk destruction of both cultural heterogeneity and environmental diversity. In *The World Is Flat* (Friedman 2005), he argued that the relentless onward march of globalization had progressively lowered all sorts of barriers to the movement of goods, services, peoples and ideas across territorial borders (hence the flatness of the world) in an increasingly connected world.

In a recent column, Friedman quotes Mohamed El-Erian: "The world is on a journey to an unstable destination, through unfamiliar territory, on an uneven road and, critically, having already used its spare tire." Agreeing with this metaphor, Friedman extends it even farther: "Nations are more tightly integrated than ever before. We're driving bumper to bumper with every other major economy today, so misbehavior or mistakes anywhere can cause a global pileup" (Friedman 2010). In that arresting metaphor, some of the cars are carrying the elements of the dark side of globalization that have been described in this book. Can the governments and international organizations of the world create effective traffic codes, regulations and systems to ensure a continually smooth flow of traffic on the global superhighway? If so, can global civil society assist the international traffic police both to keep the regular traffic flowing and to apprehend the rogue drivers and cars?

Terrorism is a subset of the dark forces threatening to overwhelm the positive force of globalization. Fortunately, in recent times Africa and Latin America have largely, albeit not totally (we must recall that 9/11 had trial runs in East Africa), managed to escape this particular pathology of globalization. They have many other problems, from gunrunning and drug trafficking (including the use of lethal force by armed criminals), to mass atrocities, including ethnic cleansing, rape as an instrument of warfare, large-scale killings and even genocide. In their chapter in this book, Garth le Pere and Brendan Vickers examine the degree to which organized crime has spread throughout Africa. There have been some instances of terrorist incidents in Africa, or some African links to terrorist incidents elsewhere. The major theatres of terrorism, however, have connected North America, Europe, the Middle East, Southern Asia and South East Asia. And the phenomenon of terrorism in turn is organically linked to other pathologies of the dark side of globalization like illegal trafficking in arms, drugs and money and training activities.

Mumbai's 26/11 as India's 9/11

One can differ about the precise parallels between the US's 9/11 and Mumbai's 11/26, two milestone events in the post-Cold War era (Roy 2009). Still, there is little doubt that in the terrorist attacks on Mumbai in November 2008 the tools of the digital age so effectively deployed on 9/11 were put to use in an even more sophisticated, if not quite as deadly a manner. If the signature feature of 9/11 was the use of the intended target's own "weapons" against the World Trade Center, one of the ultimate symbols of Western capitalism, in Mumbai it was the extraordinary combination of low- and high-tech warfare against a city that is "one of the most iconic sites of metropolitan modernity in South Asia" (Kaplan 2009). How did they do it and why did Mumbai come to epitomize "the city as target" (Bishop and Roy 2009)?

Much as 9/11 took several years of meticulous planning, so did Mumbai. But the basic concept behind it, as in all successful ventures, was simple. An initial cadre of 32 suicide terrorist recruits was trained in Pakistan in how to make bombs, survive interrogation and fight to the death (Sengupta 2009). After training, the group was pruned to 10 young men in sneakers, jeans and designer T-shirts who set sail from Karachi on 22 November using global positioning system (GPS) coordinates. On 23 November, they took over an Indian fishing trawler, all of whose crew were eventually killed, and sailed across to Mumbai, arriving on its outskirts at about 4 p.m. on 26 November. Taking instructions from handlers in Pakistan, the 10 terrorists came ashore in a motorized dinghy at about 8.30 p.m. and attacked five targets in two-man teams: Chhatrapati Shivaji Terminus (a major railway station), the Leopold Café, the Chabad House Jewish centre, and the Taj and Trident-Oberoi luxury hotels. Time bombs were left in the taxis they used, later killing hapless drivers and unsuspecting passengers. Over the next 60 hours, one terrorist was captured and nine killed, but only after their killing spree had left 166 dead, including several foreigners and many Muslims, several high-ranking police officers, and the city's top anti-terrorist cop. All this was done against a nation-state with the world's third largest army, nuclear weapons and a defence budget of US$25 billion.

The organization in charge of training the 10 terrorists for the Mumbai operations was the banned Lashkar-e-Toiba (LeT). The *New York Times*, quoting US intelligence and counterterrorism officials, reported that Pakistan's Directorate of Inter-Services Intelligence (ISI) had shared intelligence with and provided protection to the LeT (Schmitt, Mazzetti and Perlez 2008). Based in Pakistan, the LeT has evolved from being focused on Kashmir to a globally oriented terrorist organization. The radical Sunni-Deobandhi groups are "simultaneously fighting internal sectarian jihads" that pose a threat "to the Pakistani citizen and state" and "regional jihads in Afghanistan and India and a global jihad against the West" (International Crisis Group 2009). As this was the first major terrorist attack in India that received saturation coverage by the world's leading media, for the first time it brought home to a global audience that India is a frontline state against international terrorism. Although the death of fewer than 200 cannot compare to around 3,000 killed, the impact of the real-time saturation coverage on public and political opinion was such that "26/11" marks a watershed as India's own "9/11".[1] Even General David Petraeus, then Commander CENTCOM (United States Central Command) and currently Commander, International Security Assistance Force and Commander, US Forces Afghanistan, has noted that the Mumbai attacks were "a 9/11 moment" for India (*Hindu* 2009).

The slow response of Indian security was one reason the LeT group was so effective. But the main one was technology. Armed with GPS, Google maps, Blackberries and AK-47s, the group was confronted by policemen with 1950s vintage recoil rifles. Ironically, one could speak of a "digital divide" between this group of young men of peasant stock from the hills of the Pakistani countryside, on the one hand, and the metropolitan police and armed forces of one of the world's emerging powers, known precisely for its information technology and telecom prowess, on the other.

This was also "Twitter-age terrorism". Throughout the attack, the operatives were in communication with their handlers in Karachi via their mobile smartphones, keeping them abreast of developments, receiving instructions and being briefed on the deployment of the security forces around them, conveniently provided to the rest of the world by India's ubiquitous round-the-clock TV channels. In turn, some of the best coverage of the Mumbai events in those days was provided by new media and citizen-journalists, through Twitter and personal blogs.

That Mumbai should prove to be India's soft underbelly against such a deadly attack is paradoxical. Mumbai, India's "maximum city", has the dubious distinction of being the most attacked urban centre in the world, which is one reason observers take issue with the term "India's 9/11". On 12 March 1993, 15 almost simultaneous bomb explosions killed 257 people and left more than 1,000 injured; in August 2003, 46 people were killed in two bomb explosions in public places; in July 2006, several bombs exploded in suburban trains there, killing some 200 and injuring 700. If there is one Indian city that should have been prepared for another such attack, it was Mumbai. The reason it wasn't is because the November 2008 attacks upped the ante, shifting gears to a different type of terrorist operation. Instead of anonymous bombs left behind in trains or in public squares, this was about hostage-taking, machine gun spraying and hand grenade throwing.

Mumbai has not been the only Indian city targeted by jihadis. So have New Delhi, Bangalore, Hyderabad and Jaipur, among others. In fact, between January 2004 and July 2007, India had 3,900 fatal victims as a result of terrorism, more than any other country anywhere with the exception of Iraq, and more than Afghanistan and Pakistan. But Mumbai, the country's commercial and industrial capital, the one that symbolizes the achievements of the new India, the city of Bollywood and of the Birlas, of the Ambanis and the Tatas, has been the favourite objective. As Suketu Mehta (2008) has put it, "just as cinema is a mass dream of the audience, Mumbai is a mass dream of the peoples of South Asia", and thus an ideal backdrop for mass terror on the world stage.

The Mumbai attacks not only reflected the deadly use to which digital technology can be put by even small terrorist outfits – and why the age of globalization is also the age of terror – but also the key role of the media in reflecting, amplifying and multiplying on many platforms the activities of these terrorist groups, which is precisely what they crave. Mumbai broke new ground, with extraordinary scenes of reporters from television channels interrupting firemen as they attempted to save lives from the charred remains of the Taj Mahal Hotel, of television news programmes informing their audience (and thus the terrorists) about the latest deployment of the security forces, and of television channels taking calls from the terrorists themselves as the situation unfolded, calls in which they conveyed their well-crafted messages on Kashmir and other topics to anyone who would listen.

Blowback and network

Far from abating after a global war against them was formally declared after 9/11, terrorist actions, if anything, have increased in the early twenty-first century. While some argue that Al Qaeda has been weakened, this is not the case for other outfits, like LeT or the Pakistani Taliban, which may or may not be associated with Al Qaeda, but whose agenda overlaps with the latter's. The main terror theatre has thus shifted from Afghanistan in 2001 to Iraq in 2003, back to Afghanistan in 2007–8, and then to Pakistan, a nuclear weapons state, with all the attendant risks.

This fits in well, as William Coleman argues in chapter 1 of this volume, with the concept of "blowback", popularized by Chalmers Johnson, and which posits a ricochet effect, as US foreign policy actions in one place rebound and have unintended consequences elsewhere, thousands of miles away. As Coleman puts it:

> When the US has utilized its power and operated as an empire, it has accelerated the speed of globalization. In addition to networked society . . . globaliza-

tion has indirectly produced new forms of violence and networks of uncivil society as a way to combat US imperialism and the very forces of globalization, especially as the divide between rich and poor grows.

Rather than being located in a fixed abode, with set territorial boundaries and objectives determined by governments, modern jihad thus operates as a decentralized, de-territorialized network, the ultimate "non-state actors" (as President Asif Ali Zardari referred to LeT in his efforts to distance the Pakistani state from the Mumbai attacks). Traditional conceptions on how to fight such an enemy are thus bound to fail, or, even worse, generate unintended consequences that may empower the enemy further. The Obama administration's efforts to shift the Pentagon's focus on the war on terror from Iraq to Afghanistan has gone hand in hand with a radicalization of Pakistani Islamic fundamentalists and the rise of the Pakistani Taliban, thus raising the stakes on the future of South-Central Asia.

In fact, the network society brought about by the Third Industrial Revolution puts into question the very notion that the best way to fight Al Qaeda is to do so "in its home-base", i.e. Afghanistan. While some of its top leaders may be in Tora Bora or in caves on the Afghanistan–Pakistan border,[2] its cells and affiliates are spread out in many places throughout the broader Middle East and northern Africa, liaising through a variety of means, including Islamic websites.

Al Qaeda, the Taliban in its various incarnations, and entities like the Naxalite movement in India, do not only deploy the digital technology that is the driving force of globalization. They also thrive because the latter, by bringing some into the privileged circles of contemporary consumer society, also excludes others, creating an ever wider gap of inequality, of which the wave of farmer suicides in India is one tragic result. As Ajay Mehra points out in chapter 6, it should not be surprising that precisely at the moment of "the Global Indian Takeover" (as the Indian press likes to put it), vast swathes of Central India are controlled by Maoist guerrillas, who have become both more aggressive and more successful in their operations against the Indian military. In fact, the phenomena are two sides of the same coin, the bright and the dark side of globalization.

Local and global

The global-local interface has relevance even for geopolitics, as M. J. Akbar's chapter makes clear. He notes that, by definition, a superpower has a global presence and power while challenges to it tend to be regional and are therefore met with by a regional application of globally derived assets and power. But a distinctive shift in the twenty-first century, he notes, is the manner in which the challengers to the superpower too have fashioned a globalized network of assets and personnel. He highlights examples of the interconnectedness of three regional theatres, in which bilateral US relations with Iraq, Iran and Afghanistan evolve and intermingle simultaneously with the overlay of the regional dynamics. The net result, decidedly unintended, has been the weakening of US power and authority both regionally and globally and "the unlikely strengthening of Iran as a regional power". As a result: "An effective 'Shia space' now extends from Herat in west Afghanistan to the border of Syria and the northern, Shia-dense districts of Saudi Arabia." Having achieved recognition as a regional power, Iran is engaged in an intricate diplomatic game "to achieve tacit recognition of its nuclear programme as the counterpoint to Israel, much in the way that the United States accepted Pakistan's right to respond to India's nuclear weapons capability".

The interaction between global cross-currents and local actors is evident in the string of insurgencies and terrorist movements across South Asia. The Indian subcontinent is one of the places where the sunny and dark sides of globalization clash with particular force, while also highlighting the dialectic between the local and the global that is such a feature of our era. Pakistan's record of double dealing, deceit and denial of Pakistan-based attacks, in Afghanistan and India alike, has been based on four degrees of separation – between the government, army, ISI, and terrorists – whose plausibility may be fading as the separation is exploited as a convenient alibi to escape accountability. Prime Minister Manmohan Singh, by instinct circumspect in his words, believes that "given the sophistication and military precision", the Mumbai attacks "must have had the support of some official agencies in Pakistan" (*Doordarshan News* 2009). The combination of training, selection and advance reconnaissance of targets, diversionary tactics, discipline, munitions, cryptographic communications, false IDs, and damage inflicted is more typically associated with special forces units than terrorists (David Kilcullen, an Australian counter-insurgency expert who has worked with US forces, quoted in Zakaria 2008). After Mumbai's three-stage amphibious operation, even US agencies concluded that the LeT is a more capable and greater threat than previously believed (Schmitt, Mazzetti and Perlez 2008). The plot was hatched and launched in Pakistan, and while the operation was underway in Mumbai, "it was masterminded and controlled from Pakistan", according to Home Minister P. Chidambaram (Singh 2009). Senior LeT operatives Zarar Shah and Zakiur Rahman Lakhvi, indicted by the Indian police for acting as Pakistan-based handlers for the Mumbai attacks, are known to be close associates of the ISI (Parthasarathy 2009).

While the US viewed Pakistan as an ally against international enemies, the alliance was useful to Islamabad principally in an India-specific context. The two imperatives intersected with the Soviet invasion of Afghanistan. Saudi financing and American arms and training built up the mujahedin as a potent force to bleed the Soviets in Afghanistan. Over time this built up a battle-hardened jihadist army, including one Osama bin Laden, which exported terror from Afghanistan to make common cause with Islamist struggles all over the world. Yesterday's anti-Soviet mujahedin in Afghanistan is today's anti-Western jihadist everywhere.

The Saudi connection led to a spurt of madrassas spewing hatred against Jew, Christian and Hindu with equal venom. The army harnessed Islamism both against civilian political parties at home, to maintain control over Afghanistan, and against India. In power for nine years as president (1999–2008), controlling both the country and the military, General Pervez Musharraf failed to deliver Pakistan from the scourge of terrorism in part because success against the jihadists would end his utility to the West. Musharraf cut deals with extremists in the restive north-west regions of Pakistan, from where the regrouped Taliban and Al Qaeda launched increasingly deadly assaults into Afghanistan. The nightmare scenario of nuclear weapons coming under the control of Islamists has come ever closer to reality (Sanger 2009).[3] Abdul Qadeer Khan established a global nuclear bazaar that did lucrative business with Iran, Libya and North Korea (Clary 2004; Frantz and Collins 2007). The government was complicit in, connived in and facilitated, or at the very least knew about and tolerated the existence and activities of the network. When caught out, the "hero of the nation" was placed under a comfortable version of house arrest by his "friend" Musharraf. The International Atomic Energy Agency and Americans have not been permitted to interrogate Khan. Arguably, the Khan network is still active and Pakistan's nuclear weapons are not safe (Armstrong and Trento 2007; Harrison 2008; IISS 2007; Levy and Scott-Clark 2007).

Had Musharraf eliminated the threat of Islamists, his utility to Washington and the fear of the alternative would have disappeared. If he failed to show any tangible progress, he would have been toppled. So he played both ends against the middle brilliantly. But that meant that the policy contradictions ripened and threatened to burst. The Islamists survived, regrouped, built up their base and launched more frequent raids across the border in Afghanistan but also deep into the heart of Pakistan itself. Slowly but surely, Pakistan descended into the failed state syndrome (see Rashid 2008). Almost every incident of international terrorism, including 9/11, has had some significant link to Pakistan. The latest, at the time of writing, was the failed attempt to set off a car bomb in Times Square in New York on 1 May 2010. The chief suspect in that is Faisal Shahzad, a Pakistani-American believed to have received bomb-making training over several months at a terrorist camp run by militants in Waziristan in northern Pakistan (Rashid 2010).

If Al Qaeda is driven largely by religious reasons and the Naxalites by socioeconomic ones, the Liberation Tigers of Tamil Eelam (LTTE) in Sri Lanka was so by ethno-nationalism and the discrimination and aggravation exercised against the Tamil minority by the Sinhala majority.

One reason the Tamil Tigers managed to wage what amounted to a civil war for a quarter of a century against the Sri Lankan state, a remarkable feat on a self-contained island state whose topography does not lend itself to guerrilla warfare, was their technological prowess. As S. D. Muni points out in his chapter, they deployed their own shipping fleet, thus ensuring steady supply lines. They built their own navy and air force, including mini-submarines and light aircraft assembled from pre-ordered kits, from which they bombed Colombo, taking the war to the very heart of the Sri Lankan capital. In the annals of terrorism, they are also credited with the dubious distinction of having invented the suicide-bomber vest, by now widely used throughout the greater Middle East and elsewhere, as well as with having pioneered the use of female suicide bombers, and widely deployed child soldiers.

They also made the most of information technology. Their vast databases of the Tamil diaspora, especially in Western Europe and North America, allowed them to tap into the resources of the Tamil community abroad and ensure a steady income to finance their operations. In an interdependent world, the LTTE was also aware of the need to keep Western public opinion on its side, and played with great effect on the identity politics prevalent in advanced democracies. Its supreme leader, Velupillai Prabakaran, in his final stance on a small sliver of land behind a lagoon in Sri Lanka's northern-tip Vanni region, died with a side arm in one hand and a satellite phone in the other, hoping to the last minute that the international community would come to his rescue (Heine 2009).

Yet, if the LTTE's global network both empowered its insurgency and ultimately doomed it, the secret to the Nepalese Maoists' success, such as it was, was to have realized that, however ideological their struggle and internationalist their outlook, Nepal is ultimately dependent on India. They became aware that, with the murder of Rajiv Gandhi in 1991, the LTTE had burned its bridges with India and would never be able to establish its desired independent Tamil state in northern Sri Lanka, as that would be unacceptable to Sri Lanka's northern neighbour.

The Nepalese Maoists, under the leadership of Prachanda, needed to establish their strictly local roots and ambitions. The initial association with the Indian Naxalites, their ideological brethren, was thus cut off. Much the same can be said about any illusions of having Beijing as the Nepalese Maoists' patron, something that also would have been unacceptable to New Delhi. Anchored deep in the mountain kingdom's countryside, they thus waged a long war against the Nepalese state and the

Nepalese monarchy, in which they succeeded, precisely because they managed to portray themselves as a local movement embodying the last best hope to get rid of an absolute monarch, King Gyanendra, seen as corrupt, incompetent and ineffectual. They also jettisoned their revolutionary socialist programme and embraced representative democracy. This geopolitical and ideological pragmatism, as S. D. Muni shows, served them well.

As the contrasting cases of the Sri Lankan LTTE and the Nepalese Maoists show, in the age of globalization the key to the outcomes of sociopolitical processes lies in the interface between the local and the global. The global context can be a ready source of material and ideational resources to be deployed locally to great effect. Yet, and this is especially true for small, developing nations in the Global South, a single misreading of that international environment and a consequent misstep (such as the assassination of former Indian prime minister Rajiv Gandhi by an LTTE female bomber armed with one of those fabled suicide vests – itself an example of deadly blowback in that India had previously tolerated, if not permitted and supported, LTTE cells being based in India) can have devastating consequences. With a large Tamil population and an overwhelming Hindu majority, India was the one country that could have provided help and succour to the Sri Lankan Tamil struggle for autonomy and/or independence. After Rajiv Gandhi's death in Sriperumbudur, that was not going to happen.

A similar dialectic is at play in Kashmir. The India–Pakistan border has been described as the most dangerous in the world, as it joins two nuclear powers which have waged war against each other thrice in 60 years. At the heart of the India–Pakistan dispute is the fate of Kashmir, with a Muslim majority, yet part of India. On the face of it, Kashmir can seem to be to South Asia what Palestine is to the Middle East: a rallying cause for all Muslims in the region, ready to champion the cause of Kashmiri independence. Yet appearances can be deceiving. Unpacking the Kashmiri predicament is a complex endeavour. It is not evident that a majority of Kashmiris prefer independence from India, nor that they wish to become part of Pakistan, in many ways a failed state where the government has little control over what happens in much of its territory and where terrorism is rampant.

Terrorists or militants?

Rekha Chowdhary, on the other hand, questions the very use of the term "terrorism". She argues this is done in an ahistorical fashion, having become "a geo-strategic term used to justify intervention in the internal affairs of countries", while also obviating the relationship between terrorism and resistance. In her discussion of the latter in Jammu and Kashmir, she contests the notion of terrorism as an "original evil," choosing to use instead the term "armed militancy". The latter term reflects the politics of language – the Indian media as a rule don't refer to the "armed propaganda actions" in Kashmir as being undertaken by terrorists – they use the word "militants". When pressed about it, Indian journalists will readily confess that they do so under some duress – if they don't, they might lose access to sources in the "movement", or worse.

As Chowdhary puts it, taking us back to the complex interaction between the global and the local, "militancy in Kashmir has, at present, both an indigenous and a foreign face". The various groups that took up the armed struggle in the Valley form a veritable smorgasbord of the various political options on the table, from the Jammu and Kashmir Liberation Front (advocating independence), to the Hizb-ul-Mujahideen (favouring integration with Pakistan), on the local side; on the global, Islamic Jihad side, there is Lashkar-e-Toiba (lately of Mumbai fame), Harkat-ul Mujahideen and Jaish-e-Mohammad, groups led and formed by Afghanis, Arabs and Pakistanis. And it is here again that we see the "blowback", ricochet effect alluded to earlier, such a prominent feature of international conflict in the age of globalization. It is not a coincidence that political violence in Jammu and Kashmir shot up in 1989, precisely when many of these foreign jihadists came to Kashmir, after the withdrawal and defeat of Soviet forces in Afghanistan. Trained and armed by the CIA and the ISI (the Pakistani intelligence services), and finding themselves unemployed, they were ready to take on a new cause. This was to help Kashmiri militants, but also to stir the embers of the anti-India sentiment in the Valley and in Jammu, while undertaking armed actions in the rest of India – as in the attack on the Indian Parliament in 2001 and in the one on Mumbai in 2008.

Yet "blowback" works in unexpected ways. While originally welcomed to the Valley as valued help to "the boys", the "Afghan Arabs" and Pakistanis outstayed their welcome. Their disregard for local customs and their pan-Islamism soon alienated Kashmiris, in the process delegitimizing much of the basis of the local uprising, which is based on the defence of Kashmiri identity – that is, the local. Muslim Kashmir has come full circle. From the affirmation of its traditions vis-à-vis Hindu India, it is now reacting to the threat to its customs posed by Wahabi Islam.

Why has jihad taken a new lease on life in the age of globalization?

The new impetus with which jihad is waged in the early twenty-first century poses a paradox. Why is it that, precisely at a time of enormous material progress made possible by the technological advances of the Third Industrial Revolution, do we also find the rise of movements seemingly bent on turning the clock backwards? Why is it that such medieval notions as the non-education of women and the cutting of limbs for what some would consider minor infractions of the law are enjoying a resurgence in what is sometimes described as the Age of Information?

One answer to that question was given by Samuel P. Huntington in his *The Clash of Civilizations* (1998), a book whose controversial and provocative thesis has given rise to an enormous literature. Neither time nor space allows us to do full justice to either in the concluding chapter of this volume on the underside of globalization. More modestly, drawing on the contributions to this book, we would like to posit at least two reasons as to why this is the case.

1 *The dynamics of globalization is about inclusion, but also about exclusion* As we pointed out in the Introduction, globalization has brought much progress to many people around the world, raising their standard of living in ways that would have been unthinkable only a few decades ago. Anyone who compares the state of cities like Shanghai and Mumbai in the 1970s with their current condition can attest to that. At the same time, the network society on which globalization is based and which it thrives on is all about tossing out and segregating those who are not part of the network, on the reasoning that they have little or nothing to contribute to the latter. Inevitably, the excluded, many of whom can be found in parts of Africa and Asia where the Muslim religion prevails, are aggrieved, feeling they have little to lose by joining jihad. Yet, *pace* Huntington, the causal link between political violence and the Muslim religion is by no means unidirectional or overdetermined. The 150 million Indian Muslims, among whom the jihadi cause has found few takers, are the best counterfactual example of the dangers of oversimplification in this highly dangerous terrain of social science analysis.

2 *Modern jihad lends itself especially to the best and worst of globalization* As Nasra Hassan points out in her fascinating chapter, based on many years of interviewing jihadis, the apparent contradiction between the modern trappings of the digital age and the seeming backwardness of those bent on imposing Sharia law on an ever larger number of societies, preferably by force, is misleading. In fact, they complement each other rather nicely. To start with, "Muslim culture has been historically based on global networks" (Castells 2009). And, as one of Hassan's interviewees put it, "Actually, Islam introduced globalization fourteen centuries ago. Our religion exploded beyond the Arabian peninsula, into other continents. It demolished borders and 'national' rule, it did away with inequality and exploitation." There are, in fact, striking parallels between the globalization process as envisioned by its most ardent advocates, in which

markets, businesses and the laws of international supply and demand leave behind the Westphalian system based on ever more obsolete nation-states, and that of jihad and political Islam. The latter does not recognize national borders and/or legal systems and aims at unifying the whole world under Islamist rule. In addition to a similar *Weltanschauung*, they also share a commitment to the tools that have compressed time and space in the early twenty-first century, including the use of the internet and the World Wide Web. In addition to the madrassas, Islamist websites have become a key recruiting tool for jihadists.

Conclusion

We live in a world in which affairs across borders are conducted largely in an orderly, stable and predictable manner because of the reality of global governance even without world government. At the same time, there are periodic bouts of market volatility, financial crises, humanitarian emergencies, armed conflicts and even interstate wars as "pockets of apparent disorder" (Kuhn 1970: 42) amidst the generally prevailing orderly conduct of international business. It has been claimed elsewhere that part of the explanation for the stability–disorder gap lies in the existence of several disconnects (Weiss and Thakur 2010). First, while the source and scale of most of today's pressing challenges are global, and any effective solution to them must also be global, the policy authority for tackling them remains vested in states. Second, the coercive capacity to mobilize the resources necessary to tackle global problems also remains vested in states, thereby effectively incapacitating many international institutions. Third, there is a critical time lag between the emergence of collective action problems with transborder, especially global, dimensions, on the one hand, and the evolution of intergovernmental organizations to facilitate robust international responses to them, on the other. Finally, and most pertinently for present purposes, there is a disconnect between the numbers and types of actors playing ever-expanding roles in civil, political and economic affairs within and among nations, and the concentration of decision-making authority in intergovernmental institutions.

Civil society organizations (CSOs) (such as International Crisis Group, Oxfam, Amnesty International, Human Rights Watch, Médecins sans Frontières, Save the Children, World Vision, Henri Dunant Center for Humanitarian Dialogue, etc.) can often be found on the ground in unstable areas far beyond the coverage of television cameras. The information that they gather and disseminate is indispensable to generating the international will to prevent, manage and terminate conflicts. CSOs play complementary roles to intergovernmental efforts to mute the conflicts and mitigate their worst humanitarian consequences. On small arms and light weapons, the International Action Network on Small Arms, International Alert, the International Peace Bureau, the International Physicians for the Prevention of Nuclear War, the Institute for Security Studies, the Small Arms Survey and others conduct extensive research to provide state-of-the-art information and analysis. Many of them have also mounted lobbying campaigns in Nepal, Central Asia, Central America, West Africa and elsewhere. The Women's International League for Peace and Freedom has focused on the prevention of the weaponization of space, on ending the recruitment of child soldiers, and on the reintegration of ex-combatants. Working with business and governments in the Kimberly Process, CSOs have tried to delegitimize conflict diamonds which often have funded the dark side of globalization. Cross-border terrorism, as well as people, drugs and arms trafficking and money laundering, present major challenges to all governments, particularly the poorer ones. Civil society groups have tried to redress the balance between security and civil liberties. Amnesty International, Human Rights Watch and the International Committee of the Red Cross have worked tirelessly to publicize flaws in due process and physical abuses in detention centres. Human Rights Watch has also charged the United Nations Security Council with dereliction of duty as governments used the war on terror to crack down on human rights.

Because civil society is outside the formal channels of governmental and intergovernmental decision-making, its roles embrace sectors of social activity other than making and implementing public policy decisions. They attempt to influence the norms and shape the conduct of all actors engaged in the exercise of international public power through research, outreach, advocacy, lobbying, monitoring and humanitarian activities. That is, the need is greater than ever for civil society to shine the searchlight of critical scrutiny on the dark side of globalization precisely in order to ensure that the good that globalization does triumphs and its deleterious effects are mitigated. The authors in this volume have tried to identify various possible roles that civil society organizations can play to ensure that global governance translates into good governance at the international level.

Notes

1. The two acronyms reflect the respective conventions on the way dates are presented: 26 November 2008 in India, September 11, 2001 in the US.
2. The abbreviation of the region into the semi-derogatory and dismissive "Afpak" is deeply insulting and offensive to everyone in the region: Afghans, Pakistanis and Indians.

3. Secretary of State Hillary Clinton acknowledged that the "unthinkable" could happen in Pakistan: the Taliban and Al Qaeda could topple the government, giving them "the keys to the nuclear arsenal" (*Times of India* 2009). A suicide attack on a bus in Rawalpindi on 2 July 2009 was the first to single out workers of Pakistan's nuclear labs (Masood 2009).

REFERENCES

Armstrong, David and Joseph J. Trento (2007) *America and the Islamic Bomb: The Deadly Compromise*. Hanover, NH: Steerforth.

Bishop, Ryan and Tania Roy (2009) "Mumbai: City as target: Introduction", *Theory Culture and Society*, 26(7–8): 263–77.

Booth, Ken and Tim Dunne, eds (2002) *Worlds in Collision: Terror and the Future of Global Order*. Basingstoke: Palgrave Macmillan.

Borooah, Vani K. (2009) "Terrorist incidents in India, 1998–2004: A quantitative analysis of fatality rates", *Terrorism and Political Violence*, 21(3): 476–98.

Castells, Manuel (2009) *Communication Power*. New York: Oxford University Press.

Clary, Christopher (2004) "Dr Khan's nuclear WalMart", *Disarmament Diplomacy*, 76 (Mar.–Apr.): 31–5.

Doordarshan News (2009) "Isolate Pak for using terrorism as state policy: PM", *Doordarshan News*, 6 Jan.

Frantz, Douglas and Catherine Collins (2007) "Those nuclear flashpoints are made in Pakistan", *Washington Post*, 11 Nov.

Friedman, Thomas L. (1999) *The Lexus and the Olive Tree*. New York: Farrar, Straus and Giroux.

Friedman, Thomas L. (2005) *The World Is Flat*. New York: Farrar, Straus and Giroux.

Friedman, Thomas L. (2010) "Bumper to bumper," *New York Times*, 23 May.

Harrison, Selig S. (2008) "What A. Q. Khan knows," *Washington Post*, 31 Jan.

Heine, Jorge (2009) "Misapplying R2P in Sri Lanka", *The Hindu*, 27 June.

Hindu (2009) "No evidence of Indian help for militants: Holbrooke", *The Hindu*, 26 Apr.

Huntington, Samuel P. (1998) *The Clash of Civilizations and the Remaking of World Order*. New York: Simon and Schuster.

IISS (2007) *Nuclear Black Markets: Pakistan, A. Q. Khan and the Rise of Proliferation Networks: A Net Assessment*, Strategic Dossier. London: International Institute for Strategic Studies.

International Crisis Group (2009) "Pakistan: The militant jihadi challenge", Asia Report 164, 13 Mar. At <http://www.crisisgroup.org/en/regions/asia/south-asia/pakistan/164-pakistan-the-militant-jihadi-challenge.aspx> (accessed Aug. 2010).

Kaplan, Caren (2009) "The biopolitics of technoculture in the Mumbai attacks," *Theory, Culture and Society*, 26(7–8): 301–3.

Karkaria, Bachi (2008) "Our state non-actors," *Times of India*, 26 Dec.

Katzenstein, Peter J., ed. (2009) *Civilizations in World Politics: Plural and Pluralist Perspectives*. New York: Routledge.

Kronstadt, K. Alan (2009) "Terrorist attacks in Mumbai, India and implications for US interests", Congressional Research Service Report to Congress 7-5700, 19 Dec.

Kuhn, Thomas S. (1970) *The Structure of Scientific Revolutions*, 2nd edn. Chicago: University of Chicago Press.

Levy, Adrian and Catherine Scott-Clark (2007) *Deception: Pakistan, the United States, and the Secret Trade in Nuclear Weapons*. New York: Walker.

Masood, Salman (2009) "Attack in Pakistani garrison city raises anxiety about safety of nuclear labs and staff", *New York Times*, 5 July.

Mehta, Suketu (2008) "What they hate about Mumbai", *International Herald Tribune*, 30 Nov.

Parthasarathy, G. (2009) "Pakistan's future", *Daily News and Analysis* (Mumbai), 18 Mar.

Rashid, Ahmed (2008) *Descent into Chaos: The United States and the Failure of Nation Building in Pakistan, Afghanistan, and Central Asia*. New York: Viking.

Rashid, Ahmed (2010) "North Waziristan: Terrorism's new hub?" *Washington Post*, 5 May.

Roy, Tania (2009) "India's 9/11: Accidents of a moveable metaphor," *Theory, Culture and Society*, 26(7–8): 314–28.

Sanger, David E. (2009) "Obama's worst Pakistan nightmare", *New York Times Magazine*, 11 Jan.

Schmitt, Eric, Mark Mazzetti and Jane Perlez (2008) "Pakistan's spies aided group tied to Mumbai siege", *New York Times*, 8 Dec.

Sengupta, Somini (2009) "Dossier from India gives new details of Mumbai attacks", *New York Times*, 7 Jan.

Singh, Rinita (2009) "The *Indian Express* interview with Home Minister P. Chidambaram", *Indian Express* (Delhi), 5 Jan. At <http://www.indianexpress.com/news/a-crime-of-this-scale-and-size-cannot-b.../406741/> (accessed 5 Jan. 2009).

Times of India (2009) "Taliban finger on Pak N-switch has US worried", *Times of India*, 27 Apr.

Weiss, Thomas G. and Ramesh Thakur (2010). *Global Governance and the UN: An Unfinished Journey*. Bloomington: Indiana University Press.

Zakaria, Fareed (2008) "End of the line for Islamabad", *Newsweek*, 15 Dec.

Index